Great Holiness Classics
Volume 3

GREAT HOLINESS CLASSICS

in Six Volumes

Volume 1

Holiness Teaching—New Testament Times to Wesley

Volume 2

The Wesley Century

Volume 3

Leading Wesleyan Thinkers

Volume 4

The 19th-Century Holiness Movement

Volume 5

Holiness Preachers and Preaching

Volume 6

Holiness Teaching Today

* GREAT HOLINESS CLASSICS *

VOLUME 3

Leading Wesleyan Thinkers

Edited by
Richard S. Taylor

Volume Advisors:
Don Bastian
John A. Knight

BEACON HILL PRESS OF KANSAS CITY
KANSAS CITY, MISSOURI

Beacon Hill Press of Kansas City

ISBN: 083-411-0695
083-410-9093 series

Printed in the United States of America
10 9 8 7 6 5 4 3 2 1

Contents

Foreword

John Wesley is acknowledged and acclaimed as the chief architect of the doctrine of entire sanctification or Christian perfection as understood within the Holiness Movement. However, the truth this tenet expresses derives from the very heart of Scripture, and the experience and life it enshrines have been known and exemplified by the saints of every age.

Nor did Wesley give final and complete formulation of this truth. Theology is an ongoing process; it endeavors to interpret truth in language and thought-forms relevant to each succeeding generation. The creativity of the Spirit is evident in the unfolding of the doctrine from Wesley to the present. The truth of Christian holiness is so grand it defies any finality of expression.

Furthermore, since saints within every Christian tradition have found this Kingdom treasure, their witness to holiness reflects the variety of these traditions. The truth of perfect love is like a sparkling diamond—to appreciate its full beauty and brilliance we must view it from many angles.

This series of classics is designed to provide the modern reader a compact library of holiness literature. Herein you will find, along with appropriate editorial introductions and comments, many of the significant primary documents of the Holiness Movement. I commend these volumes as a devotional treasure for those who seek spiritual enrichment as well as a resource library for teachers and preachers who would deepen and enlarge their understanding of this central truth of Scripture.

—William M. Greathouse
General Superintendent
Church of the Nazarene

Understanding the Great Holiness Classics

Holiness

Christian holiness is a scriptural teaching to be understood and a relationship with God to be experienced. God is a holy God, and He asks His people to be like Him in this respect.

In the Old Testament we read, "Ye shall be holy: for I the Lord your God am holy" (Lev. 19:2). In teaching us about our responsibilities to God, Jesus summarized the first chapter of the Sermon on the Mount with the admonition: "Be ye therefore perfect, even as your Father which is in heaven is perfect" (Matt. 5:48).

Every sincere Christian wants to know what it means to be as holy as God asks us to be. Every follower of Christ feels at times yearnings to be more Christlike, to somehow realize the Christian perfection Jesus sets before us.

It is this ideal and goal taught in the Scriptures that has, across the centuries, stirred every devout Christian who has sought and experienced God's sanctifying grace. In John Wesley's *A Plain Account of Christian Perfection* he records his own experience of discovering this truth: "I tell you, as plain as I can speak, where and when I found this. I found it in the oracles of God, in the Old and New Testament, when I read them with no other view or desire, but to save my own soul" (*WW*, 11:444).

The Holiness Classics

Following in the tradition of Wesley and other devout persons who have sought and preached Christian holiness, the publishers conceived and launched this series of six volumes of *Great Holiness Classics*. The desire and purpose was, in Wesley's words, to "spread scriptural holiness over these lands" in the 20th century.

The commission given to the editors states that desire.

> To provide a representative compilation of the best holiness literature in a format readily accessible to the average minister, thus providing: (1) the preservation of the essential elements of our holiness heritage; (2) an overview of the broad scope of the holi-

ness message; (3) a norm for holiness theology, proclamation, and practice; (4) a succinct reference work on holiness; and (5) a revival of the best of the out-of-print holiness classics.

What Is a Classic?

A classic work comes from the past, but simply being old does not make it classic. To be classic, a work must have enduring excellence. Its content must be so true and persuasive that succeeding generations read it and are moved to accept the truth and to shape their lives by it. Seeking after holiness as taught in a classic, one finds the truths verified both in Scripture and in his own experience with God. A work is classic because its truths are central to revealed and to experiential Christianity.

It is this verifying of previous experience that keeps a classic alive in the consciousness of the Christian community. There is here a principle somewhat parallel to the scientific method. In science we accept as true an experiment that can be repeated under similar conditions with the same results.

Because a holiness classic represents such a verifiable and biblical promise of spiritual fulfillment, it becomes a typical example of true teaching and a dependable model of Christian experience. Other persons who ponder the Scripture and perform the experiment report comparable experiences of God. The accumulating testimony verifies the classic nature of the document.

A classic thus becomes an authoritative commentary on scriptural truth. It contains guidance that can be depended on to result in sound action and blessed results. The work therefore becomes a norm for future generations. It affirms to the reader, "If you approach God as I did and respond to Him, as by His Word and Spirit He led me to respond, you will discover that He works in your life as I testify He has worked in mine."

In a letter to Dr. Middleton, Wesley cites this appeal to holy living as characteristic of the Christian Fathers: "What the Scripture promises, I enjoy. Come and see what Christianity has done here; and acknowledge it is of God" (*WW*, 10:79).

Selection of Materials

The editors have been guided by these concepts of classic holiness writings. Works that have spoken to succeeding generations have endured; therefore, we have included them. Writings that present views widely held by other holiness writers are to be considered classic. A work that stimulates the reader to try the grand experiment is classical. In Christian literature, writings that most faithfully reflect biblical teachings are classical in the best sense of being truly Christian norms.

The materials here selected as classic, then, (1) reflect accurately the teachings of the Bible, (2) have a broad and common base of Christian testimony, (3) and are in line with the best thinking of Christian leaders who have enjoyed the experience of God's sanctifying grace.

What we have chosen, we believe gives a true account of God's plan for holy living. These writings offer a norm for Christian life that reflects God's will for His children. They lead to the greatest personal fulfillment and inspire believers to make their most effective contribution to the extension of God's kingdom.

Truth with Tolerance

Not all sincere Christians understand Bible holiness in the same way. What is here reflected is generally called the Wesleyan interpretation of entire sanctification. Even within the circle of those who follow Wesley there are some differences of interpretation. The statement of "Concepts and Identifying Terms" was drawn up as a way to reflect the widely accepted positions of the Wesleyan, Methodist tradition.

We recognize and appreciate guides to holy living from other traditions as in the Moravian, Quaker, Mennonite, and modern Keswick movements. Much of what is here included crosses all denominational boundaries. It will therefore speak to the spirits of evangelical Christians from most of the historic orthodox communions.

In order to avoid being too restrictive in our selections, we have sought the advice of a broad group of nearly 50 Bible scholars and churchmen whose names appear in the lists of editors, and of members of the editorial advisory boards. These persons have all been involved in a continuing consultation on the choice of materials to be included. We trust that the broad consensus further assures our choice of truly classic materials.

Editorial Policy

The editors were instructed to select writings "judged by the quality of the material and its ability to speak to this generation." Because many of the holiness classics, especially in the first two volumes, come from an earlier period of writing, we were further given "the right to excerpt and edit the materials, updating archaic usage as needed."

Our goal has been, insofar as is possible, to let the writers speak for themselves. In excerpting we have tried to be completely faithful to the writer's views, deleting only dated, irrelevant, or duplicated materials. Our concern has always been to present as clearly as possible what the writer believed, experienced, and taught about Christian holiness.

In order to make our selections as clear as possible for today's reader we have: (1) modernized some spelling and punctuation, (2) divided some long paragraphs for greater ease in reading, (3) prepared brief introductions and analyses of the writings included, and we have also (4) inserted center heads, side heads, and cut-in headings as brief indications of content in order to guide the reader who is looking for specific aspects of holiness teaching.

For the historical scholar who wishes to follow in our footsteps and form his own judgment of our accuracy, we have: (1) indicated our sources by title, date, edition, and page numbers from which the selection is taken (where relevant for accuracy, we have used the earliest editions of the text); (2) retained original paragraph numbers to aid the reader in locating the source of our quotations; (3) used ellipses to indicate where material has been omitted; and (4) retained italics that appear in the originals, to show what the writers sought to emphasize.

To help the reader more easily distinguish editorial comment from the classic materials quoted, we have printed the editor's additions in a slightly darker type.

Our Prayer

The prayer of the editors and publishers is that all who read these classics of holy living may come to understand "the way of God more perfectly" (Acts 18:26).

We pray "that Christ may dwell in your hearts by faith; that ye, being rooted and grounded in love, may be able to comprehend with all saints what is the breadth, and length, and depth, and height; and to know the love of Christ, which passeth knowledge, that ye might be filled with all the fulness of God.

"Now unto him that is able to do exceeding abundantly above all that we ask or think, according to the power that worketh in us, unto him be glory in the church by Christ Jesus throughout all ages, world without end. Amen" (Eph. 3:17-21).

—A. F. HARPER
Executive Editor

Concepts and Identifying Terms

At the beginning of the project the editors were mandated to "strive for balance, reflecting the various facets of holiness—crisis and process, practice and proclamation, etc."

In order to guide us and to test the inclusiveness and balance of materials chosen, it seemed necessary to devise an instrument for reminder and measurement. We therefore developed the following list of concepts and identifying terms.

The statements are designed to indicate the teachings of the church. The identifying terms are planned as a kind of shorthand device for highlighting these truths throughout the set and in the indexes.

We believe the statements faithfully reflect what the Bible teaches and what the Church has believed and taught across the centuries. The terms are biblical and/or classical in the sense that they represent the language the Church has used to describe the various facets of the experience of God's sanctifying grace.

For convenient reference, we have used these code words as cut-in heads on pages where the related concepts are explored.

A. Doctrinal

1. The requirement of entire sanctification is rooted in God's holiness. — **God's Holiness**
2. The need for entire sanctification is seen in the remaining presence of inbred sin, or carnality, in believers. The experience of entire sanctification includes cleansing from this original sin. — **Carnality/ Cleansing**
3. Entire sanctification is a gift of God's grace. — **Grace**
4. God provides the gift in the atonement of Christ. — **Atonement**

5. **Perfect Love** To be sanctified wholly means to receive grace to love God with your whole heart and to love your neighbor as yourself.
6. **Holy Spirit** At conversion, Christians receive God's Holy Spirit in regeneration, sometimes described as initial sanctification. To be sanctified wholly means to be baptized, or filled with the Holy Spirit, as happened to the disciples in the Upper Room.
7. **Christ-likeness** God offers the ministry of the indwelling Holy Spirit to make us more Christlike.
8. **Scriptural** We believe the doctrine of entire sanctification is taught in the Bible and is consistent with other salvation truths of Scripture.
9. **For All Christians** Entire sanctification is God's call to all Christians.
10. **Second Blessing** Entire sanctification is experienced as a second blessing of grace subsequent to regeneration.
11. **In a Moment** Because entire sanctification is God's gift in response to faith, it occurs in a moment of time, just as God's forgiveness comes in an instant.
12. **Names** Entire sanctification is also known as Christian perfection, perfect love, heart purity, the baptism with the Holy Spirit, being filled with the Spirit, the fullness of the blessing, full salvation, the deeper life, Christian holiness, scriptural holiness, the rest of faith, and the promise of the Father.

B. Steps to Seeking and Finding

13. **New Birth** The new birth is a prerequisite to entire sanctification.
14. **Hunger** Conviction of need is a condition for the personal quest after holiness.
15. **Consecration** Full consecration is both a precondition and a gracious fruit of entire sanctification.
16. **Faith** Faith grounded on the full-orbed purpose of Christ's death, and the fullest consecration of

which we are capable, is the human condition for entire sanctification.

17. God gives the witness of His Spirit when we are sanctified wholly. **Assurance**

C. **Living the Life of Holiness**

18. Christians grow in likeness to Christ, both before and after entire sanctification. Successful growth requires obedience, trust, deep devotion, and personal discipline. **Growth**
19. Being filled with the Spirit makes a difference in a Christian's attitudes. **Attitudes**
20. Holiness tends toward fulfillment of life and wholeness of human personality. **Wholeness**
21. Though sanctified wholly, men and women are still limited by their imperfections in judgment, personality, and conduct; they are still subject to all sorts of temptation. **Humanity**
22. Dangers to which the sanctified are especially vulnerable include spiritual pride and setting standards too high. **Dangers**

D. **Proclamation—Witnessing**

23. Testifying to God's work of entire sanctification honors God and spreads the truth. **Witnessing**
24. The truth of entire sanctification and a holy life is to be proclaimed through preaching. **Preaching**
25. Understanding of the truth of Christian holiness and hunger for the experience are communicated through teaching. **Teaching**
26. The truth of Christian holiness is spread through written testimony, exposition, and exhortation. **Writing**
27. We document and prove holiness by living holy lives and by Christian ethical behavior. **Ethics**

Editor's Introduction to Volume 3

The selections included in this volume cover much more theological ground than the particular doctrine of entire sanctification as a second work of grace because this grace cannot be comprehended apart from its linkage with the whole scope of redemption truth. The very term *holiness* derives its meaning from related concepts of sin, divine sovereignty, and free agency. Is man a pawn or a moral agent? What is the nature of grace?—God's determination to save the elect unconditionally, or His offer of salvation to all men on clearly defined moral terms?

Again, what is the true doctrine of sin? Is sin so endemic to human nature that there is no complete escape from it in this life? Or is it an accountable wrongness that may be not only forgiven but terminated? And is inbred sinfulness of nature a condition that may be corrected in this life, as a provision of the Atonement and by the agency of the Spirit?

These are questions that are central to a biblical doctrine of holiness. Only by grappling with the great principles of grace and sovereignty—the moral principles by which salvation is provided and offered—can we begin to grasp the meaning of holiness. Only then can we know whether biblical holiness is merely imputed or also imparted; a fiction or a fact; a legal relationship only or a state of character. Can the word *holiness* be invested with full moral meaning, and hence moral value? Or must it be relegated to submoral categories, by which we benefit from Christ's holiness without really participating in it?

Every such inquiry will finally come down to the irreducible issue of a partial and defective holiness over against a full and satisfactory grace. Are we to be saved from hell only, or from sin too?

Hence we have included in this anthology, especially in the earlier readings, many passages that might seem to have little immediate bearing on the doctrine of holiness. These doctrines, however, are inescapably at the very heart and core of a full salvation.

The editor makes no claim that this selection is the best possible. Some might have chosen different readings. Other influential thinkers could have been profitably used. The editors finally decided to confine the work to standard, Methodistic, and Wesleyan theologians. This eliminated some who while they influenced the general holiness movement could not properly be called leading Wesleyan thinkers.

Also we have sought to provide an anthology of *systematic theology*, in distinction from biographical, devotional, expository, or evangelistic readings. This aim, however, has not been rigidly adhered to. A more fundamental objective has been a *theological* affirmation of the Wesleyan doctrine of Christian perfection.

Unavoidably, there is considerable overlapping, even repetition, in subject matter. This would be expected in view of the scope of the theme. However, the diversity of viewpoints and emphases makes possible a challenging comparative study. All of these theologians are essentially Wesleyan, but they do not cross their *t*'s or dot their *i*'s alike. A careful reader will soon note, for example, that some stress the gradual aspects of sanctification much more than the crisis—though not denying the crisis experience. Others are urging the secondness of entire sanctification. They are very much concerned about processes and instructions that pertain to experiencing a distinct second work of grace. At this point, there seems to be some correlation between theologians more temperamentally academic and those more actively involved in proclamation and evangelistic thrust.

The editors have sought to keep editing to the minimum, and to preserve a man's personal format as far as possible. The volume will therefore not be marked by exact technical uniformity. Some changes have been made in archaic wording, paragraphing, spelling, punctuation, and the style used for scripture references. Few attempts were made to alter an author's use of scripture quotations. In some cases there seemed to be a deliberately free rendering; in others the authors had italicized words for emphasis. It was thought best to leave to the author this right.

Most of our authors used only meager documentation. No attempt has been made to track down the missing data.

Plunging directly into Watson could well be discouraging for the reader who is a novice in theological literature. In view of this, perhaps one should begin with A. F. Gray, then move to Bishops Hogue and Taylor, followed perhaps by Steele and Hills. The more complex "heavyweights" can come later—but cannot be omitted. Wiley could safely be viewed as the plumb line of the entire volume.

Those with an already acquired delight in theology will relish the depth of these readings. And it just could be that the thoughtful study of the more difficult selections may aid the newcomer to theology in acquiring such a delight.

In either case, if these classic treatments can sharpen our theological understanding and keep the holiness movement on course, they will have a significant and enduring ministry.

—RICHARD S. TAYLOR

I have made a little exposition of Methodism, but I see it will be too long to present in full. I sum it all up in one or two sentences. As to its theology, it takes the old theology of the Christian church, but it takes one element that no other Christian church has dared to put forward as a prominent feature of theology. In ours it is the very point from which we view all theology. Now listen; I want that to be understood. Knowing exactly what I say, and taking the full responsibility of it, I repeat, we are the only church in history, from the apostles' time until now, that has put forward as its very elemental thought—the great, central, pervading idea of the whole Book of God from the beginning to the end—the holiness of the human soul, heart, mind, and will.

Go through all the confessions of all the churches, and you will find this in no other. You will find even some of them that blame us in their books and writings. It may be called fanaticism, but, dear friends, that is our mission. If we keep to that, the next century is ours; if we keep to that, the triumphs of the next century shall throw those that are past far into the shade. Our work is a moral work—that is to say, the work of making men holy. Our preaching is for that, our church agencies are for that, our schools, colleges, universities, and theological seminaries are for that. There is our mission—there is our glory—there is our power, and there shall be the ground of our triumph. God keep us true.

—*John McClintock, the first president of the Drew Theological Seminary;* from an address delivered at the Methodist Centenary Celebration in New York, January 25, 1866; reported in the *Methodist*, issue of February 3, 1866. Quoted by Curtis in *The Christian Faith*, 372.

1

Richard Watson
(1781-1833)

Few, if any, have set theological standards for Wesleyans more impregnably than did Richard Watson. According to Robert E. Chiles, he "has no serious rival for theological leadership in the first half of the 19th century." Even down to 1876 his *Theological Institutes* continued in the Course of Study for American Methodist ministers.

This quiet but remarkable man was born in a saddler's humble home in an obscure village in Lincolnshire, Barton-upon-Humber, February 22, 1781. He died only 52 years later, January 8, 1833, in London. While his formal education was limited, Watson early showed unusual precocity in Latin and history. Joining the Wesleyan Methodists (British) at 15 years of age, he preached his first sermon at 16 and was ordained at 19. From then on he was indefatigable in Christian labors, as an itinerant preacher, missionary society secretary, and for one year as president of the conference. But most of all Watson served Christ through his prodigious literary output. His published writings, collected after his death, filled 13 volumes.

These include *Apology for the People Called Methodists* (1800), *Life of the Rev. John Wesley* (1831), *A Biblical and Theological Dictionary* (1831), *An Exposition of the Gospels of Matthew and Mark* (1833), and a later compilation of sermons. But most important was the *Theological Institutes*, a two-volume work that appeared between 1823 and 1829. The subtitle of the *Institutes* was: *Or a View of the Evidences, Doctrines, Morals and*

Institutions of Christianity. This is perhaps the most authentic display of the views of Watson. John Fletcher Hurst has called him "the greatest theological thinker of his day."

In *Great Holiness Classics* we have used readings only from Watson's *Institutes*, vol. 2, 1950 edition (New York: Carlton & Lanahan).

In a careful reading of this material, our minds will be stimulated by the discipline of close thinking. The logic, when followed carefully, is compelling, but the style is not easy for those accustomed to fast reading. Sometimes sentences are long and involved, perhaps even cumbersome. Nevertheless we will sense that we are in the presence of a great mind, one that is astute, penetrating, and unmistakably in earnest.

Watson is Wesleyan to the core, though less evangelistic than either Wesley or Clarke. In the words of Wiley, he "represents the more thoughtful and moderate form of Methodism." Moderate, but not deviant. One is hard put to justify some criticisms leveled against him, such as Chiles's statement that while Watson preserves "the substance" he compromises the "spirit" of Wesleyan theology.[1] Peters asserts that while Clarke tended to move toward the left of Wesley and Fletcher, Watson, by his "emphasis on the gradual," was "moving to the right"[2]—this in spite of Watson's care in declaring entire sanctification to be attainable as an instantaneous experience receivable by faith. And is Watson to be dubbed a sub-Wesleyan "scholastic," a rationalist at heart, simply because he seeks to expound and defend the teachings of his mentor (Wesley) in a reasonable, systematic, and moderate fashion? The reader must decide for himself.

Entire Sanctification[3]

It is fitting that Watson's treatment of holiness be adopted as the centerpiece of this volume. It is concise, yet comprehensive;

---

1. Robert E. Chiles, *Theological Transition in American Methodism* (New York: Abingdon Press, 1965), 48.

2. John Leland Peters, *Christian Perfection and American Methodism* (New York: Abingdon Press, 1956), 107.

3. The material is from Chap. 29, vol. 2, titled "Redemption—Farther Benefits." The discussion of entire sanctification is only a part of the chapter, 450-57.

both clear and convincing. Its structure has become the classic approach to the subject, followed to a greater or lesser degree by many Wesleyan theologians since. Watson's work is therefore eminently suited to introduce the entire subject of full salvation to any reader who may be unfamiliar with Wesleyan thought.

Two very simple objectives govern the development of this section: to show that entire sanctification is attainable in this life, and that it is attainable as an instantaneous work of grace to be appropriated by faith.

Having endeavored to establish the doctrine of the universal redemption of the human race, the enumeration of the leading blessings that flow from it may now be resumed. We have already spoken of *justification, adoption, regeneration,* and *the witness of the Holy Spirit,* and we proceed to another as distinctly marked, and as graciously promised in the Holy Scriptures: this is the ENTIRE SANCTIFICATION or the perfected HOLINESS of believers; and as this doctrine, in some of its respects, has been the subject of controversy, the scriptural evidence of it must be appealed to and examined. Happily for us, a subject of so great importance is not involved in obscurity.

SECOND BLESSING

That a distinction exists between a regenerate state and a state of entire and perfect holiness will be allowed. Regeneration, we have seen, is concomitant with justification; but the apostles, in addressing the body of believers in the churches to whom they wrote their epistles, set before them, both in the prayers they offer in their behalf, and in the exhortations they administer, a still higher degree of deliverance from sin, as well as a higher growth in Christian virtues.

Two passages only need be quoted to prove this: 1 Thess. 5:23, "And the very God of peace sanctify you wholly; and I pray God your whole spirit and soul and body be preserved blameless unto the coming of our Lord Jesus Christ." 2 Cor. 7:1, "Having therefore these promises, dearly beloved, let us cleanse ourselves from all filthiness of the flesh and spirit, perfecting holiness in the fear of God." In both these passages deliverance from sin is the subject spoken of; and the prayer in one instance, and the exhortation in the other, goes to the extent of the entire sanctification of "the soul" and "spirit," as well as of the "flesh" or "body," from all sin; by which can only be meant our complete deliverance from all spiritual pollution, all inward depravation of the heart, as well as that which, expressing itself outwardly by the indulgence of the senses, is called "filthiness of the flesh."

WHEN AVAILABLE

The attainableness of such a state is not so much a matter of debate among Christians as the *time* when we are authorized to expect it. For as it is an axiom of Christian doctrine, that "without holiness no man can see the Lord," and is equally clear that if we would "be found of him in *peace*," we must be found "without *spot* and *blameless*"; and that the Church will be presented by Christ to the Father without "fault"; so it must be concluded, unless, on the one hand, we greatly pervert the sense of those passages, or, on the other, admit the doctrine of purgatory or some intermediate purifying institution, that the entire sanctification of the soul, and its complete renewal in holiness, must take place in this world.

While this is generally acknowledged, however, among spiritual Christians, it has been warmly contended by many that the final stroke that destroys our natural corruption is only given at death; and that the soul when separated from the body, and not before, is capable of that immaculate purity that these passages, doubtless, exhibit to our hope.

If this view can be refuted, then it must follow that unless a purgatory of some description be allowed after death, the entire sanctification of believers at any time previous to their dissolution, and in the full sense of these evangelic promises, is attainable.

To the opinion in question, then, there appear to be the following fatal objections:

1. That we nowhere find the promises of entire sanctification restricted to the article of death, either expressly or in fair inference from any passage of Holy Scripture.

2. That we nowhere find the circumstance of the soul's union with the body represented as a necessary obstacle to its entire sanctification.

The principal passage that has been urged in proof of this from the New Testament is that part of the seventh chapter of the Epistle to the Romans in which St. Paul, speaking in the first person of the bondage of the flesh, has been supposed to describe his state as a believer in Christ.

But whether he speaks of himself or describes the state of others in a supposed case, given for the sake of more vivid representation in the first person, which is much more probable, he is clearly speaking of a person who had once sought justification by the works of the law but who was then convinced, by the force of a spiritual apprehension of the extent of the requirements of that law and by constant failures in his attempts to keep it perfectly, that he was in bondage to his corrupt nature and could only be delivered from this thralldom by the interposition of another. For, not to urge that his strong expressions of being "carnal," "sold under sin," and doing always "the things which he would not," are utterly inconsistent with that moral state of believers in Christ, which he describes in the next chapter; and, especially, that he there declares that such as are in Christ Jesus "walk not after the flesh, but after the Spirit"—the seventh chapter itself contains decisive evidence against the inference that the advocates of the necessary continuance of sin till death have drawn from it.

The apostle declares the person whose case he describes, to be under the law, and not in a state of deliverance by Christ; and then he represents him not only as despairing of self-deliverance, and as praying for the interposition of a sufficiently powerful deliverer, but as thanking God that the very deliverance for which he groans is appointed to be administered to him by Jesus Christ. "Who shall deliver me from the body of this death? I thank God through Jesus Christ our Lord."

This is also so fully confirmed by what the apostle had said in the preceding chapter, where he unquestionably describes the moral state of true believers, that nothing is more surprising than that so perverted a comment upon the seventh chapter, as that to which we have adverted, should have been adopted or persevered in.

"What shall we say then? Shall we continue in sin, that grace may abound? God forbid. How shall we, that are dead to sin, live any longer therein? Know ye not, that so many of us as were baptized into Jesus Christ were baptized into his death? Therefore we are buried with him by baptism into death: that like as Christ was raised up from the dead by the glory of the Father, even so we also should walk in newness of life. For if we have been planted together in the likeness of his death, we shall be also in the likeness of his resurrection: knowing this, that OUR OLD MAN is crucified with him, THAT THE BODY OF SIN MIGHT BE DESTROYED, that henceforth we should not serve sin. For he that is dead IS FREED FROM SIN."

So clearly does the apostle show that he who is BOUND to the "body of death," as mentioned in the seventh chapter, is not in the state of a believer; and that he who has a true faith in Christ "is FREED from sin."

It is somewhat singular that the divines of the Calvinistic school should be almost uniformly the zealous advocates of the doctrine of the continuance of indwelling sin till death . . . It is but justice, however, to say that several of them have as zealously denied that the apostle, in the seventh chapter of the Romans, describes the state of one who is justified by faith in Christ, and very properly consider the case there spoken of as that of one struggling in LEGAL bondage and brought to that point of self-despair and of conviction of sin and helplessness that must always precede an entire trust in the merits of Christ's death and in the power of His salvation.

PRESENT HOLINESS REQUIRED

3. The doctrine before us is disproved by those passages of Scripture that connect our entire sanctification with subsequent habits and acts, to be exhibited in the conduct of believers *before death.* So in the quotation from Romans 6, just above: "Knowing this, that our old man is crucified with him, that the body of sin might be destroyed, that *henceforth* we should not serve sin." So the exhortation in 2 Cor. 7:1, also given above, refers to the present life and not to the future hour of our dissolution; and in 1 Thess. 5:23 the apostle first prays for the entire sanctification of the Thessalonians and then for their *preservation* in that hallowed state, "unto the coming of our Lord Jesus Christ."

4. It is disproved, also, by all these passages that require us to bring forth those graces and virtues that are usually called the fruits of the Spirit. That these are to be produced during our life, and to be displayed in our spirit and conduct, cannot be doubted; and we may, then, ask whether they are required of us in perfection and maturity? If so, in this degree of maturity and perfection, they necessarily suppose the entire sanctification of the soul from the opposite and antagonist evils. Meekness in its perfection supposes the extinction of all sinful anger; perfect love to God supposes that no affection remains contrary to it; and so of every other perfect internal virtue.

The inquiry, then, is reduced to this, whether these graces, in such perfection as to exclude the opposite corruptions of the heart, are of possible attainment. If they are not, then we cannot love God with our whole hearts; then we must be sometimes sinfully angry; and how, in that case, are we to interpret that *perfectness* in these graces that God hath required of us and promised to us in the gospel?

If the *perfection* meant (and let it be observed that this is a *scriptural* term and must mean something) be so comparative as that we may be sometimes sinfully angry and may sometimes divide our hearts between God and the creature, we may apply the same comparative sense of the term to good words and to good works, as well as to good affections. Thus when the apostle prays for the Hebrews, "Now the God of peace, that brought again from the dead our Lord Jesus, that great shepherd of the sheep, through the blood of the everlasting covenant, make you *perfect* in every *good work* to do his will," we must understand this perfection of evangelical good works so that it shall sometimes give place to opposite evil works, just as good affections must necessarily sometimes give place to the opposite bad affections.

This view can scarcely be soberly entertained by any enlightened Christian; and it must, therefore, be concluded that the standard of our attainable Christian perfection, as to the affections, is a love of God so perfect as to "rule the heart," and exclude all rivalry, and a meekness so perfect as to cast out all sinful anger, and prevent its return; and that as to good works, the rule is that we shall be so "perfect in every good work" as to "do the will of God" habitually, fully, and constantly. If we fix the standard lower, we let in a license totally inconsistent with that Christian purity that is allowed by all to be attainable, and we make every man his own interpreter of that *comparative* perfection, which is often contended for as that only which is attainable.

Some, it is true, admit the extent of the promises and the requirements of the gospel as we have stated them; but they contend that this is the mark at which we are to *aim,* the standard toward which we are to aspire, though neither is attainable fully till death. But this view cannot be true as applied to *sanctification,* or deliverance from all inward and outward sin.

That the *degree* of every virtue implanted by grace is not limited, but advances and grows in the living Christian throughout life, may be granted; and through eternity also: but to say that these virtues are not attainable, through the work of the Spirit, in that degree which shall destroy all opposite vice, is to say that God, under the gospel, requires us to be what we cannot be, either through want of efficacy in His grace or from some defect in its administration; neither of which has any countenance from Scripture, nor is at all consistent with the terms in which the promises and exhortations of the gospel are expressed.

It is also contradicted by our own consciousness, which charges our criminal neglects and failures upon ourselves, and not upon the grace of God, as though it were insufficient. Either the consciences of good men have in all ages been delusive and overscrupulous; or this doctrine of the necessary, though occasional, dominion of sin over us is false.

5. The doctrine of the necessary indwelling of sin in the soul till death involves other antiscriptural consequences. It supposes that the seat of sin is in the flesh, and thus harmonizes with the pagan philosophy, which attributed all evil to matter. The doctrine of the Bible, on the contrary, is that the seat of sin is in the soul; and it makes it one of the proofs of the fall and corruption of our spiritual nature, that we are in bondage to the appetites and motions of the flesh. Nor does the theory that places the necessity of sinning in the connection of the soul with the body account for the whole moral case of men. There are sins, as pride, covetousness, malice, and others, that are wholly spiritual; and yet no exception is made in this doctrine . . . as to them. There is, surely, no need to wait for the separation of the soul from the body in order to be saved from evils that are the sole offspring of the spirit; and yet these are made as inevitable as the sins that more immediately connect themselves with the excitements of the animal nature.

INDWELLING SIN NOT A NECESSITY

This doctrine supposes, too, that the flesh must necessarily not only lust against the Spirit, but in no small degree, and on many occasions, be the conqueror: whereas, we are commanded, to "*mortify* the deeds of the body"; to "*crucify*," that is, to put to death, "the flesh"; "*to put off* the old man," which, in its full meaning, must signify separation from sin in fact, as well as the renunciation of it in will; and "*to put on* the new man."

Finally, the apostle expressly states, that though the flesh stands victoriously opposed to legal sanctification, it is not insuperable by evangelical holiness—"For what *the law* could not do, in that it was weak *through the flesh,* God sending his own Son in the likeness of sinful flesh, and for sin, condemned sin in the flesh: that the righteousness of the law might be *fulfilled* in us, who walk not after the flesh, but after the Spirit" (Rom. 8:3-4). So the notion that, so long as we are in the body, "the flesh" must of necessity have at least occasional dominion is inconsistent with the declarations and promises of the gospel.

We conclude, therefore, as to the time of our complete sanctification, or, to use the phrase of the apostle Paul, "the destruction of the body of sin," that it can neither be referred to the hour of death, nor placed subsequently to this present life. The attainment of perfect freedom from sin is one to which believers are called during the present life; and is necessary to that completeness of "holiness," and of those active and passive graces of Christianity by which they are called to glorify God in this world, and to edify mankind.

THE MANNER OF SANCTIFICATION

Not only the time, but the *manner* also, of our sanctification has been a matter of controversy: some contending that all attainable degrees of it are acquired by the process of gradual mortification and the acquisition of holy habits; others alleging it to be instantaneous, and the fruit of an act of faith in the divine promises.

That the regeneration that accompanies justification is a large approach to this state of perfected holiness; and that all dying to sin, and all growth in grace, advances us nearer to this point of entire sanctity, is so obvious that on these points there can be no reasonable dispute. But they are not at all inconsistent with a more instantaneous work, when, the depth of our natural depravity being more painfully felt, we plead in faith the accomplishment of the promises of God. The great question to be settled is whether the deliverance sighed after be held out to us in these promises as a present blessing. And from what has been already said, there appears no ground to doubt this, since no small violence would be offered to the passages of Scripture already quoted, as well as to many others, by the opposite opinion.

ATTAINABLE BY FAITH

All the promises of God that are not expressly, or from their *order,* referred to future time, are objects of *present trust;* and their fulfillment *now* is made conditional *only* upon our faith. They cannot, therefore, be pleaded in our prayers, with an entire reliance upon the truth of God, in vain. The general promise that we shall receive "all things whatsoever we ask in prayer, believing," comprehends, of course, "all things" suited to our case that God has engaged to bestow; and if the entire renewal of our nature be included in the number, without any limitation of time, except that in which we ask it in faith, then to this faith shall the promises of entire sanctification be given; which, in the nature of the case, supposes an instantaneous work immediately following upon our entire and unwavering faith.

The only plausible objections made to this doctrine may be answered in few words.

It has been urged that this state of entire sanctification supposes future *impeccability.* Certainly not; for if angels and our first parents fell when in a state of immaculate sanctity, the renovated man cannot be placed, by his entire deliverance from inward sin, out of the reach of danger. This remark also answers the allegation that we should thus be removed out of the reach of temptation; for the example of angels, and of the first man, who fell by temptation when in a state of native purity, proves that the absence of inward evil is not inconsistent with a state of probation; and that this, in itself, is no guard against the attempts and solicitations of evil.

OBJECTIONS ANSWERED

It has been objected, too, that this supposed state renders the atonement and intercession of Christ superfluous in the future. But the very contrary of this is manifest when the case of an evangelical renewal of the soul in righteousness is understood. This proceeds from the grace of God in Christ, through the Holy Spirit, as the efficient cause; it is received by faith as the instrumental cause; and the state itself into which we are raised is maintained, not by inherent native power, but by the continual presence and sanctifying influence of the Holy Spirit himself,[4] received and retained in answer to ceaseless prayer; which prayer has respect solely to the merits of the death and intercession of Christ.

It has been further alleged that a person delivered from all inward and outward sin has no longer need to use the petition of the Lord's Prayer, "and forgive us our trespasses"; because he has no longer need of pardon.

To this we reply: (1) That it would be absurd to suppose that any person is placed under the necessity of "trespassing," in order that a general prayer designed for men in a mixed condition might retain its aptness to every particular case. (2) That trespassing of every kind and degree is not supposed by this prayer to be continued, in order that it might be used always in the same *import,* or otherwise it might be pleaded against the renunciation of any trespass or transgression whatever. (3) That this petition is still relevant to the case of the entirely sanctified and the evangelically perfect, since neither the perfection of the first man nor that of angels is in question; that is, a perfection measured by the perfect law, which, in its obligations, contemplates all creatures as having sustained no injury by moral lapse, and admits, therefore, of no excuse from infirmities and mistakes of judgment; nor of any degree of obedience below that which beings created naturally perfect were capable of rendering.

---

4. While Watson does not expressly use the term "baptism with the Holy Spirit," the acknowledgment of the Spirit as the Agent of our sanctification is pervasive. It should be noted that "the sanctifying influence of the Holy Spirit" is to be "*received* and *retained* in answer to ceaseless prayer" (emphasis added).

There may, however, be an entire sanctification of a being rendered *naturally* weak and *imperfect,* and so liable to mistake and infirmity, as well as to defect in the *degree* of that absolute obedience and service that the law of God, never bent or lowered to human weakness, demands from all. These defects and mistakes and infirmities may be quite consistent with the entire sanctification of the soul and the *moral* maturity of a being still *naturally* infirm and imperfect.

REMAINING INFIRMITIES

Still, further, if this were not a sufficient answer, it may be remarked that we are not the ultimate judges of our own case as to our "trespasses," or our exemption from them; and we are not, therefore, to put ourselves into the place of God, "who is greater than our hearts." So, although St. Paul says, "I know nothing by myself," that is, I am conscious of no offence, he adds, "yet am I not hereby justified; but he that judgeth me is the Lord"; to whom, therefore, the appeal is every moment to be made through Christ the Mediator, and who, by the renewed testimony of His Spirit, assures every true believer of his acceptance in His sight.

Watson on Original Sin

Watson devotes 85 pages to a very careful discussion of the Fall and of the original sin devolving from it. While much of his exposition and polemic relates to discussions current in his day, the basic issues are timeless in both interest and importance: the nature of Adam's probation, the historicity of the Genesis account, the effects of the Fall on humankind, the internal nature of inbred sin, the mode of its transmission, and the involvement of Adam's posterity in his guilt. Inevitably the discussion refutes both Pelagianism and semi-Pelagianism.

The following three brief extracts focus on (1) the status of infants, (2) the question of deprivation versus depravation, and (3) the explanation of the observable virtues among unregenerate persons. The Wesleyan-Arminian concept of prevenient grace controls Watson's solutions.

The Status of Infants[5]

As to infants, they are not, indeed, born justified and regenerate; so that to say that original sin is taken away, as to infants, by Christ, is not the correct view of the case, for the reasons before given; but they are all born under the "free gift," the effects of the "righteousness" of one, which extended to "all men"; and this free gift is bestowed on them *in order* to justification of life, the adjudging of the condemned to live. All the mystery, therefore, in the case arises from this, that in adults we see the free gift connected with its *end,* actual justification, by acts of their own, repentance and faith; but as to infants, we are not informed by what process justification, with its attendant blessings, is actually bestowed, though the words of the apostle are express, that through "the righteousness of one" they are entitled to it.

A DIFFERENT MODE OF GRACE

Nor is it surprising that this process should be hidden from us, since the gospel was written for adults, though the benefit of it is designed for all; and the knowledge of this work of God, in the spirit of an infant, must presuppose an acquaintance with the properties of the human soul, which is, in fact, out of our reach. If, however, an infant is not capable of a voluntary acceptance of the benefit of the "free gift," neither, on the other hand, is it capable of a voluntary rejection of it; and it is by rejecting it that adults perish.

If much of the benefit of this "free gift" comes upon us as adults, independent of our seeking it; and if, indeed, the very power and inclination to seek justification of life is thus prevenient, and in the highest sense free; it follows, by the same rule of the divine conduct, that the Holy Spirit may be given to children; that a divine and an effectual influence may be exerted on them, which, meeting with no voluntary resistance, shall cure the spiritual death and corrupt tendency of their nature;[6] and all this without supposing any great difference in the principle of the administration of this grace in their case and that of adults.

But the different circumstances of children dying in their infancy, and adults, proves also that a different administration of the same grace, which is freely bestowed upon all, must take place. Adults are personal offenders, infants are not; for adults confession of sin, repen-

---

5. *Theological Institutes,* 59 ff.

6. That is, when a child dies in infancy.

tance, and trust . . . are appropriate to their circumstances, but not to those of infants; and the very wisdom of God may assure us that, in prescribing the terms of salvation, that is, the means by which the "free gift" shall pass to its issue, justification of life, the circumstances of the persons must be taken into account. The reason for pardon, in every case, is not repentance, not faith, not anything done by man, but the merit of the sacrifice of Christ.

Repentance and faith are, it is true, in the case of adults, a sine qua non, but in no sense the meritorious cause. The reasons of their being attached to the promise, as conditions, are nowhere given, but they are nowhere enforced as such, except on adults. In adults we see the meritorious cause working in conjunction with instrumental causes, and they are capable of what is required. But when we see, even in adults, that, independent of their own acts, the meritorious cause is not inert, but fruitful in vital influence and gracious dealing, we see such a separation of the operation of the grand meritorious cause, and the subordinate instrumental causes, as to prove that the benefits of the death of Christ are not, in every *degree,* and consequently, on the same principle, not in every *case,* conferred under the restraints of conditions. So certainly is infant salvation attested by the Scriptures; so explicitly are we told that the free gift is come upon all men to justification of life, and that none can come short of this blessing but those who reject it.

Deprivation Versus Depravation[7]

As to that in which original sin consists, some divines and some public formularies have so expressed themselves that it might be inferred that a positive evil, infection, and taint had been judicially infused into man's nature by God, which has been transmitted to all his posterity. Others, and those the greater number, both of the Calvinist and Arminian schools, have resolved it into privation. This distinction is well stated in the *Private Disputations* of Arminius.

ARMINIUS' VIEW

But since the tenor of the covenant into which God entered with our first parents was this, that if they continued in the favor and grace of God, by the observance of that precept and others, the gifts that had been conferred upon them should be transmitted to their posterity, by the like divine grace that they had received; but if they should render themselves unworthy of those

7. *Institutes,* 78-82.

favors, through disobedience, that their posterity should likewise be deprived of them, and should be liable to the contrary evils: hence it followed, that all men, who were to be naturally propagated from them, have become subject to death temporal and eternal, and have been destitute of that gift of the Holy Spirit, or of original righteousness. This punishment is usually called a privation of the image of God, and original sin.

But we allow this point to be made the subject of discussion—beside the want or absence of original righteousness, may not some other contrary quality be constituted, as another part of original sin? We think it is more probable that this absence alone of original righteousness is original sin itself, since it alone is sufficient for the commission and production of every actual sin whatever.

This is by some divines called, with great aptness, "a depravation arising from a deprivation," and is certainly much more consonant with the Scriptures than the opinion of the infusion of evil qualities into the nature of man by a positive cause, or direct tainting of the heart. This has been, indeed, probably an opinion, in the proper sense, with few, and has rather been collected from the strong and rhetorical expressions under which the moral state of man is often exhibited, and, on this account, has been attacked as a part of the doctrine of original sin, by the advocates of original innocence, and as making God directly the author of sin.

DEPRIVATION THE SOURCE OF DEPRAVATION

No such difficulty, however, accompanies the accurate and guarded statement of that doctrine in the sense of Scripture. The depravation, the perversion, the defect of our nature is to be traced to our birth, so that in our flesh is no good thing, and they that are in the flesh cannot please God; but this state arises not from the infusion of evil into the nature of man by God, but from that separation of man from God, that extinction of spiritual life that was effected by sin, and the consequent and necessary corruption of man's moral nature.

That positive evil and corruption may flow from a mere privation may be illustrated by that which supplies the figure of speech, "death," under which the Scriptures represent the state of mankind. For, as in the death of the body, the mere privation of the principle of life produces inflexibility of the muscles, the extinction of heat and sense and motion, and surrenders the body to the operation of an agency that life, as long as it continued, resisted, namely, that of chemical decomposition; so, from the loss of spiritual life, followed estrangement from

God, moral inability, the dominion of irregular passions, and the rule of appetite; aversion, in consequence, to restraint; and enmity to God.

This connection of positive evil, as the effect, with privation of the life and image of God, as the cause, is, however, to be well understood and carefully maintained, or otherwise we should fall into a great error on the other side, as, indeed, some have done, who did not perceive that the corruption of man's nature necessarily followed upon the privation referred to. It is, therefore, a just remark of Calvin, that "those who have defined original sin as a privation of the original righteousness, though they comprise the whole of the subject, yet have not used language sufficiently expressive of its operation and influence. For our nature is not only destitute of all good, but is so fertile in all evils, that it cannot remain inactive" *(Institutes).*

SINFULNESS MORE THAN PRIVATION

Indeed, this privation is not fully expressed by the phrase "the loss of original righteousness," unless that be meant to include in it the only source of righteousness in even the first man, the life that is imparted and supplied by the Holy Spirit. A similar want of explicitness we observe also in Calvin's own statement in his generally very able chapter on this subject, that Adam lost "the ornaments" he received from his Maker for us as well as for himself; unless we understand by these original "ornaments" and "endowments" of human nature in him, the *principle* also, as above stated, from which they all flowed; and that, being forfeited, could no longer be imparted *in the way of nature.*

LOSS OF THE HOLY SPIRIT

When the Spirit was restored to Adam, being pardoned, it was by grace and favor; and he could not impart it by natural descent to his posterity, though born of him when in a state of acceptance with God, since these influences are the gifts of God, which are imparted not by the first but by the second Adam; not by nature, but by a free gift, to sinful and guilty man, the law being irreversible, "that which is born of the flesh is flesh."

Arminius, in the above quotation, has more forcibly and explicitly expressed that privation of which we speak, by the forfeiture "of the gift of the Holy Spirit" by Adam, for himself and his descendants, and the loss of original righteousness as the consequence. . . .

This point may be briefly elucidated. The infliction of spiritual death, which we have already shown to be included in the original sentence, consisted, of course, in the loss of spiritual life, which was that principle from which all right direction and control of the various powers and faculties of man flowed. But this spiritual life in the first man was not a natural effect, that is, an effect that would follow from his mere creation, independent of the vouchsafed influence of the Holy Spirit. This may be inferred from the "new creation," which is the renewal of man after the image of Him who at first created him. This is the work of the Holy Spirit; but even after this change, this being "born again," man is not able to preserve himself in the renewed condition into which he is brought, but by the continuance of the same quickening and aiding influence.

NO SANCTITY WITHOUT A SANCTIFIER

No future growth in knowledge and experience; no power of habit, long persevered in, renders him independent of the help of the Holy Spirit; he has rather, in proportion to his growth, a deeper consciousness of his need of the indwelling of God and of what the apostle calls His "mighty working." The strongest aspiration of this new life is after communion and constant intercourse with God; and as that is the source of new strength, so this renewed strength expresses itself in a "cleaving unto the Lord," with a still more vigorous "purpose of heart." In a word, the sanctity of a Christian is dependent wholly upon the presence of the Sanctifier. We can only work out our own salvation as "God worketh in us to will and to do."

This is the constant language of the New Testament. If we are restored to what was lost by Adam, through the benefit brought to us by the second Adam; if there be any correspondence between the moral state of the regenerate man and that of man before his fall (we do not speak of *degree* but of substantial sameness of kind and quality); if love to God be in us what it was in him; if holiness, in its various branches, as it flows from love, be in us what it was in him: then we have sufficient reason to infer that as they are supported in us by the influence of the divine Spirit, they were so supported in him. Certain it is that before we are thus quickened by the Spirit, we are "*dead* in trespasses and sins"; and if we are made alive by that Spirit, it is a strong presumption that the withdrawing of that Spirit from Adam, when he willfully sinned, and from all his posterity, that is, from human nature itself, was the cause of the death and the depravation that followed. . . .

This accounts for the whole case of man's corruption. The Spirit's influence in him did not prevent the possibility of his sinning, though it afforded sufficient security to him, as long as he looked up to that source of strength. He did sin, and the Spirit retired; and the tide of sin once turned in, the mound of resistance being removed, it overflowed his whole nature. In this state of alienation from God, men are born, with all these tendencies to evil, because the only controlling and sanctifying power, the presence of the Spirit, is wanting, and is now given to man, not as when first brought into being, as a *creature;* but is secured to him by the mercy and grace of a new and different dispensation, under which the Spirit is *administered* in different degrees, times, and modes, according to the wisdom of God, never on the ground of our being creatures, but as redeemed from the curse of the law by Him who became a curse for us.

Moral Excellence in the Unregenerate[8]

NATURAL VIRTUES TRACEABLE TO THE SPIRIT

But virtues grounded on principle, though an imperfect one, and therefore neither negative nor simulated, may also be found among the unregenerate, and have existed, doubtless, in all ages. These virtues, however, are not of man, but from God, whose Holy Spirit has been vouchsafed to "*the world,*" through the Atonement.

This great truth has often been lost sight of in the controversy. Some Calvinists seem to acknowledge it substantially, under the name of "common grace"; others choose rather to refer all appearances of virtue to nature, and thus, by attempting to avoid the doctrine of the gift of the Spirit to all mankind, attribute to nature what is inconsistent with their opinion of its entire corruption.

But there is, doubtless, to be sometimes found in men not yet regenerate in the Scripture sense, not even decided in their choice, something of moral excellence. This cannot be referred to any of the causes above adduced; and is of a much higher character than can be attributed to a nature that, when left to itself, is wholly destitute of spiritual life. [God gives] compunction for sin, strong desires to be freed from its tyranny; He gives such a fear of God as preserves them from many evils [and encourages] charity, kindness, good neighborliness, general respect for goodness and good men, [as well as] a lofty sense of honor and justice. Indeed, the very command issued to them to repent and believe the gospel in order to their salvation implies a power of consideration, prayer, and turning to God, so as to commence that course which, persevered in, leads on to forgiveness and regeneration.

8. *Institutes,* 85-87.

To say that all these are to be attributed to mere nature is to surrender the argument to the semi-Pelagian who contends that these are proofs that man is not wholly degenerate. They are to be attributed to the controlling influence of the Holy Spirit; to His incipient workings in the hearts of men; to the warfare that He there maintains and that has sometimes a partial victory, before the final triumph comes, or when, through the fault of man, through "resisting," "grieving," "vexing," "quenching" that Holy Spirit, that final triumph may never come.

It is thus that one part of Scripture is reconciled to another, and both to fact; the declaration of man's total corruption, with the presumption of his power to return to God, to repent, to break off his sins, which all the commands and invitations to him from the gospel imply: and thus it is that we understand how, especially in Christian countries, where the Spirit is more largely effused, there is so much more general virtue than in others; and in those circles especially, in which Christian education, and the prayers of the pious, and the power of example are applied and exhibited.

THE SPIRIT GIVEN TO THE WORLD

The scriptural proof that the Spirit is given to the world is obvious and decisive. We have seen that the curse of the law implied a denial of the Spirit; the removal of that curse implies, therefore, the gift of the Spirit, and the benefit must be as large and extensive as the Atonement. Hence we find the Spirit's operations spoken of, not only as to the good, but the wicked, in all the three dispensations. In the patriarchal, "the Spirit strove with men"; with the antediluvian race, before and all the time the ark was preparing. The Jews in the wilderness are said to have "vexed his Holy Spirit"; Christ promises to send the Spirit to convince *the world* of sin; and the Book of God's revelations concludes by representing the Spirit as well as the Bride, the Holy Ghost as well as the Church in her ordinances, inviting all to come and take of the water of life freely.

All this is the fruit of our redemption and the new relation in which man is placed to God. As a sinner, it is true still; but a sinner for whom atonement has been made and who is to be wooed and won to an acceptance of the heavenly mercy. Christ having been made a curse for us, the curse of the law no longer shuts out that Spirit from us; nor can justice exclaim against this going forth of the Spirit, as it has been beautifully expressed, "to make gentle trials upon the spirits of men"; to inject some beams of light, to inspire contrite emotions, which, if they comply with, may lead on to those more powerful and effectual. If, however, they rebel against them, and oppose their sensual imaginations and desires to the secret promptings of God's Spirit, they ultimately provoke Him to withdraw His aid, and they relapse into a state more guilty and dangerous.

Again and again they are visited in various ways, in honor of the Redeemer's atonement and for the manifestation of the long-suffering of God. In some the issue of life; in others, an aggravated death; but in most cases this struggle, this "striving with man," this debating with him, this standing between him and death, cannot fail to correct and prevent much evil, to bring into existence some "goodness," though it may be as the morning cloud and the early dew, and to produce civil and social virtues, none of which, however, are to be placed to the account of *nature*, nor used to soften our views of its entire alienation from God; but are to be acknowledged as magnifying that *grace* which regards the whole of the sinning race with compassion and is ever employed in seeking and saving that which is lost.

A Biblical Doctrine of Imputation[9]

In chapter 19, titled "Redemption—Principles of God's Moral Government," Watson gives large attention to the question of imputation. Is Christ's active obedience *imputed*, that is, credited to us in such a way that God sees us perfectly righteous "in Christ," or is it our faith in the atonement made by Christ that is credited to us for righteousness? This was a critical issue then and equally critical today—as any informed reader of evangelical books and listener to radio and TV messages will know.

The relevance of the issue to the doctrine of holiness is twofold. First, the general Calvinistic understanding of imputed righteousness holds that because of such imputation, infractions of the moral law by believers have no bearing on eternal life; they cannot cause the forfeiture of eternal life, once that life has been given. When this is believed, antinomianism always lurks in the wings, even though officially renounced. Both Calvinists and Lutherans teach that the moral law is obligatory as a rule of life. But

9. *Institutes*, 2:215-17, 221, 228 f., 232 f., 244, 255 f.

holding the simultaneous belief that the moral law is not essential for eternal life must result in a widespread tendency toward carelessness and presumption.

Second, the entire imputation scheme presupposes that real personal holiness is neither fully possible nor absolutely necessary, therefore striving after such a holy life will be inevitably discouraged.

The following extracts from Watson's lengthy discussion will help us understand how an unbiblical concept of imputation strikes at the jugular vein of a biblical concept of holiness.

The notion, that justification includes not only the pardon of sin but the imputation to us of Christ's active personal righteousness, though usually held only by Calvinists, has not been received by all divines of that class; but, on the contrary, by some of them, both in ancient and modern times, it has been very strenuously opposed, as well as by the advocates of that more moderate scheme of election defended by Camero in France and by Baxter in England. Even Calvin himself has said nothing on this subject but which Arminius, in his *Declaration Before the States of Holland,* declares his readiness to subscribe to; and Mr. Wesley, in much the same view of the subject as Arminius, admits the doctrine of the imputation of the righteousness of Christ to us upon our believing, provided it be soberly interpreted.

There are, in fact, three opinions on this subject, which it is necessary to distinguish in order to obtain clear views of the controversy.

THE ANTINOMIAN VIEW

The first is a part of the high Calvinistic scheme and lies at the foundation of antinomianism, and is, in consequence, violently advocated by those who adopt that gross corruption of Christian faith. It is that Christ so represented the elect that His righteousness is imputed to us as ours; as if we ourselves had been what He was, that is, perfectly obedient to the law of God, and had done what He did as perfectly righteous.

1. The first objection to this opinion is that it is nowhere stated in Scripture that Christ's personal righteousness is imputed to us.[10] Not a text can be found that contains any enunciation of this doctrine; and those that are adduced, such as "the Lord our righteousness" and "Christ who is made unto us righteousness," are obviously pressed into the service of this scheme by a paraphrastic interpreta-

---

10. Arabic No. 1 was missing in the text. The editor presumes its suitability at the head of this paragraph.

tion, for which there is no authority in any other passages that speak of our redemption.

2. The notion here attached to Christ's *representing* us is wholly gratuitous. In a limited sense it is true that Christ represented us; that is, suffered in our stead, that we might not suffer; "but not absolutely as our delegate," says Baxter, justly. "Our persons did not, in a law sense, do in and by Christ what He did, or possess the habits which He possessed, or suffer what He suffered" *(Gospel Defended)*. The scripture doctrine is, indeed, just the contrary. It is never said that we suffered in Christ, but that He suffered for us; so also it is never taught that we obeyed in Christ, but that, through His entire obedience to a course of subjection and suffering, ending in His death, our disobedience is forgiven.

REFUTATION

3. Nor is there any weight in the argument that as our sins were accounted His, so His righteousness is accounted ours. Our sins were never so accounted Christ's as that He did them, and so justly suffered for them. This is a monstrous notion, which has been sometimes pushed to the verge of blasphemy. Our transgressions are never said to have been imputed to Him in the *fact*, but only that they were laid upon Him in the *penalty*. To be God's "beloved Son in whom he was always well pleased," and to be reckoned, imputed, and accounted a sinner, de facto, are manifest contradictions.

4. This whole doctrine of the imputation of Christ's personal moral obedience to believers, as their own personal moral obedience, involves a fiction and impossibility inconsistent with the divine attributes. "The judgment of the all-wise God is always according to truth; neither can it ever consist with His unerring wisdom to think that I am innocent, to judge that I am righteous or holy, because another is so. He can no more confound me with Christ than with David or Abraham" *(Wesley)*.

But a contradiction is involved in another view. If what our Lord was and did is to be accounted to us in the sense just given, then we must be accounted never to have sinned, because Christ never sinned, and yet we must ask for pardon, though we are accounted from birth to death to have fulfilled God's law in Christ. Or if they should say, that when we ask for pardon we ask only for a revelation to us of our eternal justification or pardon, the matter is not altered, for what need is there of pardon, in time or eternity, if we are accounted to have perfectly obeyed God's holy law? And why should we be accounted also to have suffered in Christ the penalty of sins that we are accounted never to have committed?

It is on this ground, that is, the absolute imputation of Christ's righteousness to us, that men who turn the grace of God into licentiousness contend that being invested with the perfect righteousness of Christ, God cannot see any sin in them; and, indeed, upon their own principles, they reason conclusively. Justice has not to do with them, but with Christ; it demands perfect obedience, and Christ has rendered that perfect obedience for them, and what He did is always accounted as done by them. They are, therefore, under no real obligation of obedience; they can fear no penal consequences from disobedience; and a course of the most flagrant vice may consist with an entire confidence in the indefeasible favor of God, with the profession of sonship and discipleship, and the hope of heaven. These notions many shamelessly avow; and they have been too much encouraged in their fatal creed, by those who have held the same system substantially, though they abhor the bold conclusions that the open antinomian would draw from it.

SECOND VIEW OF IMPUTATION

The doctrine on which the above remarks have been made is the first of the three opinions that have been held on the subject of the imputation of righteousness in our justification. The second is the opinion of Calvin himself, and those of his followers, who have not refined so much upon the scheme of their master as others, and with them many Arminians have also, in some respects, agreed; not that they have approved the terms in which this opinion is usually expressed; but because they have thought it, under a certain interpretation, right, and one that would allow them, for the sake of peace, to use either the phrase, "the imputation of the righteousness of Christ," or "the imputation of faith for righteousness," which latter they consider more scriptural, and therefore interpret the former so as to be consistent with it.

JOHN CALVIN

With Calvin the notion of imputation seems to be that the righteousness of Christ, that is, His entire obedience to the will of His Father, both in doing and suffering is, upon our believing, imputed, or accounted to us, or accepted for us, "as though it were OUR OWN." From which we may conclude, that he admitted some kind of transfer of the righteousness of Christ to our account, and that believers are considered so to be in Christ, as that He should answer for them in law, and plead His righteousness in default of theirs.

All this we grant is capable of being interpreted in a good and scriptural sense; but it is also capable of a contrary one. The opinion of some professedly Calvinistic divines, such as Baxter and his followers; and of the majority of evangelical Arminians, is, as Baxter well expresses it, that Christ's righteousness is imputed to us in the sense "of its being accounted of God the valuable consideration, satisfaction, and merit [attaining God's ends], for which we are [when we consent to the covenant of grace] forgiven and justified, against the condemning sentence of the law of innocency, and accounted and accepted of God to grace and glory" *(Breviate of Controversies).*

So also Goodwin: "If we take the phrase of imputing Christ's righteousness improperly, viz. for the bestowing, as it were, of the righteousness of Christ, including His obedience, as well passive as active, in *the return of it,* that is, in the privileges, blessings, and benefits purchased by it, so a believer may be said to be justified by the righteousness of Christ imputed. But then the meaning can be no more than this: God justifies a believer for the sake of Christ's righteousness, and not for any righteousness of his own. Such an imputation of the righteousness of Christ as this, is no way denied or questioned" *(On Justification).*

Between these opinions as to the imputation of the righteousness of Christ, it will be seen that there is a manifest difference that . . . arises from the different senses in which the term *imputation* is taken. An acceptable view takes it in the sense of accounting or allowing to the believer the benefit of the righteousness of Christ. An unscriptural view takes it in the sense of reckoning or accounting the righteousness of Christ as ours; that is, what He did and suffered is regarded as done and suffered by us. "It is accepted," says Calvin, "as though it were our own." So that though Calvin does not divide the active and passive obedience of Christ, nor make justification anything more than the remission of sin, yet his opinion easily slides into the antinomian notion. It thus lays itself open to several of the same objections, and especially to this: it involves the same kind of fiction, that what Christ did or suffered, is, in any sense whatever, considered by Him who knows all things as they are, as being done or suffered by any other person, than by Him who did or suffered it in fact.

NO BIBLICAL BASIS

For this notion, that the righteousness of Christ is so imputed as to be accounted our own, there is no warrant in the Word of God; and a slight examination of those passages, which are indifferently adduced to support either the antinomian or the Calvinistic view of the subject, will suffice to demonstrate this.

We here include only two examples of Watson's exegesis on this subject.

1 Cor. 1:30, "But of him are ye in Christ Jesus, who of God is made unto us wisdom and righteousness, and sanctification, and redemption." Here, also, to say that Christ is "made unto us righteousness," by imputation, is to invent and not to interpret. This is clear, that He is made unto us righteousness only as He is made unto us "redemption," so that if we are not redeemed by imputation, we are not justified by imputation. The meaning of the apostle is that Christ is made to us, by the appointment of God, the sole means of instructions, justification, sanctification, and eternal life.

2 Cor. 5:21, "For he hath made him to be sin for us, who knew no sin; that we might be made the righteousness of God in him." To be made sin, we have already shown, signifies to be made an offering for sin; consequently, as no imputation of our sins to Christ is here mentioned, there is no foundation for the notion that there is a reciprocal imputation of Christ's righteousness to us. The text is wholly silent on this subject, for it is wholly gratuitous to say that we are made the righteousness of God in or through Christ, by imputation or reckoning to us what He did or suffered as our acts or sufferings. The passages we have already adduced will explain the phrase "the righteousness of God" in this place. This righteousness, with respect to our pardon, is God's righteous method of justifying, through the atonement of Christ, and our being made or becoming this righteousness of God in or by Christ, is our becoming righteous persons through the pardon of our sins in this peculiar method, by renouncing our own righteousness, and by "submitting to this righteousness of God."

In neither of these passages is there, then, anything found to countenance . . . the view of imputation, which consists in the accounting the righteousness of Christ in justification to be our righteousness. It is only imputed in the benefit and effect of it, that is, in the blessings and privileges purchased by it. Though we may use the phrase, the imputed righteousness of Christ, in this latter sense, we must qualify our meaning like Paroeus, who says, "In this sense imputed righteousness is called the righteousness of Christ, by way of merit or effect, because it is procured for us by the merit of Christ, not because it is subjectively or inherently in Christ."

Yet even this matter of speaking has no foundation in Scripture, and must generally lead to misapprehensions. It will therefore be found more conducive to the cause of truth to confine ourselves to the language of the Scriptures. According to them, there is no fictitious accounting either of what Christ did or suffered, or of both united, to us, as being done and suffered by us, through our union with Him, or through His becoming our legal Representative; but His active and passive righteousness, advanced in dignity by the union of the divine nature and perfection, is the true meritorious cause of our justification.

It is that great whole that constitutes His "merits"; that is the consideration in view of what the offended but merciful Governor of the world has determined it to be a just and righteous as well as a merciful act, to justify the ungodly; and, for the sake of this perfect obedience of our Lord to the will of the Father, an obedience extending unto "death, even the death of the cross," to every penitent sinner who believes in Him, but considered still in his own person as "ungodly," and meriting nothing but punishment, "his faith is imputed for righteousness"; it is followed by the remission of his sins and all the benefits of the evangelical covenant.

This imputation of FAITH for righteousness is the third opinion we proposed to examine. That it is the doctrine taught by the express letter of Scripture no one can deny, and, as one will observe, "what that is which is imputed for righteousness in justification, all the wisdom and learning of men is not so fit or able to determine, as the Holy Ghost, speaking in Scripture, He being the great secretary of heaven, and privy to all the counsels of God." "Abraham believed God, and it was imputed unto him for righteousness" (Rom. 4:3). "To him that worketh not, but believeth on him that justifieth the ungodly, his faith is counted to him for righteousness" (v. 5). "We say that faith was imputed to him for righteousness" (v. 9). "Now it was not written for his sake alone, that it was imputed to him; but for us also, to whom it shall be imputed, if we believe on him that raised up Jesus our Lord from the dead" (vv. 23-24).

FAITH IMPUTED FOR RIGHTEOUSNESS

The nature of this faith that "is imputed for righteousness" is also examined in depth. Perhaps the gist of Watson's views is in the following:

The faith in Christ, which in the New Testament is connected with salvation, is clearly of this nature; that is, it combines assent with reliance, belief with trust. "Whatsoever ye ask the Father in *my name,*" that is, in dependence upon My interest and merits, "he shall give it you." Christ was preached both to Jews and Gentiles as the object of their *trust,* because He was preached as the only true sacrifice for sin; and they were required to renounce their dependence upon their own accustomed sacrifices, and to transfer that dependence to His death and mediation—and "in his name shall the Gentiles trust."

ASSENT AND TRUST

He is set forth as a propitiation, "through faith in his blood"; which faith can neither merely assent to the historical fact that His blood was shed by a violent death, nor mere assent to the general doctrine that His blood had an atoning quality. But as all expiatory offerings were *trusted* in as the means of propitiation both among Jews and Gentiles, that faith or trust was now to be exclusively rendered to the blood of Christ, heightened by the stronger demonstrations of a divine appointment.

To the most unlettered Christian this, then, will be most obvious, that the faith in Christ that is required of us, consists both of *assent* and *trust;* and the necessity of maintaining these inseparably united will further appear by considering, that it is not a blind and superstitious trust in the sacrifice of Christ, like that of the heathen in their sacrifices, which leads to salvation; nor the presumptuous trust of wicked and impenitent men, who depend on Christ to save them in their sins; but such a trust as is exercised according to the authority and direction of the Word of God; so that to know the gospel in its leading principles, and to have a cordial belief in it, is necessary to that more specific set of faith that is called reliance, or in systematic language, *fiducial assent,* of which cometh salvation.

The gospel, as the scheme of man's salvation, supposes that he is under law; that this law of God has been violated by all; and that every man is under sentence of death. Serious consideration of our ways, confession of our sin, and sorrowful conviction of the evil and danger of sin, will follow the gift of repentance, and a cordial belief of the testimony of God, and we shall thus turn to God with contrite hearts, and earnest prayers, and supplications for His mercy.

REPENTANCE

This is called "repentance toward God"; and repentance being the first subject of evangelical preaching, and then the belief of the gospel, it is plain that Christ is only *immediately* held out in this divine plan of our redemption as the object of trust in order to forgiveness to persons in this state of penitence, and under this sense of danger.

The degree of sorrow for sin, and alarm upon this discovery of our danger as sinners, is nowhere fixed in Scripture; only it is supposed everywhere, that it is such as to lead men to inquire earnestly, "What shall I do to be saved?" and to use all the appointed means of salvation, as those who feel that their salvation is at issue; that they are in a lost condition, and must be pardoned or perish. To all such persons, Christ, as the only atonement for sin, is exhibited as the object of their trust, with the promise of God "that whosoever believeth in him shall not perish, but have everlasting life." Nothing is required of such persons but this actual trust in, and personal apprehension or taking hold of the merits of Christ's death as a sacrifice for sin; and upon their thus believing they are justified, their faith is "counted for righteousness."

2

Jabez Bunting
(1779-1858)

Jabez Bunting was only 11 years of age when John Wesley died. It is certain his parents did not anticipate that their young son would become known as the "second founder of Methodism."

Born in Manchester, England, May 13, 1779, Bunting grew up in a home of Methodistic piety and discipline, plus economic stringency. In spite of poverty, however, his father, a tailor, managed to give his son a thorough education. Jabez's first objective was medicine, but in response to an inward call he switched to the ministry and was accepted by the Methodists when 20 years of age. After a very few years he was transferred from Manchester to London where he soon became famous as a powerful preacher and orator.

Soon also his great organizing and administrative abilities were discovered. As a consequence, much of his mature life was spent either as secretary of the Methodist Conference or as its chairman. Other administrative posts were senior secretary of the missionary society and president of the theological institute, which he helped to found. For two years he was connectional editor.

Bunting's effective advocacy of church discipline and unwavering fidelity to Wesley's teaching resulted in the final break of Methodism from the Church of England, and the formation of a close-knit ecclesiastical structure. As a consequence Bunting was often at the center of controversy. But W. L. Doughty testifies that "all parties were compelled to acknowledge his sterling Christian character and sincerity of purpose, his outstanding gifts of leadership and statesmanship, his cultured, logical mind and power in debate, his strong personality, and his popularity and power as a teacher" *(Encyclopedia of World Methodism).*

Richard Watson's monumental theology had been in print about six years when Jabez Bunting became president of the theological institute. While Watson shaped Wesleyan theology, perhaps it could be said that Bunting popularized that theology and conformed the directions of the virile young church to it.

In the following sermon (the only strictly homiletical and expository discourse to be included in this volume) Bunting is a faithful son of Wesley. He is clear in his definitions, logical in his progression, and interweaves scriptural phraseology throughout. He sees sanctification as threefold: separation from the world, purification from sin, and active dedication to God. Christ is the Sanctifier in the sense that His atonement and resurrection make the sanctifying influences of the Holy Spirit possible. These transforming influences begin at the outset of the regenerated life. Bunting's stress is clearly on the gradual, but there must be a progress that reaches purity of heart in this life, as a minimum requisite for heaven. Every measure of sanctification is to be sought by faith, yet also by prayer and "in the use of all instituted means of grace"—surely an echo of Wesley. Ignoring some exegetical details, Bunting paints with a wide brush.

The Sanctifier and the Sanctified[1]

For both he that sanctifieth and they who are sanctified are all of one: for which cause he is not ashamed to call them brethren (Heb. 2:11).

In the preceding chapter the apostle has been describing the original dignity of our Lord Jesus Christ; asserting that He was not, like Moses and the other prophets, the servant only, but the Son of God, "whom he hath appointed heir of all things, by whom also he made the worlds," "the brightness of his glory, and the express image of his

---

1. Sermon 34 in *Bunting's Sermons,* 2:117-26 (New York: Carleton & Porter, 1863).

person." In order to heighten our ideas of the Savior's uncreated majesty, he next compares Him with those who hold the most elevated rank among *created* beings, the holy angels; and infers, from His acknowledged superiority to the highest orders of the heavenly hierarchy, His true and absolute divinity:

"Being made so much better than the angels, as he hath by inheritance obtained a more excellent name than they. For unto which of the angels said he at any time, Thou art my Son, this day have I begotten thee? And again, I will be to him a Father, and he shall be to me a Son? And again, when he bringeth in the first begotten into the world, he saith, And let all the angels of God worship him. And of the angels he saith, Who maketh his angels spirits, and his ministers a flame of fire. But unto the Son he saith, Thy throne, O God, is for ever and ever: a sceptre of righteousness is the sceptre of thy kingdom" (Heb. 1:4-8).

Having thus evinced Messiah's deity, he proceeds in the second chapter to speak of His humanity and to unfold the great mystery of godliness, which teaches us that in order to deliver man, He who was the Father's Fellow did not abhor the virgin's womb but lived and died in our nature and so opened the kingdom of heaven to all believers. "For," he adds, "it became him"—it was suitable to His nature and attributes; it was worthy of His infinite wisdom and love, and honorable to His spotless purity and inflexible justice, "in bringing many sons unto glory, to make the captain of their salvation perfect through suffering"; since, by this means, "both he that sanctifieth and they who are sanctified are all of one: for which cause he is not ashamed to call them brethren." In discoursing on these words, it will be proper to consider in order,

I. The sanctification to which reference is made.
II. The Agent who effects this glorious work.
III. The union that subsists between the Sanctifier and the sanctified.
IV. The consequence and proof of that union: "He is not ashamed to call them brethren."

FORMAL HOLINESS

I. *To be sanctified*, generally speaking, is to be made and kept holy; that is, to be separated from all common uses and to be set apart and dedicated to the service of God. The term is variously applied in Scripture. Sometimes it refers to a merely relative or external holiness. Hence certain portions of time are called holy, because specially consecrated to God. Thus we read, "Remember the Sabbath day, to keep it holy." Hence, too, the vessels and other furniture of the ancient temple were styled holy, because employed exclusively in divine worship. The place in which the Jewish worship was performed was denominated, on the same account, the Lord's sanctuary, and the holy place. Lastly, the persons appointed to minister in the temple were all, in this sense, said to be sanctified; and, in particular, we read that HOLINESS TO THE LORD was inscribed in large letters on the miter of the high priest.

In all these cases the sanctification attributed is merely outward and grounded on the relations that subsisted between these times, things, places, or persons, and the God of holiness, by virtue of their dedication to His service and worship. But, in many other passages, the word *sanctification* implies that great process of spiritual renovation—that real, personal, and inherent holiness—for which it is the duty of all to seek; which it is the privilege of all to enjoy, and without which no man can see the Lord. This sanctification includes three things: (1) Separation from the world. (2) Purification from sin. (3) Dedication to God.

1. *Separation from the world.* Christians are said to be "a chosen generation, a royal priesthood, a holy nation, a peculiar people." They are called out of darkness into marvelous light. They are separated from the mass of the ungodly and unbelieving world and redeemed from the vain conversation received by tradition from their fathers. They are no longer governed by the world's false and delusive maxims, no longer in bondage to its sinful customs, no longer in love with its carnal occupations and follies, no longer polluted by its vices. Once they were children of wrath, and enemies of God, even as others; but they have been translated out of the kingdom of darkness into the kingdom of God's dear Son, and put into possession of that pure religion and undefiled, one chief part of which is to keep ourselves unspotted from the world.

This inward separation from the world is rendered visible and exemplary by the change that has taken place in the company they love to frequent, and the engagements in which they voluntarily choose to bear a part. They walk not in the counsel of the ungodly, nor stand in the way of sinners, nor sit in the seat of the scornful; but their delight is with such as fear God, with them that excel in virtue. They unite themselves, for purposes of mutual encouragement and edification, with some part of the professing church of Christ; and evince that they have passed from death unto life, because they love the brethren, and openly give them the right hand of fellowship.

It is undeniably clear from Scripture that those who have been thus sanctified from the world have always joined themselves in religious fellowship to such as had been made partakers of the same grace. For "they that feared the Lord," even of old, "spake often one to another." This separation from the wicked and the worldly is an essential constituent of evangelical sanctification: for we are expressly told that God designed, by the publication of the gospel, to take out from among the Gentiles a people prepared for His name.

That this separation from the world, first inward and spiritual, then outward and visible, and followed by the union of those thus separated with each other, is one branch of sanctification, further appears from the intercessory prayer of our blessed Lord, who mentions these things in their order and intimate connection: "I pray not that thou shouldest take them out of the world, but that thou shouldest keep them from the evil. They are not of the world, even as I am not of the world. Sanctify them through thy truth: thy word is truth. As thou hast sent me into the world, even so have I also sent them into the world. And for their sakes I sanctify myself, that they also might be sanctified through the truth" (John 17:15-19).

2. But sanctification includes also a *purification from sin.* It implies, in its lowest sense, a reformation of the life and conduct; a renunciation of all known and cherished habits of transgression. It implies a cessation not only from sinful works, but from sinful words; from foolish talking and jesting, which are not convenient; from all conversation that is licentious and impure; from all that is profane or irreverent; from all that is idle, hurtful, or slanderous.

CLEANSING

It is not only an outward, but also, and principally, an *inward* purification. It implies the purification of the understanding, not, indeed, from all error in matters unessential to piety, but from all willful blindness, all voluntary prejudice against truth and holiness, all contempt of the mysteries of God; so as to make it ready to count all things but loss for the excellency of the knowledge of Christ Jesus the Lord, and to know nothing but Christ and Him crucified.

It implies the rectification of the will; so as to free it from all rebellious opposition to the laws of God, or fretful murmuring against the dispensations of providence. It implies the due regulation of the affections and passions; their deliverance from every unlawful object and attachment, and from all sinful inordinacy as to the degree in which they are fixed even on objects lawful and proper. And it implies, when carried to its full extent, the purifying of the imagination, of the thoughts and contemplations of the mind; which ought all to be brought into captivity to the obedience of Christ, and so purged from vanity and sin, so cleansed by the inspiration of the Holy Spirit that we may perfectly love God and worthily magnify His holy name.

In fine, sanctification, as it implies a deliverance from the power and pollution of sin, extends to every member of the body and every faculty of the mind. Where sin abounded, by the pollution of the whole man, there grace is much more to abound, by the thorough cleansing both of flesh and spirit, till we perfect holiness in the fear of the Lord, till according to the apostolic prayer the very God of peace has sanctified us wholly, and our whole spirit, and soul, and body are preserved blameless, even unto the coming of our Lord Jesus Christ.

ACTIVE DEVOTION

3. A third part of sanctification is *actual dedication and devotion of ourselves to God:* "I beseech you therefore, brethren, by the mercies of God, that ye present your bodies a living sacrifice, holy, acceptable unto God, which is your reasonable service" (Rom. 12:1). To be abstracted (separated) from the world, and purified from evil, would not be sufficient, if it were not accompanied, and followed, and manifested, by the cordial and unreserved surrender of our redeemed and renewed faculties to God in Christ Jesus. Our understanding must be employed in the investigation of His works, and of His holy Word. Our will must cheerfully and promptly cooperate with His; conforming to all His revealed pleasure; entering into all His wise and merciful designs; and confidently accepting all that He enjoins or appoints, as undeniably best, because by Him approved and chosen.

Our affections must be so devoted to Him and to His cause that we shall love the Lord with all our heart, soul, and might. Our thoughts must be much engaged in devout meditation on the things that pertain to His kingdom, and in earnest aspirations after His favor and image. Yea, our eyes must read the great things of His law and gaze on the glory of His inimitable perfections as displayed in the works of His hands. Our feet must run, with willing joy and eager haste, in the way of His commandments. Our tongues must confess Him before men, and sing His goodness, and supplicate His grace. Thus are we to reckon ourselves "dead indeed unto sin, but alive unto God through Jesus Christ our Lord."

We are not only enjoined, negatively, not to yield ourselves to sin;

but positively, to yield ourselves to God, and our members as servants to holiness. Being made free from sin, we are also to become servants of God, in the discharge of every public and private, every personal and relative duty; in the exercise of every grace, and the practice of every virtue; having our fruit unto holiness, and the end everlasting life. Thus, whether we eat, or drink, or whatsoever we do we are to do all to the glory of God. Whether we live, we must live unto the Lord; and whether we die, we must die unto the Lord: whether we live, therefore, or die, we are to be the Lord's. Such is our high calling of God in Christ Jesus. Such is the mark toward which we must press, till with all saints we come unto a perfect man, unto the measure of the stature of the fullness of Christ.

SHOULD BE SOUGHT

That this sanctification ought to be sought, and may be largely experienced, in the present life, the promises, and invitations, and declarations, and precepts of Scripture that relate to it, abundantly demonstrate. The former branches of it, in particular—separation from the irreligious world, and purification from inward and outward sin—are not only essential to our present lasting comfort but indispensably requisite to our future and final salvation.

The people of God, not only on earth, but even when admitted into glory, may differ as to the degree in which they are transformed into His likeness and possessed of His fullness. But all who are now finally saved were, at the time of their decease in Christ, upon equal terms in point of *salvation from sin;* all were fully cleansed from all their idols and sprinkled from all their iniquities: since none but those who are thus made pure in heart can see the kingdom of God. Nor is it necessary that we should wait till death for the enjoyment of this purifying grace; because it is not the agony of dissolution but the blood of Jesus Christ (obtaining for us, through our faith in Him, the purifying energy of the indwelling Spirit) that cleanses from all sin. And that blood is now as efficacious as ever it can hereafter be, to all who cry to God for its application, in the exercise of ardent desire, of persevering prayer, and of active, self-denying, sin-mortifying faith.

AFTER THE NEW BIRTH

A preparation for this blessed work of sanctification is wrought even in penitents convinced of sin; who, if their conviction and contrition be genuine, will bring forth fruits meet for repentance. Properly speaking, however, the Spirit does not fully take up His abode or begin His renewing and purifying work in the soul, till we are justified by faith and have peace with God through our Lord Jesus Christ. Then the faith we have received works by love and purifies the heart. Then we first experience that principle of love to God, and to man for His sake (because He first loved us), which is the only productive seed of real and lasting holiness.

Christ is made of God unto us "wisdom" to enlighten, then "righteousness" to justify, then "sanctification" to renew, and, lastly, "redemption" to glorify. So the apostle writes to the Corinthians: "Such were some of you: but ye are washed," that is, cleansed from those external abominations, before described, in which ye once lived; and the cause of this is that "ye are sanctified," inwardly purified and transformed; and this, because "ye are justified," and, in consequence of that justification, have received the grace of holiness: all this being wrought "in the name of the Lord Jesus," for His sole merits, "and by the Spirit of our God," applying those merits to your souls, and producing in you the fruits of righteousness.

PROGRESS IN HOLINESS

And if the divine fire, thus kindled in the heart of the pardoned believer, be not chilled by relapses into sin or omissions of duty—if his faith continue to work by love, and to overcome the world—if he persists to follow Christ in the path of self-denial and mortification, constantly exercising himself unto godliness, waiting on God in the use of all instituted means of grace, and wrestling for larger measures of the Spirit and its fruits, according to his faith it shall be done unto him. Every enemy shall be vanquished, every thought shall be brought into captivity to grace; and he shall comprehend, with all saints, what is the height and depth of the love of Christ and be filled with the fullness of God. The good seed shall produce not only the blade, but the ear; yea and after that the full corn in the ear. And still shall the believer grow up into Christ his living Head in all things, by doing and suffering His will; till, when the fruit is fully ripe, angels shall put in the sickle and gather the harvest.[2]

II. The Agent who effects this glorious work.

CHRIST AS SANCTIFIER

The context proves that our blessed Savior the Lord Jesus Christ is *he that sanctifieth.* Man is naturally helpless, and dead in sin; and therefore unable to sanctify or save himself. As we are not naturally holy, but the reverse, so neither can we acquire holiness by our own natural powers or efforts. The Ethi-

2. It is obvious that Bunting is stressing continuous and progressive sanctification in this sermon and is not attempting to draw a sharp line between initial sanctification and entire sanctification, to be received by faith at a distinct point in time. *Editor.*

opian cannot change his skin, nor the leopard his spots. By grace only can we be saved, through faith; and even *that* not of ourselves. From none but the Giver of every good and perfect gift can we derive this most needful blessing. To Him it belongs to enlighten the mind, to convince the judgment, to renew the will, to bring us into the paths of holiness, and preserve us in them.

Though this work of sanctification is often ascribed in Scripture to the special agency of the Holy Spirit, yet we are not to understand those passages as excluding either the Father or the Son. It is probable that St. Paul refers to the First Person of the Trinity in his prayer for the Thessalonians: "The very God of peace sanctify you wholly; and I pray God your whole spirit and soul and body be preserved blameless unto the coming of our Lord Jesus Christ." And we elsewhere read that Christ is our "sanctification"; and that we are sanctified by faith that is in Him. The reason of these expressions, and of the corresponding phraseology of the text, is obvious.

THE TRINITY

The Holy Spirit is given to sanctify us only in consequence of the incarnation, the atonement, the ascension, and intercession of Christ. These mediatorial acts of the Son are the cornerstones of the whole covenant of grace, the whole economy of redemption. He died to procure, and He lives to dispense the Spirit by whose communion His grace flows to His mystical Body. He "loved the church, and gave himself for it; that he might sanctify and cleanse it with the washing of water by the word, that he might present it to himself a glorious church, not having spot, or wrinkle, or any such thing; but that it should be holy and without blemish" (Eph. 5:25-27). Hence the necessary instrumentality of faith in Him, in order to sanctification, as well as to justification.[3]

The text teaches us,

III. The union that subsists between the Sanctifier and the sanctified: They "are all of one."

1. There is a unity in point of *common human nature:* It was necessary that Christ should assume humanity, that He might be capable of making atonement by suffering. "Forasmuch then as the chil-

---

3. While Bunting acknowledges the place of the Holy Spirit in our sanctification, his stress is on Christ as our Sanctifier. This is in keeping with the passage he is expounding. Others, such as Daniel Steele, give more detailed attention to the Holy Spirit's function in effecting personal and experiential sanctification. *Editor.*

dren are partakers of flesh and blood, he also himself likewise took part of the same; that through death he might destroy him that had the power of death, that is, the devil; and deliver them who through fear of death were all their lifetime subject to bondage. . . . Wherefore in all things it behoved him to be made like unto his brethren, that he might be a merciful and faithful high priest in things pertaining to God, to make reconciliation for the sins of the people" (Heb. 2:14-15, 17).

ONENESS WITH CHRIST

2. There is a oneness in *exposure to earthly trials:* "For it became him, for whom are all things, and by whom are all things, in bringing many sons unto glory, to make the captain of their salvation perfect through sufferings" (v. 10).

3. There will be a oneness in point of *final reward.* If we suffer with Him, we shall be also glorified together. Christ is the firstborn of many brethren; but the firstborn will not alone enjoy the inheritance. The exclusive privileges of [being the firstborn], as sometimes admitted among men, will have no existence in heaven. All the sanctified are "children," and therefore fellow-heirs. As Christ has overcome, they shall overcome and sit down with Him on His throne. Jesus is now crowned with glory and honor; and so will His sanctified people be hereafter.

It only remains to consider,

IV. The consequence and proof of the union between the Sanctifier and the sanctified: "He is not ashamed to call them brethren."

Lest a just sense of our own great unworthiness should restrain us from drawing near to our glorious Elder Brother with humble boldness, or relying on the constant friendship to which the near relationship entitles us, He himself is pleased, with the most condescending goodness, to recognize us as one with himself, and to accost us as *brethren:* an appellation that ought to remove all our distrust and shyness and to induce our approach to Him in the full assurance of faith. Of this gracious recognition the apostle quotes three instances: "I will declare thy name unto my brethren, in the midst of the church will I sing praise unto thee. And again, I will put my trust in him. And again, Behold I and the children which God hath given me" (Heb. 2:12-13).

3

Thomas N. Ralston

(1806-91)

Thomas Neely Ralston was the first American systematic theologian of Methodism, and perhaps still the best known. The son of John and Elizabeth Neely Ralston, Thomas was thoroughly Kentuckian in birth and death, in his education, and in much of his ministry. Georgetown College was his alma mater, and Wesleyan University in Florence, Ky., bestowed upon him the honorary D.D. degree. Following his conversion at age 20, he was licensed to preach one year later and was ordained as an elder by the Illinois Conference of the Methodist church in 1834. Soon after he transferred to Kentucky, where he later cast his lot with the Southern Methodist conferences in the formation of the Methodist Episcopal Church South.

Ralston was an energetic evangelistic preacher and successful soul-winner, as well as an administrator and editor. He served as president of the Methodist Female High School in Lexington for three years, secretary of the General Conference (MES), and editor of the *Methodist Monthly.*

His first edition of *Elements of Divinity* was published in 1847, but a revised and greatly expanded edition came out in 1876.[1] This work was for many years in the course of study for licensed ministers, not only in the author's own church but in many other denominations, including the Church of the Nazarene.

---

1. *Elements of Divinity: A Concise and Comprehensive View of Bible Theology; Comprising the Doctrines, Evidences, Morals, and Institutions of Christianity.* Methodist Episcopal Church, South. Edited by T. O. Summers. 1876.

Ralston's original work, published in 1847, was confined to the doctrines of Christianity. The 1876 edition adds several chapters plus the new areas of inquiry listed in the full title. In his preface Ralston claims that the basic revision and expansion are his own.

The author's objective was to put theology in simple language. He desired to make it clear, interesting, even enjoyable to the young theologue and the alert layman. In this he admirably succeeded. Much in Ralston is exciting reading, even eloquent. The style is marked for its clarity and logical flow. In organizing the material he made a great improvement over Watson.[2]

Human Nature as Fallen[3]

Years ago Rev. H. D. Brown, a former Methodist minister who became one of the early giants of the Church of the Nazarene, said: "The doctrine of original sin is crucial to the doctrine of entire sanctification." He meant that since inbred sin as a moral bent carries over into the regenerate life, carnality in the believer is the basis for the need of a second work of grace. The cleansing from original sin is the primary objective of such a second work. It is always true that muffling and waffling on original sin will result in a gradual deprecation of second blessing teaching. The early Wesleyan theologians were vigorous and thorough in their insistence on this doctrine and in their opposition to Pelagianism in any form.

Ralston devotes six chapters to the origin and nature of sin in man; the first three to man's original state, his fall, and its penal effects. The next three are devoted to the racial effects of the Fall. In chapter 11, after proving the fact of original sin from the Scripture, he adds some observations from life. The primary intent of these observations is to disprove the notion of "Socinians, Pelagians, and Unitarians" that the prevalence of wickedness is due only to the influence of bad example and education.

---

2. Ralston had a habit of emphasizing certain words in his Bible quotations by italicizing them. We have retained his italics, even though they slightly alter the KJV.

3. *Elements of Divinity*, 135-38.

(1) To account for the general prevalence of wickedness, reliance has been placed on the influence of example and education.

EXAMPLE CANNOT ACCOUNT FOR UNIVERSAL WICKEDNESS

Here a little attention, we think, will show that the difficulty is not solved but only shifted to another quarter. If man be not naturally depraved, it will be just as difficult to account for bad example as for wickedness itself; yes, more: bad example is but another name for wickedness. Therefore, to say that general wickedness is the result of general bad example, is the same as to say that general wickedness is the result of general wickedness; or, in other words, the cause of itself, which is a manifest absurdity. Further, we might ask, How was it, upon this principle, that the first example of the various species of moral wickedness originated? Whose example taught Cain to hate and murder his brother? Whose example taught the first idolater to worship an idol? And so we might pass over the entire catalog of vices, and show that, according to this system, they never could have originated.

That we are naturally imitative beings, to a great extent, we readily admit; but if this alone leads to a course of wickedness, it would follow, upon the same principle, that there should be quite as much potency in good as in bad example. But, we ask, Is this the case? Why did not the piety of righteous Noah lead all his sons and their descendants, from generation to generation, in the pathway of duty and obedience?

Again, is it not frequently the case that the children of pious parents fall into habits of immorality? If example alone shapes their character, surely the pious example of their parents, which they see almost constantly before their eyes, should be more powerful than the wicked example of others more remote from them, and perhaps but seldom witnessed. Allow to example all the influence it can possibly wield, still it would follow that if man is naturally innocent and pure, there should be more virtue than vice in the world; but if, as some contend, the soul is naturally indifferent—a perfect blank, tending neither to good nor evil—then we might expect to find virtue and vice pretty equally balanced. But the fact of the world's history is contradictory to all this.

(2) But now look at the second fact—*the strength of the tendency in man to evil.*

Who has not felt this in his own heart? "When I would do good, evil is present with me." The turbulence of evil passions is such that the wise man has said, "He that ruleth his spirit is better than he that taketh a city." The strength of this native tendency in man to evil is so great that, to counteract it, an effort is required; the cross must be taken up, right hands cut off, right eyes plucked out, and a violent warfare upon the impulses of our own nature must be waged. Now contemplate the absurdity of supposing that bad example could originate this tendency to evil. If such were the case, good example would produce a similar tendency to good; but such is evidently not the fact. The native tendency of the human heart is invariably to sin; so much so that in no case can it be counteracted but by the "crucifixion" of "the old man."

(3) The third fact is *the early appearance of the principle of various vices in children.*

Although entirely separated from their species, native instinct will lead the young lion or tiger to be fierce and voracious; and with equal certainty, pride, envy, malice, revenge, selfishness, anger, and other evil passions have been found invariably to spring up at a very early stage in the hearts of children, whatever may have been the example or education with which they have been furnished. Nay, the evils have more or less frequently exhibited themselves before the opportunity would have been afforded for the influence of example. Now, how can this be accounted for but upon the supposition that the seeds of these vices are sown in our nature?

(4) The fourth fact is, that *every man is conscious of a natural tendency to many evils.*

All men are not prone alike to every species of vice. Some have a strong constitutional tendency to pride, others to anger, others to cowardice, others to meanness, and others perhaps to avarice or sensuality. Now, if we deny the native depravity of man, we necessarily deny this constitutional tendency to one vice more than another; for if man has no native tendency to evil in general, it is clear he can have no native tendency to any particular species of evil. Every whole includes all its parts.

(5) The fifth fact is the *general resistance to virtue in the heart; it renders education, influence, watchfulness, and conflict necessary to counteract the force of evil.*

Vice in the human soul, like noxious weeds in a luxuriant soil, is a spontaneous growth. It only requires to be left alone, and it will flourish. Not so with virtue. Its seeds must be sown, and, like the valuable grains produced by the assiduous care and toil of the husbandman, it

NATURAL RESISTANCE TO VIRTUE

requires an early and persevering culture. Hence the necessity of a careful moral training—the value of a good education.

What powerful influences are requisite to be wielded in the promotion of virtue! Motives of gratitude, interest, honor, benevolence, and every consideration that ought to weigh with an intelligent mind, are presented as incentives to virtue. The closest vigilance is necessary at every point to keep the object of good from being entirely forgotten or neglected; and, withal, a perpetual conflict must be kept up with surrounding evil, or the thorns and thistles of vice and folly will choke the growth of the good seed and lay waste the blooming prospect. Why, we ask, is this the case? Deny the doctrine of the native depravity of man, and it is utterly unaccountable. If example were the only influence, and man had no greater tendency to evil than to good, might we not as well expect to find virtue the spontaneous and luxuriant growth, and vice the tender plant, requiring all this toil and care for its preservation and prosperity?

SINFULNESS CANNOT BE TRACED TO WRONG EDUCATION

Those who have endeavored to account for these *facts* on the principle of *education* find in their undertaking no less difficulty than those who attribute them to the influence of *example.* Education, in too many instances it must be confessed, has been greatly defective; but never so bad as to account for all the evil passions and sinful practices of men. So far from this being the case, its general tendency, defective as it may be, is of an opposite character. Men are generally wicked, not so much for the want of good precept, as in spite of it. Instruction has generally been better than example; so that, if bad example cannot account for the proneness to evil in men, much less can education.

Who taught the first murderer his lessons in the crimes of shedding his brother's blood? Which of the prevalent vices of mankind had its origin in imparted instruction? What crime is it that can only exist and prevail where special schools are established for its culture? The influence of education, it must be admitted, is very great; but the difficulty to be accounted for is this: Why is it that man is so *ready* in the school of vice and so *dull* in the school of virtue? Deny the doctrine of our native corruption, and why might we not, with far more reason, expect that education should produce general virtue than vice? Thus have we seen that experience and observation only confirm the Scripture doctrine of the native and total depravity of man.

Repentance[4]

It should be a truism among us that our feeling toward holiness will in large measure be determined by the depth of our repentance. An abhorrence of sin, and a radical turning from it, will induce a corresponding hunger for holiness and a resolute commitment to it. Preachers who slight repentance will gather a people who slight holiness.

In chapter 26 Ralston provides a clear outline of basic biblical truth on this vital subject. He calls it "Repentance—Its Nature, Means, and Necessity." Here he distinguishes between reformation and sorrow for sin. Also he departs from Watson, his mentor, in distinguishing between conviction and repentance. Furthermore he clarifies the sense in which repentance is the gift of God and the sense in which it is the act of the sinner. The following is Section I, "The Nature of Repentance."

I. In endeavoring to ascertain *the Scripture doctrine in reference to the nature of repentance,* which is the point proposed as first to be discussed, we hope to be conducted by the plain teachings of the Bible to such conclusions as shall be clear and satisfactory to the candid mind.

1. In inquiring for the Scripture import of repentance it is natural that our first appeal be made to the *etymology of the word.*

Here we find that two different words in the Greek Testament, varying in their signification, are rendered "repent." These are *metamelomai* and *metanoeō*. The former implies *a sorrowful change of the mind,* or properly, *contrition for sin;* the latter implies all that is meant by the former, together with *reformation from sin*—that is, it implies *a sorrow for,* and a consequent *forsaking of, or turning away from sin.* Macknight, in reference to these words, makes the following critical remarks: "The word, *metanoia,* properly denotes such a change of one's opinion concerning some action which he hath done, as produceth a change in his conduct to the better. But the word, *metameleia,* signifies the *grief* which one feels for what he hath done, though it is followed with no alteration of conduct. The two words, however, are used indiscriminately in the LXX (Septuagint), for *a change of conduct,*

4. *Elements of Divinity,* 343-49.

and for *grief* on account of what hath been done." (See Macknight on 2 Cor. 7:10.)

Here it may be observed that, although there is a diversity, there is no opposition of meaning in these two words. The only difference is, the one implies more than the other. *Metanoeō* implies all that is implied by *metamelomai,* together with something further. It is worthy of notice that with us, in common conversation, we frequently use the English word *repent,* merely to denote the idea of sorrow or contrition for the past, whether that sorrow be accompanied by any change of conduct or not. But in the investigation of the Scripture meaning of repentance, the distinction above made is important to be kept in mind.

In reference to the repentance of Judas, spoken of in Matt. 27:3, a form of the verb *metamelomai* is used, from which we conclude that there is no evidence from that expression whether his repentance was further than mere contrition or not. But generally, where repentance is spoken of in Scripture, connected in any sense with salvation, the word used is a derivative of *metanoeō.* Hence we conclude that the proper definition of *evangelical repentance,* or that repentance which the gospel requires, includes both *contrition* and *reformation.*

REPENTANCE

2. In accordance with what we have said, we find the correct definition of repentance, as adopted by Dr. Thomas Scott, to be as follows: "A genuine sorrow for sin, attended with a real inclination to undo, if it were possible, all we have sinfully done; and consequently an endeavor, as far as we have it in our power, to counteract the consequences of our former evil conduct; with a determination of mind, through divine grace, to walk for the future in newness of life, evidenced to be sincere by fruits meet for repentance—that is, by all holy dispositions, words, and actions" (Scott's *Works,* 4:43).

Substantially the same, but perhaps better expressed, is the definition of repentance given by Mr. Watson in his *Biblical Dictionary.* Thus: "Evangelical repentance is a godly sorrow wrought in the heart of a sinful person by the Word and Spirit of God, whereby, from a sense of his sin, as offensive to God and defiling and endangering to his own soul, and from an apprehension of the mercy of God in Christ, he with grief and hatred of all his known sins, turns from them to God as his Savior and Lord."

By attention to the above definitions, as well as from the etymology of the word as already given, it will appear that all that is implied by evangelical repentance is properly embraced under one or the other of the two general heads presented—that is, *contrition* and *reformation.* There may be both contrition and reformation, but if they are not of the right kind—if either of them be spurious—the repentance is not genuine. We may suppose the contrition to be genuine, yet if the genuine reformation does not ensue, the repentance is not evangelical. Or we may suppose a thorough reformation to take place, at least so far as externals are concerned, yet, if it does not proceed from a right source—if it does not flow from a "godly sorrow, wrought by the Spirit of God"—the repentance cannot be genuine.

It may, however, be necessary to enlarge somewhat upon the definitions given.

(1) First, then, in reference to that part of repentance that we have termed *contrition,* we observe, that it always presupposes and flows from *conviction.*

What we think to be a little inaccuracy of expression has occurred with most theological writers, whether Calvinistic or Arminian, in reference to this point. It has generally been represented that conviction constitutes a part of repentance.

CONVICTION IS NOT REPENTANCE

Mr. Watson, than whom, we believe, a more discriminating divine, and one more critically correct, has never written, in speaking of repentance, uses, in his *Biblical Dictionary,* the following words: "Taken in a religious sense, it signifies conviction of sin, and sorrow for." Now, that *conviction* must necessarily precede repentance, and is indispensable to its existence, we readily concede; but that it constitutes a part of repentance, we think is so palpably unscriptural, that it is a little surprising that critical divines should so generally have passed over this point in such haste as to adopt the inaccuracy of expression in which, as we have seen, the penetrating Watson has, though inadvertently, we believe, followed them.

That conviction cannot be a part of repentance, we may clearly see when we reflect that God has never promised to repent for any man. "God is not the son of man that he should *repent,*" but He "has commanded *all men* everywhere to *repent.*" Again: conviction is a work that the Lord performs by the agency of the Holy Spirit, which is promised "to reprove (or convict) the world of sin." Now, we see from these passages, as well as from the whole tenor of Scripture, that God is the Agent who convicts, and man is the agent who, under that conviction, and through divine grace, is called upon to repent. God has never commanded us to convict ourselves, but He has commanded us to repent. Hence we infer that conviction constitutes no part of repentance.

Again: that conviction cannot be a part of repentance is clear, not only from the definitions quoted from Scott and Watson, but also from the etymology of the word *repent,* as already shown. According to all these, "repentance is a sorrow for sin." Now, "sorrow for sin" is not conviction but an effect of conviction. Conviction, unless resisted, results in repentance; it leads to it but does not constitute a part of it.

(2) Again, we remark that *contrition, the first part of repentance when not stifled or resisted by the sinner, results in, and leads to, reformation—the second part of repentance.*

This may be seen from the words of the apostle, in 2 Cor. 7:10: "For godly sorrow worketh repentance to salvation not to be repented of." Some have concluded from this passage that "godly sorrow" cannot be a part of repentance, because it is said to "work repentance," and "repentance," say they, "cannot be said to work, or produce, itself." This seems to be rather a play upon words.

We readily admit that a thing cannot be both effect and cause at the same time and in the same sense; and consequently, in this acceptation, repentance cannot be the cause of itself. But one part of repentance may be the cause of the other; and this we believe is the clear meaning of the passage, quoted, "Godly sorrow (that is, contrition, or the first part of repentance) worketh (or leadeth to the second part of repentance—that is, the completion of repentance—or, as it is expressed in the text) repentance to salvation."

Although "godly sorrow" is repentance begun, yet no repentance is "repentance to salvation" till it is completed; or till it extends to a thorough reformation of heart and life. Hence we say with propriety that repentance begun worketh repentance completed or, which is the same thing, "godly sorrow worketh repentance to salvation."

(3) Repentance presupposes *the sinful condition of man.*

NEED FOR REPENTANCE

"A just person needeth no repentance." As none can repent of their sins till they are first convicted, so none can be convicted of sin but such as have sinned. The general position here assumed—that sinners and such only are proper subjects for repentance—is clear from the Scriptures. One or two quotations may be allowed. In Matt. 9:13 the Savior says: "I am not come to call the righteous, but *sinners* to repentance." In Luke 13:2-3: "Jesus answering said unto them, Suppose ye that these Galileans were *sinners* above all the Galileans, because they suffered such things? I tell you, Nay: but, except ye repent, ye shall all likewise perish." Here the argument is that as all are sinners, therefore they must repent, or perish.

(4) The last question we shall discuss concerning the nature of repentance *relates to its connection with faith and regeneration.*

Upon this subject, between Calvinists generally, and Arminians, there is a great difference of sentiment. But this difference relates not to the abstract but to the relative nature of repentance. They agree with regard to what repentance is, considered in itself; but differ with regard to its relative character, as connected with faith and regeneration. The Calvinistic doctrine is that faith and repentance both flow necessarily from and are always preceded by regeneration.

CALVINISTIC VIEW

The Calvinistic view on this subject is clearly presented in Buck's Dictionary, thus: "1. Regeneration is the work of God enlightening the mind and changing the heart, and in order of time precedes faith. 2. Faith is the consequence of regeneration, and implies the perception of an object. It discerns the evil of sin, the holiness of God, gives credence to the testimony of God in His Word, and seems to precede repentance, since we cannot repent of that of which we have no clear perception, or no concern about. 3. Repentance is an afterthought, or sorrowing for sin, the evil nature of which faith perceives, and which immediately follows faith. Conversion is a turning from sin, which faith sees, and repentance sorrows for; and seems to follow, and to be the end of all the rest" *(Art. Faith).*

Here we see that, according to the above, which is the view of Calvinists generally, there is, in reference to these graces, in point of time, the following order: (1) Regeneration; (2) Faith; (3) Repentance; (4) Conversion.

ARMINIAN VIEW

Arminians think the Scriptures present a different order on this subject. They contend that, so far from repentance and faith being preceded by regeneration, and flowing from it, they precede, and are conditions of regeneration. But our business in the present chapter is with the subject of repentance. We shall endeavor to show that it precedes both saving faith and regeneration.

Now observe, we do not contend that repentance precedes the enlightening, and, to some extent, the quickening, influence of the Holy Spirit, and some degree of faith; but we do contend that repentance precedes justifying faith and the new birth, which constitute an individual a new creature, or a child of God.

We shall examine this subject in the light of Scripture.

SCRIPTURE EVIDENCE

1. It appears evident from *the total depravity of human nature,* as taught in Scripture, that the soul must first be visited by the convicting grace of God, and that a degree of faith must be produced before the first step can be taken toward salvation. This we find also clearly taught in the Word of God. In Heb. 11:6, we read: "But without *faith* it is impossible to please him: for he that cometh to God must *believe that he is,* and that *he is a rewarder* of them that diligently seek him." To show that at least a degree of conviction and of faith must necessarily precede evangelical repentance, many other texts might be adduced; but as this is a point that will scarcely be disputed, we deem the above sufficient.

We proceed now to show that evangelical repentance precedes justifying faith and regeneration. It should, however, be remembered, we do not contend that there is no repentance after faith and regeneration. It is freely admitted that repentance may and does continue in some sense and to some extent, as long as there are remains of sin in the soul, or perhaps as long as the soul continues in the body; for even if we suppose the soul to be "cleansed from all sin," a sorrowful remembrance of past sins, which constitutes one part of repentance, may still be properly exercised. But the point of controversy is not whether repentance may succeed, but whether it precedes justifying faith and regeneration. A few passages of Scripture, we think, may determine the question.

2. The general custom with the sacred writers, wherever repentance is spoken of in connection with faith or regeneration, *is to place repentance first.*

Thus we read, Acts 20:21: "Testifying both to the Jews, and also to the Greeks, *repentance* toward God, and *faith* toward our Lord Jesus Christ." Acts 5:31: "Him hath God exalted with his right hand to be a Prince and a Saviour, for to give *repentance* to Israel, and *forgiveness of sins.*" Mark 1:15: "*Repent* ye, and *believe* the gospel." In these passages *repentance* is placed *before faith* and *forgiveness.* Now, although we would not rest our argument simply on the fact that repentance is placed invariably foremost by the inspired writers, yet upon the supposition that it is always preceded by faith and regeneration, it would be difficult to account for the general observance of this order in the Scriptures.

Again; the Scriptures frequently speak of repentance as the first step or commencement of religion. The dispensation of John the Baptist was introductory or preparatory to the gospel; and his preaching was emphatically the doctrine of repentance. He called on the people to repent and be baptized with "the baptism of *repentance*," and this was to prepare the way for Christ—to prepare the people by repentance for the reception of the gospel by *faith.* In Heb. 6:1, we read: "Not laying again the *foundation of repentance* from dead works, and of faith toward God." Here repentance is not only placed before faith, but it is spoken of as the "foundation," or commencement in religion.

3. In Acts 2:38, St. Peter says: "*Repent,* and be baptized every one of you in the name of Jesus Christ for the *remission of sins,* and ye shall receive *the gift of the Holy Ghost.*" These persons could not have been regenerated believers, for if so, their sins must have been already remitted; but they were commanded to "repent and be baptized," in order to remission. Hence it is clear that with them repentance preceded remission; but, as remission always accompanies faith and regeneration, their repentance must have preceded faith and regeneration. It is said in Matt. 21:32: "And ye, when ye had seen it, repented not afterward, that ye *might believe* him." Here repentance is presented as a necessary antecedent of faith.

Quotations on this point might be greatly extended, but we will add but one text more—Acts 3:19: "*Repent* ye therefore, and be converted, that your sins may be blotted out, when the times of refreshing shall come from the presence of the Lord." Here repentance, so far from being presented as "an afterthought," following saving faith and regeneration, is presented as one of the conditions in order to remission: and, consequently, in order to faith and regeneration.

4. We here simply add that the Calvinistic scheme, in requiring regeneration and justifying faith to precede repentance, appears to be not only not countenanced by the general tenor of Scripture, but is likewise seriously objectionable on other grounds. As "all men everywhere" are "commanded to repent," and that, not after they shall become regenerated, but "now"—at this moment—it follows either that they are commanded to do what God knows they cannot do, or that repentance may precede regeneration.

Once more: as all men are required to repent, and warned that "except they repent, they shall perish," it follows, that if they cannot repent till they are first regenerated, and if regeneration be a work in which "the sinner is passive," as the Calvinists teach, then the finally impenitent may urge a fair excuse for neglecting to repent; they may say: "Truly we never repented, but we are not to blame; repentance could not precede regeneration, and we were compelled to wait for Thy regenerating grace."

We deem it useless to pursue this subject further. We have endeavored to illustrate the nature of repentance, both by considering what it implies in the abstract and by noticing its relation to faith and regeneration.

Duty Toward Our Neighbor[5]

That holiness should be moral and practical is axiomatic. Entire sanctification completes the process of ridding the soul of its lawless elements and unites the entire being in thoroughgoing goodwill. This goodwill is directed to the family, immediate neighbors, the church, fellow workers, employers as well as employees, and toward society in general. Such goodwill is not a spineless softness. It is a positive seeking of human welfare, and it sees that such welfare can be achieved only within the framework of the moral laws of God. Holiness obeys the law from the heart, because one is motivated by Christian love and seeks honestly the fulfillment of the law's intent.

Holiness people need all the help they can get in thinking through the ethical implications of their holiness position. Therefore Ralston's perceptive discussion of the second section of the Ten Commandments is perennially relevant.

THE MORAL LAW

Agreeably to our Lord's comment on the moral law, our duty to God, which we have already considered, was embraced in the *first* of the two tables of stone, and our duty to our neighbor in the *second*. The former is all fulfilled in *loving God supremely;* the latter in *loving our neighbor as ourselves.*

To the latter branch of this duty, or to the second table of the Decalogue, we now call attention. In our Savior's epitomized presentation of the moral law, the six commandments of the second table are

---

5. *Elements of Divinity,* 815-24. This selection is chapter 10 of Part III (The Morals of Christianity) and is titled "Our Duty to Our Neighbor—Its General Principles Considered."

all comprised in this sentence, "Thou shalt love thy neighbour as thyself"; and also in our Savior's golden rule (Matt. 7:12).

St. Paul comments on the moral law in perfect accordance with our Savior's teachings. He says: "He that loveth another hath fulfilled the law. For this, Thou shalt not commit adultery, Thou shalt not kill, Thou shalt not steal, Thou shalt not bear false witness, Thou shalt not covet; and if there be any other commandment, it is briefly comprehended in this saying, namely, Thou shalt love thy neighbour as thyself. Love worketh no ill to his neighbour: therefore love is the fulfilling of the law" (Rom. 13:8-10).

Thus it appears that all moral obligation—our duty to God, ourselves, and others—is comprised in one word—LOVE. Here is the grand center and source whence all duty is derived—love to God and love to man. How sublimely simple and comprehensive is this comment of Christ; and how beautiful the illustration of St. Paul! In considering this moral code, so far as it relates to *love to our neighbor,* two things are to be noticed—

LOVE AND LAW

I. THE GENERAL PRINCIPLES EMBRACED

II. THEIR APPLICATION TO SPECIAL CASES AND CONDITIONS

In this chapter we will consider *the general principles embraced.*

These are all comprised in the six commandments of the second table; and no more simple and correct method of analyzing and illustrating the subject can be adopted than to consider each of these commandments separately.

I. The *fifth* commandment—the *first* in the second table—reads thus: "Honour thy father and thy mother: that thy days may be long upon the land which the Lord thy God giveth thee" (Exod. 20:12).

FAMILY DUTIES

Although this commandment only specifies the duty of children to parents, yet, according to its scope and bearing, it should be understood as covering the whole ground, not only of the obligation of children to parents, and of parents to children, but of inferiors to superiors, and superiors to inferiors. . . .

II. The sixth commandment is, "Thou shalt not kill."

1. This commandment *forbids* the taking of life—either our own, or that of our fellow creatures—except in case of *public justice* by process of law, necessary *self-defense,* or *justifiable war* lawfully waged.

SANCTITY OF HUMAN LIFE

In reference to the first exception here specified, there can be little controversy. All will admit that, for a capital offense, the law of the land may rightfully take the life of the criminal.[6] This is only carrying out the ancient precept delivered to Noah and his family: "Whoso sheddeth man's blood, by man shall his blood be shed" (Gen. 9:6).

It must also be understood that *treason,* because it is of the essence of murder, and necessarily leads to its commission, is here constructively embraced as a crime included with murder and may rightfully be involved in the same penalty of forfeiture of life.

But as to crimes and misdemeanors of less magnitude, and for the perpetration of which there is no warrant in the Word of God for inflicting the penalty of death, should any state attach such penalty and the officers of the law carry out the sentence and execution accordingly, the state itself then becomes the violator of the sixth commandment, by taking the life of man without authority from God who gave it.

In a case of this kind, the state itself is the offender in the sight of heaven, and, as may be apprehended, will sooner or later be visited with judicial punishment. There can be no question that it is the duty of all civil officers, whether judicial or executive, while holding office under government, to carry out the constitution and laws of that government faithfully, according to their official oath. So long as they are not convinced of any discrepancy between the civil and the divine law, they are blameless in so doing. But should they be required as civil officers, to sanction or perform what they are convinced is contrary to the law of God, then they can no longer act as officers of the law without being identified with the state as *particeps criminis.* Their only proper remedy, then, is, "for conscience' sake," to resign.

2. That *self-defense,* when our own lives are attacked or in imminent danger, is a duty, there can be no question. The law of nature dictates it. Nor is it inconsistent with the duty of "loving our neighbour as ourselves." Yet even the plea of self-defense cannot justify us in taking the life of another person unless that self-defense be strictly necessary and not brought about by our own willful act. If we have voluntarily brought the difficulty or danger upon ourselves, or if we can see a way of escape from it by any other means, we cannot, without guilt, save ourselves by destroying others.

3. It is generally conceded that the taking of life in *war* is not murder. St. Paul says: "Let every soul be subject unto the higher pow-

---

6. Today it is no longer true that the propriety of capital punishment is a universal assumption. *Editor.*

ers. For there is no power but of God: the powers that be are ordained of God. Whosoever therefore resisteth the power, resisteth the ordinance of God" (Rom. 13:1-2).

Human governments, then, are the ordinances of God—not, however, in such sense that God sanctions all their principles or measures. They are frequently cruel, unjust, and vicious. As such, God may tolerate, but He cannot sanction or approve them. Yet that human governments should exist, notwithstanding their imperfections, is according to the divine will, and that, as a general rule, they should be treated with respect and submission is also a maxim of revelation. But as in the nature of things, human governments in the present state of the world cannot be maintained without war, it necessarily follows that war is sometimes justifiable; and if so, then the taking of life in war, according to the rules of honorable warfare, is not a violation of this commandment.

But if the war, though justifiable in itself, be conducted on principles of cruelty, and human life be wantonly and uselessly destroyed, contrary to the rules of honorable warfare, so far as this is the case, the taking of life in war is as really murder as in any other instance.

Again, if the war itself be unjustifiable—if it be commenced and carried on through wicked motives, merely through worldly pride and ambition—through the lust of power or gain, or to gratify a spirit of revenge—in all such cases, the war, from beginning to end, is but a wholesale murder—it is a plain violation of the precept, "Thou shalt not kill."

In an unjustifiable war, the nation bringing it on is guilty of a national offense against God and man, for which, as a nation they will be likely to be visited with appropriate punishment. The individuals composing the nation waging such a war, so far as they may voluntarily engage in it, with a proper understanding of its character, are personal violators of the sixth commandment, and are really guilty of murder; but so far as their participation is not *voluntary,* but unavoidable, they are individually innocent or excusable. . . .

5. *Suicide.* Some of the ancient Greek and Roman philosophers at times expressed very correct notions in reference to this crime. Plato says, "We men are all by the appointment of God in a certain prison, or custody, which we ought not to break out of, or run away." Cicero says, "God, the supreme governor of all things, forbids us to depart hence without His order. All pious men ought to have patience to continue in the body as long as God shall please who sent us hither;

and not force themselves out of the world before He calls them, lest they be found deserters of the station appointed them by God."

But Cicero, in another place, appears as the apologist of this crime, and Seneca was also its advocate; while Demosthenes, Cato, Brutus, and Cassius all encouraged it by their example. Hence it is manifest that the Bible alone can establish us firmly on the right foundation in reference to this question.

That the divine law, as exhibited in the sixth commandment, clearly prohibits suicide, may be seen both from the letter and spirit of that precept, "Thou shalt not kill." Surely, to take my own life is as literal a transgression of this law as to take the life of my neighbor! Our Savior's version of the law, "Thou shalt do *no* murder," is still more emphatic in the prohibition of suicide and every conceivable species of murder. . . .

6. According to the admitted maxim, that "the greater comprehends the less," the command, "Thou shalt not kill," not only prohibits *murder,* but all *offenses of less magnitude* whose natural tendency leads to the perpetration of murder.

Under this head may be embraced—*sinful anger, hatred or malice, revenge, strife, excess*—in relation to food, drink, or labor—*unnecessary exposure of our own life or that of others,* and the *neglect of the necessary means of preserving life,* under any circumstances.

(1) *Sinful anger.* As the indulgence in *this* often results in murder, it is forbidden by this commandment. It cannot be supposed that the pure and holy nature of God is susceptible of anger, as a perturbing or agitating passion, in the sense in which this emotion often exists in man. Yet, in His nature He is immovably opposed to sin. This fixed opposition, this holy disapprobation and hatred of sin, and this determination to punish the sinner, are expressed in Scripture by the term *anger.* Hence we read, "God is *angry* with the wicked every day." From this fact we may rationally infer that *anger* is not, under all circumstances, sinful; but that in the sense in which it is commonly indulged, it is sinful.

That it is in direct antagonism to the great law of love in which the essence of Christianity is embraced, is clearly set forth in the Bible. St. Paul says: "Let all bitterness, and *wrath,* and anger, and clamour, and evil speaking be put away from you, with all *malice*" (Eph. 4:31). In the same apostle's enumeration of "the works of the flesh," he embraces not only "murders," but also *strife, variance, hatred,* and *wrath.* And St. John testifies: "Whosoever hateth his brother is a murderer" (1 John 3:15). Anger, if permitted to carry us beyond a calm and holy indignation against sin, or if allowed a permanent lodgment in the heart, becomes sinful and pernicious, destroying the peace of him who indulges in it, and divesting him of that amiability of temper and behavior that is essential to the Christian character.

(2) *Revenge* is also interdicted by this law. St. Paul says: "Recompense to no man evil for evil. . . . Dearly beloved, avenge not yourselves, but rather give place unto wrath: for it is written, Vengeance is mine; I will repay, saith the Lord. Therefore if thine enemy hunger, feed him; if he thirst, give him drink: for in so doing thou shalt heap coals of fire on his head. Be not overcome of evil, but overcome evil with good" (Rom. 12:17, 19-21). How attractive, how sublime, are the mild precepts of the gospel, when contrasted with the selfishness and cruelty of human philosophy! Lord, endue us with that mind which was also in Christ Jesus!

(3) *Strife, contention, disputation,* and *quarreling,* originating in an unholy temper and conducted in a vainglorious or ambitious spirit, are forbidden by this law and are inconsistent with Christian character and hurtful to society. "Follow *peace* with all men" (Heb. 12:14) is the gospel rule. And again: "Do all things without *murmurings* and *disputings*" (Phil. 2:14). Again: "Let nothing be done through *strife* or vainglory" (Phil. 2:3). St. Paul also (2 Cor. 12:20) speaks in condemnation of "envyings, *wraths, strifes,* backbitings, whisperings, *swellings, tumults,*" showing that all such things are uncongenial to the spirit of Christianity.

(4) In a word, this commandment prohibits all *injurious excess* tending to the enervation or destruction of the health, vigor, and activity of our bodily powers or mental faculties. This not only interdicts all drunkenness and dissipation, in the common acceptation of the term, but also excess in the use of food, in labor, in recreation, or amusement, or whatever would tend to impair the constitution, or deprive us of the possession of . . . a sound mind in a healthy body.

(5) Again, if we neglect the means that we believe to be essential to the preservation of our own lives or the lives of others, and life is lost through that neglect, we are guilty of murder. If we see a blind man unconscious of his danger, about to step over a precipice where he will inevitably be destroyed, and have it in our power to save his life, either by giving him timely warning or by pulling him from the danger, and fail to do so, we are as really guilty of murder as though we had

directly taken his life by our own overt act. "Lord, have mercy upon us, and incline our hearts to keep this law!"

III. "Thou shalt not commit adultery."

The sin here forbidden, embracing every violation of the law of conjugal fidelity, and of chastity in general, will be considered in connection with the obligations pertaining to the conjugal relation. Hence we will not enter upon the subject in this connection.

IV. "Thou shalt not steal."

Under the head of *theft,* as the term is here used, much more is implied than the overt act of stealing in the sense of the civil law. In a legal sense, *to steal* is to take from another his property, goods, money, or possessions, in a secret and fraudulent manner. It differs from robbery in that the one is performed in a secret or hidden manner and the other by violence or force.

The divine law penetrates more deeply, and scrutinizes more closely, than civil statutes can do, having cognizance of the secret thought as well as the overt act. It is understood here not only to forbid the crime of *theft,* in its literal, civil acceptation, but also *robbery,* the receiving of stolen property, knowing it to be such. [This law forbids] all fraudulent dealing—using false weights and measures, removing landmarks, injustice or unfaithfulness in contracts between man and man, and breach of trust, any act of oppression, extortion, bribery, unjust and vexatious litigation, trespassing upon property, engrossing commodities so as to enhance the price, gambling, or any other method of taking from others their property or possessions, without due and adequate compensation for the same. How full and comprehensive is the law of God as here exhibited; and with what simplicity and beauty is it expressed by our Savior in His golden rule of "doing to others as we would that they should do unto us"!

It may be a question of some doubt whether the crime of *slander* more properly falls under the condemnation of *this* or the *next* commandment, which prohibits false testimony. It seems clearly condemned by both precepts. As it speaks falsely against our neighbor, it is "bearing false witness," and is condemned by the *ninth* commandment; but as it thereby *steals* away his *good name,* which is "rather to be chosen than great riches," it properly comes under the head of *theft.* It is written: "Whoso privily *slandereth* his neighbour, him will I cut off" (Ps. 101:5). In describing wicked apostates who were to come, St. Paul gives it as one of their characteristics, that they will be found "speaking *lies* in hypocrisy" (1 Tim. 4:2). And he says to the Ephesians (4:31): "Let all evil speaking be put away from you." In describing the atrocities of the unconverted pagans, he characterizes them as "backbiters" (Rom. 1:30). The crime of slander has been forcibly described in the familiar lines of the poet:

Good name in man and woman
Is the immediate jewel of their souls:
Who steals my purse steals trash;
But he that filches from me my good name
Robs me of that which not enriches him,
And makes me poor indeed.

"Lord, have mercy upon us, and incline our hearts to keep this law!"

V. "Thou shalt not bear false witness against thy neighbour."

This, like all the other precepts of the divine law, grows out of the principle of *love.* Hence, as we should "love our neighbour as ourselves," we should take the same care to refrain from speaking so as to injure him, either in his property or reputation, as we would take in reference to ourselves.

This duty forbids, not only testifying falsely against our neighbor when called on to render legal evidence, but also condemns falsehood and deception in every shape. It prohibits forgery, concealing the truth, undue silence in a just cause; all tale-bearing, whispering, detracting; all rash, harsh, and unjust censuring—it condemns all concealing, excusing, or extenuating sins, and all raising or circulating false rumor, and even all countenancing evil reports concerning our neighbor, whether true or false, when the object is, not to do good to others, but injury to him. "Lord, have mercy upon us, and incline our hearts to keep this law!"

VI. "Thou shalt not covet thy neighbour's house, thou shalt not covet thy neighbour's wife, nor his man-servant, nor his maid-servant, nor his ox, nor his ass, nor any thing that is thy neighbour's."

This commandment is directly opposed to that *love of the world,* which is represented by St. John as inconsistent with the love of God. "If any man love the world," saith the apostle, "the love of the Father is not in him" (1 John 2:15). To *covet* is *earnestly to desire* or long after an object that we may possess and enjoy it. It may be taken in a good sense, as in the passage, "Covet earnestly the best gifts"; but when it has for its object the property of our neighbor, and amounts to a desire unlawfully to possess that which belongs to another, it is founded in practical injustice and is one of the most widely extended and pernicious sins. It is at the root of nearly all dishonesty and fraud. Indeed, it comprehends "the love of money," which, the apostle teaches, "is the root of all evil" (1 Tim. 6:10).

As an eminent author has said: "This is a most excellent moral precept, the observance of which will prevent all public crimes; for he who feels the force of the law that prohibits the inordinate desire of any thing that is the property of another, can never make a breach in the peace of society by an act of wrong to any of even its feeblest members." "Lord, have mercy upon us, and write all these, thy laws in our hearts, we beseech thee."

Christian Perfection[7]

At the outset Ralston makes it clear that he considers the three major terms expressive of this doctrine in the New Testament are *holiness, sanctification,* and *perfection.* He holds these terms to be synonymous, especially in the forms "perfected holiness, entire sanctification, and Christian perfection."

Ralston develops the chapter in his typical, well-organized manner:

I. How may the doctrine of Christian perfection be proved by Scripture?

II. The attainment of Christian perfection

III. Objections answered

As was common among early holiness theologians, Ralston treats the second work of grace as maturity, rather than discerning the sharp distinction between purity and maturity, as later writers came to affirm.

I. How may the doctrine of Christian perfection be proved by Scripture?

1. By the *divine precepts.* "Walk before me, and be thou perfect" (Gen. 17:1). "Hear, O Israel: Thou shalt love the Lord thy God with all thine heart, and with all thy soul, and with all thy might" (Deut. 6:5).

---

7. From chapter 37, *Elements of Divinity.* The reprint begins with section II and covers pp. 462-72.

"And now, Israel, what doth the Lord thy God require of thee, but to fear the Lord thy God, to walk in all his ways, and to love him, and to serve the Lord thy God with *all thy heart* and with *all thy soul*" (Deut. 10:12). "Serve God with a *perfect heart* and with a willing mind" (1 Chron. 28:9). "Be ye therefore *perfect,* even as your Father which is in heaven is perfect" (Matt. 5:48). "He that loveth another hath fulfilled the law. . . . therefore *love* is the fulfilling of the law" (Rom. 13:8, 10). "Now the end of the commandment is charity out of a *pure heart,* and of a good conscience, and of faith unfeigned" (1 Tim. 1:5). "Thou shalt love the Lord thy God with *all thy heart,* and with *all thy soul,* and with *all thy mind*. . . . Thou shalt love thy neighbour *as thyself.* On these two commandments hang *all the law* and the prophets" (Matt. 22:37, 39-40).

Here Jehovah explicitly commands Abraham to be "*perfect.*" This demonstrates that, with him, perfection was attainable. God could not command an impossibility. And this perfection related to Abraham's future life, embracing his entire history from that hour to the end of his earthly course. "Walk before me," said God, "and be thou *perfect*"—that is, be *perfect* in thy *walk*—thy entire character and life.

None can read the foregoing scriptures without seeing that *loving God with all our ability* is an express command of both Testaments; of Moses and the prophets; of Christ and the apostles. Now, as this love to God and our neighbor comprises the whole law of God, and as it is solemnly and explicitly enjoined, it follows, first, that it is a duty *possible* for all to comply with; secondly, that in complying with this broad requirement, they fulfill their *whole duty,* and, of course, attain unto that high religious state implied in perfected holiness, entire sanctification, or Christian perfection.

2. This doctrine is proved by *the divine promises.*

"The Lord thy God will circumcise thine heart, and the heart of thy seed, to love the Lord thy God with all thine heart, and with all thy soul, that thou mayest live" (Deut. 30:6). "Come now, and let us reason together, saith the Lord: though your sins be as scarlet, they shall be as white as snow; though they be red like crimson, they shall be as wool" (Isa. 1:18). "Then will I sprinkle clean water upon you, and ye shall be clean: from all your filthiness, and from all your idols, will I cleanse you. A new heart also will I give you, and a new spirit will I put within you: and I will take away the heart of stone out of your flesh, and I will give you a heart of flesh. And I will put my spirit within you, and cause you to walk in my statutes, and ye shall keep my judgments, and do them" (Ezek. 36:25-27). "Blessed be the Lord God of Israel; for he hath . . . raised up an horn of salvation for us, as he spake by the mouth of his holy prophets, that we, being delivered out of the hands of our enemies might serve him without fear, in holiness and righteousness before him, all the days of our life" (Luke 1:68-75). "If any man love me, he will keep my words: and my Father will love him, and we will come to him, and make our abode with him" (John 14:23). "If we confess our sins, he is faithful and just to forgive us our sins, and to *cleanse us from all unrighteousness*" (1 John 1:9).

In these promises, the Christian is abundantly assured of all the gracious assistance to enable him to obey the divine precepts. Indeed, were these promises not thus expressly given, the fact that the command is given, were enough. Each command of God implies the promise of grace to obey it. God here promises so to "circumcise," or change, the heart that the great command of perfect love shall be complied with. He promises that, under the gospel dispensation, believers shall be "cleansed from *all their filthiness,* and *from all their idols.*"

Again, Zacharias prophesied that, under the reign of Christ, His followers would be enabled to "serve him without [tormenting] fear, in *holiness,* and *righteousness* before him, *all the days of their life.*" Surely, here is the promise of *perfected holiness,* entire sanctification, and Christian perfection!

And how full are the promises of Jesus! To every one that loves Him, He and His "Father will come," and they will make their "abode with him"; thus filling his heart with the fullness of His presence and grace.

Again: we are not only promised that "if we confess our sins" they shall be forgiven, but we shall be *"cleansed from all unrighteousness."* Is not this complete deliverance? Can it imply less than entire sanctification—than perfected holiness—than Christian perfection?

3. The *prayers of Scripture* prove this doctrine.

"That they all may be one: as thou, Father, art in me, and I in thee, that they also may be one in us. . . . I in them, and thou in me, that they may be made *perfect* in one" (John 17:21, 23). "God dwelleth in us, and his love is *perfected* in us" (1 John 4:12). "And the very God of peace *sanctify you wholly;* and I pray God your whole spirit and soul and body be preserved *blameless* unto the coming of our Lord Jesus Christ. Faithful is he that calleth you, who also will do it" (1 Thess.

5:23-24). "Create in me a clean heart, O God; and renew a right spirit within me" (Ps. 51:10). "For this cause I bow my knees unto the Father of our Lord Jesus Christ, of whom the whole family in heaven and earth is named, that he would grant you, according to the riches of his glory, to be strengthened with might by his Spirit in the inner man; that Christ may dwell in your hearts by faith; that ye, being rooted and grounded in love, may be able to comprehend with all saints what is the breadth, and length, and depth, and height; and to know the love of Christ, which passeth knowledge, that ye may be filled with all the fulness of God" (Eph. 3:14-19).

In reference to our Savior's prayer, we ask, Can this prayer be answered, and Christians not be entirely sanctified—perfected in holiness and in love? St. John says God's "love is perfected in us." Now, if the blessing of "perfect love" be not the privilege of Christians under the gospel, what sensible construction can be put upon this text? Look also at the prayers of David and St. Paul—a "clean heart," to be sanctified "wholly," and to be "filled with all the fulness of God," are the objects for which they pray. Did they pray according to the will of God? Are we authorized to assume that they prayed for impossibilities, and thus, under the divine influence, offered up solemn petitions for things that it was absolutely impossible—contrary to God's will—that they should obtain? Shall we assume that this solemn mockery was dictated by God's Spirit? As if designedly to silence this impious cavil, St. Paul adds to his petition these words of assurance: "Faithful is he that calleth you, who also *will do it.*"

Hence we conclude that if Christ and His holy prophets and apostles have not set the example of absurdly praying for blessings, contrary to God's will, knowing that it was impossible for their prayers to be answered, then the blessing of perfected holiness, entire sanctification, or Christian perfection is the birthright of every Christian who will seek it with his whole heart.

4. The *exhortations of Scripture* prove this doctrine: "Let us go on unto *perfection*" (Heb. 6:1).

"Having therefore these promises, dearly beloved, let us cleanse ourselves from all filthiness of the flesh and spirit, *perfecting holiness* in the fear of God" (2 Cor. 7:1). "I beseech you therefore, brethren, by the mercies of God, that ye present your bodies a living sacrifice, holy, acceptable unto God, which is your reasonable service" (Rom. 12:1).

"But let patience have her perfect work, that ye may be *perfect* and *entire, wanting nothing*" (James 1:4).

Here St. Paul exhorts Christians to "go on unto perfection"; to "cleanse" themselves from "all filthiness of the flesh and spirit, perfecting holiness in the fear of God"; and St. James exhorts his brethren to aim at the attainment of a state in grace so exalted that they shall be "*perfect* and *entire, wanting nothing.*" Did they exhort them to aim at impossibilities? Did they mock their brethren, by knowingly exciting in them vain, delusive hopes? Or were these inspired apostles ignorant on the subject of which they wrote? Either they were themselves deluded, they willfully deluded their brethren, or the blessing of perfected holiness, entire sanctification, or Christian perfection is attainable under the gospel.

5. The examples *recorded in Scripture of persons having attained Christian perfection,* may be adduced as proof of the doctrine.

"By faith Enoch was translated that he should not see death; and was not found, because God had translated him: for before his translation he had this testimony, that he pleased God" (Heb. 11:5). It is recorded that Job "was *perfect* and *upright,* and one that feared God, and eschewed evil" (Job 1:1). It is said also that Zacharias and Elizabeth "were both *righteous* before God, walking in *all the commandments and ordinances* of the Lord *blameless*" (Luke 1:6). Of Nathanael our Savior exclaimed: "Behold an *Israelite indeed,* in whom is *no guile!*" (John 1:47). St. Paul says: "Howbeit we speak wisdom among them that are *perfect*" (1 Cor. 2:6). "Let us therefore, as many as be *perfect,* be thus minded" (Phil. 3:15).

Enoch, "before his translation"—that is, while living in the world —"had this testimony, that *he pleased God.*" Not that he pleased God in *some things;* that were faint praise; but that "he pleased God"—without qualification—no exception is intimated; and we are not authorized to suppose any. And as a seal and reward of his upright and blameless character and conduct, he "was translated that he should not see death."

If our Savior pronounced Nathanael "an Israelite *indeed,* in whom is *no guile,*" who shall lay any thing to the charge of that elect saint? But St. Paul speaks of *living* Christians who were "perfect." Either, then this inspired apostle was deceived as to the character of the persons to whom he referred, or he taught the doctrine of Christian perfection.

II. The *attainment* of Christian perfection

1. *When* may this great blessing be attained? On this question

there has been much dispute among Christians. Many have contended

WHEN AVAILABLE

that Christian perfection is not attainable till the hour of death; others, while denying that it is the general privilege of Christians in this life, have admitted that it may be the privilege of a favored few, to whom God, for special reasons, may see fit to grant peculiar favors; but even in such cases they consider it impossible for this blessing to be retained except for a short period.

Some of the insuperable objections to this last theory are the following:

1. It is entirely unsupported by Scripture.

That this high state of grace is intended only for a favored class of Christians is nowhere intimated in God's Word. Surely no Christian should feel at liberty to patronize a religious theory thus destitute of any Scripture basis!

2. This theory is contrary to the general tenor of Scripture on the subject. As we have already shown, the precepts, the promises, the exhortations, and the prayers, relating to this high state of religious attainment, are without restriction. The command to "love God with all the heart," and to "love our neighbour as ourselves," and to "be *perfect*, as our Father who is in heaven is perfect"; the promise, "From all your filthiness, and from all your idols, will I cleanse you," and "he is faithful and just to forgive us our sins, and to cleanse us from all unrighteousness"; the exhortation, "Let us go on unto perfection," and "Let us cleanse ourselves from all filthiness of the flesh and spirit, perfecting holiness in the fear of God"; and the prayer, "The very God of peace sanctify you wholly," and, "that ye may be filled with all the fulness of God"—all these commands, promises, exhortations, and prayers are general, and unrestricted to classes of Christians, in their character and application. They pertain alike to the Jew and to the Gentile, to the high and to the low; to all classes and to all orders. Indeed, in this respect, the "ways of God are equal." Such are the principles on which the gospel system of salvation is conducted, that the highest state of religious experience is within the reach of "the least of all saints."

But is this state in religious attainment possible in this life? Should we seek it, aim at it, pray for it, and expect it, in this life; or must we consider it impossible for us to attain to it, till the hour of death? Here is an important practical question, which demands a careful consideration.

That Christian perfection, entire sanctification, or perfected holiness (whichever of these terms we choose to use) is attainable in this life whenever we comply with the conditions prescribed in the gospel, we firmly believe, for the following reasons:

AVAILABLE NOW

1. This doctrine harmonizes with the great principles on which God's moral government over mankind, as exhibited in the gospel, is conducted. Everywhere man is treated as a moral agent. Good and evil, life and death, are set before him; and he is commanded to reject evil and death, and to choose good and life. Where is it intimated that, in this requirement, there is any restriction? that he only has ability through grace, to reject the evil and to choose the good, to a *partial* extent? that when he has advanced to a certain stage in this process, the wheels of his chariot are so locked that he can progress no farther? Has his free agency been destroyed because he has become a child of God? While in the guilt of sin, was he free, through grace, to repent, believe, and be converted; but now that he is a justified child of God, has he lost his free agency; or has the grace of God been so far withdrawn from him that he cannot go on from one degree of faith, and zeal and love, and holiness, to another, till he shall appear *perfect* before God, exhibiting in their *fullness, maturity,* and *perfection,* all the graces of the Christian character?

Unless God has made a radical change, either in the character of man, or in His government over him, if we were free before conversion to reject evil and choose good, we cannot be less so after conversion. If, through grace, we forsake *one* sin, we *may* forsake *all* sin. If we may be cleansed from *one sin,* we may be cleansed from *all sin.* If we may keep *one* commandment, we *may,* through grace, "keep the whole law"—that is, the law of faith and love, under which we are placed under the gospel. Again: if it is impossible for us to avoid sinning, how can we be held responsible for that which is unavoidable? If we may advance to one degree of holiness or sanctification, which we attain when we are justified, why may we not, on the same principle, "go on unto perfection"?

It is a maxim of the gospel, as clear as the sun, that there is no excuse for sin. Even the heathens, amid their idolatry, are "without excuse." If justified persons are unable to attain "perfected holiness" in this life, what but sin can prevent it? and if that sin is unavoidable, what better apology for sin can be imagined? No just law, human or divine, can punish an intelligent agent for an unavoidable act. If continuing in sin, "that grace may abound," after conversion, is a necessity from which we cannot es-

SIN NOT NECESSARY

cape, then, for that sin, we cannot be punished. Yea, more, the very position involves an absurdity. Sin, to be personal and actual, so as to deserve punishment, must be avoidable. Hence we conclude that unless the moral agency of man, or God's government over him, is radically changed when we are justified, we *may,* from that hour, "go on unto perfection"; and whenever we comply with the conditions prescribed in the gospel—that is, whenever we exercise the requisite degree of faith, be it one day or ten years after our conversion—*that moment* God will *"cleanse us from all unrighteousness."*

2. That Christian perfection is attainable in this life, at any period, we believe, because the contrary hypothesis is inconsistent with the commands, promises, exhortations, and prayers connected with the doctrine in question.

ATTAINABLE IN THIS LIFE

All the commands, promises, exhortations, and prayers, recorded in Scripture, except where the context explicitly shows to the contrary, are in the present tense—they are intended to take effect from the moment of their delivery. If God says, "Be ye holy," He does not mean when we die, or next year; nay, nor tomorrow: He means *now*—"today, if ye will hear his voice"—"*now* is the accepted time; behold! *now* is the day of salvation." *Now* is emphatically God's time. Anyone may perceive that the Scriptures referred to cannot, without the utmost violence, be construed as not applying to the *present* time. When our Savior said, "Be ye therefore perfect," how absurd to suppose He merely intended to teach the necessity of perfection at death! It would be no worse to contend that when He said, "Seek, and ye shall find; ask, and ye shall receive; knock, and it shall be opened," He only designed to instruct His disciples in reference to their duty in the hour of death.

Equally absurd would it be, without authority, to construe the promises, entreaties, or prayers in the same way. When our Lord promised, saying, "Come unto me, all ye that labour and are heavy laden, and *I will give you rest*" (Matt. 11:28), who ever dreamed that He was merely promising rest at death? When St. James (1:4) exhorted his brethren saying, "Let patience have her *perfected work,* that ye may be *perfect and entire, wanting nothing,*" how preposterous the supposition that he was merely encouraging them in reference to their deathbed duties! When David prayed, "Create in me a clean heart, O God," was he looking forward to the hour of death for an answer to his petition? How absurd the hypothesis! Even so, to construe all these commands, promises, exhortations, and prayers, referring to the blessing of perfect holiness, perfect love, or Christian perfection, as not contemplating any realization this side the hour of dissolution, would be the climax of absurdity.

3. Our next reason for believing that Christian perfection is attainable in this life is founded on *the explicit declarations of Scripture.*

(1) The Scriptures connect with the attainment of this blessing, the performance of subsequent duties that can only pertain to the conduct through life—entirely inapplicable to the hour of death.

St. Paul, speaking of the *destruction of the body of sin,* adds, "that *henceforth* we should not serve sin"—that is, *through all subsequent life,* extending from the hour in which this great triumph over sin is gained, to the hour of death. In a passage already quoted (1 Thess. 5:23), the apostle, after having prayed for his brethren that they might be sanctified "wholly," prays further, that they may "be preserved *blameless unto the coming of our Lord Jesus Christ.*"

(2) Again: the fruits of the Spirit, which, all must admit, Christians are required to exhibit in their maturity and perfection, are, in their nature, such that they can be thus produced only in life. These fruits are thus enumerated: "But the fruit of the Spirit is love, joy, peace, longsuffering, gentleness, goodness, faith, meekness, temperance" (Gal. 5:22-23). No sober-minded Christian can suppose that it is intended that this constellation of Christian graces shall shine forth in its maturity only in death. But if we are to exhibit these fruits in life, then, of necessity, to the same extent must we be exempt from the opposite evils. And if Christianity does not require us to bring forth these fruits unto perfection during life, then it will follow that we are not required to be delivered from the opposite evils. Thus, if we are not required to be perfect in love, we may indulge in sinful anger; if we are not required to be perfect in temperance, then we may indulge in intemperance, and so of the rest.

That these fruits of the Spirit are required to be exhibited, not *partially,* but in their perfection, in the lives of Christians cannot be controverted, without the utmost violence to the Scriptures. And if so, then Christian perfection, which implies these fruits in their maturity, is attainable in this life.

(3) If Christian perfection be not attainable till death, then it must follow, either that *death,* "the last *enemy* that will be destroyed," is the efficient agent in the work, or that the blood of Christ, and the

influence of the Holy Spirit, are more efficacious in death than they can be in life—both of which positions are too unscriptural to be entertained.

(4) The Scriptures explicitly teach, in so many words, that this blessing is attainable in this life. St. John declares: "Herein is our *love made perfect,* that we may have boldness in the day of judgment: because *as he* [Christ] *is, so are we in this world*" (1 John 4:17). In this passage, the apostle, as though he had foreseen that some would oppose this doctrine, has furnished us as direct an answer to the objection now before us, as language can express. "If we love one another, God dwelleth in us, and his *love is perfected in us*" (1 John 4:12). The apostle was evidently here speaking of *living* Christians, including himself in the number, and not of such only as were on the bed of death. "And every man that hath this hope in him *purifieth* himself, *even as he* [Christ] *is pure*" (1 John 3:3). "But if we walk in the light, as he is in the light, we have fellowship one with another, and the blood of Jesus Christ his Son cleanseth us from all sin" (1 John 1:7). This entire cleansing from sin is not promised at death, but evidently takes place *now*—while "we walk in the light." "Follow peace with all men, and *holiness,* without which no man shall see the Lord" (Heb. 12:14). The *holiness* here spoken of can only mean "perfected holiness"; and this is to be *followed,* not at death, but *now,* while mingling with the affairs of this life.

Such, according to God's Word, are the glorious privileges of all the children of God, even in this world. They not only "know God" in the remission of "past sins," but following "on to know the Lord," they may "know the love of Christ, which passeth knowledge," and "be filled with all the fulness of God." It matters but little whether this eminent state of holiness be gained by a bold, energetic, and determined exercise of faith and prayer, or by a more gradual process—whether it be *instantaneous* or *gradual,* or both the one and the other.[8] The great matter is, with each and all of us, that we lose no time, but arise at once and "press toward the mark for the prize of the high calling of God in Christ Jesus."

---

8. It really matters a lot! Whether one walks *now* in the light, and presses his way into a victorious experience, or limps along for years, is not a matter of indifference. To treat it as such is to encourage believers to follow the path of least resistance and elect, by default, the "more gradual process." And where are the witnesses to a clear experience of entire sanctification attained by the gradual process? *Editor.*

III. Objections answered

1. It is objected that entire sanctification is impossible in this life because of *the union of the soul with the body.*

It is assumed that the body is so depraved by sin, that so long as the soul remains in the body, sin must remain in the soul.

We ask, Where is the scripture proof of this position? Several texts are relied on for this purpose; but it can easily be shown that unless perverted, they furnish not the slightest support to the position in question. The language of St. Paul to the Romans is quoted: "For we know that the law is spiritual: but I am carnal, sold under sin. For that which I do I allow not . . . but what I hate, that do I. . . . For I delight in the law of God after the inward man: but I see another law in my members, warring against the law of my mind, and bringing me into captivity to the law of sin which is in my members" (Rom. 7:14-15, 22-23). Again: "The carnal mind is enmity against God: for it is not subject to the law of God, neither indeed can be. So then they that are in the flesh cannot please God" (Rom. 8:7-8).

The argument against Christian perfection, deduced from these scriptures, is this: That the apostle, in this place, is describing his own condition as one "sold under sin," even while he is the converted apostle; and as *he,* converted apostle as he was, could not escape the dominion of sin, because he was still in the flesh, so neither can any others, so long as they remain in the body.

Now we venture to affirm that this is a gross perversion of the scripture in question. The apostle, in the seventh chapter to the Romans, is *not* describing his own state, as the converted apostle, but he is personating the *convicted sinner,* seeking in vain for *deliverance from sin under the bondage of the law.* It is only necessary for us carefully to read the sixth and eighth chapters of Romans, in connection with the seventh, and the truth of this remark will be seen. In the sixth chapter, the justified believer is "*freed from sin*"—"his old man" (sinful nature) is crucified with Him (Christ) that *the body of sin might be destroyed,* that henceforth he should *not serve sin*—he is "made *free from sin*" and has his "*fruit unto holiness.*" Could the apostle so flatly contradict himself, as in the next chapter, to represent the same character as "*sold under sin,*" and in "*captivity to the law of sin*"? The hypothesis is inadmissible.

Another error in this argument against perfection is, that the term *flesh* in the phrase, "They that are in the *flesh* cannot please God," means *the body.* It certainly cannot mean *the body;* for then no *living man* could ever please God. It means the *sinful, depraved nature*—the "carnal mind"— the "old man"—that must be "put off," or "crucified with Christ," before we can "walk in newness of life."

2. It is objected against Christian perfection that "the attainment of it in this life *would render the atonement of Christ no longer necessary.*" Surely not. Whatever be our state in grace, we are dependent on Christ, from moment to moment, for all we have and are. And in proportion as we cease to exercise, or cast off, that faith in the merits of Christ by which the blessing in question has been received, at the same time, and to the same extent, will that blessing be withheld; so that the most advanced Christian may ever exclaim—

Every moment, Lord, I want
The merit of Thy death!

3. It is objected that *"this doctrine of Christian perfection destroys the possibility of any further advancement in religion."*

PERFECTION AND GROWTH

Certainly it does not. Adam in paradise may have been as perfect in his character as the purest and most exalted angel, yet he was probably far below the holy angels in capacity, whether for loving God or enjoying happiness. In nature, perfection in any particular department does not close the door against all farther advancement; then why should it in religion? A perfect *seed* may advance, first to a perfect *blade,* then to a perfect *ear,* and then to perfect *corn* in the ear. Just so the Christian, though "perfected in love"—loving God with all his capacity—may still continue to "grow in grace, and in the knowledge of our Lord and Saviour Jesus Christ"; and while his capacity thus enlarges, while his knowledge increases, and his spiritual powers expand, he may still be advancing in grace, sinking deeper and still deeper in the depths of infinite holiness and love; and rising higher and still higher in the heights of ineffable joy and felicity.

Indeed, we have no authority to fix any limit on the advancement of redeemed and sanctified spirits, either in this world or the next. It is their duty and privilege ever to be advancing, not only to "perfect holiness in the fear of God," but ever after to be reaching forth unto still more exalted degrees of perfection in holiness, and knowledge, and love, and bliss, till released from the tenement of clay and entered upon the glories of immortality, they shall, to all eternity, be approximating nearer and still nearer to the source and fountain of finite perfection and bliss and glory.

4

Luther Lee

(1800-1889)

It is a rare person who, with no formal education, and who at 19 years can scarcely read the Bible, nevertheless achieves prominence and wide influence both as an educator and a theologian.

Such a person was Luther Lee. He began life in Schoharia, N.Y., November 30, 1800. His illiterate parents could not help him with an education. Fortunately, he was converted and joined the Methodist church, then at 25 years of age married a schoolteacher, Mary Miller. In addition to bearing him five sons and two daughters she "gave him all the education he ever received" *(Encyclopedia of World Methodism).*

He began his ministry as a circuit rider in the Genesee Conference (N.Y.). Nine years later (1836), having transferred to the Black River Conference, he was rapidly becoming a leader, with intense reforming instincts and strong debating ability. For five years (1838-43) these talents were channeled into the abolition movement. As an agent for the Massachusetts Anti-Slavery Society, he assisted in the organization of the Liberty Party.

When in 1843 the Wesleyan Methodist Connection was organized, Lee joined that movement. Within a year he was president of their first General Conference. In addition to pastoring several Wesleyan churches in New York and Ohio, he edited for eight years their official magazine, the *True Wesleyan.* From 1864-67 he served as a professor in Adrian College, a Wesleyan school. After the Civil War, however, he rejoined the Methodist

Episcopal church and spent the last 10 years of his active ministry as pastor of Methodist churches in Michigan.

His books are said to have had a large sale. They include *Universalism Examined, Immortality of the Soul,* and his *Autobiography of Luther Lee, D.D.* While president of Leoni Theological Institute, Lee published his systematic theology, with an extended title, *An Exposition of the Divine Origin, Doctrines, Morals, and Institutions of Christianity.*[1] It is divided into four books in the one volume and contains approximately 600 pages. His style is marked by simplicity and clarity, and his thought shows admirable theological acumen.

Lee retired in 1877, and died in Flint, Mich., December 13, 1889.

Sanctification—Initial, Progressive, and Entire[2]

While Lee gives the simple title "Sanctification" to this section, the expansion above more precisely indicates the ground he covers. The first several pages are devoted to proving that sanctification begins with regeneration and in fact is in essence no different. This he does, not by argument but by a long list of quotations. Most of his authorities come down so heavily on sanctification as a gradual unfolding of regeneration that the net impression is a doctrine of holiness solely by growth.

Fortunately, when Lee takes up in earnest the question of the distinction between sanctification as begun in regeneration and that sanctification that may be called "entire," he achieves a better balance between process and crisis. He says, "This progressive work may be cut short and finished at any moment, when the intelligence clearly comprehends the defects of the present state, and faith, comprehending the power and willingness of God to sanctify us wholly, is exercised."[3]

In respect to the psychological nature of entire sanctification, Lee differs sharply with his contemporary (and probably friend), Charles G. Finney, who sees the will as the sole nexus of either sin

1. Luther Lee, *Elements of Theology* (New York: Miller, Orton & Mulligan, 1856).
2. This is Section 5 of Chap. VIII, Book II, 207-8, 211-19.
3. Also quoted by H. Orton Wiley, *Christian Theology*, 2:477.

or holiness: the "states of the sensibility," while needing control, are virtually irrelevant, at least in defining the current moral character. Lee insists that whether these nonvolitional irregularities are called physical (and amoral) depravity or original sin, "the thing itself must be corrected or removed before there can be an entire consecration of all the soul to God, or before the man can be said to be wholly sanctified." In other words, the entire nature must be brought into "harmony with the enlightened judgment, and sanctified will, and all be in harmony with the divine law." Entire sanctification extends to the mental and emotional dispositions as well as to the consciously willed intentions.

Lee's formal definition of sanctification is worthy of being prequoted here: "Sanctification is that renewal of our fallen nature by the Holy Ghost, received through faith in Jesus Christ, whose blood of atonement has power to cleanse from all sin; whereby we are not only delivered from the guilt of sin, which is justification, but are washed entirely from its pollution, freed from its power, and are enabled, through grace, to love God with all our hearts, and to walk in His holy commandments blameless."

The doctrine of sanctification is approached with a large degree of solicitude, not on account of any doubts in regard to it, but in view of its vast practical importance, in connection with the fact that there exists a great diversity of views on the subject. No question in theology is of greater practical importance to every Christian, and yet there are few, if any points, in regard to which the views of Christians appear less clear, and perfect. It is, doubtless, in some sense, plain in experience to those who enjoy it, but so to put it upon paper as to render it plain to those who have never experienced the blessing, or who have experienced it only in a very limited degree, is not the easiest task that the author of a system of theology has to perform. A work like this would be incomplete without an examination of the subject, and as difficult as it may be to present it, so as not to add obscurity to what has already been rendered too obscure, the task must be undertaken.

I. *Sanctification Has Its Beginning in Regeneration*

INITIAL SANCTIFICATION

This point is universally admitted. Whatever controversies have arisen in regard to other aspects of sanctification, it is believed that no evangelical writer has denied that sanctification begins with regeneration, and that every regenerate person is, in part, sanctified. . . .

II. *The Way Is Now Prepared to Inquire What Is Entire Sanctification, More than Is Implied in Regeneration*

To make the matter as plain as possible, it will be necessary to explain what sanctification is, and then point out wherein it transcends regeneration.

Before attempting an explicit answer to this question, it is proper to notice the primary sense of the terms employed to express the thing after the nature of which we inquire.

To sanctify is to separate a thing from common use and to devote it exclusively to holy or religious purpose. It contains the two ideas, that of separation and of consecration. Christians are sanctified by being separated from the world and by being devoted to God. It implies real holiness, hence, to sanctify is to purify and make holy.

The Hebrew word rendered *sanctify* is *kadash,* and it signifies "to cleanse, purify, make holy."

The Greek word rendered *sanctify* is *hagiazō.* It is derived from *hagios,* which signifies "holy," hence *hagiazō* signifies "to consecrate, separate, set apart, purify, cleanse from pollution, make holy." This word occurs 20 times in the New Testament; twice it is rendered *hallowed,* once it is rendered *be holy,* and in all the other cases it is rendered *sanctify, sanctified,* and *sanctifieth.*

The noun rendered *sanctification* in Greek is *hagiasmos.* This is derived from the same, *hagios,* "holy." This word occurs only 10 times in the New Testament; in 5 cases it is translated *holiness,* and in 5 it is translated *sanctification.* As specimens of the texts in which the word is rendered by each of these English words, the following is sufficient.

Heb. 12:14—"Follow peace with all men, and *[hagiasmon]* holiness, without which no man shall see the Lord."

1 Cor. 1:30—"Who of God is made unto us wisdom, and righteousness, and sanctification *[hagiasmos],* and redemption."

These explanations, though not essential to the argument, clearly show that to be sanctified is to be made holy, to be cleansed from sin. The way is now prepared to give a definition of *sanctification,* which shall be done in as few and clear words as possible. Sanctification is that renewal of our fallen nature by the Holy Ghost, received through faith in Jesus Christ, whose blood of atonement has power to cleanse from all sin; whereby we are not only delivered from the guilt of sin, which is justification, but are also washed entirely from its pollution, freed from its power, and are enabled, through grace, to love God with all our hearts and to walk blamelessly in His holy commandments.

This definition is in harmony with the established fact that sanctification commences with regeneration, because it includes all that is ascribed to that change, while, in extent, it expresses a higher state than all regenerate persons can be said to enjoy, at the commencement of their Christian experience.

But what does sanctification embrace more than is implied in regeneration?

It is not to be understood that sanctification adds any new virtues that are not present in every regenerate soul before entire sanctification. It was said, while treating of regeneration, that it reverses the current of the affections, and so renews the whole soul that all the Christian graces exist.

They may not all exist in an equal degree of strength, but they are all there, though some of them may be as the shining of a faint light. None of them is likely to exist in a full degree of maturity and power at the moment of regeneration.

The power of sin is broken, the tyrant is dethroned, and his reign ceases in the soul at the moment of regeneration; yet, sin is not so destroyed as not to leave its mark upon the soul, and even yet struggle for the mastery.

A REMAINING WARFARE

There is still a warfare within, and however clear the intellect may be to see what is right, and however determined the will may be to execute the decision of the judgment, there will be found an opposing element in the sensibility of the soul, which, though it no longer controls the will, often rebels against it and refuses to obey it. That this depravity does not lie exclusively in the will but also in the perverted passions and appetites is too plain to be denied; and that these struggle for unlawful indulgence after regeneration is too universal in Christian experience to need proof. This state of things, as a matter of fact, must be admitted by all, yet theologians explain it in the light of their different creeds and different systems of philosophy. Hence some call it the remains of original sin, some call it indwelling sin, and some say it is the depravity that remains after regeneration.

Rev. Charles G. Finney denies that it is moral depravity, and hence he denies that there is any sin or moral depravity remaining in the soul after regeneration. He denies that any moral quality pertains to the sensibility of the soul, and hence he does not include the subjugation of the passions to the sanctified will in his ideas of entire sanctification, beyond the mere fact that the will is not governed by them and does not endorse or execute any of their irregular motions. His words are, "It is evident that sanctification in the Scripture, and proper sense of the term, is not a mere feeling of any kind. It is not a desire, an appetite, a passion, a propensity, an emotion, nor indeed any kind or degree of feeling. It is not a state or phenomenon of the sensibility. The states of the sensibility are, like those of the intelligence, purely passive states of mind, as has been repeatedly shown. They of course can have no moral character in themselves. The inspired writers evidently use the terms which are translated by the English word sanctify, to designate a phenomenon of the will, or a voluntary state of mind."[4]

If the above be all true, the conclusion appears undeniable, that every man is entirely sanctified the moment he wills right, and as Mr. Finney contends for the freedom of the will, that man has natural power to will right, all can sanctify themselves by an act of will in a moment. Perhaps Mr. F. and his friends will feel no desire to escape this conclusion, for it really appears to be the result aimed at. Mr. Finney's view of sanctification, as above given, appears to be defective. While, "it is evident that sanctification is not a *mere* feeling of any kind," it is no less evident that it includes all right feelings, and excludes all wrong feelings. While, "it is not a desire, an appetite, a passion, a propensity, an emotion, nor indeed any kind or degree of feeling," it comprehends and implies a right state of all the desires, appetites, passions, propensities, emotions, and every kind and proper degree of right feeling.

HOLINESS MORE THAN RIGHT WILLING

While "the states of the sensibility are, like those of the intelligence, purely passive states of mind," still while they rebel and struggle against the dictates of the intelligence, and the decisions of the will, they mar the perfection of the sacrifice that the worshiper is bound to make of his entire self to God, and their rebellion is inconsistent with what many at least believe to be a state of entire sanctification. While sanctification is "a voluntary state of mind," so far as to exist only as a sequence to the determination of the will, it includes much more than right volition and more than volition has power to effect.

The fact cannot be overlooked that Mr. Finney's view of sanctification differs very materially from that commonly held by all other schools of theology. It differs by being grounded upon a denial that moral depravity extends to the states of the intelligence and sensibility

4. *Systematic Theology*, 2:200.

of the soul, depravity being confined wholly to the state of the will.

It differs by being made to include, according to the above view, only a right state of the will, while others hold that it includes a right state of all the powers and susceptibilities of the soul.

Mr. Finney denies that there is any sin or moral depravity remaining in the soul after regeneration, but this he does by denying that the states of the sensibility, in which they war against the right determinations of the will, and clamor for indulgences the will cannot allow without sin, involve sin or moral depravity. This makes the discussion turn upon the mere name by which a mental state is called, and not upon the fact of the existence of the state. That such states of the sensibility exist after regeneration all must admit, but while old school men call it depravity remaining after regeneration, Mr. Finney denies that it is sin, or moral depravity, and affirms that it is physical depravity, referring to the same mental state that others call remaining sin after regeneration, allowing regeneration to take place instantaneously with justification. It is not necessary to take issue with Mr. Finney on the use of terms, since the thing called by different names is now understood. Allowing Mr. Finney to be right in calling it physical depravity, it is then maintained that entire sanctification includes the removal of this physical depravity so that in all purely mental states the sensibility shall be in harmony with the enlightened judgment and sanctified will, and all be in harmony with the divine law.

CORRECTION NEEDED

What Mr. Finney calls physical depravity must be admitted to be a consequence of the Fall and also to be greatly aggravated and made worse by sinful practices. All propensities and passions, and appetites that prompt to evil, gather strength in the direction of evil, as they are indulged by the practice of evil. Now, whether we call them sin, original sin, moral depravity, or physical depravity, the thing itself must be corrected or removed before there can be an entire consecration of all the soul to God, or before the man can be said to be wholly sanctified.

SINFUL ANGER

Let this point now be illustrated. The passion of anger results from an original susceptibility of the soul; the susceptibility is not wrong in itself, it is God's work for a good end. A depraved or perverted development of this susceptibility is seen when anger is produced by what should produce a feeling of complacency. This is often the case, as when one sinner is angry because another sinner gives his heart to God. Another depraved development of this susceptibility is seen when real wrong, which ought to produce a feeling of detestation toward the act, rather awakens a feeling of anger toward the actor, wrong in kind and degree, and prompting to wrong acts toward him. So far as the will does not acquiesce, Mr. Finney, if he is understood, calls it physical depravity. But with sinners, the will does acquiesce, often at least. This propensity to anger becomes stronger as it is indulged.

Now, suppose a person naturally given to passion, and who has never restrained his anger, is converted at the age of 40, and the sin of anger will be found to have left its mark upon the soul after regeneration, in this increased susceptibility to anger or increased liability to become angry. The first time the man is insulted, he will feel the very pulsation of anger throb within him, whether the will consents or not. If the will is not carried away by the storm of feeling, but maintains its right position, the storm will soon lull, and he will have gained a victory. In this conflict it is supposed that he cried in his heart to God, in the name of Jesus Christ, and when the conflict is over he feels that he has been preserved from a great fall. Yet he is impressed with his own weakness and is dissatisfied with himself and feels the necessity of having a still deeper work wrought within him. If he remains watchful and prayerful, under the next provocation, the impulse of anger will be less powerful, and the victory over it will be achieved with greater ease, and so on, until the propensity is wholly subdued.

Apply the principle and operation here evolved, to the entire soul with all its powers and susceptibilities, so far as applicable, and the reader will have spread before him the work and process of gradual sanctification, after, and above, and beyond what is implied, necessarily, in regeneration. This, however, needs to be further guarded and explained as follows:

1. This progress is made in the strength of God, by grace constantly supplied through faith in Christ, and by the influence of the truth, and the power of the Holy Spirit, who is the efficient agent in sanctification.

PROCESS AND CRISIS

2. It is gradual, as above described, not in the sense of making equal and even progress, through each day, week, month, or year, but in the sense of a succession of victories over our internal foes, and a succession of larger and larger blessings, or deeper and deeper baptisms of the Holy Spirit, until the work is finished, in the full sense of the definition of sanctification, which has been previously given.

3. This progressive work may be cut short and finished at any moment, when the intelligence clearly comprehends the defects of the present state, and faith, comprehending the power and willingness of God to sanctify us wholly, and do it now, is exercised. This faith, of course, is exercised in God, through our Lord Jesus Christ, relying upon the merits of His death, and expecting the work to be wrought by the agency of the Holy Spirit, which He promises to send, and which He has sent, and does send.

This view explains how sanctification may be both gradual and instantaneous. It may not be safely affirmed that it cannot take place at the moment of regeneration, yet it is clear that it very rarely does. If the intelligence did then comprehend the necessity of the entire work, and faith was exercised accordingly, it would take place, but this is not likely to be the case. The awakened sinner has his mind mainly directed to the guilt of his sin and his inability to save himself without God, and he cries to God for pardon and a new heart. Faith is limited by the view his intelligence takes of his necessity; the work wrought, and the blessing obtained, are according to the faith exercised.

WHY SUBSEQUENT TO CONVERSION

With most persons it may be presumed that their view of the whole subject, at the time of their conversion, may be expressed in these few words, "I am a sinner lost, Christ is a Savior, who died to save me; able and willing to save now. Lord, for Christ's sake, save me this moment." Subsequently, the necessity of a deeper work, as illustrated in the supposed case of the man of passion, converted at the age of 40, is seen and felt. At any time when the intelligence comprehends what is wanting to constitute a state of entire sanctification, and faith is exercised, the work will be finished. The end may be reached by a succession of these instantaneous advances toward it, as light increases and faith is exercised; or it may be reached at once, when light and faith are sufficiently clear, comprehensive, and powerful.

4. This state of entire sanctification does not place the sanctified beyond the power of temptation from influences without; it only subdues and expels all the foes within. Adam could have had no foes within until they were admitted from without, and so may it be with those who are sanctified wholly, in spirit, soul, and body. In this state, all is right and peace within.

NOT BEYOND TEMPTATION

The will is right at the moment of regeneration, and it must remain right, or willful sin will be the result, and justification will be lost; but while the will is right, the propensities, passions, and appetites may struggle against the decisions of the will and keep up a warfare within, and these must be subdued. The will can and does resist them in a regenerate state, but it cannot silence them, renew, or change their direction, by an act of volition. These belong to the soul, and must be brought into harmony with right, and the sanctified will, before the whole soul can be said to be sanctified, or to be entirely consecrated to God. When this work is wrought, then the war within will cease, and there will be a development of all the Christian virtues, in such a state of strength and maturity, as to exclude the opposite vices. There will be love without hatred, submission without rebellion, faith without unbelief, humility without pride, meekness without anger, patience without impatience, and peace without contention, strife, or wrath.

5. This state of entire sanctification does not preclude a further growth. It ends the warfare within and leaves the whole soul, with all its passions, to be led on in the path of holiness, while increasing intelligence points out the way, as it obtains clearer and higher views of human duty and destiny, and the regenerated will presses the whole soul on to know and enjoy more of God. When the embarrassments are thus removed out of the soul itself, progress will be more rapid, every virtue may increase in strength and brightness, and the will may become stronger and stronger in its determination in the direction of holiness.

GROWTH

6. As a concluding remark under this head, let it be observed, that the above exposition of entire sanctification appears to accord with Christian experience. It accords with the experience of those who have not reached the state. If the whole number of Christians were consulted at or near the time of their conversion, few, if any, would be found to believe themselves to have been wholly sanctified at the time of their conversion, or to have been freed from all depravity. Yet they feel confident that their sins have been forgiven and that they love God. Whatever may be their creed, whatever may be their philosophy of regeneration and sanctification, if they are real Christians, experience has but one language; they are conscious that they love God and enjoy His favor, yet that they have not attained all that is implied in entire sanctification, as taught in the Scriptures, and as it has been explained above.

If the experience of those who have obtained this great blessing of entire sanctification were consulted, it would doubtless be found to accord with the explanation above given. But this is a point that is likely to be fully comprehended by those only who enjoy a state of entire sanctification, and need not be further pressed.

III. *The Proof That Entire Sanctification May Be Attained and Enjoyed in This Life*

1. *God is able to sanctify believers wholly*

It will not be denied that God is omnipotent, and of course can do anything and everything that comes within the bounds of moral propriety. If it be right and desirable that saints should be wholly sanctified in this life, omnipotence can do it. We also have a practical development of this power in the work of regeneration. It has been seen that all agree that regeneration is sanctification in part and that every regenerate person is in part sanctified. It is admitted that the guilt of sin is removed and that the power of sin is broken, so that sin ceases to have dominion over the regenerate. This being admitted, the greater part of the work is done, so far as the power of God is concerned. If God has moral might to break the power of sin in the soul, and deliver the soul from its control, He must be able to deliver entirely from all sin. If God can save men from most of their sins, and from the greatest of their sins, He must be able to save from the smaller number and from the least in magnitude. This reasoning would appear conclusive, if left to make its own impression upon the common sense of the reader, but the fact is clearly asserted in the Scriptures.

2 Cor. 9:8—"And God is able to make all grace abound toward you; that ye, always having all sufficiency in all things, may abound to every good work."

2 Cor. 10:5—"Casting down imaginations, and every high thing that exalteth itself against the knowledge of God, and bringing into captivity every thought to the obedience of Christ."

Eph. 3:16-21—"That he would grant you, according to the riches of his glory, to be strengthened with might by his Spirit in the inner man; that Christ may dwell in your hearts by faith; that ye, being rooted and grounded in love, may be able to comprehend with all saints what is the breadth, and length, and depth, and height; and to know the love of Christ, which passeth knowledge, that ye might be filled with all the fulness of God. Now unto him that is able to do exceeding abundantly above all that we ask or think, according to the power that worketh in us, unto him be glory."

The above scriptures clearly comprehend the blessing of entire sanctification, and declare that God is able to bestow it.

2. *God has clearly promised a state of entire sanctification*

This blessing was promised under the Old Testament covenant. Gen. 17:1-2—"The Lord appeared to Abram, and said unto him, I am the Almighty God: walk before me, and be thou perfect. And I will make my covenant between me and thee."

This covenant was with Abraham and his seed forever. Now as God on entering into covenant commanded him to walk before Him and be perfect, the covenant itself must have secured the blessing of a perfect state of all such as take hold upon it by faith to the extent of its provisions. In perfect accordance with this view of the covenant, do we find the gracious promise of God. Deut. 30:6—"And the Lord thy God will circumcise thine heart, and the heart of thy seed, to love the Lord thy God with all thine heart, and with all thy soul, that thou mayest live."

This clearly includes what is called being made perfect in love. Ezek. 36:25-27—"Then will I sprinkle clean water upon you, and ye shall be clean: from all your filthiness, and from all your idols, will I cleanse you. A new heart also will I give you, and a new spirit will I put within you: and I will take away the stony heart out of your flesh, and I will give you an heart of flesh. And I will put my spirit within you, and cause you to walk in my statutes, and ye shall keep my judgments, and do *them*." 1 Thess. 5:23-24—"And the very God of peace sanctify you wholly; and I pray God your whole spirit and soul and body be preserved blameless unto the coming of our Lord Jesus Christ. Faithful *is* he that calleth you, who also will do *it*."

This text implies a promise. Paul prays for the blessing of entire sanctification, and true prayer is based upon the covenant promises. But the declaration that God is faithful and will do it implies that God has promised it and shows that Paul had his eye on the promise when he uttered the prayer. When God is said to be faithful, it is always with reference to His covenant and promises. 1 John 1:8-9—"If we say that we have no sin, we deceive ourselves, and the truth is not in us. If we confess our sins, he is faithful and just to forgive us *our* sins, and to cleanse us from all unrighteousness."

The expression, "he is faithful and just," clearly implies that the thing is secured by promise and that the promise not only reaches to the pardon of sin but also comprehends the act of cleansing us from "all unrighteousness."

3. *God has commanded us to be sanctified wholly, to be perfect, to be holy*

Matt. 5:48—"Be ye therefore perfect, even as your Father which is in heaven is perfect." Rom. 12:1-2—"I beseech you therefore, brethren, by the mercies of God, that ye present your bodies a living sacrifice, holy, acceptable unto God, which is your reasonable service. And be not conformed to this world: but be ye transformed by the renewing of your mind, that ye may prove what is that good, and acceptable, and perfect, will of God."

This text contemplates nothing short of entire conformity to the will of God.

2 Cor. 7:1—"Having therefore these promises, dearly beloved, let us cleanse ourselves from all filthiness of the flesh and spirit, perfecting holiness in the fear of God."

This text was addressed to Christians, and it is therefore clear that there is a state of purity from all filthiness of the flesh and spirit, and of perfected holiness, which may be reached in this life, which they had not attained, or which it was possible, that they as Christians had not attained. When a Christian is cleansed from all filthiness of the flesh and spirit and has perfected holiness in the fear of God, he has reached a state of entire sanctification.

2 Cor. 13:11—"Finally, brethren, farewell. Be perfect, be of good comfort, be of one mind, live in peace; and the God of love and peace shall be with you."

If Paul aimed at expressing any definite idea by being perfect, he must have meant being made perfect in love, or a state of entire consecration to God.

Heb. 6:1—"Let us go on unto perfection." What can we understand by perfection unless it be entire sanctification?

James 1:4—"But let patience have her perfect work, that ye may be perfect and entire, wanting nothing."

This is very comprehensive and expresses the idea by three different terms. They were to be perfect, which denotes all they were required to be, just what they ought to be. Then they were to be entire, which denotes every part of what was necessary to make them perfect. And then to make the sense still more full if possible, the apostle adds, "wanting nothing." Those who are wanting in nothing to complete their Christian character or state must be entirely sanctified.

1 Pet. 1:15-16—"But as he which hath called you is holy, so be ye holy in all manner of conversation; because it is written, Be ye holy; for I am holy."

In the light of the above scriptures it cannot be denied that Christian perfection, entire sanctification, or consecration to God is commanded as a Christian duty.

4. *The Scriptures teach that the attainment of a state of entire sanctification is a proper subject of prayer.* This is principally taught by example, in the prayers of inspired men.

PRAYERS FOR HOLINESS

In the prayer of our Lord Jesus Christ, which He offered upon the eve of His passion, we have these remarkable words in regard to His disciples. John 17:23—"I in them, and thou in me, that they may be made perfect in one; and that the world may know that thou hast sent me, and hast loved them, as thou hast loved me."

Perfection in unity is the principal thought in this text.

Ps. 51:2, 7, 10—"Wash me throughly from mine iniquity, and cleanse me from my sin. . . . Purge me with hyssop, and I shall be clean: wash me, and I shall be whiter than snow. . . . Create in me a clean heart, O God; and renew a right spirit within me."

It may be said that David was fallen at the time he uttered this prayer, and that he prayed for pardon. This may be true, but still his prayer comprehends more than pardon. He appears to charge his fall upon his innate depravity, which still remained in him, and now he prays for a more thorough work. He asks for a clean heart, and no heart is clean where any degree of sin remains.

Col. 4:12—"Epaphras, who is one of you, a servant of Christ, saluteth you, always labouring fervently for you in prayers, that ye may stand perfect and complete in all the will of God."

The object of his prayers was that they might enjoy and maintain perfection and completeness in all the will of God. This certainly must exclude all sin.

1 Thess. 5:23—"And the very God of peace sanctify you wholly; and I pray God your whole spirit, and soul, and body be preserved blameless unto the coming of our Lord Jesus Christ."

Here Paul clearly prayed for entire sanctification on behalf of his brethren at Thessalonica.

Heb. 13:20-21—"Now the God of peace, that brought again from the dead our Lord Jesus, that great shepherd of the sheep, through the blood of the everlasting covenant, make you perfect in every good work to do his will, working in you that which is wellpleasing in his sight, through Jesus Christ; to whom be glory for ever and ever. Amen."

Such a text needs no comment to make it express the doctrine of entire consecration to God. The state of Christian attainment prayed for is looked for as the result of the work of God within.

It will hardly be affirmed that we are thus encouraged to pray for what is not attainable.

Mark 11:24—"What things soever ye desire, when ye pray, believe that ye [will] receive them, and ye shall have them."

This text is a sufficient comment upon all the prayers offered up for entire sanctification.

5. *The Scriptures teach us that some did attain to a state of entire sanctification in olden times*

Gen. 5:24—"And Enoch walked with God: and he was not; for God took him." It would be a fair inference to conclude that he was wholly consecrated to God. We are told in verse 22 that "Enoch walked with God three hundred years."

2 Kings 2:11—"And it came to pass, as they still went on, and talked, that, behold, there appeared a chariot of fire, and horses of fire, and parted them both asunder; and Elijah went up by a whirlwind into heaven."

It would not be an unwarrantable inference to conclude that Elijah was sanctified wholly on earth.

Job 1:1, 8—"There was a man in the land of Uz, whose name was Job; and that man was perfect and upright, and one that feared God, and eschewed evil. . . . And the Lord said unto Satan, Hast thou considered my servant Job, that there is none like him in the earth, a perfect and an upright man, one that feareth God, and escheweth evil?"

It is certain that God found no fault with Job. How much remaining sin would be found, if one like Job was put in the crucible of modern theology and tested?

Luke 1:6—"And they were both righteous before God, walking in all the commandments and ordinances of the Lord blameless."

This is said of Zacharias and Elizabeth. Some have supposed that Zacharias could not have been perfect, because he did not believe the angel as described in verse 20. If it be allowed that moral dereliction is involved, it does not prove that they were not perfect prior to that interview with the angel. The doctrine of perfection under consideration does not pretend to secure the perfect against the possibility of a relapse.

6. *But the Scriptures teach that some have been perfect in the sense of entire consecration to God, in another and more general manner*

It is by referring to unnamed persons as perfect, as though the fact that there is such a class were understood.

Ps. 37:37—"Mark the perfect man, and behold the upright: for the end of that man is peace."

Ps. 119:2-3—"Blessed are they that keep his testimonies, and that seek him with the whole heart. They also do no iniquity: they walk in his ways."

Prov. 2:21—"For the upright shall dwell in the land, and the perfect shall remain in it."

Prov. 11:5—"The righteousness of the perfect shall direct his way: but the wicked shall fall by his own wickedness."

1 Cor. 2:6—"Howbeit we speak wisdom among them that are perfect: yet not the wisdom of this world, nor of the princes of this world, that come to nought."

Phil. 3:15—"Let us therefore, as many as be perfect, be thus minded: and if in any thing ye be otherwise, God shall reveal even this unto you."

1 John 1:7—"But if we walk in the light, as he is in the light, we have fellowship one with another, and the blood of Jesus Christ his Son cleanseth us from all sin."

1 John 2:5—"But whoso keepeth his word, in him verily is the love of God perfected: hereby know we that we are in him."

1 John 3:3—"And every man that hath this hope in him purifieth himself, even as he is pure."

1 John 4:17-18—"Herein is our love made perfect, that we may have boldness in the day of judgment: because as he is, so are we in this world. There is no fear in love; but perfect love casteth out fear: because fear hath torment. He that feareth is not made perfect in love."

A special comment upon each of the above texts is unnecessary; they clearly teach that there were persons in the times of the writers who were perfect, in the Bible sense of perfection as applied to the children of God. This perfection was a perfection in obedience, a perfection in love, a being "cleansed from all unrighteousness, and from all sin." This is all that is claimed, and at this state let both writer and reader aim, and never rest satisfied short of its full enjoyment. Amen.

5

Samuel Wakefield

(1799-1895)

Born in Huntingdon County, Pa., March 6, 1799, Samuel Wakefield was of English-Irish descent. His parents, together with three young Irishmen by the name of Simpson (one of whom became the famous Bishop Matthew Simpson), comprised the first Methodist "class" in the county.

When Samuel was only seven the family moved to a wilderness area farther west, where the boy worked along with his father to clear 70 acres. His formal schooling amounted to a bare seven months; but his thirst for knowledge was so great that after working from dawn to dusk he would study far into the night by the light of a candle.

When 20 years of age he was converted at a Methodist camp meeting. Three months later he preached his first sermon and 10 months later, March 21, 1820, was licensed as a local preacher. During these years he studied Greek and Latin under a Presbyterian minister, and also studied medicine.

He achieved wide acceptance as a leader and preacher, serving several times as a delegate to the General Conference, pastoring for some years the prestigious Liberty Street congregation (Uniontown), and leading as presiding elder of the Uniontown district.

Wakefield was equally well known as a singer, hymn writer, and compiler of hymnals and songbooks.

His literary work included *An Essay on Justifying Faith,* a grammar of the English language, and his most enduring work, a systematic theology, which was introduced into the Methodist course of study and was widely known as "Wakefield's Theology." Fifteen years before his death he was included in the *Cyclopedia of Methodism.*[1]

H. Orton Wiley comments that Wakefield's theology (like Ralston's) is a "revision of Watson's *Institutes* with some valuable material added. The purpose was to furnish a clear and comprehensive outline of scriptural theology."[2]

Allegheny College bestowed on him the D.D. degree and many years later the LL.D. He died at 96 years of age, September 13, 1895.

Free Will and Free Grace

Robert E. Chiles, in *Theological Transition in American Methodism,* takes Watson and Miley to task for allegedly departing from Wesley on the subject of free will. But Chiles reveals a curious twist in thinking even by the title of his chapter: "From Free Grace to Free Will." Implied here is a substantive antagonism between the two concepts, as if free grace were orthodoxy while free will were heresy.

There may be between Wesley and his successors a shift in emphasis but not a change in direction. The uniform position of all Wesleyan thinkers is that only free will can respond to free grace. Grace without freedom is irresistible grace, and hence necessitarian. Such grace not only carries with it the whole train of deterministic doctrines, but also blanks out all meaningful personal responsibility.

The antithesis implied by Chiles between free grace and free will is valid only if free will implies freedom from the need of grace. To assume such an implication is arbitrarily to fasten on only one concept of free will and to ignore other possibilities. It would be an unjustifiable error to read into Wesleyan theologians this one-sided meaning.

---

1. Rev. ed.; Matthew Simpson, ed. (Philadelphia: Louis H. Everts, 1880).
2. Unpublished course notes, Pasadena College.

Such a limited concept is to see free will as completely incompatible with an impaired moral will. The implicit supposition is that the moral *inability* implied in original sin, requiring grace, is contradictory to the moral *ability* implied in free will. But no such contradiction exists. A human will may be free yet morally weak and subjectively impotent. Man's freedom may not be abridged by God—either by decree, predestination, selective grace, or by any other external control. But at the same time it may be impaired by the damaging effects of the carnal mind, so as to require the enabling and reinforcing of divine grace.

In establishing an anchor point for Wesley's thought, Chiles (p. 134) seizes upon the concession to Calvinism made in Conversation II at Bristol, Friday, August 2, 1745.

"Wherein may we come to the very edge of Calvinism?" is the question raised. Part of the answer is: "In denying all natural free-will and all power antecedent to grace." The second half of the sentence explains the first half. By "natural free-will" Wesley obviously means unimpaired moral power sufficient to achieve righteousness and thereby eternal life. Wesley thus repudiates Pelagianism *in toto.* He just as obviously does not mean that unregenerate persons have no capacity for independent moral action. This is confirmed by the care with which Wesley characteristically denies *irresistible* grace (*Works,* 10:254 ff., et al.). Only free will can resist the Spirit.

True Wesleyanism neither denies free will nor the impairment caused by original sin. Rather, it teaches that prevenient grace sufficiently energizes the sin-weakened will so that moral choices can again be made in practical freedom. Scriptural grace is not a free grace that obviates free will. It is a free grace that respects free will.

The earnest discussions of free will by Methodistic theologians in the last century were necessary to break the shackles of an enervating and responsibility-canceling determinism. The vigorous affirmations of freedom and responsibility were not deviant forms of Wesleyanism, though they may have exhibited a shift of emphasis.

The following discussions by Wakefield, which both echo and clarify Watson, are samples of the line of reasoning followed by these writers.

MAN'S MORAL AGENCY[3]

A *free moral agent* is one who is the real author of his own moral actions, without being determined to will or to act by an extrinsic cause.

An action is rendered *moral* by two circumstances: *first,* it must be free or voluntary. "If, in any action," says Dr. Reid, "an agent has power to will what he does, or not to will it, in that action he is free. But if, in every voluntary action the determination of his will is the necessary consequence of something involuntary in the state of his mind, or of something in his external circumstances, he is not free; he has not the liberty of a moral agent, but is subject to necessity."[4]

But *secondly,* it is essential to a moral action that it has respect to some rule or law that determines it to be right or wrong. Moral agency, therefore, implies moral law, a comprehension of moral distinctions, and some degree of practical judgment. "For, if a person has not the judgment to discern one determination to be preferable to another, either in itself or for some purpose which he intends, what can be the use of a power to determine? His determinations must be made perfectly in the dark, without reason, motive, or end. They can neither be right nor wrong, wise nor foolish."[5]

No one can deny, without running into great absurdity, that a self-active and free agent may exist. To deny this is either to deny the existence of God, or, if His existence be allowed, to deny that He is a free agent. But to suppose that God cannot act without being impelled thereto by a power back of His own is to suppose a power greater than His, on which the exercise of His omnipotence depends. By a parity of reason we should be compelled to suppose another power still back of that, and so on, *ad infinitum,* which would be both absurd and impious. Hence we are forced to the conclusion that God is a free agent in this fullest sense of the term, being self-active and wholly independent of all extrinsic influences whatever.

Now, as it is evident, beyond all controversy, that God is a self-active agent, it is rational to believe that when He created man in His own image, He endowed him with *self-active power;* or, in other

---

3. This selection is taken from *A Complete System of Christian Theology* (Cincinnati: Cranston and Stowe, 1869), chapter 4, 314-18.

4. Reid's *Works,* 3:173.

5. Ibid.

MAN A FREE AGENT

words, made him capable of acting without being necessitated to act by some extrinsic efficient cause. Nor is it more difficult to conceive that man possesses self-active power than that such a power belongs to God; for though in man's case this power is limited and dependent, and in God infinite and independent, yet in both, so far as the simple question of free agency is concerned, it is the same. We hold, then, that the volitions and moral actions of men are purely their own and not determined by any extrinsic cause, and therefore, that men are truly *free moral agents.*

When we claim for man a self-active power in the exercise of volition we do not mean that the will is altogether uninfluenced by motives. We know that he is the subject of appetites and passions connected with his animal nature; that there are within emotions and desires, reasonings and judgments, moral perceptions and convictions, and that he is graciously visited by the influences of the Holy Spirit. But in no case can motives efficiently cause volition. Amidst influences for good on the one hand and for evil on the other, it belongs to man to choose. God has endowed him with the faculty of free volition, and while that faculty remains, no power extrinsic to himself can necessitate his choice.

If it be said, in advocacy of the determining power of motives, that every volition must have a sufficient cause, the only necessary reply is that man, in the exercise of willing, is a sufficient and independent cause. He may be acted upon by a thousand influences, but he does not necessarily yield to any of them. He is a free agent—the real author of his own actions, and not a mere instrument, acting only as he is acted upon. . . .

1. *Argument from the testimony of consciousness* . . .

But the testimony of consciousness becomes still more interesting when we consider it in relation to the phenomena of our moral

THE SENSE OF MORAL OBLIGATION

constitution. It is a matter of universal experience that men are capable of comprehending moral distinctions, or of perceiving that there is a real difference between right and wrong conduct, and that they feel themselves to be under a moral obligation to do what they believe to be right, and to refrain from doing that which they believe to be wrong. These facts are necessarily implied in the very existence of the faculty we call conscience, or the moral sense; and this faculty, in its practical operations, as necessarily implies our free moral agency.

All men are conscious, in a greater or less degree, of moral obligation; but there cannot be a sense of moral obligation where there is no sense of moral freedom. Let a man be convinced that all his volitions and actions are determined by some cause over which he has no control, and at once his sense of obligation must cease. It would be absurd to suppose that he could feel morally bound to pursue any given course of action, if he did not believe himself to be morally free.

Men are often the subjects of self-condemnation; but they cannot be without recognizing the fact that they have power to control their own moral actions. What is *self-condemnation* but a consciousness on the part of a free moral agent that he has voluntarily and unnecessarily transgressed a known law? Convince him that the act was unavoidable, and his self-condemnation is at an end. He can no more blame himself for having committed it than he can blame the tornado for having destroyed his neighbor's property. That remorse for past offences, which accompanies evangelical repentance, depends for its very existence upon the conviction that we are free, and not impelled, in our moral actions, by any law of absolute necessity. We conclude, therefore, that our consciousness clearly establishes the doctrine of man's free moral agency. To set aside its testimony would be as unphilosophical as to conclude that it is midnight when we behold the blaze of the meridian sun. But the doctrine in question may be argued:

2. *From the common consent of mankind*

That men of all countries and in all ages of the world have generally acknowledged the freedom of the human will is a position clearly indicated by many historical facts. To a few of these, and only to a few, we will briefly direct the reader's attention.

(1) There are, in all languages, so far as we can learn, words and phrases in regard to human conduct expressive of obligation, of moral agency, of right and wrong, of innocence and guilt, of praise and blame. Now, as the language of a nation is always indicative of its common sentiments, this fact cannot be accounted for in any rational way, unless we admit that there is a general agreement among men in favor of the doctrine for which we contend—the free moral agency of man.

(2) The existence of civil government is another fact that merits our consideration. This supposes not only constitutional provisions, but the enactment of specific laws for the direction and regulation of human conduct. But would not such enactments be most absurd if

men did not possess the power of self-control? We might as well frame a code of laws for the government of the lower animals. Hence, in the very existence of these laws we have decisive proof that the uncontrolled freedom of the human will is generally acknowledged.

All laws are enforced by penal sanctions; for a law without a penalty is, in fact, no law at all. But in every penal sanction it is taken for granted that the subjects of the law have power either to obey or disobey it. If they had no power to disobey the law, the penalty would be a useless appendage; and if they had no power to obey the law, the penalty would be unjust and cruel. That men have power to control their own moral actions is therefore acknowledged in the enactment of legal penalties and is thus shown to be the common belief of the world.

(3) It is a fact of universal notoriety that men are in the habit of projecting plans of future operation they resolve to pursue. This proves, beyond a doubt, that they believe themselves to be free, and to be able to direct their volitions and actions to a certain end. . . . Men could not make promises and enter into contracts that look to the future, if they did not verily believe that their volitions and actions are their own and uncaused by any power extrinsic to themselves. Thus we come to the conclusion that the doctrine of moral liberty is one of common consent.

3. *We argue this doctrine from the teachings of the Holy Scriptures.*

When we turn to the sacred volume and investigate its teachings in regard to man's moral agency, we find its testimony so abundant, and at the same time so variant in manner, that we can only note a few leading features in the general argument. We may remark,

(1) That the freedom of the human will is everywhere acknowledged in the Scriptures. "I call heaven and earth to record this day against you, that I have set before you life and death, blessing and cursing: therefore *choose* life, that both thou and thy seed may live" (Deut. 30:19). "*Choose* you this day whom ye will serve" (Josh. 24:15). Here men are exhorted to *choose,* which is the same as to *will,* or to put forth an act of *volition;* but if the will were not free—if every volition of the human mind were necessarily determined and unavoidable, it would be impossible to reconcile such exhortations with either sincerity or common sense.

Our Lord said to the Jews, "How often would I have gathered thy children together, even as a hen gathereth her chickens under her wings, and ye *would not!*" (Matt. 23:37). And again, "Ye *will not* come to me, that ye might have life" (John 5:40). These plain and inspired passages clearly recognize the fact that men have power to control their own volitions, and that they are therefore justly punishable if they refuse to comply with the divine will. But if the doctrine of moral necessity were true, that the volitions and actions of men could not be different from what they are, all men would be perfectly innocent; for surely no one in his right mind will suppose that men can be *guilty*, and therefore justly punishable, if their actions and volitions are necessary and unavoidable.

Our blessed Lord, in closing up the sacred canon, issued this remarkable proclamation: "And *whosoever* WILL, let him take the water of life freely" (Rev. 22:17). Here again, the freedom of the human will is manifestly acknowledged; and the doctrine is virtually taught, moreover, that the salvation of men depends on their voluntary acceptance of the terms on which it is proposed. Now, as it does not require the eye of a philosopher to see the antagonism between the theory of moral necessity and the teachings of the holy Scriptures, so it cannot be difficult to determine which we should adopt. We must conclude, according to the latter, that man has power to control his own voluntary actions—that he can obey or disobey the divine law, and that he is therefore a free moral agent.

(2) This doctrine is evinced by the fact that man is under moral government, and in a state of probation. God is the Governor both of the world of matter and the world of created and intelligent mind; but He does not govern both in the same way. He governs the material world by certain fixed, invariable, and necessary laws that cannot be resisted; and hence its phenomena are nothing more nor less than a succession of necessary causes and effects.

But when we turn our attention to that government which He exercises over intelligent creatures, we find it to be of a very different character: it is one that involves the idea of moral distinctions, of right and wrong, of rewards and punishments, and, consequently, of laws that may be either obeyed or disobeyed. In a word, it is a *moral government;* the only kind that is suited to moral creatures.

That God has placed the human family under this kind of government is everywhere taught in the sacred Scriptures. When He created man He gave him a moral law, enforced by a suitable penalty. That he violated the law, and incurred its penalty, are matters of history. But had he power to obey it? To say he had not is to charge God with injustice, in imposing upon him a law he could not obey, and then punishing him for his disobedience. But if he had power to obey the law, then he was a free moral agent.

Here it is proper to observe that the advocates of moral necessity suppose their theory to be perfectly consistent both with man's free agency and with his moral accountability. They hold that men are free in the proper sense of the word, when they have power to act according to their own volitions, and that they are justly responsible for their moral conduct, because they act voluntarily and are free from natural necessity. But it is certainly a very defective view of human liberty to suppose that it consists solely in freedom from coaction, or in the opportunity that men have to act according to their volitions.

Will any man say that civil liberty consists in the mere privilege of obeying laws? Surely not; for this would be to say that men may enjoy civil liberty while in a state of slavery. No one will deny that even slaves have liberty to obey the law under which they are placed; but can they be persuaded that for this reason they are properly free? We know they cannot; and yet this is the only kind of freedom that the theory of moral necessity allows to man. He is free, not in the exercise of willing—for in this everything is determined—but in being at liberty to act according to his necessitated volitions.

Now, we deny that this kind of freedom forms a just ground of moral responsibility. We take it to be an incontrovertible truth that a

MORAL ACCOUNTABILITY

man's power is the proper measure of his moral accountability. This principle is admitted by all, in regard to such actions as are controlled by natural necessity. If a man were made the instrument, by natural necessity, of destroying the life of his neighbor, he could not be justly punished as a criminal; and for this simple reason, that he had no power to do otherwise. But will not the same principle apply to *moral* necessity? Suppose a man resolves to do some wicked act. If every volition is a necessary effect, how is he guilty and justly punishable in this case any more than in the other? Had he power to will otherwise? If he had, the doctrine of moral necessity is false, and he is justly chargeable with crime; but if he had not, he can no more be accountable for a necessary *volition* than for a necessary *action*.

From the whole of this reasoning, we feel ourselves safe in the conclusion that the theory of moral necessity cannot be reconciled with man's accountability and the retributions of the Judgment Day. Men may talk as they please about moral agency, and the freedom of the human will; but unless man possesses a self-controlling power over his own moral actions, he can no more be justly rewarded or punished than the beasts that roam in the forest. This controlling power can only be exerted in acts of volition; and hence we contend that the *will of man is essentially free.*

Holiness and Christian Ethics

Holiness as a state is inward conformity to the will of God, but as a life it is outward conformity to that will. The will of God for mankind generally is expressed in the form of law, that is, specific statutes of command or prohibition by which man's ethical conduct is to be directed and governed. Whatever may be said respecting divine law and the pagan world, the Judeo-Christian ethic sees the Decalogue as the authoritative base with love as law's enfleshment. Wesleyan theologicans typically have not viewed the gospel and law as mutually exclusive, but as complementary. The gospel is the Good News, not only that infractions of the law may be forgiven, but the good news that a grace is available whereby the law may be kept in freedom—joyfully, consistently, and from the heart. The following discussion by Wakefield is a reasonably representative statement of a Wesleyan approach.

THE MORAL LAW[6]

Morality in a general sense denotes *virtue,* or *the practice of moral duties.* In a strictly theological sense it means a voluntary conformity of our moral actions to the will of God. By the *morals* of Christianity, therefore, we are to understand the practical duties that Christianity requires. Hence it becomes a matter of importance to know both what these duties are and how they ought to be performed. But before we proceed to investigate them in detail we will offer some remarks in regard to that system of moral law on which they all depend, and by which they are prescribed.

By *moral law* we understand a law that prescribes to men their religious and social duties; or, in other words, the duties we owe to

6. This is chapter 1, "The Moral Law" of Book 5, "Morals of Christianity," 467-71.

God and to one another. Such a law, in its highest degree of perfection, is contained in the Scriptures of the Old and New Testament, and in them only. . . .

Philosophers have entertained various and conflicting opinions in regard to what constitutes the *ground of moral obligation;* but all Christians will agree that the will of God, which is ever in perfect accordance with rectitude, is the *standard* of right for all moral creatures, and ought to be obeyed. And as the holy Scriptures are the only authoritative revelation of the divine will, we will proceed to inquire into the manner in which they make known to us a system of moral law. . . .

1. *The morals of the Scriptures are not generally proposed to us in the form of a regular code.*

Even in the books of Moses, which, to a great extent, have the legislative form, all the principles and duties that constitute the full character of *godliness* under that dispensation are not made the subjects of formal injunction by particular precepts. They are partly unfolded in general principles, or often take the form of injunction in an apparently incidental manner, or as matters of obvious inference. A preceding code of traditionary moral law is also all along supposed in the writings of Moses and the prophets, as well as a customary ritual and a doctrinal theology, both transmitted from the patriarchs.

This, too, is eminently the case with the Christian Scriptures. They suppose that all who believe in Christ admitted the divine authority of the Old Testament, and they assume the perpetual authority of its morals as well as the truth of its fundamental theology. The constant allusions in the New Testament to the moral rules of the Jews and patriarchs, either expressly as precepts or as the data of argument, sufficiently guard us against the notion that what has not in so many words been reenacted by Christ and His apostles is of no authority among Christians.

In a great number of instances, however, the form is directly preceptive, so as to have all the explicitness and force of a regular code of law, and is, as much as a regular code could be, a declaration of the sovereign will of Christ, enforced by the sanctions of eternal life and death.

2. *The moral law is summarily comprehended in the Decalogue or Ten Commandments.*

These were written by the finger of God on two tables of stone, and delivered to Moses on Mount Sinai. These tables were deposited in the sacred chest, called the ark of the covenant, but copies of them were transcribed into the Pentateuch in Exod. 20:1-17, and in Deut. 5:6-21.

This giving of the law on Mount Sinai was the most solemn transaction that ever took place between God and man, and, therefore, it was introduced in the most solemn manner. In the morning of the day on which this law was given, the presence of Jehovah became manifest by thunders and lightnings, a dense cloud on the mountain, and a terrific blast of a trumpet, so that all in the assembly were struck with terror and dismay. Shortly after, the whole mountain appeared on fire, columns of smoke arose from it as the smoke of a furnace, and an earthquake shook it from top to base; the trumpet continued to sound, and the blast grew longer and louder. Then Jehovah, the sovereign Lawgiver, came down upon the mount and called Moses to ascend to the top that he might receive His law.

In this summary of moral law we have the most complete and perfect arrangement and specification of human duties that has ever been made, and one that will probably never be improved. Its division into two distinct parts or tables was not accidental, but a matter of design, and was made for most important reasons. The first table comprehended the four precepts that enjoin our duty to God and the second the six that prescribe our duty to men. It is called the moral law because the subject of its injunctions is not ceremonial observances but moral actions, and to distinguish it from the positive laws, which were only of temporary obligation.

3. *The moral precepts of the Old Testament are received into the Christian code.*

When our Lord, in His Sermon on the Mount, says, "Think not that I am come to destroy the law or the prophets. I am not come to destroy, but to fulfill"—that is, to confirm or establish the law—the entire scope of His discourse shows that He is speaking exclusively of the moral precepts of THE LAW, eminently so called, and of the moral injunctions of the prophets founded upon them, and to which He thus gives an equal authority.

In like manner St. Paul, after having strenuously maintained the doctrine of justification by faith alone, anticipates an objection by asking, "Do we then make void the law through faith?" and subjoins, "God forbid; yea, we *establish* the law"; meaning by this term, as the context and his argument show, the *moral* and not the ceremonial law.

After such declarations it is worse than trifling for anyone to contend that, in order to establish the authority of the moral law of the Jews over Christians, it ought to have been formally reenacted. Indeed, the summary of the law and the prophets, which is to love God with all our heart, and to love our neighbor as ourselves, is unquestionably enjoined and even reenacted by the Christian Lawgiver.

When our Lord was explicitly asked by "one who came unto him and said, Good Master, what good thing shall I do, that I may have eternal life?" the answer shows that the moral law contained in the Decalogue is so in force under the Christian dispensation that obedience to it is necessary to final salvation: "If thou wilt enter into life, keep the commandments." And that He refers directly to the Decalogue is manifest from what follows. "He saith unto him, Which? Jesus said, Thou shalt do no murder. Thou shalt not commit adultery. Thou shalt not steal" (Matt. 19:17-18). Here we have all the force of a formal reenactment of the Decalogue, a part of it being evidently put for the whole.

Nor would it be difficult to produce passages from the discourses of Christ and the writings of the apostles, which enjoin all the precepts of this law separately by their authority, as indispensable parts of Christian duty, and that, too, under their original sanctions of life and death. So, then, the two circumstances that form the true character of LAW in its highest sense, DIVINE AUTHORITY and PENAL SANCTIONS, are found as truly in the New Testament as in the Old. It will not, for instance, be denied that the New Testament enjoins the worship of one God alone; that it prohibits idolatry; that it forbids false and profane swearing; that St. Paul uses the very words of the fifth commandment preceptively when he says in Eph. 6:2, "Honour thy father and mother; which is the first commandment with promise"; or that murder, adultery, theft, false witness, and covetousness are prohibited under pain of exclusion from the kingdom of God.

Thus, then, we have the whole Decalogue brought into the Christian code of morals by a distinct injunction of its separate precepts, and by their recognition as of permanent and unchangeable obligation; the fourth commandment (concerning the Sabbath) only being so far excepted that its injunction is not so expressly marked. This, however, is no exception in fact; for (1) Its original place in the two tables sufficiently distinguishes it from all positive, ceremonial, and typical precepts, and gives it a moral character in respect to its *ends;* which are, first, *mercy* to servants and cattle, and secondly, the undisturbed *worship of God;* (2) It is necessarily included in that "law" which our Lord declares He came "not to destroy," or abrogate; in that "law" which St. Paul declares to be established by faith; and, (3) It was recognized in the practice of the apostles, who did not cease to keep holy one day in seven, but gave "the Lord's day" that eminence and sanctity in the Christian Church, which the seventh day had in the Jewish, by consecrating it to holy uses.

4. *The New Testament contains a fuller revelation of moral law than the Old.*

It is important to remark that though the moral laws of the Mosaic dispensation pass into the Christian code, yet they stand there in other and higher circumstances. In particular,

NT ADVANCE OVER OT

(1) They are more expressly extended to the heart, as by our Lord in His Sermon on the Mount; who teaches us that the thought and inward purpose of any offense is a violation of the law that prohibits its external and visible commission.

(2) The principles on which they are founded are carried out in the New Testament into a great variety of duties, which, by embracing more perfectly the social and civil relations of life, are of a more universal character; and there is an enlarged injunction of positive and particular virtues, especially of such as belong to the Christian temper.

(3) All overt acts are inseparably connected with those corresponding principles in the heart that are essential to acceptable obedience; which principles suppose the regeneration of the soul by the Holy Spirit. This moral renovation is, therefore, held out as necessary to our salvation and promised through Christ.

(4) The precepts of the gospel are connected with peculiar promises of divine assistance, are illustrated in the perfect example of our Lord, and are enforced by sanctions derived from the clearer revelation of a future state, and the more explicit promises of eternal life, and threatenings of eternal punishment.

It follows, therefore, that the gospel contains the most complete and perfect revelation of *moral law* that has ever been given to man. It contains a law that is of universal obligation, the law that was given to Adam in paradise, and from which his subsequent apostasy could not release him. This law has no relation, therefore, to times and places or to one age or nation more than another; but being founded in the relations of men to their Creator and to one another, it retains its authority under all dispensations.

The great principle involved in all acceptable obedience to moral law is LOVE—*love to God* and *love to man.* When the lawyer inquired, "Master, which is the greatest commandment in the law? Jesus said unto him, Thou shalt love the Lord thy God with all thy heart, and with all thy soul, and with all thy mind. This is the first and great commandment. And the second is like unto it, Thou shalt love thy neighbour as thyself. On these two commandments hang all the law and the prophets" (Matt. 22:36-40). So also St. Paul testifies, that "love is the fulfilling of the law" (Rom. 13:10). It is on this grand principle of universal love that all moral law is founded; and its particular precepts only point out the various ways in which this love is to be manifested.

THE PRINCIPLE OF LOVE

To the revealed will of God we may now turn for all necessary information on the interesting subject of Christian morality. But as the gospel is a message of mercy to a sinful and rebellious race, and as it requires of all men, as indispensable conditions of their salvation, "*repentance* toward God and *faith* toward our Lord Jesus Christ," it seems both proper and necessary that we should in the first place direct our attention to a consideration of these important evangelical requirements.

6

Miner Raymond

(1811-97)

Raymond was born August 29, 1811, at Rennselaerville, N.Y. Because of a limited education he turned to the trade of shoemaker. But while still a very young man God impressed him with a call to the ministry. He promptly left the tools of his trade forever, and entered Wesleyan Academy in Wilbraham, Mass., where his natural mental endowment soon became obvious. He was appointed as helper and instructor under the well-known teacher Wilbur Fisk. Later, in 1848 after three short pastorates in Massachusetts, he was elected principal of Wilbraham at 37 years of age. The academy prospered under his leadership.

But his most productive years were as professor of systematic theology at Garrett Biblical Institute of Evanston, Ill., to which he was elected in 1864. While there he wrote his three-volume *Systematic Theology,* published first in 1877. Though in academia, he remained active in Methodist church administration. The high regard with which he was held was evidenced by over 50 votes received for bishop in 1872.

After the death of his first wife, the mother of his six children, he married Mrs. Isabella Hill Binney, widow of Amos Binney, author of *Binney's Theological Compend.* This made him stepfather-in-law to Daniel Steele, who had married Binney's daughter. Raymond's *Systematic Theology* came out two years following Steele's first book, *Love Enthroned.*

As was the case with so many in this volume, Raymond's work was for a while used in the Methodist course of study for ministers.

Nature and Origin of Sin[1]

Raymond's style is both concise and lucid. There is intensity of close reasoning combined with compactness and economy of expression. This reflects his philosophical approach to theology. He is reasoning more than researching and makes minimal use of supporting references. Even Bible quotations are few, though apt.

Representative of Raymond's style is this discussion on the nature and origin of sin. It is moral philosophy based on biblical foundations. The distinction made between wrong acts and evil motives is clear. Wrong acts carry inescapable natural consequences; but whether they also carry demerit and condemnation depends on the personal factors that together constitute accountability. In his approach, Raymond is typical of 19th-century Methodist theologians in their earnest efforts to be rational without being rationalistic.

The primary idea designated by the term *sin* in the Scriptures is want of conformity to law, a transgression, a transgression of law, a doing that which is forbidden or a neglecting to do that which is required. The term used in the Greek Testament for this specific thought is *anomia; a*, privative, and *nomos*, law—without law, or contrary to law. Some writers denominate the doing of that which is forbidden a sin of commission, and neglecting to do that which is required a sin of omission.

In this view, sin pertains exclusively to conduct, not, however, to mere muscular activities; the thoughts, emotions, desires, affections, and volitions of the mind may be what they ought not to be, may not be conformed to law, may be transgressions of law, may be sin in the primary sense of the term.

In a secondary sense the term applies to character; not to what one does—to what he thinks, desires, wills—but to what he is. A man may be what he ought not to be, what the law forbids he should be,

---

1. The following selection is from *Systematic Theology* (Cincinnati: Hitchcock and Walden, 1877), 2:54-63.

or he may not be what the law requires him to be. This want of conformity to law in character is in the Greek Testament usually termed *hamartia,* though in 1 John 3:4 it is used as a synonym with *anomia.* "Sin is a transgression of the law," *hamartia* is *anomia.* In Rom. 7:20, "Now if I do that I would not, it is no more I that do it, but sin that dwelleth in me," it is evident that the term *sin, hamartia,* is used to signify some defect, disorder, disease, derangement, depravity, whatever it may be called, in the state and condition of the mind; it pertains to character, to what the man *is.*

In a word, it is sufficiently accurate, though not perfectly so, to say that in New Testament use the term signifies, generically, *want of conformity to law,* and that under this generic sense there are two species, one having respect to conduct and the other to character. The former is sometimes called in common discourse actual transgression, and the latter, to distinguish it from the former, is called original sin, natural depravity, inherited or inherent unrighteousness. Man regarded with reference to the first is said to be a sinner, with reference to the second, sinful.

TWO KINDS OF SIN

The term *sin,* as above defined, may be taken abstractly or concretely.[2] If the former [abstract], it refers solely to the thing done as actually performed, and to the character as actually existing. If the latter [concrete], it takes into account, in addition to the deed done and the character sustained, the personal relations of the agent to these. Abstractly, a man may be both sinful and a sinner, and yet not be responsibly such. If depravity be outside of his control, and if under its influence his conduct be necessitated, he is sinful and a sinner in the sense that his character and conduct are not conformed to law; but he is not a guilty sinner, is not under obligation to punishment for his sins. It might be said that he is not a sinner in such a case, because . . . he is not under law, and therefore cannot be a sinner in any proper sense of the word. This would be . . . true and scriptural as to doctrine, but not in exact conformity with the scriptural use of terms. The Scriptures do use the terms *righteousness* and *unrighteousness, holiness* and *sin* in the abstract sense of conformity and nonconformity to law.

Before we can fully fix the sense of the term *sin,* and define the nature of that which is intended, it is necessary to inquire, What is

2. What others designate as legal versus ethical sin, or objective versus subjective, Raymond indicates by the terms *abstract* versus *concrete.*

law? Perhaps it is sufficient for our present purpose to say God's will is man's law. God, as Creator and Preserver, has the natural right of proprietorship. He has in man, as in all things He has made, the absolute right of unlimited possession; and man is therefore naturally under the obligation of universal obedience.

It is sometimes asked whether this is right because God wills it, or does He will it because it is right? It is impossible for finite thought to get anterior or exterior to God. There can be nothing to the infinite antecedent in time or external in space, that limits Him, or by constraint determines what His will shall be. It is therefore in accordance with truth, and sufficient for all purposes of science to say that this is right because God commands it, and its opposite is wrong because God has forbidden it.

GOD'S WILL

The will of God is the ground of moral obligation, and yet it is impossible to think that right and wrong depend upon the will of God, in such a sense as that we could conceive a reversal of the case possible. We cannot think that a volition of the divine mind could make ill will among social beings right, and goodwill wrong. There is a sense in which moral principles are as eternal and immutable as God, and the will of God is immutably in harmony with them.

How does God make known His will? How does this law become a law to man? By natural conscience, by the works of God in nature, by the ways of God in providence, and by the words of God in revelation. Man is the conscious subject of various impulses—impulses that constitute to him grounds of action, motives or movers toward volition. Some of these are in his own estimation higher than others. He sees that a greater good will be secured by action in accordance with the higher.

GOD'S WILL MADE KNOWN

Under these circumstances, from the necessities of his nature, he must feel an obligation to choose the higher. He feels what is expressed in English by the words *ought* and *ought not.* This is more than a verdict of propriety or fitness. It is the recognition of a superior, who has a right, authoritatively, to command obedience. It is an acknowledgment of law and of obligation. By experience and observation man finds that obedience to the higher impulse is useful, to the lower injurious, and he hence infers that He who established this order of things wills that the good should be chosen and the evil rejected. This also is recognizing law, recognizing an established order of sequence between actions and their results, and is also a recognition of obligation to obedience.

In the book of revelation God has distinctly in words said, thou shalt and thou shalt not. Thou shalt love God supremely and thy neighbor as thyself. These voices of God in natural conscience, nature, providence, and revelation harmonize with each other; separately and collectively they make known what is right and what is wrong. God's will, then, made known is man's law; conformity therewith in conduct and character is righteousness, a want of conformity is sin.

BIBLE STANDARDS

But it is manifest that under the limitations of human knowledge man may think he knows God's will when, in fact, he is mistaken; so that that may obligate his conscience, which is not conformed to law. Here the case will be better understood by observing the distinction between a right action and a righteous agent, between a wrong action and a guilty agent.

The right or wrong of an action depends upon its relations to the will of God. The guilt or innocence of an agent depends upon his intentions. If a man performs a right act, one that corresponds with his relations and is in accordance with the laws of his being, in any case the natural result of such an act will accrue to him; but the judicial results thereof will depend upon the motives with which he did it. If, because of ignorance of the law or in indifference to it, he performed the act without reference to moral obligation, he has no reward. The act is not to him an act of righteousness, he has not a righteous man's reward.

ACTION VS. INTENT

It is not certain that he is even innocent, for if he might have known his duty, he was obligated by it and is censurable for his neglect of moral obligation; if, in his misapprehensions of relations and law, he supposed the act wrong in itself, and did it with the intent to do a wrong thing, he is guilty and may be justly punished for the sin of an evil intent.

Again, if a man do a wrong thing—that is, an act in violation of relations and laws—the natural results inevitably follow, but the judicial results will depend upon the motives with which he did it. If he did not and could not know his duty in the case, or if knowing the right he was necessitated to do the act by any constraint, either physical or mental, he is innocent. Yea more, if in unavoidable misapprehensions of duty he supposed the act a right one and did it from a sense of duty, he is virtuous and may be justly rewarded for his righteous intent.

The same principles and distinctions apply to character as to conduct. The distinctions here are more clearly marked by the use of terms *automatic excellence* and *moral desert.* When a man is what he is by creation, by inheritance, by any necessity, by any thing beyond his control, he is automatically excellent, or the reverse; when he is what he is by voluntary self-culture, then moral desert attaches to his character. If he has disciplined himself in holy thoughts, affections, and purposes, so that by reason of such discipline holiness has become the habit of his mind, become a trait of his character, and if he has done so under a recognition of moral obligation, he is entitled to a reward for his inhering excellencies. Contrariwise, if a man is a bad man, because of voluntary neglect of the means of culture and voluntary disregard of his duty in this respect, he is to be blamed, and may be justly punished because of his inherent badness.

MORAL CHARACTER

Natural results follow goodness and badness, irrespective of their source and moral deservings. God and all right-minded beings will esteem and treat all persons and things according to their worth. As a man will place a higher estimate upon a good watch than upon a worthless one, so will all right-minded persons esteem and treat a good man according to his excellence, whatever be the source of his inherent worth. As a man kills a snake because he is a snake, not because he is to blame for being a snake, so will he refuse to take a bad man into his confidence, whether the man be to blame for his badness or not. The natural results of goodness and badness are not of the nature of rewards and punishments. Automatic excellence, with its results, is a different thing from moral desert and its results.

What are the elements of a moral action? Power, intelligence, free will, and an apprehension of moral obligation. Power, executive efficiency, causation, ability to bring something to pass. Intelligence, ability to apprehend an end, and the means adapted to its accomplishment. Free will, alternative power, first cause, power to volitionate in the absence of constraint, both in the choice and in the endeavor. Apprehension of obligation, a sense of duty, a feeling of ought and ought not.

REQUISITES FOR MORAL ACTION

These principles of law and of obligation, as stated above, are to our thought, obviously correct, and they make obvious what is the nature of sin, taking the term in what we have called its primary sense; sin properly so called. It is as St. John has defined it, a transgression of the law. This postulates a righteous commandment, issued by righteous authority, adequately made known to the subject; the subject being fully endowed with the power of obedience, which power is itself alternative, equally efficient for obedience or disobedience, and the subject also endowed with a clear apprehension of personal responsibility and obligation.

To sin, then, is to intelligently, freely, and morally volitionate contrary to the requirements of a known righteous and acknowledged commandment. If this be an explication of the *nature* of sin properly so called, then it is also an explication of the *origin.* Sin originated in the abuse of free will; it was the act of an unconstrained first cause, a creation *de nihilo* of a free moral agent.

ORIGIN OF SIN

So far as the human race is concerned, sin had its beginning in the minds of Adam and Eve, in that volition that caused the outward act of partaking the forbidden fruit. Should it be here remarked that sin had its beginning among the angels who by it fell from their first state, and that our first parents sinned because they were tempted by Satan in the form of a serpent, we reply, the remark is not pertinent. First, because if admitted it only removes the discussion backward from Adam to the first sinner, whoever he might be, whenever and wherever he might have sinned, and the principles determining the case would be the same as if we consider Adam the first sinner.

Again, the temptation was not causative; it was not a necessitating persuasion, it was only one of the constituents of environment, one of the ingredients in the conditions of the case—not in itself, nor in its connections determinative. The case is the same as if the agency of Satan were left out of the account.

The Relation of Adam to His Posterity[3]

All students of theology know that the relation of Adam's sin to the sin of the race is an intricate and controversial, but very crucial, area. The phase of this issue most helpfully unfolded by Miner Raymond is the question of covenants. He shows that the Calvinistic notion of God's covenants being solely with Adam as the representative of the race and with Christ as the representative of the elect is completely untenable. He shows fully and logically

3. This selection is from 2:99-111.

that the full consequences of their respective actions could not accrue unconditionally. With a repudiation of this concept of covenants goes also the denial of the doctrine of imputation flowing from it. The entire subject is highly relevant to the doctrine of holiness, and also to contemporary teachings within evangelicalism.

The doctrine of original sin, as set forth in these pages, and as maintained by the Church, with inconsiderable exceptions, during the whole period of ecclesiastical history, involves the assertion that death, with all that it includes and implies, was brought into the world by the first sin. Physical, intellectual, moral, and religious disabilities have been inherited, are common to the race, and are consequent upon the first transgression. This assertion naturally gives rise to the following inquiries: What possible relation of Adam to his posterity can be the cause or occasion of such vast results to the one from the single act of the other? What is the philosophy of this connection? Wherein does its fitness, its propriety, its justice appear?

Among believers in the doctrine of innate depravity there are three theories, affirming severally identity (if that is not a misnomer), representation, and parentage. The first affirms that the relation of Adam to his posterity is that of a genus to its species. Adam *is* the race. The second, that of a representative to his constituents: Adam represents his race. The third, that of a parent to his children: Adam is the father of his race.

THEORY OF IDENTITY

The theory of identity postulates the doctrine of realism; namely, that genera are really existing things, entities. This doctrine is a mere theory, not supported by any facts or conclusive arguments, and is wholly repugnant to common sense. Therefore, the assertion that Adam was the race or that each individual of the race existed generically in him is founded in a bad philosophy.

Again, we affirm that this theory is resorted to by the theologian in the interests of error. It is asserted that the transmitted results of the first sin are of the nature of punishments, and as under the government of God none can be punished but the guilty, it is therefore asserted that the posterity of Adam are guilty of his sin. The question, How can this be? forces itself for an answer, and the theory of generic existence, generic transgression, and generic guilt is resorted to for a reply. The posterity of Adam are punished for his sin because they were in him, were identical with him in the sin, that is, they sinned.

We deny that inherited infirmities are punishments. Mankind is responsible for what he is no further than his character is self-imposed; what comes necessarily by transmission from ancestors is no fault of those upon whom they come. They may be said to be of the nature of penal sanctions, so far forth as they express God's displeasure with sin; but they are not punishments. The theory is therefore founded in a bad philosophy and is resorted to as an apology for an assumption of what is erroneous. But what is worse than all this is, it is made the basis of what vitiates the whole science of anthropology.

INFIRMITIES NOT PUNISHMENTS

The assumption that Adam was the race is made the ground of an affirmation that all of the race have passed their probation, are under the doom of eternal death, and that their salvation depends not at all, in any sense, upon themselves, but results entirely, in the case of such as are saved, from an arbitrary decree of unconditioned election. The theory of generic existence in the first man asserts very strongly the doctrine of traducianism, to which we make no objection; besides this, it has no merit whatever. It is asserted by but a very few and deserves no further consideration.

The theory of representation is more plausible but is nevertheless objectionable. Its characteristic thought is that the first man was a federal head, a natural representative of his race, and that therefore his posterity are responsible for his acts, in the same way as a nation is responsible for the acts of its representative or minister plenipotentiary in a foreign court. Again, some affirm that Adam was a federal head, a representative with full power to act for his constituents, not only by his natural relations as the father of the family but also by the will and appointment of God. Here much is said about a covenant of works, supposed to be made with the race in Adam, which is also contrasted with a supposed covenant of grace made with the elect in Christ. Respecting this term, *covenant of works,* because of the prominence given to it, rather than because of any merit in it, it may be needful to indulge a brief discussion.

THEORY OF REPRESENTATION

It is a matter of history that God said to Adam, "Of the tree of the knowledge of good and evil, thou shalt not eat of it: for in the day that thou eatest thereof thou shalt surely die" (Gen. 2:17). That is, God promised life on condition of obedience, and threatened death on condition of disobedience. This is of the nature of a contract or covenant and may be so called, if it pleases.

More is *implied* in the covenant than is expressed. The simple act of eating fruit was representative of universal obedience, and being a positive command, and a case where the only obvious reason for obedience was that it was a divine law, it was the most fitting test of loyalty. It was an impressive setting forth, in a fact of history, of the whole economy of the divine government. It recognizes man as a subject of government, under the obligations of unlimited obedience, with assurances of suitable retributions. This is manifestly the covenant under which all moral beings are created, a covenant common to all the intelligences of the universe capable of moral responsibility. It is the universal law of supreme love to God, and mutual, equal love among equal social beings. It is the promise of God to all His creatures that if they, on their part, voluntarily keep all His commandments, He on His part will give them eternal life. This covenant regards the creature in his normal condition and relations, and summarily stated it is, *do and live.*

COVENANT OF GRACE

Under the economy of redemption, the creature is regarded as a sinner, rendered by his sins incapable of the perfect obedience required of him when in his normal state; and eternal life is conditioned, not on works but on faith. He that believeth shall be saved. He that believeth on the Son of God hath eternal life; or, summarily, *believe and live.* The economy of salvation, under the scheme of redemption, or, in other words, the promise of eternal life on condition of faith, is called in the New Testament a new covenant, which is adequate Scripture authority for calling the promise of eternal life on condition of good works the old covenant. The condition in the one case is good works, and the covenant may therefore be called the covenant of works; in the other case the condition is faith, and the covenant may be called the covenant of faith. It is, however, losing sight of the antithesis, generally called the covenant of grace.

PROBATION ONLY IN ADAM

So far, all is well enough, but those who evince a partiality for those formulas go further, and so use the terms employed as to make them teach what, to our thought, is a false view of the doctrine of federal headship. According to the theory in question, the parties to the covenant of works are God on the one part and the race, in the person of Adam, on the other. In like manner the parties in the covenant of grace are God on the one part and the elect, in the person of Christ, on the other. Adam acts for the race; his acts are their acts, and the results of his action accrue to the race. Also, Christ acts for the elect; His acts are their acts, and the results of His acts accrue to them. So that it, of course, follows that man's only probation began and ended in the garden. If Adam had been obedient, he and his posterity would have been immediately placed in eternal life, beyond the possibility of sinning; but being disobedient, he and his posterity fell immediately under the doom of eternal death. No member of the human family ever had, has, or can have, any other probation. All fell in Adam, all are doomed to eternal death, because of his transgression.

PROBATION IN CHRIST

In the covenant of grace it was promised, on the part of God on condition of Christ's obedience unto death, that His elected people should have eternal life. Their salvation from death and elevation to eternal life was made dependent, not at all on anything they should be or do, but wholly on the active and passive righteousness of Christ. No son or daughter of the first pair has any part, either in their perdition or their salvation. Those that are lost were lost in Adam; those saved, saved in Christ. The lost were doomed to a necessity of sinning, and the saved were elected to a necessity of repenting, believing, and loving; they were elected to faith, to holiness, and to salvation. The covenant of works and the covenant of grace cover the whole ground; the one was commenced and consummated in Eden; the other on Calvary. Adam and Christ are the only active agents in the whole matter. The history and destiny of the entire race was determined by the individual acts of the first and second Adam.

REFUTATION

Now, can the refutation of such a theory require argument? To our thought, it is so repugnant to our intuitive sense of justice, honor, and right, that to state it seems sufficient for its rejection. Adam, being a father, might act for his children, but certainly within limits. The natural relation of parent to child cannot in justice convey the right to make a final disposal of all that pertains to the child; certainly not to seal his eternal destiny. The child, as an individual, has personal rights that the parent cannot invade without injustice.

As the natural relation of parent to child is not the ground of federal headship, in the sense of the theory here disputed; so, neither is the office of representative or minister plenipotentiary the ground or reason of any such power to dispose of the interest and welfare of constituents. The posterity of Adam never were his constituents in any such sense. They certainly never conferred upon him such powers, and if in any sense, and by any authority, he sustained an official relation as a representative of his race, his powers could not extend to the disposal of eternal destiny. No such office could be justly constituted by any authority in the universe.

But the abettors of this theory are so zealous for its maintenance that they do even assert that the first man was such a federal head, such a representative by divine appointment. If this thing had not been said by some very pious people, we should be disposed to pronounce it blasphemy. Certainly it is difficult to conceive of any conduct more dishonorable to God than to conceive that He has made the eternal destiny of uncounted millions of intelligent and sentient beings depend upon the single volition of an individual man.

Connected with this view of federal headship is the doctrine of imputation, so called. This, also, on account of its prominence in theological discussions, cannot be passed unnoticed. Imputation, in the theory under discussion, has three applications: (1) Adam's sins are imputed to his posterity. (2) The sins of the elect are imputed to Christ. (3) The righteousness of Christ is imputed to the elect. That is to say, God thinks of Adam's race as guilty of Adam's sins, of Christ as guilty of the sins of the elect, and of the elect as having performed the active righteousness of Christ, and in Christ's person been obedient unto death.

IMPUTATION

The second of these three views, that God thinks of Christ as guilty of all the sins of all for whom He died, is too horrible to be endurable, and therefore does not often appear. But the first, that God imputes the sins of Adam to his race, and the third, that He imputes the righteousness of Christ to the elect, are quite popular, and, in a proper sense, deservedly so. But, taken in the sense above alluded to—namely, that by imputation Adam's act was the act of his posterity, and that therefore they deserve eternal death; that God thinks of the race as committing the first sin, and, so thinking, therefore punishes them for it—is simply abhorrent to common sense.

God thinks of things as they are. The whole doctrine of imputation, taken in the sense that God thinks of one individual as having done what another did, that He punishes one for the sins of another, is evidently so contrary to the common convictions of mankind as to what is just, right, honorable, and godlike, that it may be fairly affirmed that but for excessive zeal in the support of mere theory, such an idea had never been entertained. The doctrine of imputation, in the sense here objected to, is of no service except to form an apology for the "horrible decree" of unconditional personal reprobation to eternal death.

But it will be said that the doctrine of imputation is a Bible doctrine. Similar terms are frequently used in the Scriptures. The doctrine in its proper sense will be discussed where it belongs, under the head of justification by faith. Justification, the pardon of sin, the forgiveness of sin, the remission of sin, the nonimputation of sin, and the imputation of righteousness are synonymous terms, and all mean exemption from the punishment due to sin.

THE BIBLICAL DOCTRINE

When it is said that God doth not impute iniquity, the meaning plainly is that as the executive of law He orders the nonexecution of the penalty due to sin. In Rom. 4:7-8, "Blessed are they whose iniquities are forgiven, and whose sins are covered. Blessed is the man to whom the Lord will not impute sin," it is evident that imputation and pardon are the same thing. Not to impute sin, is not to think that the accused did not commit sin, but it is to pardon sin, to grant exemption from punishment. Whatever countenance, therefore, the Scriptures may give to the idea that God imputes the Adamic transgressions to Adam's posterity, which by the way is not a Bible formula, does not warrant the thought that God regards the race as guilty of the first sin, and therefore punishes them for it, but simply, that in some way, in some sense, the consequences of Adam's sin accrue to his posterity. In what way, and in what sense, remains to be stated.

We think it has been clearly shown that the relation of the first man to the race is not the relation of a genus to its species and is not such a relation of a representative to his constituents as involves unlimited power in the representative to dispose of every interest of his constituents. We feel no partiality for the idea of federal headship or representation; but, with proper explanation, it may be admitted; it is at best but a figurative illustration and is of doubtful service.

Adam was the head of his race and represented his race just as a father is the head and representative of his family. Consequences of the character and conduct of parents naturally accrue to their children. The physiological, the psychological, the aesthetical and moral characteristics of the parents (those characteristics that belong to the parents naturally, not those that come by grace) are inherited by the children; parents beget children in their own likeness. Again, if parents are idle and improvident, the children suffer the deprivations of poverty; if they are vicious, the children are affected by the detrimental influences of bad example and a vicious education. But can any man say that these disadvantages are *punishments*? Does God consider the children guilty of their parents' sins? Certainly not.

But, still, it is said, since these are consequences of *sin,* are even of the nature of penal sanctions, how can any suffer them unless the sufferer be guilty? This question is the same as the question, how can the innocent ever be allowed to suffer at all? That the innocent do, under the providence of God, oftentimes suffer with the guilty is a matter of well-known fact. The justification of God's ways with man, in this respect, is the same as in the case of the permission of evil, at any time, in any degree, and under any circumstances; it is the question of theodicy.

WHY DO THE INNOCENT SUFFER?

Our answer is in . . . the doctrine of the divine goodness. God's goodness in the permission of these things is vindicated by the fact that He not only has provided an adequate remedy but also has provided means by which these evils may themselves be rendered blessings—afflictions may be made to work a far more and exceeding and eternal weight of glory. The wrath of man may be made to praise God. All things may be made to work together for good.

7

William Burt Pope

(1822-1903)

William Burt Pope was a Canadian by birth but an Englishman by residence from 7 years of age onward and by education and lifelong ministry. He was a theological student in Hoxton College at the early age of 18, and from then on he never laid aside the theological enterprise. While his earlier ministry was in the pastorate, his later years were spent as a professor (lecturer) in theology at Didsbury College, Manchester. In temperament he was melancholy, in vocation a disciplined workman, in life an irreproachable saint, in thought an astute logician and perceptive analyst.

Pope's scholarship was authentic, as attested by his translation from German to English of Stier's *Words of the Lord Jesus,* and of Haupt's commentary on First John (for Schaff's *Commentary*). Other works include four volumes of sermons, *Prayers of St. Paul,* and *The Person of Christ.* His best-known and most enduring works, however, were his three-volume opus in systematics, *A Compendium of Christian Theology,* and its pithy digest, *A Higher Catechism.* The fuller work is as discursive as the subject matter requires. In the *Catechism* the mature conclusions are distilled into lucid questions and answers. According to Herbert McGonigle, Pope himself believed the *Catechism* to be his best work.[1]

1. *Nazarene Preacher,* June 1972, 9.

Pope was no mere echo of Watson, but a profoundly original thinker, with a broad and comprehensive grasp of the Christian faith—and primarily of Wesleyanism as a religious system. Robert E. Chiles comments, "Pope stands out as one of the towering figures in all of Methodist theology who with remarkable fidelity recaptures the essence of Wesley's theology."[2] In an earlier study John L. Peters had claimed that Pope's *Compendium* was the "work which came to be most influential during this period" (that is, in America, 1865-1900).[3]

These evaluations were in spite of the fact that Pope was a foreigner competing in America with the likes of Whedon, Summers, and Miley. His theology was in the Methodist course of study for eight years, 1880-88.

Prevenient Grace in Relation to Free Will[4]

This discussion comes from a major division of the *Compendium* called "The Administration of Redemption." It is reproduced here only in part, and the focus is on the question of man's accountability to respond to the gospel. The entire treatment constitutes what Herbert McGonigle believes to be "Dr. Pope's most original contribution to Wesleyan theology."

FREEDOM

The prevenient grace of the Spirit is exercised on the natural man: that is, on man as the Fall has left him. As the object of that grace man is a personality free and responsible, by the evidence of consciousness and conscience. As fallen he is throughout all his faculties enslaved to sin; but knows that sin is foreign to his original nature and that the slavery is not hopeless nor of necessity. His will is still the originating power or principle of self-determination, under the influence of motives originated in the understanding and feeling, but capable of controlling those motives. And his whole nature, as fallen —whether regarded as intellect, sensibility, or will—is under some measure of the influence of the Holy Spirit, the firstfruits of the gift of redemption.

---

2. *Theological Transition in American Methodism: 1790-1935*, 34.

3. *Christian Perfection and American Methodism*, 158.

4. This excerpt is taken from the *Compendium*, second edition, published in London by the Wesleyan Conference Office, 1880, 2:363-67. The marginal notes retained are from the original edition.

These several propositions are in themselves clear and simple and true. They are in harmony with all sound psychology, with common sense, and with the tenor and tendency of all Scripture. Their difficulty is felt only in relation to the theological speculations that have been connected with the influence of the Holy Spirit and the metaphysical speculations with which the doctrine of election has surrounded them.

PERSONALITY

1. Prevenient grace is exercised on the personality of man, free and accountable: not upon any particular element of his nature, but upon himself. That personality is the . . . responsible author of all that he does: not his will, nor his feeling, nor his intellect; but the hidden man, the *autos ego,* the central substantial person who is behind and beneath all his affections and attributes. That influence of the Spirit, directly or through the Word, is exercised upon the agent whom St. Paul describes as the active I or the passive me of every religious feeling that precedes regeneration.

FREE WILL

2. The person or personality of the natural or unregenerate man is free, inasmuch as no power from without controls his will. It is the very nature of will to originate volition: otherwise, if constrained, will is no more will; the possessor of it is not accountable; and volition is only a misnomer for the obedience, only in appearance spontaneous, to a natural or physical law. Consciousness and conscience alike attest that the sinner—for of the sinner we are now speaking—is free and responsible: his consciousness in its first elements is that of a free agent; and his conscience, or MORAL CONSCIOUSNESS, asserts his responsibility, not only for actions but for words and thoughts and the whole posture of the mind.

BONDAGE TO EVIL

3. Again, that person is bound and enslaved to sin. Naturally the bias to evil and the aversion from the moral law are so universal that, even apart from New Testament teaching, common consent allows that human nature is bound to what is wrong: so bound that none can escape without a direct divine intervention; and bound so universally in actual experience as to warrant the induction that none will ever be born without it. In the case of actual trangressors, the effect of habit invariably both proves the original innate bondage and deepens its strength.

4. But the slavery is not absolute. It is conscious slavery, and not submitted to without reluctance. It is not so much a fetter on the will itself, as the ascendency of a sinful bias over the motives that actuate the conduct by governing the will: the feelings and desires of the

affection, and the thoughts of the mind. The will is not bound; but the understanding that guides it is darkened, and the affection that prompts its exercise is corrupted by sense. Now here comes in the doctrine of prevenient grace. It is not needed to restore to the faculty of will its power of originating action: that has never been lost. But it is needed to suggest to the intellect the truth on which religion rests and to sway the affections of hope and fear by enlisting the heart on the side of that truth.

The Relation of Grace to the Freedom of the Will

The grace of God and the human will are cooperant, but not on equal terms. Grace has the preeminence, and that for many reasons. First, the universal influence of the Spirit is the true secret of man's capacity for religion. Second, His influence, connected with the Word, is universal, inevitable, and irresistible, as claiming the consideration of the natural man. And, lastly, He gives the power, whether used or not, to decide against sin and submit to God. These facts assure to grace its supremacy in all that belongs to salvation. But the cooperation of the will is real: because in this last stage it rests with the free agent himself whether the influence of the Spirit be repelled or yielded to. This is the uniform and unfailing testimony of Scripture; the consideration of which will prepare the way for a brief review of ecclesiastical opinions and dogmas on the subject.

COOPERATION

I. The general truth of a cooperation between the Spirit and the will of man is a postulate of the entire Scripture. Like some other fundamental truths, it is not demonstrated but taken for granted; and that very fact is sufficient evidence of our proposition. This cooperation may be viewed negatively or positively.

1. Negatively, there is no reference in the only authority to an arbitrary divine power reigning over the things that accompany salvation. He who works in us to will is never represented as working so absolutely upon us that nothing is left to personal responsibility. *Turn thou me* is followed by *and I shall be turned* (Jer. 31:18). And both parts of the sentence must have their force. There is no saying in the Word of God that, fairly expounded, represents the divine Spirit as overruling the energy of the human object of His grace.

2. Positively, and in the most express manner, the Scripture represents divine prevenient grace as operating through and with man's free concurrence. Figuratively this is expressed by the *good ground*

that receives the seed (Matt. 13:23). Everywhere it is assumed that the first application of truth is probationary, detecting a character in the hearer that in some sense decides all. But it must always be remembered that this hearer of the Word has a preliminary grace in the roots of his nature, which he yields to or resists in the very act of resisting or yielding to the appeal of heaven.

We find it, literally, in all those passages that declare that believers themselves voluntarily receive the Word of God or of Christ or of grace. So, in Thessalonians: *Having received the word (dexamenoi* answering to *paralabontes)* (1 Thess. 1:6; 2:13). This last expression is used concerning the reception of Christ: *As ye have received Christ Jesus the Lord* (Col. 2:6). Another and cardinal text is: *We then, as workers together with him, beseech you also that ye receive not the grace of God in vain* (2 Cor. 6:1). Here there is cooperation of the apostles with God; but it is equally certain that there is a cooperation of believers with both.

II. That the Spirit has the preeminence is equally the doctrine of all the Scripture, as indeed it is of common sense.

1. The fact that man is, since the Fall, still a free agent is not more essentially a necessity of his moral nature than it is the effect of grace.

FREEDOM IS OF GRACE

Redemption is universal and goes back to the root of the nature. Its universality has this for its result, that all who are born into the world are born into a state of probation: otherwise the human spirit would have fallen back under the law of physical necessity or into that of diabolic bondage to evil.

Unredeemed spirits are responsible; but their responsibility is no longer probationary: they are responsible for a state of guilt that has become determined by their own first act, and then become habitual. The difference put between them and us is the mystery of redeeming mercy. The children of men are in bondage to sin; this is the character that is stamped upon them by inheritance. But the bondage is not hopeless nor is it to any mortal necessary; they have a natural capacity of freedom to act as well as to choose, to perform as well as will; and this their very nature is itself a gift of grace.

2. Grace has the preeminence inasmuch as its influence when the Word is preached, whether directly or indirectly, is inevitable and irresistible.[5] Prevenient grace moves upon the will through the affections

---

5. By *irresistible* Pope would mean that the preached Word cannot fail to exert its influence. He is not intending to say that the hearer cannot resist the appeal of the truth.

of fear and hope; and these affections are necessarily moved by the truths that the understanding perceives. But the understanding is under the necessary influence of the Word, while, apart from the understanding, in some sense, the passions are under the control of the Spirit. However obstinately and effectually the truth may be resisted as a ruling power, as truth it cannot be resisted.

INFLUENCE INEVITABLE

3. Moreover, in the secret recesses of man's nature the grace is given, thus disposing and enabling him to yield. Though the will must at last act from its own resources and deliberate impulse, it is influenced through the feeling and the understanding in such a manner as to give it strength. It is utterly hopeless to penetrate this mystery: it is the secret between God's Spirit and man's agency. There is a divine operation that works the desire and acts in such a manner as not to interfere with the natural freedom of the will. The man determines himself, through divine grace, to salvation: never so free as when swayed by grace.

ULTIMATE SECRET OF GRACE

Faith, Repentance, and Salvation[6]

Pope here stresses the element of trust in saving faith and shows that faith is possible only in the presence of true penitence.

6. Faith as the Instrument of Salvation

1. What is the faith that brings salvation?

It is that act or habit of the penitent by which, under the influence of the divine grace, he puts his trust in Christ as the only and the sufficient Savior.

2. Does not this definition give a limited view of faith?

As a condition of salvation it must be thus limited: it is an exercise of a common faculty directed to special objects; the act of the penitent only; as specially aided by the Spirit; as resting on Christ; and as including trust in Him.

---

6. This reading, and the next on sanctification, are taken from *Higher Catechism of Theology* (215-18) published in New York by Phillips & Hunt; no date—but apparently after the *Compendium.*

3. Is there a more general view of faith given in Scripture?

Yes: in each of these five respects a wider faith may be noted, out of which the saving faith springs.

4. Explain this more fully as to the first.

Faith is a primary faculty of human nature, which apprehends and believes in and trusts the invisible: all men to a certain extent walk by faith and not by sight alone. But saving faith is that faculty directed to the entire compass of the revelation of saving truth.

5. How is it the act of the penitent only?

There is a mere intellectual belief or credence of which the truths of revelation are the object: their external and internal credentials may win men's assent without attracting their hearts. This faith every intelligent being shall sooner or later possess. But the supernatural order has in it a gospel revealed only to the faith of the penitent: it is adapted to repentance as light is to the eye.

6. What is its special relation to divine grace?

Saving faith is exercised under the influence of that general prevenient grace without which man can do nothing good: that grace here reaching its highest point.

7. But is not faith said to be of the operation of God?

No, faith is said to be *in the working* and operation of the God who raised Christ from the dead: it is nowhere declared to be wrought in us directly and independently (Col. 2:12).

8. Is not faith one of the fruits of regeneration, and a gift of the Spirit?

The former is a special grace of the new life, and the latter one of the extraordinary charisms of the Spirit.

9. Does saving faith make Christ its only object?

Christ is certainly the first and nearest object where the gospel is preached. God is however always and most necessarily the ultimate object of all saving faith: *For he that cometh to God must believe that he is, and that he is a rewarder of them that seek after him* (Heb. 11:6). But the revelation of Christ is the revelation of God; and thus where God is the object—as in justifying faith—Christ is implied: and, where Christ is the object, God is implied.

10. What measure of knowledge must precede this faith?

Belief cometh of hearing (Rom. 10:17). It is therefore not a vague trust in the mere name of Jesus. But, as the sole condition of our being saved, faith requires no more than a knowledge of Christ as the appointed Mediator between God and men.

11. Why is the trust of faith made so emphatic?

Because, first, it is the person of a living God and Savior that is behind all nearer objects of faith; and, second, it is simple trust of the heart that distinguishes saving faith from all other belief.

12. Does the idea of trust inhere in every description of saving faith?

That it does so may be seen by examination. The word *pisteuein* is used in certain varieties of phraseology: (1) followed by the dative, it means belief of the words of God or of His Son, and this is reliance on divine authority; (2) followed by *epi* or *eis* it strongly marks repose on a sure foundation; (3) indirectly connected with *en* it expresses the trust that is really one with its object. Take these in their order: *Abraham believed God* (Gal. 3:6); *He that believeth in the Son hath everlasting life* (John 3:36); *Ye are all sons of God in Jesus Christ, through faith* (Gal. 3:26).

13. How is this seen in the figures used to describe faith?

Seeking refuge in Him, coming to Him, beholding Him, eating His flesh and drinking His blood, following Him: all these current illustrations, which almost cease to be figures, have personal trust at their root.

14. Is not this trust full assurance?

It is an assured trust; but the assurance of having its object does not belong to the essence of faith as a condition of salvation. To trust without this assurance is the strength of faith; to be followed by assurance is its privilege and glory.

15. How does this agree with the definition of Heb. 11:1?

That definition, which precedes a catalog of the triumphs of faith, includes, and indeed makes preeminent, the assurance that animates the work of faith. Moreover, it is not the specific faith that precedes salvation, but the general principle of faith in God, which is there intended.

7. Repentance and Faith

1. In what sense does repentance precede faith?

The self-loathing, self-renouncing, and self-despairing penitent alone is capable of saving faith.

2. In what sense does faith precede repentance?

None can thus repent without faith in the testimonies of God's Word concerning sin, with its punishment and remedy.

3. How are they, in their unity, related to justification?

The penitent convicted of sin pleads guilty, trusts in the atoning Reconciler, and his faith is reckoned for righteousness.

4. How related to regeneration?

The penitent, acknowledging his spiritual death, receiving the Son of God as the new life of his soul.

5. How to sanctification?

The penitent, confessing his unholiness before the altar and trusting in the virtue of the sprinkled blood, is purged from his defilement and accepted on the altar of consecration.

6. Are repentance and faith only preparatory to salvation?

They both enter the regenerate life and are perfected in it: repentance as the constant remembrance of past forgiven sin, with zealous use of all the means of self-mortification; and faith as the grace that works by love in the pursuit of perfection, always deepening as its range enlarges.

Christian Sanctification[7]

The key to understanding Pope's concise outline in these readings is his differentiation between external and internal sanctification. His own synonymous alternative would be *objective* and *subjective.* Sanctification is first of all positional: it is a hallowedness based on a relation of sonship with God. But it must also be personal, an inwrought sanctity of character. Other pairs of terms sometimes used are: Standing and State, Declarative Grace and Operative Grace, Relational and Substantive. Both aspects of sanctification are concomitants of justification. The distinction between sanctification as consecration (in the case of entire sanctification) and sanctification as purification is also relevant.

---

7. Readings from the *Catechism* (250-62).

1. Sanctification

1. What do we mean by Christian sanctification?

The whole estate of believers as they are made partakers of divine holiness and consecrated to the fellowship and service of God through the Mediator.

2. How is this related to the two former estates?

Righteousness regards the regenerate as conformed to the law of God and sanctification as conformed to the divine nature. In other words the new life is in the former set right with law, and in the latter is united with God himself.

3. Is sanctification, then, only a distinct branch of the common Christian privilege?

In one sense it must be studied as such. But in another it covers the whole ground, and all religion may be expressed in terms of sanctification. For the regenerate life is the Spirit of holiness in the nature, making regeneration and sanctification really one; while our sanctification is *the will of God* (1 Thess. 4:3), as expressed in law, and our being cleansed from *all unrighteousness* (1 John 1:9) and kept blameless. The three are profoundly one.

4. How is this further illustrated by the terminology?

All the terms of sanctification—such as consecration to God, purification from sin, holiness, with many expressing the means by which these are attained and their relations to each other—were used in the Old Testament to describe the full covenant relations of Jehovah with His people, especially as He was manifested in His temple. They are all hallowed afresh in Christ, with a deeper meaning and with the same comprehensiveness of range.

5. How with a deeper meaning?

(1) Sanctification—whether as washing or laying on the altar—was in the Levitical economy chiefly, though not wholly, external for the purifying of the flesh and keeping the people as such dedicated to God. In the New Testament *Ye shall be holy!* never rests short of interior union with God: *As he which hath called you is holy, be ye holy in all manner of living* (1 Pet. 1:15).

(2) Moreover, in the new covenant, righteousness and the new life in Christ throw their deep meaning on sanctification.

6. What are the two leading ideas in holiness?

Separation FROM sin and UNTO God; these being necessarily one, but by equal necessity viewed as distinct, though not to be divided in time. The one must imply the other.

7. Is not holiness the internal quality as shown in a holy life and character?

Yes, when viewed in the ethics of Christianity: we now consider it only or chiefly as the application of the Atonement by the Spirit.

8. But is not the external or objective application of the Atonement our justification?

Yes, as the Atonement is an obedience offered to justice; but as it is a sacrifice of expiation its application is both our external and our internal sanctification.

9. Are there two classes of terms for this external and internal sanctification?

The terms are not sharply defined any more than in external and internal righteousness and sonship. *Hagiazein,* to sanctify or hallow to God, embraces both; so does *katharizein,* to cleanse or purify; and *hagiasmos,* sanctification, like *hagios,* saint, unites the two. But the external and internal meanings of all these terms are almost always actually or virtually blended.

10. How may we sum up this before we proceed?

We must remember that the estate of the Christian, in the inmost sanctuary of the new covenant, is both an external status or position and an internal character. As a child of God he has the real new life and is in a state of sonship; as righteous he is in the state of justification and has the law written on his heart; as sanctified to God, his state is that of a consecrated person and his quality or inward condition is that of purity. But the external in all these gives him his name: he is a justified and consecrated son of God.

11. It follows, then, that all who are regenerate and justified are sanctified also?

Most assuredly. They have, through that common grace, acceptance as pardon at the bar, acceptance as the adoption of sons, and acceptance on the altar as the consecrated property and servants of God: in all these senses they have the grace *which he freely bestowed on us in the Beloved* (Eph. 1:6).[8]

---

8. In this answer Pope speaks of sanctification in its positive and relational sense. See below for his defense of entire sanctification.

2. Sanctification as External

1. Have we any instances of the external or objective application in Scripture?

(1) Whatever is set apart from common to sacred use is said to be sanctified: as time in the Sabbath; place in the temple and city of Zion; and everything laid on the altar *that sanctifieth the gift* (Matt. 23:19). (2) The holy NAME, or *Christ as Lord,* is to be hallowed, as already holy, in the human heart (Matt. 6:9). (3) The persons of believers are holy as separated from the world (1 Pet. 3:15; 2:9).

2. Does this last illustration hold good?

Christians are called saints *(hagiois),* just as they are called children of God and righteous, apart from their internal character, although it is the supposition of that internal character that justifies the name. Christians are *sanctified in Christ Jesus, called to be saints:* TO BE is not in the text, but it represents the truth. God makes us what He reputes us to be (1 Cor. 1:2).

3. To sanctify to God being the divine term, what is the corresponding human?

We dedicate to God, present at the altar, consecrate in intention, what only the Holy Spirit sanctifies to God.

4. Then external sanctification is the consecration by the Spirit of what man presents?

The sinner conscious of defilement offers himself to God and is accepted for the sake of the Atonement he pleads; that acceptance is his cleansing from sin or sanctification.

5. Is this the same as pardon and adoption?

Yes: *dikaioun,* or justify in the court, is *katharizein,* or cleanse in the temple. So the accepted worshiper in the temple is the son in the house, and before the bar he is justified.

6. How is sin viewed in this connection?

As defilement or spot *(macula):* that uncleanness or vileness that God hates because it is not like His own nature. In external sanctification He does not see that spot or take account of it; just as in justification He does not reckon the offense. The Atonement has shown why.

7. What terms express the application of the Atonement?

Terms derived from the old economy: sprinkling the blood,

cleansing the conscience, washing from iniquity, purifying the heart, or purging the conscience.

8. Sprinkling and washing may be external: can cleansing and purifying be so too?

In such passages as *Purifying their hearts by faith* (Acts 15:9); *The blood of Jesus Christ his Son cleanseth us from all sin* (1 John 1:7); *Cleanse your hands, ye sinners* (James 4:8), the same word *katharizein* is used and must have an external rather than an internal meaning.[9] But purging and purifying are commonly used rather of the internal work.

9. In what sense is the conscience said to be purged?

The conscience [consciousness] of guilt is also the conscience of defilement. When the offering of Christ is said to *purge* (or *cleanse*) *our conscience from dead works* (Heb. 9:14) the meaning is that the believer's heart is delivered from the sense of both guilt and of defilement from which *dead works* could not deliver, *to serve the living God.* It may be added that the old judicial term—expurgation from guilt—helps us to understand this external purging of the conscience. Another and stronger word is used by the apostle when the more internal cleansing is meant: Purge out the old leaven *(ekkatharate)* from the church (1 Cor. 5:7).

10. Then we are sanctified to the service of God?

Sanctification negatively is cleansing from sin, positively it is consecration to God's fellowship and possession. The former, that is, communion with God, belongs rather to internal sanctification; the latter, that is, the being set apart to divine use, belongs rather to external or objective sanctification.

11. In what sense is Christ made unto us sanctification?

He is made unto us *hagiasmos,* not *hagiōsunē:* our sanctification to God by himself, not by our inward holiness. Of the latter He is the indirect source, as He accomplishes our holiness by His Spirit and with our cooperation; of the former, as of our justification, He is the

---

9. Acts 15:9 does not fit the category of external sanctification as do the others. (1) It is a purifying of the heart, not the "hands" (as in the James reference). (2) It is accomplished by the Father by means of the outpouring of the Holy Spirit and is not here directly accredited to the Blood. (3) It is intended to be seen as the New Covenant form of circumcision—an inward circumcision by faith that obviates the external circumcision by works, thus fulfilling Deut. 30:6. (4) The actual purifying experienced at Pentecost by Peter and others was not external, but internal. *Editor.*

direct source and only ground. Thus we have a justifying and a sanctifying God in Christ alone. [Cf. Watson, supra, p. 46.]

3. Sanctification as Internal

1. What are the evidences that sanctification is an internal process running parallel with the external?

Those passages that represent it as progressive and perfected; and some words that have an interior meaning.

2. Is outward consecration spoken otherwise?

Throughout the Old Testament and the New, things and persons dedicated to God are regarded as His through one act of giving and receiving on the altar, *the altar that sanctifieth the gift* (Matt. 23:19). It is an acceptance once for all.

3. Is there a change of phrase to denote the distinction between external and internal sanctification?

Generally, there is not; but the construction of the words and the context show the difference with sufficient clearness.

4. Give some illustrations of this.

(1) Our Lord is said to have once *made purification of sins,* and to have *put away sin by the sacrifice of* himself (Heb. 1:3; 9:26). Both of these terms include the provision for the outward and inward application of His sacrifice.

(2) Hence cleansing and washing and purifying are used of both; but *Wash away my sins* (Acts 22:16), refers rather to the external putting away of sin, while *Wash me throughly from mine iniquity* (Ps. 51:2) and *Cleanse us from all unrighteousness* (1 John 1:9) seem also to carry the process into the inner man.

5. Where have we the process and the end of sanctification combined?

Let us cleanse ourselves from all defilement of flesh and spirit, perfecting holiness in the fear of God (2 Cor. 7:1). Here holiness is the end or *telos,* and cleansing the process which, though not precisely as gradual here, aims at it.[10] And the saints are spoken of as *hagiazomenoi, those who are in course of sanctification* (Heb. 10:14).

---

10. It is doubtful if any gradual process is here. The plain import seems to be that their holiness is defective due to the contamination that the Corinthians have allowed. They are to decisively cleanse themselves of this defect in their holiness, thus perfecting it. See Ralph Earle, *Word Meanings in the New Testament,* 4:136. See also Procksch in Kittel's *Theological Dictionary of the New Testament,* 1:114. Cf. *God, Man, and Salvation,* 468, n. 13. *Editor.*

6. Do not these passages connect sanctification with ethical duty and personal discipline?

Yes: it is remarkable that the word *cleanse,* or *purify,* strictly appropriate only to the Spirit's work, should be assigned to man's act. But so it is; and everywhere our gradual sanctification is bound up with our Christian discipline.

7. But are there no words that belong only to internal or subjective sanctification?

(1) The adjective pure or clean has an interior meaning: *Blessed are the pure in heart* (Matt. 5:8). (2) Another verb is also used, *hagnizein,* which goes to the inmost nature: *Every one that hath this hope set on him purifieth himself, even as he is pure* (1 John 3:3). Observe that to the Lord himself the words that denote internal purification are never applied. *Hagnos* here is a peculiarity.

8. What is meant by entire sanctification?

This is the work of the Holy Spirit alone, applying the virtue of the Atonement in the removal of the last trace of the indwelling or pollution of sin and consecrating the entire nature of the believer to God in perfected love.

9. Where is this promised?

Generally by all the assurances of salvation or redemption for sin; but, in reference to sanctification itself, especially by the apostle's prayer, *The God of peace himself sanctify you wholly* (1 Thess. 5:23), with its pledge of divine fidelity for full assurance.

10. What is the force of this passage?

Two words are used in it that express completeness: *holoteleis,* meaning that the subjects of this sanctification are perfectly sanctified; and another, *holoklēron,* which shows that the former referred to the individual as composed of body and soul and spirit, *preserved entire, without blame.*

11. What preeminence is here observable in sanctification?

It is a hallowing of the whole nature of man. Our righteousness before God is in the spirit: *the spirit is life because of righteousness* (Rom. 8:10). Our sonship leaves the body *dead because of sin;* but our sanctification views even the perishing physical frame as entirely the Lord's: *Know ye not that your body is a temple of the Holy Ghost which is in you?* (1 Cor. 6:19).

12. Do not some other passages teach the entireness of sanctification?

(1) There are some that refer to the crucifixion of the flesh and the destruction of the body of sin: these really belong not to sanctification but to the growth of the regenerate life.

(2) Others that allude to the law as fulfilled in us belong to the life of righteousness.

(3) We have to do now with sanctification proper, which is simply and solely the removal of the spot or defilement that is contrary to the holiness of the divine nature.

13. But to return: What is meant by the Spirit's application of the virtue of the Atonement?

The virtue or efficacy of the Atonement is direct or indirect: direct in the abolishing of the alienation or wall of partition between man and God, which is its virtue proper; and indirect, in obtaining the power of the Holy Spirit which carries its virtue into the inner man.

14. Is the gift of the Spirit, as the virtue of the Atonement, more than purification from inward sin?

Yes, it is the secret of communion or fellowship with God, of which purification is the condition. We are made, through the *communion of the Holy Ghost* (2 Cor. 13:14) gradually to *become partakers of the divine nature* (2 Pet. 1:4) and *partakers of his holiness* (Heb. 12:10).

15. What means or instrumentalities are generally connected with internal sanctification?

(1) The word of truth: *Sanctify them in the truth: thy word is truth* (John 17:17). But the truth is the instrument of salvation under every aspect of the estate of grace.

(2) Sacramental means seal the covenant of sanctification: these are still the word as expressed in act, and as such convey the grace of which they are signs. Here also we must remember that every blessing of the new covenant is included.

(3) If such language may be used, the sacred presence of the Holy Trinity in Christ is the means of sanctification, and necessarily of entire sanctification. The prayer for the indwelling of Christ has this object, *that ye may be filled unto all the fulness of God* (Eph. 3:19).

(4) In a very important sense, the might of divine love is the instrument of this as of every effect of divine grace: *His love is perfected in us* (1 John 4:12).

16. What is the relation of repentance and faith to entire sanctification?

Repentance is in the consecrated soul a habitual loathing of sin as a remaining defilement; faith is the conviction that it may be entirely removed, and the instrument in man that obtains its removal: actively laying hold of the promise and passively receiving its fulfillment.

17. Does any promise encourage this faith?

(1) When, under the influence of the Spirit, faith beholds Christ as having in himself *no sin,* and as *manifested to take away our sins* (1 John 3:5) it has promise enough for its encouragement.

(2) *By grace are ye saved through faith* (Eph. 2:8): salvation is redemption from all sin in this world, since there is no purgatorial purification after death.

(3) Faith, therefore, *working through love* (Gal. 5:6) as a condition, is the final and only instrument in man for the attainment of the Spirit's grace in the utter destruction of evil as defilement and all that is called sin.

4. Historical

1. How has the doctrine of sanctification been held in the Christian Church?

It is found in every system of teaching; but its development has been clouded by many misconceptions, and as a doctrine it has not had a sufficiently distinct place.

2. What was the first error observable?

(1) In early times it was not distinguished from Christian perfection generally, of which however it is only one aspect. (2) Internal righteousness and internal sanctification were regarded as one and the same thing. (3) Both these errors are found in various forms down to the Reformation and have not been wanting since.

3. What effect has the former had?

Besides throwing the terminology of the New Testament into confusion, it tended in earlier times to abolish the Spirit's sanctifying office, by making sanctification only the progress of the soul towards ethical perfection: of which more hereafter.

4. What have been the effects of the latter?

They may be traced in three lines:

(1) In medieval and Tridentine theology, sanctification is no other than progressive justification. The inherent grace infused, or the

indwelling of Christ by His Spirit, is the common source of both; but without remembering that the common fountain sends forth separate streams.

(2) In Lutheran theology, justification is mainly limited to the imputation of Christ's righteousness, and sanctification is actually or virtually limited to the good works that are the fruits of justification. Hence in its dogmatics and expository books sanctification, as such, occupies a small place.

(3) In the Reformed or Calvinistic theology, sanctification is either the gradual development of the holy dispositions implanted in the new birth, and therefore progressive regeneration; or it is the imputation of Christ's holiness as His perfect obedience to the law. In both cases sanctification loses its specific character as the removal of unholiness.

5. How are we protected from these several errors?

From all alike by remembering that the three estates of covenanted salvation are mutually complementary, each being perfect and complete in itself. But, particularly:

(1) Righteousness is our conformity to the justice of God guarding His righteous law; sanctification is our conformity to His holiness, which guards His holy nature.

(2) The new life is not developed in sanctification. It simply grows up into Christ: sanctification is not the deepening of life but the hallowing of that life to God.

(3) Good works, which all these systems place under the head of sanctification, have no more to do with it than with righteousness or the new life. They belong to ethics, being the common condition and result of all.

6. But does not the New Testament invariably go on from justification through the new life to the good works of holiness?

Much theology travels in that course; but the New Testament never does. The idea of law is predominant in the Epistle to the Romans; that of holiness in the Epistle to the Hebrews; but good works in the newness of life belong to both. Good works *are the fruits of righteousness* (Phil. 1:11); we are *created in Christ Jesus for good works* (Eph. 2:10); and these righteous evidences of the Spirit of life are *fruit unto sanctification* (Rom. 6:22); not so much fruits of sanctification as themselves to be sanctified, *eis hagiasmon.* Mark how the three estates are united: We are enjoined to *put on the new man, which after*

God hath been created in righteousness and holiness of truth (Eph. 4:24).

7. What was the early doctrine of the Arminians on this subject?

Arminius was among the first to distinguish clearly between sanctification and justification: teaching that the former is a gradual purification from sin. But he also confounded it with the gradual death of the old man; and left it uncertain whether or not the death of the body is the final end of sin in the nature. Nor was this point decided by his followers.

8. Where else is the same confusion to be seen?

In both Lutheran and Reformed theology, which regard death as the sanctifier and hold that *the flesh lusteth against the Spirit* to the end (Gal. 5:17); a subtle relic of Gnosticism.

9. But is not St. Paul's teaching in the same strain?

He introduces the conflict only to show its effect in this, *that ye may not do the things that ye would.* Meanwhile, *they that are of Christ Jesus have crucified the flesh* (Gal. 5:17, 24), and crucifixion is unto death. But this has to do directly with regeneration, and with sanctification indirectly: so far that is as the flesh cannot as tainted with sin enter into heaven, any more than flesh and blood.

10. Has the present privilege of deliverance from the last taint or spot of sin been ever taught in the Christian Church?

Not explicitly by any branch of it until the Methodist theology made this entire sanctification prominent.

11. Was it then implicitly taught by any?

Yes, by all; but not as a privilege attainable during the probation of life. The highest teaching from Augustine downwards made the reservation that the conflict with the remainder, however slight, of sin, is a necessary part of the probation of the believer's humility.

12. How does Methodist theology deal with this?

(1) By insisting that the perfect love of God is shed abroad in the heart, and that this must needs extinguish the very principle of self, which is the true defilement of original sin; (2) by its doctrine of Christian perfection generally.

13. What is the doctrine?

That the Christian covenant makes provision for the completeness of the estate of believers in every relation, entire sanctification being only one of these. This will be our next subject: for this completeness is Christian perfection.

14. Meanwhile, what tendencies to error are still to be guarded against in the doctrine of entire sanctification?

(1) Entire consecration to God is sometimes held to be the whole of sanctification, whereas it is the external act of the Spirit, which, however blessed in itself, is to be followed by an internal purification from the last remains of the carnal mind.

(2) This internal purification, though in its completeness an instant and decisive act of the same Spirit, is the crown of penitent faith. The believer's repentance must bring forth its own fruits in the mortification of indwelling sin, *fruit unto sanctification* (Rom. 6:22). There is danger of neglecting this condition of the supreme gift.

(3) It may be added that there is danger also of forgetting the distinction between sanctification and entire sanctification: as if holiness or consecration to God were a second blessing bestowed at some interval after believing. Its entireness may be called a second blessing, but holiness itself begins the life of acceptance. The Holy Spirit as a sanctifier is given, not after an interval, but when we believe. *In whom, having also believed, ye were sealed with the holy Spirit of promise, which is an earnest of our inheritance,* as we are children, and, as we are sanctified, *unto the redemption of God's own possession* (Eph. 1:13-14).[11]

(4) A distinct assurance, connected with the moment of final deliverance from sin, and as it were apart from the silent seal of the indwelling Spirit, is sometimes looked for without any express warrant of Scripture.

(5) Other safeguards lead us to our next subject, the doctrine of Christian perfection.

The Methodistic Doctrine of Entire Sanctification[12]

This is a remarkable statement. In all Wesleyan literature there can scarcely be found a more balanced, comprehensive, or

11. Steele and Wiley identify the sealing of the Spirit with the second work of grace. See below.

12. In this reading we return to the *Compendium,* 3:96-99. Pope's résumé, which we have just left, is here in the *Compendium* found in its original unabridged form.

perspicuous summary of the unique genius of original Wesleyanism. It provides a plumb line for authenticity.

3. Reviewing the whole, we may conclude that, while the substance of the Methodist doctrine of entire sanctification is the same that has been aimed at in all the purest types of practical theology, it has some points of difference, or specific characteristics of great importance.

LOVE AND LAW

(1) It connects the fulfillment of the evangelical law with the effusion of divine love in the heart more strictly and consistently than any other system of teaching. The mystical and ascetic teachers of perfection have generally made love, and that the love of God, their keynote. But they seldom gave a good account of the relation of that love to the obedience that is essential to perfection. Some of them erred by making the absolute moral law the standard; and then the highest result was a striving toward a perfection that death only could introduce. Others lost all thought of law in the contemplation of the holiness of Christ, and their perfection was the gradual transformation of the character into His image.

Others rightly viewed love as the fulfilling of the law; and supposed that its value in the sight of God was such as to obtain a meritorious acceptance beyond that of mere obedience to any law: forgetting, meanwhile, that the preciousness of love as a grace springs from its faith in the merit and strength of the Redeemer. Others separated between the righteousness of the law, which is unattainable and must be reckoned to the believer, and the perfection of love, which he may attain in his own person: thus dividing what the Scripture joins.

But the Methodist doctrine boldly declares that the righteousness of the law is fulfilled in believers, that is the righteousness of the new law of faith; and that as faith is reckoned for righteousness, so faith working by love is reckoned for perfection.

DESTRUCTION OF SIN

(2) The Methodist doctrine is the only one that has consistently and boldly maintained the possibility of the destruction of the carnal mind, or the inbred sin of our fallen nature. It is true that certain of the mystics held, as we have seen, something almost equivalent to this doctrine; and that the Pietists of the school of Spener included the annihilation of the old Adam among the privileges of God's children. But the utmost contemplated by them was the gradual suppression of the evil nature through the ascendency of love. Now it is undeniable that a very large portion of the Methodist teaching takes that ground. On the same principle that

the shedding abroad of love is made the spring of regeneration, its perfect effusion is made the strength of entire sanctification. In many passages of sermons and hymns the Wesleys expressly taught this. But they failed not to look deeper into the heart than the region of its affections. They knew that life is more even than love; and that, as the regeneration of the Spirit is the gift of a new life capable of loving God, so the perfection of that love toward God is possible only where the original death of the soul is altogether changed into life.

Hence the fervor with which the hymns appeal to the Holy Spirit for the destruction of inbred sin, and the almost equal earnestness with which the sermons urge on believers the prayer for faith in the omnipotent power of God, not only to shed abroad His perfect love but to finish the death of the body of sin. The combination of the two elements, the negative annihilation of the principle of sin and the positive effusion of perfect love, is, it may be said, peculiar to Methodist theology as such.

(3) The original teaching of Methodism was peculiar also in its remarkable blending of the divine and human elements in the process of entire sanctification. It invariably did justice both to the supreme divine efficiency and to the cooperation of man. The charge brought against it, sometimes malevolently, sometimes thoughtlessly, that it stimulates believers to expect this supreme and most sacred blessing at any time, irrespective of their preparatory discipline, is contradicted by the whole tenor of the authoritative standards of this doctrine. Wesley's sermon on "The Scripture Way of Salvation" contains an elaborate discussion of this point; and it must be taken as a whole by those who would understand the subject. The sum of all is in the following sentences:

COOPERATION

> Experience shows that, together with this conviction of sin *remaining* in our hearts, and *cleaving* to all our words and actions; as well as the guilt that on account thereof we should incur were we not continually sprinkled with the atoning blood; one thing more is implied in this repentance; namely, a conviction of our helplessness. . . .
>
> "But what good works are those, the practice of which you affirm to be necessary to sanctification?" First, all works of piety; such as public prayer, family prayer, and praying in our closet; receiving the supper of the Lord; searching the Scriptures, by hearing, reading, meditating; and using such a measure of fasting or abstinence as our bodily health allows.
>
> Secondly, all works of mercy. . . . This is the repentance, and these the "fruits meet for repentance," which are necessary to full

> sanctification. This is the way wherein God hath appointed His children to wait for complete salvation. . . .
>
> Yet they are not necessary either in the same sense with faith, or in the same degree. . . . [because] this repentance and these fruits are only *remotely* necessary—necessary in order to the continuance of his faith, as well as in the increase of it; whereas faith is *immediately* and *directly* necessary to sanctification. . . .
>
> To this confidence, that God is both able and willing to sanctify us now, there needs to be added one thing more—a divine evidence and conviction that He doeth it. In that hour it is done: God says to the inmost soul, "According to thy faith be it unto thee!" Then the soul is pure from every spot of sin; it is clean "from all unrighteousness." The believer then experiences the deep meaning of these solemn words: "If we walk in the light as He is in the light, we have fellowship one with another, and the blood of Jesus Christ His Son cleanseth us from all sin."[13]

The intense, absorbing, patient, human preparations of the heart in man are from the same Spirit who at length gives the divine evidence of the unspeakable power of God to save from all sin.

Here it is to be observed that Mr. Wesley passes from the perfect shedding abroad of love in the heart to the application of the supreme efficacy of the Atonement to take away the evil of the nature: it is "the moment wherein sin ceases to be." It is more, therefore, than the spirit of entire consecration to which many of those who have received his teaching limit it; it is more even than the abundant effusion of love that may fill the heart's sensibilities without purifying its hidden depths: a distinction his own words refer to: "How clearly does this express the being perfected in love! How strongly imply the being saved from all sin!"

MODERATION

(4) Finally, the doctrine that runs through the works and the whole career of the Wesleys is marked by its reasonableness and moderation as well as its sublimity. The far greater part of the definitions of it are taken up with defining what it is not. It is not absolute perfection, nor the perfection of angels, nor even that of unfallen Adam: it is a perfection that has come up from much tribulation and bears the scars of infirmity to the end. It is not immunity from temptation, and the possibility of falling, and the remainders of ignorance and shortcoming in the presence of the perfect law the rigor of which is not applied to it in Christ.

It is a perfection that is no other than a perfect self-annihilating life in Christ: a perfect union with His passion and His resurrection,

---

13. Wesley's *Works*, 6:50-53.

and the perfect enjoyment of the value of His name of Jesus, as it is salvation from sin. It is the perfection of being nothing in self, and all in Him. It is a perfection for which the elect with one consent have longed from the apostles downwards: neither more nor less than the unuttered, groaning desire of the children of God in every age; the common deep aspiration, with only one note more emphatic than has been always heard, though even that has not been always wanting, the destruction of the inbred sin of our nature. He who searcheth the heart hath always known the mind of the Spirit even when its deepest desire has not been clearly uttered. And He will yet, we dare believe, remove the last fetter from the aspirations of His saints and give them one heart and one voice in seeking the destruction of the body of sin as well as the mortification of its members.

Christian Ethics: Love and Law[14]

In no area of theology is there greater danger of drifting into antinomianism on the left or legalism on the right than in the attempt to determine the relationship of love to law. This selection breaks into Pope's discussion of liberty and law. It will be helpful to give the last few sentences of that discussion as a transition to Love and Law.

Christ has reenacted His law as an evangelical institute by which all shall be tested. The antinomian proper is one who treats the requirement of perfect holiness as met by Christ, and refuses to measure his conduct by any law whatever. To him obedience is only a matter of expediency, and propriety, and it may be reward; but not a matter of life and death. His disobedience may be chastised by a Father, it cannot be eternally punished by a Judge. The law is no longer a condition of salvation: obedience not being a condition of acceptance as to the past or negative salvation, neither is it a condition of acceptance as to the future, or positive salvation. There is also a still more prevalent practical antinomianism, which uses liberty as an *occasion to the flesh* (Gal. 5:13). This may be, or may not be, connected with the theoretical renunciation of law. It is found in all communities: the disgrace of all creeds and confessions.

---

14. The following readings are from the *Compendium,* 3:174-85, and belong to the section titled "Christian Ethics," which is in the larger division, "The Administration of Redemption."

The written commandments are a safeguard against both forms of the common enemy. The noblest and best corrective is, as will be seen, *but by love serve one another.* But besides the gentle protest of charity there is the stern protest of law with its sanctions. He who knoweth our frame has protected us, if need be, against ourselves. As the gospel disarms the law in one sense, it arms it again in another; they are a mutual defense. *He that despised Moses' law died without mercy under two or three witnesses: Of how much sorer punishment, suppose ye, shall he be thought worthy* (Heb. 10:28-29).

But we need not fill up the quotation; suffice that it is a denunciation of those who *sin wilfully after that we have received the knowledge of the truth* (v. 26). The law protects the gospel by protecting itself. If Christian people recite their creed to keep in memory the things they surely believe, not less necessary is it that they should recite the Commandments also to keep in memory what they must do to enter into life.

In the following discussion of Love and Law we have one of the most astute and penetrating theological essays in the English language. It is a profound and exciting exposition of the nature of Christian love. Love is seen as a force so dominating and pervasive that in its presence antinomianism and pharisaism become impossible. Only love is sensitive to the inner meaning and purpose of law; moreover, love not only fulfills law but goes beyond it. "It fills up the interstices by a running commentary, and adds an undertone of subsidiary precepts that perfect the directory of duty. It interlineates the written code within and without, inserting its own boundless variety of unwritten commands" (pp. 180 f.).

Love and Law

Love has been seen, in the doctrine of sanctification, to be the principle and strength and perfection of consecration to God. In ethics we have to consider it rather as the fulfilling energy and the fulfilled compendium of law, and the unity of these two.

Love, the Complement or Fulfillment of Law

Love is the complement or filling up of all that is meant by law: the summary of all possible duty to God and man.

1. Generally, this may be said to have been our Lord's authoritative compendium. He honored the principle as it had never been honored before. He made it the source of all the merciful dealings of

God with man. He assumed its perfection for himself: His love and His humility being the sole graces that He called His own. He made it the badge of His discipleship: the one bond of community between His people and their Lord.

This thrice-honored grace the Redeemer also made the epitome of all duty in its two branches, toward God and toward man. He was not only rebuking the pharisaic computation of the value of precepts, but spoke for all time, when He said that *on these two commandments* —that is on the supreme love of God, and the love of the neighbor as self—*hang all the law and the prophets* (Matt. 22:40). He did not enact these laws, or this twofold law, as new; nor did He assign them a new importance in themselves. He simply declared that these were the sum of all duty and gave them a new significance in ethical systems. In the Old Testament they seemed to be AMONG the precepts; now they are OVER them.

After the Lord had thus set the example, it is not to be wondered at that every writer in the New Testament has paid his tribute to love. St. James leads the way by his *nomon basilikon,* the *royal law* (2:8), limited by him, however, to the love of our fellows. St. Paul's great expression is that *love is the fulfilling of the law* (Rom. 13:10). In both instances of its use, the meaning is limited, as in St. James, to the love of the neighbor. Again and again the New Lawgiver and His apostles sum up all duty, not as two kinds and orders of love, but as love generally. St. Peter makes charity or love absolute, the crown of the graces introduced into the life and sustained there by faith: *Add . . . to brotherly kindness charity* (2 Pet. 1:7), a grace therefore that is directed both to God and to man; and, if not precisely the sum of duty, yet the crown and consummate of all.

St. Paul is still more express: in his hymn to charity, the noblest ethical strain of the New Testament, *agapē* is evidently the substance of all personal religion; nor is there an internal grace or an external duty that is not regarded as an expression of love. The same may be said of his epitome afterwards given: *Now the end of the commandment is charity* [love] *out of a pure heart, and of a good conscience, and of faith unfeigned* (1 Tim. 1:5). As the end of the law is Christ, so the end of the commandment is charity: a declaration of large compass. Inverting the order of the words, pure faith leads to a cleansed conscience and purified heart, the abode of perfect love. But it is St. John who carries the tribute to its highest point. He makes the ethical divine nature charity, *God is love;* and the perfection of this grace the perfection of all religion, which is, like him who possesses it, *made perfect in love* (1 John 4:16, 18).

2. Charity in its full meaning in Christian ethics is therefore the substance of all obligation to God and our neighbor: it might suffice to say to God; for there is no real and essential obligation but to the Supreme Lawgiver. There is no possible act of the soul that is not an act of love, as love is the return of the soul to its rest. It expresses all homage and reverence to the divine Being, with every affection of heart that makes Him its object; all delight in His holy law; all devotion to His service. Love to man is purely ethical as it is the reflection of the divine love. The neighbor is united with the self as a creature; and as self, literally understood, is lost in love. Love views all creatures and self included as one before God. Hence all the variety of our duty to our fellows is the expression of charity, aiming supremely at the Supreme, but reflected on all men for His sake. But we are permitted to speak of obligation as summed up in charity, which, negatively, *worketh no ill to his neighbour* (Rom. 13:10), and, positively, loves *his neighbour as himself* (Matt. 22:39).

COMPREHENSIVENESS OF LOVE

3. The fulfillment of law in a perfect character may be regarded as the formation in the soul of a holy nature. Love is the *plērōma* of religion as well as of law; the sum of all interior goodness: a life governed by this grace is necessarily holy; for all the faculties and energies of the being are united and hallowed by charity. It expels every opposite affection; it sanctifies and elevates every congenial desire. It regulates and keeps from affinity with sin every emotion. It rules with sovereign sway, as the royal law within, the will and intention that governs the life. Where pure charity is there can be no disobedience to heaven and no injury to neighbor; there must be all obedience to God, and all benevolence to man: therefore the whole of goodness is in the perfection of this grace. When it thus reigns within it diffuses its influence over the intellect and its judgments: the mind conducts its operations under the authority and restraint and sure intuitions[15] of charity, and the heart is united in God.

LOVE THE HOLY CHARACTER

4. The love, however, that is the *anakephalaiosis*, or summing up, of all law, is of necessity perfect love, such as neglects no injunction, forgets no prohibition, discharges every duty. It is perfect in passive as

15. Pope may have placed too much faith in the intuitive wisdom of love as a sufficient guide in questions of right and wrong. See comments by Wesley and Fields, p. 185. *Editor.*

well as active obedience. *It never faileth* (1 Cor. 13:8); it insures the existence of every grace adapted to time or worthy of eternity. It is *the bond of perfectness* (Col. 3:14). Therefore it is that the term *perfect* is reserved for this grace. Patience must *have her perfect work* (James 1:4); but love alone is itself perfect, while it gives perfection to him who has it.

Love the Fulfiller

Love is the fulfiller of law, as well as the fulfillment. This general truth, which is not so directly declared as the former, is often indirectly laid down and is very important in many ways.

THE SOUL'S STRENGTH

1. It is the energy of the regenerate soul that the Spirit uses: *faith which worketh by love* (Gal. 5:6). When the Holy Spirit dethrones the self in the renewed spirit He makes His agent the principle that is most contrary to self, charity. Strictly speaking all men are actuated by love; but the love by which faith worketh is turned away from self and looks outward. Hence it is the strongest power in our nature sanctified and set on its highest object.

IN MAN

(1) What love is cannot be defined. As we must think to know thought, and feel to know feeling, and will to know volition, so we must love to know the meaning of love, though even then it passeth knowledge. Something of which love in man is the highest expression is found to be as universal as life: it is as mighty in animated nature as gravitation in the world of matter. As instinct, or as merely natural affection, it achieves or seems to achieve unconsciously almost incredible wonders. But when regenerated and made the energy of living faith, under the Holy Spirit, it is capable of the utmost task that can be laid upon it, even a full obedience to the divine law. It is in fact the indwelling of Christ, the indwelling of God by the Holy Spirit: *he that dwelleth in love dwelleth in God* (1 John 4:16).

Under such a condition, what is impossible? Hence it is obvious, that love as the Spirit's instrument is more than that affection of human sensibility that generally bears the name. It is the bond of all the attributes and perfectness of our nature. Though it is not literally the regenerate life—any more than the essence of God is love—it is the strength of that life. It is the outgoing of the soul toward its one Supreme Object; and this movement or energy is transmitted into every manifestation of force in the moral sphere.

All that is true in the physical theories of CORRELATION of forces and CONSERVATION of energy may be transferred to the domain of ethics: save that in the omnipotent energy of the Spirit poured into the Church, and into its individual members, there is a perpetual increase of the living power that governs the moral world of Christendom. Love in the Christian life is simply and solely seeking its way back to God: that is its centripetal force. The spirit is kept from being lost again in its Creator because of the original fiat that gave it personality: that is its centrifugal force. Hence the orbit of holy duty.

Love is the very strength of the Holy Spirit in the inner personality of the regenerate. It is behind the intellect and the sensibilities and the will: ruling the man who is the possessor of these. Though it derives its name from one of the middle class of these three elements of human nature, it is exalted to be over them all. And, though it has not a new name, it has a new nature and a new prerogative, for *love is of God* (1 John 4:7). This is said of no other grace as such.

(2) But the strength of love as a principle of obedience may be viewed in its particular relation to God. It has all the power of gratitude: *We love him, because he first loved us* (1 John 4:19). *If ye love me, keep my commandments* (John 14:15). *If God so loved us, we ought also to love one another* (1 John 4:11). In these sentences, combined in this order, we have the highest tribute to the strength of gratitude, as the noblest form of love. It is worthy to be the response of the divine charity to sinful man. To it as a sentiment of grateful devotion is committed the obedience of the regenerate life. And the manifestation of this love to those around us, in imitation of the supreme charity, gives the highest nobility to virtue.

It is moreover the principle of delight in the divine character, which inspires the desire to imitate and become like God: a desire that is capable of being intensified to unlimited strength and may become one of the mightiest impulses of the soul in man. This is either a silent, instinctive necessity of being transformed into the image of Him whom love adores, or an active energy that has in it the potentiality of all holiness. The law, which is a transcript of the divine nature, becomes itself the object of love: *O how love I thy law* (Ps. 119:97) is the note of the psalm that sings the praises of God's Word. As the divine character and law are both embodied in the Incarnate Son, human love set upon Him is the strength of all holiness. Here our own words fail, and we take refuge in St. Peter's: *Whom having not seen, ye love; in whom, though now ye see him not, yet believing, ye rejoice with joy unspeakable and full of glory* (1 Pet. 1:8).

2. Charity is the guardian of obedience: the evangelical and better form of the rabbinical "hedge about the law." There are two leading enemies of the righteousness of the gospel against both and each of which it is the only and effectual safeguard. ANTINOMIANISM cannot stand in the presence of love. Its grosser and more refined forms are alike repelled. Theological dogmatic argument says, *Is therefore Christ the minister of sin?* (Gal. 2:17). *How then can I do this great wickedness, and sin against God?* (Gen. 39:9). The heart's best enforcement of both is, *O how love I Thy law!* (Ps. 119:97).

THE GUARD

PHARISAISM, whether the spirit of a vain dependence on mechanical external obedience, or in its milder form the hireling sentiment, is utterly rejected of love. Its ethical precept warns: *Thou shalt not tempt the Lord thy God* (Matt. 4:7). This grace knows nothing of its *own righteousness* (Phil. 3:9), never being able to forgive itself for sin against God, and all the less because so much has been forgiven. The query, *What shall we have therefore?* (Matt. 19:27), is replaced by another, *How much owest thou unto my lord?*—unto THE LORD! (Luke 16:5).

3. Love also is the expositor of the law, which it keeps and defends. It is the scribe well instructed within the heart.

THE EXPOUNDER

(1) The enlightened and regenerate reason is of course the interpreter of the commandments; but love is the ever-present secretary of the judgment, and renders the meaning of every law with an infinite grace peculiar to itself. This heavenly authority explains the phraseology of ethics in its own sense; and defines the terms of its vocabulary in its own spirit. It does not relax the meaning of any of the most rigid of them. The must and ought and shall have their full significance; the language of threatening and sanction is not softened; nor is the Moral Governor of the universe reduced to a personification of mere good nature. But charity, without abolishing or really qualifying the ethical ideas of the Scripture, transfigures both them and the language that expresses them. Yet this is only by giving the commandments their deeper meaning: the spiritual interpretation, as we call it, is really the generous interpretation of love.

When the New Lawgiver ascended the Mount and opened His mouth, Love Incarnate then first disclosed the hidden mysteries of ethics; and its deep interpretation pervades the whole Sermon. Applied to the commandments generally, and to the Decalogue in particular, it reveals a new world of morals. The precepts of the first table, literally interpreted, seem cold and hard and limited: but let love interpret them according to its sentiment of perfect devotion! So it is with the other table. Let the injunctions to remember the Sabbath, to abstain from stealing, and murder, and adultery, and false witness be severally expounded by perfect charity, and how their spiritual meaning searches the heart, quickens the pulse of duty, and inflames the soul's desire!

SUPPLEMENTS ALL CODES

(2) Again, love supplies the omissions of every statute and code; being quick to discern, where the law is silent, its unexpressed meaning and inference. Love is the fulfilling or the COMPLEMENT of the law, and its SUPPLEMENT also. It fills up the interstices by a running commentary, and adds an undertone of subsidiary precepts that perfect the directory of duty. It interlineates the written code within and without, inserting its own boundless variety of unwritten commands.

(3) It is also the arbiter that settles every difficulty. There are many complications in the application of ethical principles. From the beginning there has been a special department that, under the name of CASUISTRY, presides over anomalies in morals, conflicting precepts, collision of duties, and seeming incompatibilities of obligation. Here Love abounds *in all judgment* (Phil. 1:9), or discrimination. It stands by the side of conscience, ever ready and seldom at a loss for the right exposition. Seldom: for there will be instances after all, cases of conscience that no casuistry will decide; scruples and doubts that no human authority can determine; and that perplex and embarrass even the sure instincts of love. But, generally, this interpreter keeps the honest Christian, who simply and only aims at perfection, right.

This Casuist, sent by a heavenly commission into the court, lays down three general principles for the extrication of the embarrassed soul that desires to do its duty: first, God, the highest object of obedience, must invariably and at all costs have the preeminence; secondly, the most generous interpretation of every questionable obligation is to be preferred; and, thirdly, self as an end is always to be utterly rejected, or, so far as it is admitted subordinately as an end, it is always the self of eternity rather than the self of time.

The application of these standing bylaws is illustrated by the Supreme Sovereign himself, much of whose legislation had to do with collisions of duty. For instance, the disciple who says, *Suffer me first to go and bury my father,* is bidden, *Let the dead bury their dead: but go thou and preach the kingdom of God* (Luke 9:59-60). The voice of

Christ, who is God in His kingdom, must be supreme over every other, even the most powerful claim.

In every such case of severe collision between the pure, natural instincts and the service of God, God must be first, and He will hold His servant harmless. The earliest lesson from the lips of Jesus enforced this. Between what seemed His duty to His mother and His new vocation there was a collision: *Wist ye not that I must be about my Father's business?* (Luke 2:49).

COLLISION OF DUTIES

Again, when His disciples blamed the loyal woman of the alabaster box, the Redeemer taught them a lesson: on His person, while He was yet with them, it was impossible to be too profuse in gifts, and she who seemed too lavish was shielded: *Why trouble ye the woman?* (Matt. 26:10). Her large and liberal interpretation of duty, with the decision to which pure love brought her, was defended and commended to all the world.

Lastly, of the third principle also He set in His own person the great example: He *pleased not himself* (Rom. 15:3). And when the greatest of all conflicts in ethics occurred, between the care of His own innocence and the salvation of guilty men, He surrendered the former: *Not my will, but thine, be done* (Luke 22:42); and suffered himself to be *numbered with the transgressors.* In Him infinite charity expounded duty. It must do the same office in us. No other principle of exposition will carry us safe through the complications of life. Expediency, common sense, reason may err: love, armed with these principles, NEVER FAILETH (1 Cor. 13:8).

Love, the Unity of Fulfiller and Fulfillment

The perfection of the Christian system of ethics is seen in the combination of love the fulfiller and love the fulfillment of law: law and obedience to law are one in charity. To borrow terms in modern use, here is the unity of objective and subjective: a unity that impresses its various and most important influence on the whole study of New Testament morals.

1. It explains the fact that the Christian revelation is comparatively indifferent to legal codes and formal enactments. It does not dwell so much on the enforcement of specific obligations as on the vigorous maintenance of the principle of charity. Love is the strength of the MUST, which at once prescribes obedience and gives the fullness of the commands to which obedience is due. It is obvious, therefore, that Christianity cannot have, like the old covenant, the distinction of

moral and ceremonial and political law. Its legislation extends only where love can reign: that domain cannot be one of mere ceremonial observances; nor can it be the sphere of civil government, where charity is not the viceregent of God.

The old economy, which contained indeed latently a hint of this in *Be ye holy!* (Lev. 20:7) and *Thou shalt love the Lord thy God!* (Matt. 22:37), has vanished with all its legislation. Even its DECALOGUE, as such, is retained only because our Lord has himself and by His apostles exempted it from the operation of that principle and incorporated it in the Christian statute book. Introduced into the legislation where charity is supreme, it is by our Lord reduced to one twofold principle, the love of God and the love of neighbor. It is in other respects dealt with in a free spirit. It is rearranged, abridged, and its spirit extracted; it undergoes also a change in the fourth commandment, a spiritualization everywhere, and has an endless supplement added.

ACTIVE AND ONE

2. Love is an active principle, the law of the movement of the *whole of man* toward God. And, therefore, if love is both the fulfillment and fulfiller, all holiness must be no other than one concentrated and active outgoing of the strength of the whole nature of him who obeys. It does not pause to distinguish between what is forbidden and what is commanded. *I will run the way of thy commandments, when thou shalt enlarge my heart* (Ps. 119:32). There is no mere obedience to prohibitive ordinance.

The spirit that hates evil loves holiness; and, in going to the limit of every interdict, it runs to the other side and finds the perfect opposite. It avoids sin only on its way to holiness. Its resistance to evil is the resistance of love. There is no fear in love, but there is deep wrath: an anger that sins not, but abhors that which is evil and will not be content with anything less than the abolition of the sin.

Hence, further, charity, as an eternal and ever-growing activity, pursues every precept into all its ramifications. Here we have again the spiritual interpretation. . . . It cannot ask the question: *Which is the great commandment in the law?* (Matt. 22:36). And it cheerfully consents to that strong word of the moralist among the apostles: *Whosoever shall keep the whole law, and yet offend in one point, he is guilty of all* (James 2:10). The ethics of love makes provision everywhere *that God may be all in all* (1 Cor. 15:28), that the very least ordinance shall be sustained by all the majesty of heaven. *He that is faithful in that which is least is faithful also in much* (Luke 16:10). It is impatient of greater and less in duty.

3. Here we may recall the *law of liberty* (James 2:12), which is royal and perfect: royal and sovereign, in virtue of its being perfect.

LIBERTY

The law was given by Moses, but grace and truth came by Jesus Christ (John 1:17): the grace of the gospel is the truth of the law; and of those who receive it we read: *against such there is no law* (Gal. 5:23); which means more than that they are uncondemned by the statute. But the very liberty is itself law. *He taketh away the first,* the outer code, *that he may establish the second,* the inner (Heb. 10:9).

Nevertheless, the law, as we have seen, remains for a testimony, and for the conviction, and for perpetual incentive. Its uses are thus summed up by the old theology: its political use, to regulate common life; its theological use, to convince of sin; its teaching use, to instruct in morals.

The true Christian, however, is *not under the law, but under grace* (Rom. 6:14). He is not indeed over law in the sense of being independent of it. His emancipation is only so far as grace or mercy effects it through forgiveness; but that very grace disciplines or teaches him to walk according to the strictest principles of morality. The law is neither over nor beneath the believer: it is, like the Kingdom itself of which it is the rule, within us.

4. Christianity has introduced what is sometimes called the new law: it is *the law of Christ;* or *the law of faith* (Rom. 3:27; Gal. 6:2).

PERFECTION

Now if all law is love, and all fulfillment is love, it is obvious that there may be a *righteousness of God* (Rom. 10:3) attainable unto perfection: that *the righteousness of the law might be fulfilled in us* (Rom. 8:4). Love presides over ethics, which are adapted to a disordered constitution and a lost estate. It covers a multitude of past sins and enables the believer to present what is accepted as a full obedience. Thus is that saying true: *Mercy rejoiceth against judgment* (James 2:13). If strict justice should proceed in its inquisition according to the standard of heaven and unfallen creatures, mercy or love cries, *Have patience with me, and I will pay thee all* (Matt. 18:26): these my children shall be made perfect in duty. Meanwhile, its perfect work is judged according to the evangelical standard of grace: *it is accepted according to that a man hath, and not according to that he hath not* (2 Cor. 8:12). *Whoso keepeth his word, in him verily is the love of God perfected* (1 John 2:5).

5. Lastly, this teaches that there cannot possibly be any works of supererogation. For, as law is love, love is also law. There can be no

such thing as overpassing the limits of obligation. The spirit of divine charity seems to suppress the terminology of ethics, and to change its character; but only to revive it into higher life. The vows of poverty, chastity, and obedience, so far as they are Christian, are not in reality voluntary vows, but obligatory laws. *Blessed are the poor in spirit* (Matt. 5:3), *Blessed are the pure in heart* (v. 8), *Blessed are they which do hunger and thirst after righteousness* (v. 6), are benedictions pronounced upon the three severally as expressing the true Christian character. Every counsel of perfection is a commandment with promise. And, as to the whole theory on which these are founded, it may be said that Jesus, the universal Lawgiver, is the One DIRECTOR OF SOULS: THERE IS ONE LAWGIVER (James 4:12), who is GOD-MAN, the Lord; and His law is love, whether as to the perfect principle that keeps it, or as to the sum of the commandments that it must keep.

8

Benjamin Field

(1827-69)

Benjamin Field was born in Sevenoaks, Kent County, England, of devout Wesleyan Methodist parents. For half a century his father served as a faithful local preacher. Benjamin, the first-born son, very early showed both a precocious intellect and a sensitive spiritual-mindedness. At only 16 years of age he was licensed to preach, and soon thereafter he entered the Theological Institution in Richmond.

When young Field graduated three years later he was ordained and appointed as a missionary to India. But after a disappointing four years, due to recurrent and prostrating fever (probably malaria), he was compelled to return to England. Here he entered on a series of six short but highly successful pastorates, the last two being in the London area.

Despairing of regaining his health in England, he and his wife emigrated to Australia in 1865. Here he quickly captured the love and respect of the Australian Wesleyan Methodists, who did everything possible to care for the ailing minister. Unable to preach, he edited the *Wesleyan Chronicle*, in the absence of its regular editor, Rev. John C. Symons. It was during these difficult years that Field wrote *The Student's Handbook of Christian Theology.* The task was begun at the strong urging of editor Symons. Field finished the work only 10 months before his untimely death at 42 years of age.

Field's life was marked by almost continuous calamities and physical weakness. He lost two wives, one child, and left upon his death one 18-year-old son and two very small children by his second wife. Possessing an extremely conscientious and sensitive spirit, he was frequently tortured by depression and feelings of inadequacy. Yet his preaching was powerful—often in spite of extreme weakness—and his soul-winning efforts were markedly successful. In all places where he served, he was deeply loved.

Lesser men would have surrendered to their infirmities. But Field used what strength he had in disciplined labor. When he could not call or preach he studied and wrote. Perhaps his major life's work, the *Handbook,* would never have been produced if he had been robust.

As a clear, understandable, and comprehensive compendium, the *Handbook* was enormously successful, selling over 23,000 copies before it was revised by John C. Symons in 1886. For an author whose formal theological education was limited, the volume shows a clear grasp of issues, sound scholarship, and a surprisingly wide acquaintance with the literature of both Wesleyans and other theologians. The style is plain and unadorned, yet often vivid, always logical, and highly literate.

Field's documentation often leaves much to be desired. Relying heavily on Wesley, and to a lesser extent on Watson and Fletcher, he sometimes quotes without indicating the fact. At other times he indicates that he is quoting but gives no reference. Generally, however, the references he gives are adequate pointers for further checking.

Adoption and the Witness of the Spirit[1]

It is impossible to build a solid experience of full salvation on a foundation of uncertainty. We must know we are children of God before we can with confidence and boldness exercise faith for entire cleansing. Therefore the question of belonging to God, made sure by the clear witness of the Spirit, is directly relevant to a second work of grace. Field's chapter "Adoption and the Witness of the Spirit" is thus appropriate. Wesley himself held that the

---

1. The following readings are from the Revised Edition of 1886, *The Student's Handbook of Christian Theology,* published at New York and Cincinnati by the Methodist Book Concern. These selections were not touched by Symon's revision. "Adoption and the Witness of the Spirit" is chap. 11, 208-15.

witness to our sanctification is similar in nature, and as clear as God's witness to our justification.

I. What is adoption?

Adoption is an act of God's free grace, whereby, upon the forgiveness of sins, we are received into the number, and have a right to all privileges, of the sons of God[2] (Rom. 7:15; Gal. 4:5; Eph. 1:5).

It is used by St. Paul to express the privileges to which regeneration under the new covenant introduces believers, as they are the children of God.[3]

II. In what respect does it differ from pardon and justification?

The terms refer to one and the same act of the divine mind, though they place that act under different aspects. *Pardon* leads us to think of God simply as our *Sovereign*, remitting all our past transgressions. *Justification* embraces an allusion to His character as the righteous yet merciful *Judge*, who, even in the act of remitting the penalty of sin to the believer in Jesus, maintains the principles of His just and holy government. But *Adoption* is an act of God, viewed as our compassionate *Father*, by which He accepts the returning prodigal, admits him to filial communion, and reinstates him in the possession of all the privileges of his house and family.[4]

III. What are the special privileges belonging to this state?

Freedom from servile spirit (Rom. 8:15; Gal. 4:7); the guidance of the Holy Ghost (Rom. 8:14); filial confidence in God (Rom. 8:15; Gal. 4:6); a propriety in all He has and is (1 Cor. 3:21-23); and a right and title to eternal life (Rom. 8:17; Gal. 4:7; 1 John 3:2).

IV. Is it possible that the believer can be assured of his adoption?

1. *The practical importance of such assurance is presumptive evidence that he may.*

ASSURANCE

If left in darkness as to his acceptance, his mind would be a prey to endless anxieties. No emotions of ardent gratitude and filial joy would spring up within him. He could not pray in full assurance of faith, nor joy in God through our Lord Jesus Christ, nor rejoice in hope of the glory of God. All the love, and joy, and peace of a Christian heart spring from a "knowledge of salvation."

---

2. Wesleyan *Catechism* (old ed.).
3. Dr. Pope.
4. Dr. Hannah.

It is reasonable, therefore, to suppose that the God who pardons iniquity, and receives the penitent to favor, would by some means attest the fact in man's own heart and not leave it to conjecture, or assumption, or inductive reasoning.

2. *The Scriptures everywhere assert that such assurance is attainable.*

They abound with examples of those who have lived in the enjoyment of it. Under the patriarchal dispensation there were Abel (Heb. 11:4); Enoch (Heb. 11:5); and Job (Job 19:25). Under the Jewish dispensation, David (Pss. 32:5; 103:1, 3, 12); Hezekiah (Isa. 38:17); Isaiah (6:7); and Daniel (9:23). And in the dispensation of the gospel, "the knowledge of salvation by the remission of sins" is one of the distinguishing features of the new life.

BIBLICAL EVIDENCE

Our Lord was anointed "to comfort all that mourn" (Isa. 61:1-3). He continually honored the faith of the humble by an assurance of forgiving mercy (Matt. 9:2; Luke 7:47-48; 10:20). He has provided for His Church "another Comforter," whose perpetual work it is to testify to the adoption of His believing people (Rom. 8:15). The converts in apostolic times showed by the gladness they felt that they knew they were of God. See the Pentecostal believers (Acts 2:46); the Ethiopian (Acts 8:39); the jailer (Acts 16:34). And St. Paul always assumes that those to whom he wrote knew themselves to be forgiven (Rom. 5:11); otherwise his descriptions of their character would be false . . . and his admonitions altogether inapplicable (2 Cor. 13:11; Phil. 3:1; 4:4; 1 Thess. 5:16-18).

V. By what means is this assurance of our spiritual sonship attained?

There is a twofold witness granted (Rom. 8:16): First, that of the Spirit himself or rather *the same* Spirit *(auto to pneuma)* of which the apostle had spoken in the foregoing verses; "the Spirit of Christ," "the Spirit of God," "the Spirit of adoption." Secondly, that of "our spirit"—our true self, the spiritual, intelligent, accountable, and deathless part of our nature. There is a *conjoint* testimony of these two witnesses. "The Spirit himself is a *fellow-witness* with our spirit." Such is the import of the Greek word *summarturei,* which is employed here. Now, although the witness of God's Spirit comes first in the order of thought and in point of fact, it will be advantageous to consider, at once, the nature of the other witness.

TWOFOLD WITNESS

VI. What is the witness of our own spirit?

It consists in the testimony of our individual consciousness that we possess the character of the children of God, as that character is portrayed in God's Word. In the language of Dr. Hannah, it is "that rational inference which, proceeding from a careful examination of the scriptural marks of the children of God, and a satisfactory persuasion that these marks are produced in us by the presence and agency of the Holy Spirit, confirms us in the grateful conclusion that we are the children of God."

THE INDIRECT WITNESS

And in the language of Mr. Wesley, "it is nearly, if not exactly, the same with the testimony of a good conscience towards God; and is the result of reason and reflection on what we feel in our own souls. Strictly speaking, it is a conclusion drawn partly from the Word of God and partly from our own experience. The Word of God says every one who has the fruit of the Spirit is a child of God; experience or inward consciousness tells me that I have the fruit of the Spirit; and hence I rationally conclude, therefore I am a child of God."[5] The following scriptures appear to refer to the subject: 2 Cor. 1:12; 1 John 3:14, 18-19; 5:10. Now, as this experiential witness proceeds from the Spirit of God and is grounded on what He works in us, it is sometimes called the Spirit's *indirect* witness, to distinguish it from the other testimony, which is properly direct. "The testimony of our conscience" is, however, a phrase on every account preferable to this.

VII. What is the witness of the divine Spirit?

THE DIRECT WITNESS

It consists in a communication made by the Holy Spirit to the believer's mind of the fact that his sins are forgiven, that he is reconciled to God, and that the filial relation, which was destroyed by disobedience, is now restored by grace through faith. Mr. Wesley's definition is very clear and full: "By the testimony of the Spirit, I mean an inward impression on the soul, whereby the Spirit of God immediately and directly witnesses to my spirit that I am a child of God, that Jesus Christ hath loved me and given himself for me, that all my sins are blotted out, and I, even I, am reconciled to God."[6]

In accordance with this are the words of Dr. Hannah: "The witness of the Holy Spirit is that which directly ascertains to us the

5. Sermon 11.
6. Sermons 10, 11.

bl--sing of our acceptance with God, and which, impressing on our ; a sense of His paternal love towards us in Christ Jesus, creates n us that great element and principle of the new nature—love to n return." The following scriptures refer to this subject: Rom. 6; Gal. 4:6; 1 Cor. 2:12; 1 John 4:13. And the doctrine is clearly ..pied in such passages as Rom. 5:1, 5; 8:1; Isa. 12:1-2.

VIII. By what arguments is it proved that this testimony is direct and immediate?

1. *It is proved by the meaning of the word that is employed.*

"The Spirit beareth *witness.*" Now, a witness is not an inferential deduction, however logical in its process; not a conjecture, however well founded. It is a direct, implicit testimony, given with the greatest care and distinctness.

2. *It is proved by the subject matter of the testimony.*

PROOFS OF DIRECT WITNESS

The witness is to our adoption, to the forgiveness of sin, the blotting out of the handwriting that was against us. Now, this is not anything that originates in our minds, nor is it anything perceptible to the evidence of our senses. It is an act of God, a mighty secret buried in the recesses of our Father's heart, locked up more closely than the most hidden of human thoughts, one of "the deep things of God," which can be known to us on earth only by a supernatural communication (see 1 Cor. 2:11). Unless, therefore, the Holy Spirit will tell us what has taken place in the mind of God, whether He has pardoned our sins and written our name in the Book of Life, we must live in sorrow and in gloom all the days of our life. But the arrangement is made; and what we could not know by the use of our reason or the evidence of our senses, "God hath revealed unto us by His Spirit." Essentially divine, that Spirit "searcheth all things, yea, the deep things of God." He knows the moment when adopting love welcomes home the prodigal, and away He hastens on His dovelike mission to reveal the glorious fact to the anxious soul, thus becoming to that soul "the Spirit of adoption," whereby he cries, "Abba, Father."

3. *It is proved by the experience of the children of God.*

Dr. Chalmers says that he could not, without making his doctrine outstrip his own experience, vouch for any other intimation of the Spirit of God than that which He gives in the act of making the Word of God and the state of our own hearts clear to us.[7] . . .

---

7. Lec to the Romans.

Dr. Watts gives, as the result of *his* experience, a very different view. Says he, "There is an extraordinary witness of the Spirit, when, in an immediate and powerful manner, He impresses the soul with an assurance of divine love, and gives the heart of the saint a full discovery of his adoption, without the more slow and argumentative method of comparing the dispositions of their souls with some special characters of the children of God in Scripture."

We could bring forward a great multitude, far inferior, perhaps, to these men in learning and genius, but well instructed in the deep things of God, and they can tell by experience how the Holy Spirit wrought in their soul when first they believed. They were not conscious of any of the fruits of the Spirit. In fact, all their thoughts and reflections were turned from themselves to the Cross. But there was a secret consciousness, a testimony mysteriously sent into the soul, the whisper of a voice that could not be heard beyond the confines of the soul, but which there spoke thrillingly and impressively, "Thy sins, which are many, are all forgiven thee." At once they felt the joy of salvation and exclaimed in full assurance of faith, "I am my Beloved's, and my Beloved is mine."

4. *It is proved by the fact that nothing but this can make our happiness simultaneous with our adoption.*

If left to infer only on the basis of our principles, we are pardoned, and only from the reality of the change we have undergone, some portion of time must necessarily elapse. There must be time for temptation to test us, and opportunities for . . . the graces that are within, to develop before we can decide on their genuineness. And the length of time that will transpire will be very much proportioned to a man's natural temperament. Those who are constitutionally depressed and melancholy will be for a long season in gloom, slow and cautious in admitting anything that tends to their comfort; and only the sanguine will enter speedily into liberty, and rejoice in the Lord.

And in the very best case the decision will be pronounced in heaven, that the heir of hell is received among the faithful, while he himself is groaning, "O that I knew where I might find Him!" Surely, there is nothing in the gospel to warrant such a belief as this. No; as soon as the three thousand gladly received the word, as soon as the Ethiopian embraced Him of whom the prophet spake, as soon as the jailer believed in the Lord Jesus, the Comforter sped away with the tidings of their pardon. And in the very same moment in which it is pronounced in the courts above, "Thy sins be forgiven thee," there is the echo in the believing heart, "Go in peace." And this can arise from nothing else than the direct and immediate testimony of the Holy Spirit.

IX. How is it proved that this testimony of the Spirit of God must be antecedent to the testimony of our own spirit?

From this single consideration, we must be holy in heart and holy in life, before we can be conscious that we are so, before we can have the testimony of our spirit that we are inwardly and outwardly holy. But we must love God before we can be holy at all, this being the root of all holiness. Now, we cannot love God till we know He loves us. "We love him *because* he first loved us." And we cannot know His pardoning love to us till His Spirit witnesses it to our spirit. "Since, therefore, this testimony of His Spirit must precede the love of God and all holiness, of consequence it must precede our inward consciousness thereof, or the testimony of our spirit concerning them."[8] Thus, also, the point is stated by Mr. Watson: "These fruits (love, joy, and peace) cannot result from anything but manifested pardon: they cannot themselves manifest our pardon, for they cannot exist till it is manifested. God, conceived of as angry, cannot be the object of filial love; pardon unfelt supposes guilt and fear still to burden the mind; and guilt, and 'joy,' and 'peace' cannot coexist."[9] The relation in which these "fruits of the Spirit" stand to "the witness of the Spirit" is that of the effect to its cause.

PRIORITY OF DIRECT WITNESS

X. How may this testimony of God's Spirit be distinguished from the impressions of an excited imagination, and from the delusion of the devil?

There are certain marks by which it may be known.

1. *The testimony of the Holy Ghost is always preceded by hearty, genuine repentance.*

Its consolations are unknown till the spirit has been humbled and is contrite; till iniquity has been abandoned, and the cry extorted, "God, be merciful to me a sinner." But with this deep and penitent humiliation of heart, presumption is unacquainted. And we therefore press this inquiry upon all who think they have the Spirit of God, have you felt a godly sorrow for sin—sorrow that has led you to hate it as the worst of evils, and to put forth every power in forsaking its prac-

8. Wesley's *Sermons,* No. 10.

9. *Institutes,* chap. 24.

tice? If the believer has, the Spirit who is leading him will not suffer him to be deceived: but if he have not, the cry of Abba, Father, is from no divine testimony. He is saying peace, where there is no peace.

2. *Where the Holy Spirit bears His witness, He invariably produces a holy character.*

The inward testimony causes to spring forth that beautiful cluster of Christian graces that the apostle calls "the fruit of the Spirit" (Gal. 5:22-23). Fruits like these are never produced by a fantasy or a delusion. They grow nowhere but in a heart that has undergone the great regenerating change. Where they are found, the witness from above, and the witness from within, bear a united testimony, which may be received without suspicion and without fear.

XI. Is this witness of the Spirit the common privilege of believers?

Many regard it as the privilege only of a highly favored few of saints of the first order, and not even to be granted to them till just at the close of life. But this notion has not even a pretext of scriptural footing. In Gal. 4:6 St. Paul makes it a part of "the common salvation," as truly as adoption itself. "Because ye are sons"—not because you are singularly holy, or have come to hoary hairs, or are on the verge of the grave, but "because ye are sons God hath sent forth the Spirit of his Son . . . that we might receive the adoption of sons." It is not a good service reward, but a birthright; not a crown of distinction, but a joy of adoption.

A UNIVERSAL PRIVILEGE

And every part of the New Testament makes the sense of adoption a near, present good, which babes in Christ may grasp and the meekest of the earth may feel, which is offered to the prodigal when he returns from his wanderings, and to the publican when first justified from his sins. Let the following passages, which were addressed to believers of every age and rank, be duly pondered: Rom. 5:1-5; 8:15-16; 1 Pet. 1:8-9. Besides these there is an almost endless variety of texts holding out to believers the promise of rest and peace (Matt. 11:28; John 15:26-27; Rom. 14:17).

And can the enjoyment of rest and peace, such as that which is here described, coexist with doubt and misgiving as to our acceptance in the Beloved? No; it can arise from no influence but that of the Holy Spirit, the Comforter, who reveals to us the mercy of God in Christ. If these things are so, the sense of adoption is not a privilege of such high and transcendent saintliness as to be attainable only by the few. It is a common privilege of our common faith. In the heart now throbbing for the first time under the inspirations of spiritual life, there is the same cry as in the heart of the aged saint on whose face is falling the light of a brighter world than this. Each can say, "Abba, Father; my Lord and my God."[10]

XII. Can this witness of the Spirit be held in uninterrupted enjoyment?

Certain it is that it may be lost. And unless we learn to live by the faith of the Son of God, and maintain diligence in Christian duty, it is impossible to retain it. Besides this, there may be times of very severe and heavy trial; the mind may be depressed through bodily disorders, or be in heaviness through manifold temptations; and the great adversary may use all his skill to inject unbelieving thoughts. In such circumstances it may be very difficult to retain the full assurance of faith, especially for one who is naturally of a melancholy temperament.

MAY BE CONTINUOUS

But it may be done. It is obviously God's will that His children should "*abide*" in His love (John 15:9-10); should "rejoice in the Lord always" (Phil. 4:4; 1 Thess. 5:16); should "*walk* in the light" (Isa. 2:5; 1 John 1:6-7); and should "joy in the God of salvation," even in seasons of greatest providential darkness (2 Cor. 6:10; Hab. 3:17-18).

But are there not what are called *sovereign* hidings of God's countenance? that is, does not God withdraw the witness from His children in the mere exercise of His sovereign pleasure? We often meet with this idea in Calvinistic writers; but we venture to affirm that it is totally groundless, without one prop in Scripture. God is faithful, unchangeable to His covenant engagements, and never leaves His people, even for a moment, while they are faithful to His grace. The withdrawal of His favor and peace is the chastisement for disobedience (Isa. 59:2).

XIII. What is to be said of persons, humble, prayerful, consistent, who are evidently brought into darkness through constitutional depression?

"We reply, constitutional depression may prevent the soul from exercising faith in Christ; and as faith is the instrument by which we receive the Spirit's witness, the absence of that instrument, through depression, will, of course, be the occasion of our being destitute of the Spirit's witness. As mental depression affects our perceptions generally, it will doubtless affect

TIMES OF DEPRESSION

10. See Arthur's *Tongue of Fire,* chap. 5.

and distort our religious perceptions; and, in instances deeply exacerbated, may so fix and concentrate the soul's attention on what is gloomy, as to create for itself a region of darkness in which it cannot see the benign features of God's character, or the mercy so brightly revealed in the gospel. Thus, through a mental infirmity obscuring our views, our confidence fails; and our confidence failing, our evidence fails too. Such cases, however, are to be regarded as evidence of mental disease, and not to be regarded as a standard for others whose minds are in a healthy state."[11]

In viewing the whole subject, we may say, in the words of Mr. Wesley, "Let none ever presume to rest in any supposed testimony of the Spirit which is separate from the fruit of it. And let none rest in any supposed fruit of the Spirit without the witness. . . . In our being favored with a two-fold testimony there is evidently great practical utility, as it is a protection against presumption on the one hand, and despondency on the other. Our Maker has placed a double guard around our spiritual and eternal interests. As He has provided that where one bodily sense mistakes an object, another sense may correct it; so in reference to the important subject of saving religion—its evidence is placed both in our consciousness of the Spirit's witness, and the conviction of our own judgment." The one is the echo of the other, responding to the same blessed testimony. "What 'the Spirit itself' makes evident to our *consciousness*, 'our spirit' makes evident to our *reason*. What the former reveals by an immediate impression, the latter demonstrates by inference and argument; both unite in declaring that now are we the sons of God."

Entire Sanctification: Its Nature and Possibility[12]

The following two selections are taken from Chapter XIII, the full title of which is "Christian Perfection; or, Entire Sanctification." The first three questions summarize a rather standard exposition and defense of Christian perfection.

---

11. On this subject Mr. Wesley's sermon on "The Wilderness State" should be carefully read. (However, this sermon does not contain the foregoing lengthy quotation. *Editor.*)

12. This section comes from pages 226-32.

Question 4 begins a discussion of this state viewed as entire sanctification. At the outset the writer speaks of this level of sanctity as a "maturity of grace." This language can be misleading if it is allowed to blur the great difference in real experience between God's gift of sanctifying purity and our subsequent growth in maturity. In his answers to questions VI and VII Field makes his own position clear on the second work and the instantaneous nature of entire sanctification.

IV. The same maturity of grace is often spoken of as entire sanctification. Does that phrase suggest any other views of this state of holiness?

ENTIRE SANCTIFICATION DEFINED

The verb "to sanctify" in its etymological meaning signifies to separate from a common and profane use to an appropriate and special service. In this sense it is applied to the Sabbath (Gen. 2:3); to the Jewish tabernacle and temple and the utensils of the divine service (see Exodus 30); and to Aaron and his sons and their successors in office.

The term, thus used in a ceremonial sense, is applied in a high spiritual sense to all justified and regenerate men (1 Cor. 1:2, and other places) denoting their separation from sin and their dedication to the service of God. And from this it is easy to see what is involved in that matured and perfected degree of the Spirit's work, which St. Paul calls being sanctified "wholly" (1 Thess. 5:23). It consists in an entire separation from sin and an entire dedication to God.

1. *Entire separation from sin.*

By this we mean, first separation from all *outward* sin, all violations of the law of love that relate to our outward conduct; and, secondly, from all *inward* sin, all violations of the law of love that relate to the intellect, sensibilities, and the will. And is not the absolute necessity and easy possibility of this entire separation from sin most clearly insisted upon throughout the Revelation of God? Let the following passages be duly pondered: Ps. 130:5-6; Ezek. 36:25-27; Rom. 6:6-11; 2 Cor. 7:1; Eph. 5:25-27; 1 John 1:7, 9; 3:8.

It must be observed, however, that if sin were defined in its most absolute and strict sense as including, not only every transgression of the divine law, but every defect by which we come short of its requirements, "there is no man that sinneth not." But defect and infirmity—which are, in a sense, transgressions of the perfect law, and from which no one is clear till he lays down this corruptible body—are not charged upon the conscience and imputed as sin in the case of a man whose heart is clean, and whose intentions, affections, and principles are swayed by love; for "love is the fulfilling of the law" (Rom. 13:10).

2. *Entire dedication to God.*

We mean a complete acquiescence in His will and reference to His glory; using and enjoying all as He wills we should, disclaiming any rights that conflict with His rights; pursuing such business and in such measure as from our best light we believe He approves; loving only those objects that He loves, and in that degree which He allows; and discharging every duty, in the world or in the church, at home or abroad, in willing and acknowledged reference to the honor of His name. This is entire sanctification. And who will say that by the grace of God it is not possible? It is enjoined, Rom. 1:1; 12:1-2; 1 Cor. 6:19-20; and it is exemplified, Rom. 14:6-8; Gal. 2:20.

BIBLICAL DESCRIPTION

The man who is thus entirely cleansed and entirely dedicated has that mind in him "which was also in Christ Jesus" (Phil. 2:5); he is "filled with the fruits of righteousness" (Phil. 1:11); his speech will "be always with grace, seasoned with salt" (Col. 4:6); he "will set no wicked thing" before his eyes (Ps. 101:3); his bodily appetites will be used only for the purposes for which they were designed (1 Cor. 9:27); he rejoices evermore, prays without ceasing, and in everything gives thanks (1 Thess. 5:16-18); the law of love, as described in 1 Corinthians 13, is written on his heart; and he moves amidst the scenes of life "blameless and harmless, the son of God, without rebuke" (Phil. 2:15).

Such an one can say, in some humble and distant sense, what his divine Master said, "The prince of this world cometh, and hath nothing in Me"; and when God comes to inspect the soul, He finds all that it possesses to be in harmony with himself—a throne on which He reigns without a rival, an empire wherein He exercises undisputed dominion. This is entire sanctification—this is Christian perfection. And we may sum up the whole in the words of Dr. Hannah, "It denotes the extirpation of our remaining sin, and the mature growth of regenerate life; or, in other words, that pure and perfect love of God, and of all others for His sake, which is now attainable through faith in our Lord Jesus Christ, and which is strictly consistent with the acknowledged infirmities of our present mortal condition." And this suggests another inquiry:

V. What limits or qualifications are we to assign to this state of grace?

1. *Does it include infallibility, exemption from errors of judgment, or intellectual perfection of any kind?*

No; while we remain in the body we are liable to be imposed upon by deceptive appearances, to arrive at false conclusions; to be misled by unfaithful memory, illusory observations, erratic imaginations; to form unauthorized surmises and suspicions; to entertain incorrect opinions about many things. This is a natural consequence of the soul's dwelling in flesh and blood. But a man may be filled with pure love, and yet be subject to ignorance and mistake.

2. *Does it suppose that the conduct and feelings will be always free from improprieties and irregularities?*

No; from imperfect knowledge or mistake in judgment there may frequently result an improper conduct and feeling. For instance, wrong information concerning an upright and honest neighbor may lead me to regard and to treat him as a vile and disreputable man. The prejudice of education may induce me to flagellate the body, or to confine myself to the cloisters of a monastery. "And a thousand such instances there may be, even in those who are in the highest state of grace. Yet, where every word and action spring from love, such a mistake is not properly a sin."[13]

HUMANITY

3. *Does it imply freedom from temptation?*

No; a state of temptation is compatible with the highest state of holiness; for Adam, in his primeval innocence, was tempted; and the Savior, who knew no sin, was tempted in all points like as we are; and so long as our probation lasts, we shall be liable to temptation from a variety of sources. But so long as it is promptly, and with the full and hearty concurrence of the soul, repelled, there is no indication of inward sympathy, and there is no sin.

4. *Does it imply an exemption from the danger of falling away?*

No; the most holy Christians are not in this respect above Adam . . . or above angels in heaven. The one fell into sin from the summit of his paradisaical excellence, and the others from the height of their celestial perfection. So may those believers whose hearts have been purified by faith gradually depart from the faith and even fall so low as to count the blood of the covenant, wherewith they were sanctified, an unholy thing.[14]

13. Wesley's *Plain Account of Christian Perfection.*

14. Fletcher's *Last Check.*

5. *Does it preclude the possibility of further advancement?*

No; the word *perfection* indicates that the graces of the Spirit exist in the sanctified soul without alloy, without mixture—that there is nothing within contrary to them—that they exist in measure corresponding with the present capacity of the soul possessing them; but it does not indicate an attainment beyond which there is no progress. As the defects and infirmities of this mortal state are overcome or removed, as the capacities continue ever and endlessly to enlarge, as the mind expands and unfolds its energies, so will the sublimities of its moral perfection wax brighter and brighter. Through time and throughout eternity the soul will continue to receive fresh supplies from the fullness of its glorified Lord, "changed from glory into glory."

GROWTH

VI. Is this state of Christian perfection attained when the believer is justified? In other words, is regeneration identical with entire sanctification?

This opinion was strenuously advocated, more than a century ago, by the celebrated Count Zinzendorf, and many of our countrymen imbibed it from him. And still there are a few—a very few—who contend that at the moment of regeneration the believer is completely and thoroughly sanctified; and that if he should afterward be conscious of inbred corruption, he has, in a measure, fallen from grace.

It may be conceded, first, that in very exceptional cases, especially in the cases of those who are saved just at the close of life, the work is "cut short"; and the penitent believer is at once forgiven and cleansed from all unrighteousness: secondly, that in the holy transports of his first love, the justified man *imagines* that all sin is gone—"he feels no sin, and therefore fancies he has none; it does not stir, therefore it does not exist; it has no motion, therefore it has no being"; thirdly, that the regenerate man "is delivered from the dominion of outward sin, and, at the same time, the power of inward sin is so broken that he need no longer follow or be led by it." But it is by no means true that inward sin is then totally destroyed; that the root of pride, self-will, anger, love of the world, is then taken out of the heart; or that the carnal mind, and the heart bent to backsliding, are entirely extirpated. These, to some extent, remain under the control of a stronger gracious power implanted, but still making resistance and indicating the need of a further work.

SUBSEQUENT TO NEW BIRTH

Take the following scripture proofs that there is sin still existing in the heart of the justified believer.

BIBLICAL PROOFS

1 Cor. 3:1-3: The persons here addressed were "babes in Christ," and were, therefore, born again of the Spirit, they were Christian brethren, "sanctified in Christ Jesus" (1 Cor. 1:2); and yet they were in a measure "carnal," of which there were tokens enough to disturb the peace and prevent the prosperity of the church.

2 Cor. 7:1: This exhortation plainly teaches that the believers to whom it was addressed were still the subjects of spiritual pollution from which the soul must be cleansed before they could answer the great purposes of their Christian calling.

Gal. 5:17: The apostle directly affirms that the "flesh," the evil nature, opposes the Spirit, even in believers; that even in the regenerate there are two principles "contrary the one to the other."

1 John 1:7: In this passage we are supposed to be "in the light," but not yet cleansed from sin; this entire cleansing is still held out as an object to be aimed at in all the holy exercises of the soul.

The whole tenor of New Testament teaching leads to the same conclusion, "that there are two contrary principles in believers, nature and grace, the flesh and the Spirit. Almost all the directions and exhortations in St. Paul's epistles are founded on this supposition; pointing at wrong tempers or practices in those who are, notwithstanding, acknowledged by the inspired writers to be believers. And they are continually exhorted to fight with and conquer these, by the power of the faith which was in them."[15]

What, then, is the difference between regeneration and entire sanctification?

"Regeneration is the beginning of purification; entire sanctification is the finishing of that work. A regenerate man is kept from voluntarily committing known sin; which is what is commonly meant in the New Testament by 'committing sin.' But he yet finds in himself the remains of inbred corruption or original sin; such as pride, anger, and envy. The person fully sanctified is cleansed from all these inward involuntary sins. He may be tempted by Satan, by men, and by his own bodily appetites, to commit sin; but his heart is free from those inward fires, which, before his full sanctification, were ready to fall in with

---

15. See Wesley's sermon on "Sin in Believers," where this subject is treated at length.

temptation, and lead him into transgression. The Holy Spirit has cleansed him from all these pollutions of his nature."[16]

VII. If Christian perfection is thus a distinct work from regeneration, is it to be attained gradually or instantaneously?

That there is to be a gradual growth to the maturity of the Christian life is plain. Hence the commands, 2 Pet. 3:18, and the figures by which the work of grace is illustrated: it is leaven (Matt. 13:33); it is the mortification of sin (Col. 3:5); it is the rising from infancy to manhood (1 John 2:12-13); and it is a race, "a going on" (Heb. 6:1; 12:1). But though there is a progress toward perfection in every justified believer, yet its attainment is not a mere ripeness, insured by natural growth, but is instantaneously wrought in the soul by the direct agency of the Holy Spirit. It is by faith (Acts 15:9), and, therefore, at any time when the requisite faith is exercised, the reward will be granted. . . .

INSTANTANEOUS

VIII. What is the scripture proof that this state of moral and spiritual excellence is attainable?

1. *It is proved from the fact that God commands it.*

Read Deut. 6:5, compared with Luke 10:27; Matt. 5:48; Rom. 6:11; 2 Cor. 7:1; Heb. 6:1; 12:14; James 1:4; 1 Pet. 1:15-16. If it is not attainable, then God has issued a command that it is impossible to obey—made a requirement of His creatures that they have no power to perform. Who is prepared for this conclusion?

2. *It is proved from the fact that God promises it.*

Read Deut. 30:6; Ezek. 36:25-29; Matt. 5:6; 1 Thess. 5:23-24; 1 John 1:7-9. If it is not attainable, then God's promise will fail; but "He is not a man that he should lie."

3. *It is proved from the fact that holy and inspired men prayed for it in behalf of the Church.*

Read John 17:20-23; Eph. 3:14-21; Col. 4:12; 1 Thess. 5:23; Heb. 13:20-21; 1 Pet. 5:10. If it is not attainable, the men who offered these prayers were deluded by the Holy Spirit, and inspiration is not to be trusted!

4. *It is proved from the fact that the Bible points to it as the great object of all God's dealings with men.*

It is the object of Christ's mediatorial work (Luke 1:68-75; 1 John 3:8; Eph. 5:25-27; Titus 2:14); of the institution of the Christian

16. Bishop Hedding, of the M.E. Church of America.

ministry (Eph. 4:11-13; Col. 1:28); of the promise of the gospel (2 Pet. 1:4); and of the afflictions of life (Heb. 12:10). To suppose that it is not attainable is to cast contempt on the provisions of grace, and above all, to dishonor the meritorious sacrifice of Christ.

5. *It is proved from the fact that the Scriptures present us with examples of those who have realized it.*

Enoch (Gen. 5:24); Noah (Gen. 6:9); the disciples on the Day of Pentecost (Acts 2:4); Barnabas (Acts 11:24); St. John (1 John 4:17); the apostles who labored among the Thessalonians (1 Thess. 2:10); and St. Paul (Phil. 3:15).[17] Now, if an instance can be found in the Bible of one individual who, at any period of his life, was perfect, blameless, free from sin, or entirely sanctified, the attainableness of such a state is clearly proved. And it would make nothing against this doctrine if a charge of moral delinquency could be afterward proved against him; because, as we have already shown, Christian perfection does not imply impeccability, or certain perseverance in that state to the close of life.

IX. If the blessing of perfect love is thus proved to be attainable, may we look for it in the full vigor of life?

The general opinion of Calvinistic divines is that it cannot be attained until death. The great and good Matthew Henry teaches this doctrine; and Dr. Dodd says, in his note on Rom. 6:7, "The body of sin in believer's is, indeed, an enfeebled, conquered, and deposed tyrant, and the stroke of death finishes its destruction." We, on the contrary, believe that the entire sanctification of our nature may take place long before death and be exemplified in whatever position Providence may place us. Our reasons for this conclusion are—

1. We find no intimation in the Bible that we cannot be cleansed from sin while in life and health; and in no one passage is it hinted that the glorious transformation must be postponed to the end of our career. All the commands and promises that relate to this subject are so worded as to convey the idea of a *present* application.

---

17. The words of Paul, in Phil. 3:12-14, have often been adduced as his own acknowledgment that he was not wholly sanctified. But the context shows that the perfection of which he was speaking in verse 12 consists in the obtaining of the reward to which, as a Christian racer, he was aspiring. He was looking for the crown of martyrdom and the resurrection to eternal life and was led to view everything as imperfect or unfinished till these were attained. And he calls upon all who, like himself, were "perfect," in the sense of being cleansed from indwelling sin, to "be like minded" in pressing forward to the goal. *Editor.*

2. We are nowhere taught that the soul's connection with the body is a necessary obstacle to its entire sanctification. Indeed, it is explicitly declared that the body, with all its appetites, powers, and members, is to be sanctified to God (Rom. 6:13; 1 Cor. 6:19-20; 2 Cor. 7:10-11; 1 Thess. 5:23; Heb. 10:22).

3. It is the blood of Christ, and not "the last enemy," that cleanseth from all sin (1 John 1:7; Rev. 1:5). And it would be an insult to Christ and to His precious blood to suppose that He cannot save His people from their sins while soul and body are united.

4. The Scriptures connect our entire sanctification with subsequent habits and acts to be exhibited in the conduct of believers before death (Rom. 6:6, 19, 22; 2 Cor. 7:1; 1 Thess. 5:23).

5. The Scriptures also require us to bring forth the graces and virtues which are usually called the fruits of the Spirit. That these are to be produced during the life, and to be displayed in our spirit and conduct, cannot be doubted; and we may then ask whether they are required of us in perfection and maturity. If so, in this degree of perfection and maturity, they necessarily suppose the entire sanctification of the soul from the opposite and antagonistic evils.

We conclude, therefore, as to the time of our complete sanctification, that "now is the accepted time, now is the day of salvation."

Objections to the Doctrine of Christian Perfection[18]

It would be difficult to find more cogent refutations of objections to the doctrine of Christian perfection than Field here develops.

XI. What are the leading objections raised against the doctrine of Christian perfection?

Obj. 1. *The doctrine cannot be true, because many Christians, and even many learned and pious divines, do not receive it.*

To this we reply, that although it be true that great names in vast numbers might be arrayed in opposition to the doctrine, as above stated, yet other names equally distinguished for learning and excellence can be arrayed as its zealous defenders. This, however, does not

18. This discussion is from pp. 233-39.

settle the difficulty. The question is not dependent on human opinions, however respectable and worthy of attention. "To the law and to the testimony!" One "thus saith the Lord" is more conclusive than all the opinions of all the great and learned men the world ever contained. If the doctrine is in the Bible, let us embrace it, whoever may oppose; if it is not, let us reject it, whoever may be its defender.

Obj. 2. The doctrine cannot be true, because there are no examples of it.

If the fact asserted in this objection were conceded, the attainableness of perfection might still be maintained. What God wills us to be can never be inferred from what we are. Let us mournfully confess that every Christian since the world began had lived beneath the privileges of his vocation, rather than charge God with requiring anything from us that we cannot perform, or promising anything to us that He will not bestow.

But we cannot concede that the universal experience of the Church is against the doctrine. How many, in modern times, have humbly but confidently affirmed that they could "reckon themselves dead indeed unto sin, but alive unto God through Jesus Christ." And those who lived in closest communion with them have told "how holily and justly and unblamably they behaved themselves." Read the memoirs of Fletcher, Bramwell, Carvosso, Mrs. Fletcher, Mrs. Rogers, and Lady Maxwell. Was there anything in their experience contrary to the Word of God? Did they not understand the character of their experience? Did they in the general movements of life give any signs of mental aberration, from which we might conclude that they were self-deceived?

But the Holy Scriptures, as we have already shown, present us with examples of those who have realized this full salvation. Enoch and Elijah must have enjoyed it; they loved God with all their heart, and lived in full preparation for their translation to glory. The disciples, after the baptism of Pentecost, must have enjoyed it. They were so filled with the Holy Spirit that love reigned alone, to the extinction of every antagonistic principle and affection, rendering life itself one continued sacrifice of praise. Stephen must have enjoyed it. The benignity, the tenderness, the boldness, the spirituality of that man of God, as he stands before the council, and his Christlike regard for his murderers as he sinks to rest, show that his soul was filled with love to God and man.

The apostle John must have enjoyed it. His epistles are the breathings forth of that "perfect love" of which he so sweetly writes. And St. Paul must have enjoyed it. See how he loved his hostile countrymen (Rom. 9:1-3); how he realized the efficacy of the Savior's death (Gal. 6:14); how he esteemed all worldly things, that Christ might be all in all (Phil. 3:8-9); how contentedly he submitted to the will of God in every dispensation of His providence (Phil. 4:11-13); how fully he discharged the duties of his calling (Acts 20:20-21, 26); how pure and single was his aim (Acts 20:24); how blameless his deportment (1 Thess. 2:10); how strong his faith (2 Tim. 1:12); and how perfect his meetness for the heavenly inheritance (Col. 1:12; 2 Tim. 4:5-8). Is not this the experience of one who stands "perfect and complete in all the will of God"?

And if ministers, instead of advocating the cause of imperfection, were to display more fully before their people the beauties of holiness, the infinite efficacy of the precious blood, and the duty of being filled with the fullness of God, can we doubt that there would be many living witnesses in all our churches that Christ our Savior is able to save to the uttermost?

Obj. 3. *The doctrine cannot be true, because it is promotive of pride and self-righteousness.*

Strange mistake! He who is cleansed from all unrighteousness is, above all other, "clothed with humility." He has become a willing and ready disciple of Him who was "meek and lowly in heart"; and whatever good thing he enjoys he ascribes to the free, unmerited grace of God in Christ Jesus. Holiness and pride are far as the poles asunder.

Obj. 4. *The doctrine cannot be true, because it would exclude the necessity of a Mediator.*

The abundant blessings that a holy man has received from the mediation of the Savior invests that mediation with all possible attractiveness. His life of holiness is a "life of faith in the Son of God." And all his fruits of holiness flourish only as he abides in the Vine. He rejoices in Christ Jesus (Phil. 3:3); he walks in Him (Col. 2:6); he glories in His cross (Gal. 6:14); whatsoever he does, he does all in His name (Col. 3:17); he looks with ardent longing for His glorious appearing (Titus 2:13); and never does he so fully apprehend the preciousness of Jesus as when he has put away the evil and bitter thing that Christ hateth.

Obj. 5. The doctrine cannot be true, because the Scriptures explicitly and pointedly assert the necessary existence of sin within us to the close of life.

Let us examine the passages referred to:

1. 1 Kings 8:46; 2 Chron. 6:36. These passages, taken in the fullest sense of which they are capable, only assert that there is no man who is not a sinner. If they were intended to assert—as our opponents imagine—that there is no man who does not, and cannot, live without committing sin, then why say, "If they sin against Thee"? The true meaning, however, is that no man is placed beyond the possibility of sinning. "The Hebrew has no mood to express words in the permissive or optative way; but to express this sense it uses the future tense." And hence the text should be translated: "Should they sin against Thee, for there is no man that may not sin—no man who is impeccable, none infallible, none that is not liable to transgress."[19] The same remarks will apply to Eccles. 7:20 where the verb *to sin* is in the future and is properly rendered subjunctively, with the negative particle, "There is not a righteous man upon earth who does good, and may not sin." Dr. Peck says, "The rule of Hebrew syntax authorising this rendering may be found in all good Hebrew grammars; and in the application of the rule to the passages under consideration we are supported by some of the best critics—Romish, Lutheran, Calvinist, and Arminian."

THE "NECESSITY" OF SIN

2. Prov. 24:16 is often adduced. But this passage is totally irrelevant; for there is here no mention of sinning, and no reference to sin. Read the context, and it will soon appear that Solomon is speaking of the adversities into which a good man may fall, but from which God delivereth him.

3. Prov. 20:9. Shall we conclude from this question that *God* cannot make our hearts clean? Would not this be a direct contradiction to such passages as Ps. 51:7-10; Ezek. 36:25-26; 1 John 1:7? The passage is simply an affirmation that all have sinned; that no man can with truth say, with respect to his past life, I am guiltless, my heart is clean, I have not sinned.

4. James 3:2. The force of the objection, arising from this text, lies in the supposition that James is speaking personally, including himself with those whom he was addressing; but it is a well-known custom for speakers to use the pronoun *we* in statements where the

---

19. For a learned examination of this point, see Dr. Peck on *Christian Perfection.* See Dr. Clarke's note *in loco.*

including of themselves would involve the most preposterous consequences. If James must be supposed to refer to himself always when he uses the word *we,* it must be granted that he was exposed to the greater condemnation (v. 1); that he was a horsebreaker (v. 3); that his tongue was set on fire of hell (v. 6); that he was a common swearer (v. 9). But this supposition is too gross to be admitted; yet it is just the principle on which men allege the former passage against the doctrine of entire sanctification.

But even if St. James *had* designed to include himself in that statement, the utmost it could prove would be that he and those whom he addressed were imperfect; but no number of cases of unfaithfulness on the part of men could disprove that the privilege of perfect holiness was placed before them. James was a full believer in the doctrine of Christian perfection, as is evident from the subsequent part of the verse, and from 1:4. What he intends by the statement, "in many things we offend all," is that the "many masters" or teachers who thrust themselves into the office, affecting that for which they are not qualified, are causes of offense and stumbling to all, and shall receive greater condemnation. Therefore, "be not many teachers, let no more of you take this upon you than God thrusts out; seeing it is so hard not to offend in speaking much."[20]

5. 1 John 1:8. Dr. Wardlaw asks, "Is not the plain meaning, that if at any time we say we have no sin, we are deceiving ourselves?" We reply, certainly not. The passage explains itself. Read verses 8, 9, 10, where the meaning evidently is: "I have before affirmed that the blood of Christ cleanseth from all sin. And no man can say, I need it not; I have no sin to be cleansed from. If we say that we have no sin, that is, that we have not sinned (v. 10), we are under the most dreadful of all deceptions and the truth of the gospel is not in us, the whole of which is founded on this most awful truth, that all have sinned. But if we confess our sins, from a deep sense of their guilt and demerit, He is faithful and just, not only to forgive the sin, but also to purify the heart, that we may go and sin no more."[21] There is nothing in this text, therefore, to favor the necessary existence of sin. It is rather one of the strongholds of those who contend for the entire cleansing of the soul by the precious blood of Christ.

6. Rom. 7:14-25. No passage has been more usually resorted to, as furnishing proof of the necessary continuance of indwelling sin,

---

20. Wesley's note *in loco.*
21. See Wesley and Clarke.

ROMANS 7

than this. It is argued, "If the great Apostle was 'carnal, sold under sin,' how can any one expect to reach a state of freedom from its guilt and power?" But it remains to be proved that St. Paul, in this chapter, is describing his character and feelings as a regenerate man. To us this notion appears perfectly untenable, because neither his own experience, nor that of any regenerate person, can be reconciled with the description here given. A regenerate man yields his members as instruments of righteousness unto God (6:13); but this man with his flesh obeys the law of sin (v. 25). A regenerate man does not commit sin (1 John 3:9); but this man is sold under sin (v. 14). A regenerate man is spiritual (6:4); but this man is carnal (v. 14). A regenerate man has his fruits unto holiness (6:22); but this man brings forth fruit unto death (v. 5). A regenerate man exults in his liberty (8:2); but this man groans by reason of his bondage (v. 24). So that there is no agreement or resemblance at all between the regenerate man and those described in this chapter.

If it be asked, whom then does the apostle describe? we reply, he is either personating a Jew who is struggling with sin, but through resting in the law is unable to conquer; or he is showing what his own state was when his conscience was awakened, but knowing nothing of a Savior, he found himself enslaved to the practice of sin, which he abhorred. Convinced by many unavailing efforts that he could never extricate himself from his bondage by the deeds of the law, he cries out from the depths of his wretchedness for a deliverer, whom at length he found in the person of "Jesus Christ our Lord."

The chief reason why St. Paul is supposed to speak of himself as a regenerate man is that he uses the first person and the present tense throughout the passage. But it should be recollected how common it is with the inspired writers to speak as if they included themselves, when in reality they did not intend it. Thus Hosea (12:4) says, "There (viz., in Bethel) God spake with *us,*" whereas he was not in existence when God spake with Jacob there. The Psalmist, speaking of the dividing of the Red Sea, says, "There did *we* rejoice in him"; and yet he was not present when that event occurred. Instances of the same thing occur in Paul's writings (Rom. 3:7; Gal. 2:18; 1 Thess. 4:17). It was a method of avoiding, as much as possible, the giving offense to the Jews, when dwelling on subjects concerning which they would be peculiarly sensitive.

"That St. Paul does not speak these words of himself, but, under his own borrowed person, describes the state of a carnal, unregenerate person was the opinion expressed by St. Irenaeus and Origen, by Tertullian and St. Basil; by Theodoret and Chrysostom; by St. Jerome, and sometimes by St. Augustine; by St. Ambrose and St. Cyril; by Macarius and Theophylact."[22] The same sentiment is held, "as far as we know, by all the evangelical commentators of the present time on the continent of Europe; most of the English Episcopal Church, also, for many years; and not a few of the Scotch, Dutch, and English Presbyterian and Congregational divines have adopted the same interpretation."[23]

And "it is difficult to conceive how the opinion could have crept into the church, or prevailed there, that the Apostle speaks here of his regenerate state; and that what was, in such a state, true of himself must be true of all others in the same state."[24] No, there is nothing in the whole of this chapter, when rightly interpreted and applied, that is inconsistent with the scriptural doctrine of Christian perfection.

Obj. 6. The doctrine cannot be true, because the Scriptures uniformly speak of believers as fighting a good fight; whereas, if inbred sin is destroyed, the conflict is finished.

THE CHRISTIAN WARFARE

This idea is not less absurd than to suppose that, because civil dissension has no existence in a besieged city, therefore the inhabitants may sit secure, though the enemy is at their gates, attacking their outworks, and striving to make a breach in the walls. Has not the most perfect Christian an unfailing adversary in the devil, who goeth about as a roaring lion? (1 Pet. 5:8-9). Are not principalities and powers and the rulers of the darkness of this world, engaged for his destruction? (Eph. 6:11-12). And is not the world, in which he sojourns, full of temptations? Surely, then, there can be warfare, fierce and dreadful enough, without the remains of sin in the heart. Was not the blessed Savior free from sin? And yet He maintained a conflict with the devil for 40 days in the wilderness. The disciple is not above his Master.

Obj. 7. The doctrine cannot be true, because the Savior has taught us to pray, "Forgive us our trespasses," whereas, if we live without sin, that prayer has neither use nor meaning.

It may be sufficient to reply that the same prayer teaches us, in two of its petitions, to ask for ourselves and others an entire deliv-

---

22. Dr. Jeremy Taylor, "Sermon on Rom. 7:19."

23. Dr. Bloomfield.

24. Dr. A. Clarke's note on Romans 7.

erance from sin. What else can be the meaning of "Thy will be done on earth as it is in heaven," and "deliver us from evil"? Besides, it should not be forgotten that, though we do not sin according to the evangelical sense of that term, but fulfill the law by pure love to God and man (Rom. 13:10), there are many involuntary improprieties of speech and behavior into which we may be drawn through ignorance, mistake, or infirmity. These may be regarded as "trespasses," though not charged upon the conscience and imputed as sin; and of them we should ask the forgiveness of our Father in heaven. Moreover, in the Lord's Prayer we are regarded as being linked in the bonds of brotherhood with the sinners of our race; and not for ourselves only, but for them, do we pray, when we say, "Forgive *us our* trespasses." But take what view we will of the meaning of the petition, would it not be a strange and sorry argument that we must continue in sin, because, being sinners by nature, we are taught to ask for pardon?

XII. If the doctrine of Christian perfection be true, are the offspring of sanctified parents holy from the birth?

CHILDREN OF SANCTIFIED PARENTS

It has been said, "Like produces like. If the nature of original corruption is totally destroyed in parents, it is impossible but that their children must be also perfectly pure." Whatever support such a sentiment might be supposed to derive from philosophy, it certainly has none in the Bible. "The Scripture hath concluded all under sin." The relation of the entire race to fallen Adam—a fact on which the great argument in Romans 5 rests—is independent of all intermediate descent. Moreover, the holiest parents are not now in the condition of our unfallen ancestor. The whole nature—bodily, mental, and moral—is deteriorated by the Fall; and sanctification by the Holy Spirit does not restore these powers to a state of Adamic perfection even in the parent himself who enjoys this sanctification. If the parent himself is not thus restored, how can he transmit that perfection to his posterity?

Besides this, the maxim that "like produces like" is true of *nature* and *capacity* but not true in any sense of *acquired* endowments, or *superinduced* qualities. The sons of an astronomer have no innate knowledge of the stars; and Milton's daughters added no books to his immortal epic. As the acquirements of the intellect cannot be transmitted from sire to son, so neither can the piety of the heart. This has been obtained by grace, through faith in Christ Jesus; and can only be obtained by the successive generations of men, however holy their immediate parentage may be, as the result of the same personal repentance and faith. Hence it is said, "Except a man"—the phrase is as general as can be found, a man, of whatever lineage, or rank, or training, or education—"except a man be born again, he cannot see the kingdom of God."

The Peril of Final Apostasy[25]

Field's title, "The Final Perseverance of the Saints," doesn't quite match the author's development. He first declares that believers may "deeply and finally fall." He then cites and answers the leading arguments against the impossibility of apostasy.

Nothing could be more germane to a biblical doctrine of holiness than the relation of free will to final perseverance, and the effect of sin after the new birth. If sin after regeneration has no bearing on final destiny, then final salvation has some basis other than moral. To declare the imputation of Christ's righteousness an adequate moral basis for ultimate salvation is to say that a substitute holiness is acceptable.

A moral basis for salvation requires a redemptive plan that provides for real personal holiness, not a fictional accrediting. The Atonement is a moral basis for divine pardon, but it cannot be a moral basis for tolerating persistence in sin.

I. What are the two views that are held upon this subject?

1. *The Calvinistic view*—namely, that all who have received the grace of God, being born again of the Spirit, shall certainly persevere to the end and be eternally saved. In other words, they shall never fall either totally or finally from a state of grace. This doctrine follows, as a necessary sequence, from the doctrine of personal election.

2. *The Arminian or Wesleyan view*—namely, that those who were once justified and regenerated, may, by grieving the Spirit of God, fall away and perish everlastingly. In other words, their perseverance in the ways of righteousness, and their glorification in heaven, are strictly conditional.

---

25. This is chap. 14, and Field gives it the title "The Final Perseverance of the Saints" (242-46).

II. By what arguments do we sustain the view that a Christian may deeply and finally fall?

1. *It is clearly implied in the solemn injunctions that the Bible contains to a faithful perseverance in the ways of God.*

Read Matt. 24:13; 26:41; John 15:4; 1 Cor. 9:24; 10:12; Col. 1:22-23; Heb. 3:14; 4:1; 1 Pet. 5:8-9; 2 Pet. 1:10-11; Rev. 2:10. It will be seen that many of these texts expressly connect our future blessedness with the faithful observance of the conditional precept. The end can only be secured as the means are observed. But this can be true only on the principle that we are still in a probationary state, and that our eternal happiness, so far from being fixed by an irrevocable decree, is contingent on our faithfulness to God.

2. *It is proved by the repeated warnings of the Bible against apostasy from God, such apostasy, with its general consequences, being announced as fearfully possible.*

Read Ezek. 18:24-26; Matt. 5:13; John 15:2, 6; Rom. 11:19-22; 1 Cor. 10:3-12; Heb. 10:38; 2 John 8; Rev. 3:11. In full accordance with these passages is St. Paul's language, descriptive of his own conduct and fear (1 Cor. 9:27). All these texts would be without meaning if our admission to heaven were unalterably secured.

3. *It is proved by the affecting descriptions and examples of apostasy that the Bible presents as monitory signs and beacons of the people of God.*

Read Matt. 12:43-45; 1 Tim. 1:18-19; 2 Pet. 2:20-22; Heb. 6: 4-6; 10:26-29. No terms could be found that more clearly describe and designate a state of salvation than those employed in these texts, as descriptive of the former condition of these apostates. The unclean spirit had gone out of them; they had faith and a good conscience; they had escaped the pollutions of the world through the knowledge of the Lord; they were enlightened, and tasted of the heavenly gift, and were made partakers of the Holy Spirit. Yet so total is their fall that their hearts become again the dwelling place of wicked spirits; they make shipwreck of faith; they are again entangled in, and overcome by, the pollutions of the world; they crucify to themselves the Son of God afresh, even counting the blood wherewith they were sanctified an unholy thing. On this account their final doom is the "fiery indignation which shall devour the adversaries."

BIBLE EXAMPLES OF APOSTASY

Surely, here is proof enough that no man, however deep his piety, is the subject of an unconditional or absolute appointment to eternal life. While in this world, he is in a state of probation that implies danger, and can only obtain the recompense of the reward, "*if* he continue in the faith, grounded, and settled, and be not moved away from the hope of the gospel."

III. What are the leading arguments adduced in opposition to this doctrine?

1. *It is alleged that there are "promises and declarations insuring or implying the communication of grace to the end."*

We must consider John 4:14; 6:39-40; Heb. 13:5, and many others. True, God is faithful; He cannot deny himself. But all these promises directly express or clearly imply some condition, the violation of which, on man's part, will sacrifice the promised good. For example, the first of these passages expresses the permanence of the gift, but it is only to him that "drinketh of the water." Let him wander from the fountain, and cease to drink, and the living water will no longer refresh his soul.

As to the second, it is a clear expression of "the Father's will." But is that will never frustrated by the sin of man? (See Matt. 23:37, and 1 Tim. 2:4, compared with John 5:40.) And was it not directly frustrated by the sin of Judas? He, like the rest, was given to Christ but was "lost" to Christ and heaven (see John 17:12). As to the third, while God promises His abiding presence with His saints, other scriptures teach that that presence will be withdrawn from the disobedient and unfaithful (2 Chron. 15:2; 24:20). And so every promise of grace is contingent upon the faith and obedience of them to whom it is given.

2. *It is alleged that there are texts in which the strongest confidence is expressed as to the certainty of final salvation, and that these would be the utterance of foolhardy assurance were the Arminian doctrine true.*

Those who argue thus, quote Rom. 8:35-39; 2 Cor. 5:1; Phil. 1:6; 1 Pet. 1:4-5. We reply, that it is the privilege of every Christian to live in "full assurance of hope" (Heb. 6:11). Heaven is prepared for him (Matt. 24:34; John 14:2); divine grace is sufficient to meet the exigencies of his condition (2 Cor. 12:9); God has promised to supply his need through all the changes of his life (Phil. 4:19); he has in the graces of the Spirit an earnest of the inheritance (2 Cor. 1:22; Eph. 1:14); and God is faithful, who will not suffer him to be tempted above that he is able (1 Cor. 10:13). Hence he has reason enough to "rejoice in hope of the glory of God" (Rom. 5:2); and in proportion as he advances in holiness will he "abound in hope by the power of the Holy Spirit" (Rom. 15:13).

But let hope be as confident as it may, it is still *but* hope and cannot have all the absolute certainty of possession. Certainty leaves no room for fear; hope may. And in our probationary state, though "begotten again to a lively hope," we are to "pass the time of our sojourning here in fear" (1 Pet. 1:17); a fear such as that which existed in Paul (1 Cor. 9:27); and which, from a due apprehension of danger, will prompt to the mortification of the flesh (1 Cor. 9:27), to incessant watchfulness and prayer (Matt. 26:41), and to holy diligence (2 Pet. 1:10; 3:14). It is, therefore, neither presumption nor foolhardy assurance to "hope to the end." This is, indeed, enjoined as a duty. But while "rejoicing in hope," "let us also fear, lest, a promise being left us of entering into his rest, any of you should seem to come short of it" (Heb. 4:1).

3. *It is alleged that there are texts that contain affirmations still more direct that the righteous shall finally obtain eternal life.*

Texts such as Rom. 8:28-30; John 10:28; and 11:25-26 are cited. The first of these texts is supposed to be the stronghold of the Calvinistic doctrine. But does the apostle mean that the blessings there mentioned invariably and unavoidably follow each other, so that no person who receives the first blessing ever fails to receive the second, or the third? He cannot mean that. The statement of our Lord, in Matt. 22:14, proves that many have been "called," who were never "justified"; and the awful instances of apostasy named in Heb. 6:4-8, and 2 Pet. 2:20-22, prove that there have been men who were once "justified," and yet were never "glorified."

DESTINY NOT FIXED

The apostle, in enumerating these Christian privileges and marking their sequence, is speaking of the gracious "purpose" of God in its gradual development and its ultimate consummation. These successive blessings are designed for Jews and Gentiles; they constitute so many steps from a state of nature to eternal glory. All who are glorified in heaven have advanced by these steps. Being "foreknown" as true believers, they were "predestinated"—predesigned (so the *proorizō* in this text means)—to be conformed to the image of Jesus, in the holiness of their present character, and in their final glorification. This was the great blessing that God marked out for them as believers.

They were, therefore, "called"—invited—by the gospel to this state of benefit. The calling being obeyed, they were "justified"; and being justified, and continuing in that state of grace, they were "glorified"; for "he that shall endure unto the end, the same shall be saved" (Matt. 24:13). This is the plain and obvious course of the amplification pursued by the apostle. Except in direct opposition to other parts of Scripture, it cannot be designed to teach that these privileges follow each other with absolute and never-failing certainty in the experience of everyone who is called by the gospel.

The great mistake with regard to this text, and the others referred to, viz., John 10:28, "My sheep shall never perish"; and John 11:26, "Whosoever liveth and believeth in me shall never die," arises from supposing that they relate to a certain number of persons as *men*, whereas they relate to persons as existing under some particular *character.* To such character the promises are sure. Let the character be sacrificed, and the promise is made void. God himself has made this point plain in Ezek. 33:13, to which, as furnishing a key to many texts of Scripture, I must specially refer the reader: "When I shall say to the righteous, that he shall surely live," I speak to him as a righteous man, and the promise depends on his retaining his righteous character; for "if he trust to his own righteousness, and commit iniquity, all his righteousness shall not be remembered; but for his iniquity that he hath committed, he shall die for it." Here you discover the principle that runs through the whole of Scripture: "Wherefore let him that thinketh he standeth take heed lest he fall."

4. *It is alleged that the Arminian doctrine makes God changeable.*

By no means. With Him is no variableness. A change of character would be a cessation of divinity. "But this," as Dr. Wardlaw . . . observes, "is quite consistent with changes in the relation in which His moral and accountable creatures stand to Him, and in the consequent state of His mind towards them. Surely no one will imagine that when any man from being loyal becomes rebellious, the relation between him and God can continue the same as before, or that the state of the divine mind remains unchanged towards him." It is evident that complacency must come to an end when men "turn from the holy commandment delivered unto them." And as governor, He who "is angry with the wicked every day" cannot retain the same relative position to man in his guilt that He had sustained to him as His "willing and obedient" child.

But a change in the relations between the creature and the Creator is not, properly speaking, a change in the Creator himself. Indeed, the very change in the judicial relation arises from the unchangeableness of God and the mutability of man. The change comes upon man.

He "draws back" from God, to whom he has pledged his devotion; and if God is unchangeably true, his "soul shall have no pleasure in him"; if He is unchangeably pure, "the foolish shall not stand in His sight"; if He is unchangeably just, He will reward the man according to his works. It is, therefore, because He retains all the unsullied purity of His holiness; because He retains all His truth and righteousness, as the principles of His moral administration that He can no longer "hold him guiltless" who sins willfully after he has received the knowledge of the truth. And we throw back the charge of imputing changeableness to God upon those who hold the doctrine we oppose.

5. *It is alleged that the Arminian doctrine is destructive of spiritual comfort, repressing all the buoyancy of generous and confiding love.*

THE BASIS OF TRUE COMFORT

This view is certainly not in harmony with experience. The Christian's comfort arises from his conscious interest in Christ, from the unfailing efficacy of the Atonement and intercession of his Lord, and from his hope of the heavenly inheritance. And that comfort can never be destroyed while he cleaves to the Lord with purpose of heart. The thought that he may "fall away," and that his "latter end" may be "worse than the beginning," is repressing to all the buoyancy of presumption, but is one of the most powerful motives to filial duty. And if, under the impulse of salutary fear he "gives diligence to make his calling and his election sure," he will realize the happiness of him "that feareth alway" (Prov. 28:14); "the joy of the Lord will be his strength"; he will never fall: "For so an entrance shall be ministered unto him abundantly into the everlasting kingdom of our Lord and Savior Jesus Christ."

9

John Miley
(1813-95)

It was as professor of theology at Drew Theological Seminary, from 1873 until his death in 1895, that Miley reached the zenith of his intellectual powers and theological influence. During this period he published his two major works. *The Atonement in Christ* (1879) and *Systematic Theology* (two volumes, 1892 and 1894).

When he entered upon his teaching career he was, however, already a seasoned and mature thinker, having been in the Methodist ministry for 35 years. His first publication, at 38 years of age, was a treatise on *Class Meetings,* in which he revealed the depth of his pastoral concerns. He was known as an able preacher, as well as a cogent writer. In addition to the two major works there flowed from his pen scores of theological articles of concern to the Methodism of his day.

John was born in Butler County, Ohio, on Christmas Day, 1813. He earned the A.B. degree in 1834 and the A.M. in 1837, both from Augusta College. Entering the pastoral ministry of the Methodist Episcopal church in 1838, he served various churches, first in Ohio and then in the New York East Conference. The vacancy at Drew, which Miley was called to fill, was created when Randolph S. Foster was elected bishop.

Robert E. Chiles reports strong commendation for Miley's work by his contemporaries. Southern Methodist John Tigert wrote, "As a whole, a most creditable and satisfactory exhibition

of the theology of our common Methodism" (*Theological Transition in American Methodism,* 59).

Regeneration[1]

Here Miley deals with what he calls the "Deeper Principle of Interpretation." Having granted that regeneration is "the inception of new life," he proceeds to affirm that the analogy of natural generation does not sound the deepest note. Rather, the deepest note is in "the fact that the offspring is in the likeness of the parentage" (p. 330). In the new birth we "receive the impress and likeness of the Holy Spirit." This is Miley's ground for defining regeneration as "subjective holiness," and accounts for his difficulty in the next chapter in finding any very significant difference between regeneration and sanctification.

4. *Deeper Principle of Interpretation.* Underlying the points of comparison usually presented in the analogical treatment, there is a deeper fact that gives us the true nature of regeneration. It is the fact that the offspring is in the likeness of the parentage. This principle rules in all forms of propagated life. It is the determining law of species. It here suffices that we merely state this law, as it was sufficiently discussed in our anthropology. We there found it a valid and sufficient ground for the genetic transmission of depravity from Adam down through the race. This is the principle that opens the clearer view of regeneration. As by natural generation we inherit from the progenitors of the race a corruption of the moral nature, so by the new birth we receive the impress and likeness of the Holy Spirit.

This is our interpreting principle. Nor is it fetched from afar, but is right at hand in the classical passage on regeneration: "That which is born of the flesh is flesh; and that which is born of the Spirit is spirit" (John 3:6). In the first part the truth is deeper than the derivation of a body of flesh in the form and likeness of the parental body; it means the inheritance of a corrupt nature. . . . In this corruption of nature lies the necessity for the new birth. It was on the ground of this fact that Christ said to Nicodemus: "Marvel not that I said unto thee, Ye must be born again." But such a necessity can be met only by a

1. The following excerpts are from *Systematic Theology,* 2:327-53. Chapter 6, "Regeneration."

divine operation within the moral nature, which shall purify it and transform it into the moral likeness of the divine. All this is the meaning of the words of Christ: "That which is born of the Spirit is spirit" —spirit, not essentially, but in the sense of a spiritual or holy quality. As the depravity of the original parentage is transmitted through natural generation, so through regeneration we are transformed into the moral likeness of the Holy Spirit. This meets the necessity for regeneration. There is no other way in which it can be met. Thus we find the real meaning of being born of the Spirit.

The nature of the regeneration is thus manifest. It is a state of subjective holiness. We state the characteristic or predominant fact, without reference to the proper distinction between regeneration and entire sanctification. It must be a state of subjective holiness because it is the result of an operation of the Holy Spirit that as really transforms the soul into the moral likeness of himself as the laws of nature determine the likeness of the offspring to its parentage.

There is no mystery in this doctrine that should in the least discredit it with any who believe in God. Just what it is in the inner nature of a mineral, a plant, or an animal that determines its peculiar cast, we do not know; but God knows, and it was easy for Him to so determine the nature in each. So did He make man, even in His own image; and, after he has fallen into a corrupt state, God can renew him in holiness after His own image. If this is not possible, no agency of God is possible in either creation or providence.

5. *Other Forms of Presentation.* Regeneration, or that moral renovation that it represents, is expressed in other forms of thought, but the deeper idea of a moral transformation into the likeness of the divine holiness is ever present. A few instances will answer for illustration; and we shall thus bring other texts into service in setting forth the nature of regeneration.

CLEANSING

"Then will I sprinkle clean water upon you, and ye shall be clean: from all your filthiness, and from all your idols, will I cleanse you. A new heart also will I give you, and a new spirit will I put within you: and I will take away the stony heart out of your flesh, and I will give you an heart of flesh" (Ezek. 36:25-26). Here is a state of moral corruption and of insensibility to spiritual things. The filthiness and the heart of stone can mean nothing less. Such is the subject of the moral renovation. The renovation is a purification, and the inception of a new spiritual life. Such is the meaning of the sprinkling with clean water, the cleansing, and the new heart and new spirit. Such is the work of regeneration.

"Therefore if any man be in Christ, he is a new creature: old things are passed away; behold, all things are become new" (2 Cor. 5:17). To be in Christ, as here expressed, is to be in living union with Him. This is the state of an actual salvation, and the same as the regenerate state. To be thus in Christ is to be a new creature, or a new creation. By such a new creation we are transformed into a state of holiness like unto the primitive holiness wherein man was made in the likeness of God. This is the same deep sense of regeneration.

NEW CREATURE

"That ye put off concerning the former conversation the old man, which is corrupt according to the deceitful lusts; and be renewed in the spirit of your mind; and that ye put on the new man, which after God is created in righteousness and true holiness" (Eph. 4:22-24). The old man is both a corrupt nature and a vicious habit of life. The new man is the opposite in both respects. This is plain from the contrast in which they are placed. It is manifest in the fact that the new man is created in righteousness and true holiness. The old man and the new are such that the former can be put off and the latter put on only through a renewal in the spirit of our mind. This must be a thorough moral transformation. It is such in fact, for it is being created anew in the image of God. This is the same deep truth of regeneration that we found in its representative terms. St. Paul expresses the same truth elsewhere, and in very similar words: "Seeing that ye have put off the old man with his deeds; and have put on the new man, which is renewed in knowledge after the image of him that created him" (Col. 3:9-10).

NEW MAN

6. *The New Life.* Regeneration is the ground of a new spiritual life, a life in righteousness. In the very nature of it, as set forth in the Scriptures, it must be such.

It is expressed as a new birth or a being born of God. "If ye know that he is righteous, ye know that every one that doeth righteousness is born of him"; "Whosoever is born of God doth not commit sin"; "Beloved, let us love one another: for love is of God; and every one that loveth is born of God, and knoweth God"; "For whatsoever is born of God overcometh the world" (1 John 2:29; 3:9; 4:7; 5:4). Or is regeneration a being born of the Spirit? "For the law of the Spirit of life in Christ Jesus hath made me free from the law of sin and death. . . . That the righteousness of the law might be ful-

NEW BIRTH

LIFE AFTER THE SPIRIT

filled in us, who walk not after the flesh, but after the Spirit" (Rom. 8:2, 4). "But the fruit of the Spirit is love, joy, peace, longsuffering, gentleness, goodness, faith, meekness, temperance: against such there is no law" (Gal. 5:22-23). Such are the fruits of regeneration; for the Holy Spirit plants His grace, not in the vicious soil of the flesh, but only in the soul that by regeneration is morally transformed into the likeness of himself.

As regeneration is a new creation whereby we become new creatures in Christ, so old things pass away, and all things become new; a good life replaces the evil life (2 Cor. 5:17). "For we are his workmanship, created in Christ Jesus unto good works" (Eph. 2:10). In regeneration the old man is put off, and not only as a corrupt nature, but also as an evil life; and the new man is put on, not only by the purification of the moral nature, but also in the habit of a new life in righteousness and true holiness (Eph. 4:22-24).

Further, regeneration is expressed as at once a crucifixion and a resurrection with Christ; and on these grounds a new spiritual life,

ALIVE WITH CHRIST

a truly Christian life, set forth as both a privilege and a duty (Rom. 6:5). By such crucifixion we die to sin; and by such a resurrection we are made alive in Christ. Such is the deep meaning of Paul when he says: "I am crucified with Christ: nevertheless I live; yet not I, but Christ liveth in me" (Gal. 2:20). Only a truly spiritual or Christian life can properly answer to the life in Christ attained in regeneration.

The Agency of the Spirit

Very strongly Miley pivots regeneration on the supernatural and immediate action of the Holy Spirit. He repudiates the Campbellite notion that the truth is the effective agent in producing regeneration. Without the direct action of the Spirit upon the nature, Miley is saying, regeneration becomes only conversion and is reduced to a phenomenon that is explainable in psychological terms.

3. *The Only Efficient Agency.* Whatever may be conditional to regeneration, or whatever must precede or accompany it, still it is efficaciously wrought solely by the power of the Holy Spirit.

The error of baptismal regeneration has widely prevailed. It is thoroughly the doctrine of Romanism; predominantly, of Lutheranism and Anglicanism. But the effect is impossible to such a cause. No man can rationally think it possible that the outward application of water to the body should effect the interior renovation of the soul. Baptism is the sign of an interior purification by the power of the Holy Spirit, but can have no part in the efficacious agency whereby it is wrought. It is true that the Scriptures verbally place baptism close to regeneration (John 3:5; Acts 2:38; Eph. 5:26; Titus 3:5; Heb. 10:22). In like manner they place baptism equally close to justification or the remission of sins (Acts 2:38; 22:16). But is it possible in fact? Or can anyone rationally think it possible that the application of water in baptism should cancel the guilt of sin? Justification, or the forgiveness of sins, is definitely and only the act of God; and baptism can have no part in it, except as a sign or confession of the faith wherein the gracious forgiveness is granted. Baptism is equally without efficacy in itself for our spiritual regeneration.

Some hold that we are regenerated by the power of the truth. Such is the common rationalistic view. It is definitely the doctrine of the Disciples, or Campbellites. Some in the fellowship of thoroughly orthodox churches hold the same view.[2] The fact is not really other because the Scriptures are designated as an instrumental agency, nor because there is also set forth an agency of the Holy Spirit. The real point is that [by Anderson] an efficient agency is assigned to the Scriptures in the work of regeneration. In verification of this position we cite a single passage: "The change of heart in regeneration is produced by a previous change of judgment. The erroneous opinions of the sinner are corrected, and that corrects his feelings. He receives new information, and that gives another direction to his affections. Plainly, the Bible removes his delusions, and, in showing him the true nature of objects, makes him love many things which he formerly hated, and hate many things which he formerly loved. When he believes its report; when he takes Bible views of objects, looks at them through its telescope, looks at them through its microscope, looks at them through its atmosphere; when he looks at God, looks at Christ, looks at himself, looks at his soul, looks at this world, looks at death, looks at eternity in Bible light, the look revolutionizes him. See what a commotion has been produced among the affections of his spirit, so soon as this heavenly light, altering the decisions of his judgment, has dawned on his mind! He is now with ardor pursuing objects which he

2. Anderson, "Regeneration," sec. III.

formerly despised, or feared, or abhorred; and fleeing, as when a man flees from the plague, or from his house on fire, from objects which he formerly considered harmless, or in which his soul delighted. The Bible light has disclosed friends where he thought there were none but foes, and foes where he thought there were none but friends."[3] This passage cannot mean anything less than an efficient agency of divine truth in the regeneration of the soul. And what is true of it is equally true of the fuller discussion.

Those who maintain this doctrine assume to find the proof of it in the Scriptures themselves. Some texts are seemingly in their favor (John 15:3; 17:17; James 1:18; 1 Pet. 1:23). That divine truth, as revealed in the Scriptures, fulfills important offices in the attainment of salvation and the maintenance of a truly spiritual life, is not to be questioned. That it possesses in itself the power of regenerating the soul, must be denied as at once unscriptural and impossible. The texts that seemingly attribute regeneration to the power of the truth cannot be interpreted as actually so meaning without placing them in opposition to the many that definitely ascribe that work to the divine agency, and in a manner to mean that it is the only efficient agency. There is no need of an interpretation that involves such an opposition of texts. The many services of the truth in our attainment of salvation, and in our maintenance of a true Christian life, will, without any notion of its regeneration power, easily interpret the texts adduced in proof of such a power.

It is not in the nature of truth, not even of divine truth, that it should possess the power of regeneration. The Scriptures, which contain this truth, give us a knowledge of divine things; but such knowledge has no direct power over our moral nature. They contain many holy precepts, enough indeed for our guidance into all duty; but precepts have not in themselves the power of ruling our lives; and much less have they the power of sanctifying our nature. Wherein, then, lies the great power of the Scriptures in the religious life? The answer is obvious: It lies in the practical motives embodied in the great religious truths that they reveal. Such motives may act upon our moral and religious feelings, and through them become a ruling force in our religious life. But such is the only mode of their power; consequently, they can never reach the moral nature with any power of regeneration.

We have no power of self-regeneration. The nature of inherited

3. Ibid., 82-83.

depravity precludes its possibility. As a subjective state it is as really in us and of us as if original to our nature. Hence a power of self-regeneration would be the same as a power of changing one's own nature. There can be no such power. It is the sense of Scriptures respecting our natural state that we have no such power (John 3:6; Rom. 7:5, 14, 18, 21; 8:3-8). In this moral impotence lies the necessity for the economy of redemption. Regeneration is a true sphere of the divine monergism.

There is also a sphere of synergism. Regeneration is not an absolute work of the Spirit. We have already shown its conditionality. There are prerequisites that cannot be met without our own free agency. There must be an earnest turning of the soul to God, deep repentance for sin, and a true faith in Christ. Such are the requirements of our own agency. There is no regeneration for us without them. Yet they are not possible in the unaided resources of our own nature. Hence there must be a helping work of the Spirit prior to His work of regeneration. There is such help. The Holy Spirit enlightens, awakens, and graciously draws us. All this may be without our consent, and even despite our resistance. We may finally resist, or we may yield to the gracious influences and be born of the Spirit. Here is the sphere of synergism.

Sanctification[4]

Both in his chapter on regeneration and in the chapter on sanctification Miley leans heavily on John 3:6, "That which is born of the flesh is flesh; that which is born of the Spirit is spirit." He interprets *flesh* as depravity and *spirit* as holiness. He assumes that the birth of the Spirit is not only *necessitated* by inherited depravity, but that this birth of the Spirit is designed to *correct* the depravity.

But Miley may be misapprehending the true import of Jesus' statement here. Perhaps the contrast intended in "flesh" and "spirit" is not depravity and holiness, but death and life, or the natural versus the spiritual. Jesus is really saying that natural generation does not include spiritual life; such life can be created only

4. This material is Chap. 8, pp. 354-84.

by the Spirit. Flesh procreates flesh. It takes the Holy Spirit to procreate spiritual life.

The Spirit birth supplements the natural birth but does not cancel it. The reborn believer remains born of the flesh, but with his spiritual deficiency supplied. From our natural parents we receive our human nature, but a nature void of spiritual life because of the Fall. If this lack is to be supplied, we must be born of the Spirit. Only then is our human nature restored to its true humanness, by the restoration of the spiritual dimension. But while restored to true humanness in the sense of being once again a three-dimensional being with body, soul, and spirit, we are not yet restored to full holiness.

In spite of this defect, and several footnoted deviations from classic Wesleyan interpretations, much value remains in the chapter. Miley's deviations are perhaps prompted by an irenic spirit rather than by a spirit of compromise.

In his section III, "The Life of Holiness," the distinction between purity and maturity is most helpful. He is strong here, at the very point where many others have been weak. It is only on the basis of this distinction that the notes of crisis and process can in turn have their proper due.

The term *sanctification* is in frequent use, particularly with Methodists, for the expression of a full salvation or a completeness of the Christian life. It is not itself adequate to such expression, for the reason that it is often used in Scripture in a lower sense, or without the idea of completeness.[5] Hence in its doctrinal use it is often accompanied with the word *entire;* so that the full expression is entire sanctification. This is not without warrant in the words of St. Paul wherein he prayed that the Christians of Thessalonica might be wholly sanctified (1 Thess. 5:23).

Other words or formulae are also in use; such as holiness, Christian perfection, the higher Christian life, Christian purity, love enthroned; but such formulae are merely representative of the doctrine, not the full expression of its content. Hence, which shall be used is a matter of mere individual preference. The doctrine itself is the question of interest.

5. Wesley, *Plain Account of Christian Perfection*, 50-51.

I. *Meaning of Sanctification*

Holiness in man is a moral or religious state; sanctification, a gracious work of God whereby that state is produced. The idea of the divine holiness underlies that of human holiness. Without the former there is no place for the latter. That God is holy is a reason for holiness in ourselves: "Because it is written, Be ye holy; for I am holy" (1 Pet. 1:16). There was no such idea in Greek thought; not even the idea of the divine holiness. This being the case, there could be no such reason in the Greek mind for personal holiness. Hence new meanings were necessary to the Greek words appropriated for the expression of these purely biblical ideas.[6]

THE IDEA OF HOLINESS

As the divine holiness is a reason for Christian holiness there must be a likeness between the two. This is possible notwithstanding the infinite fullness of the one and the narrow limitations of the other—just as it was possible for man to be originally created in the image or likeness of God. However, no true view of the subject can ever overlook that difference. There is another point of difference; the divine holiness is an eternal possession, while Christian holiness is always an attainment. The latter fact gives propriety to the use of the word *sanctification,* which means a holiness wrought in us by a gracious work of God.

A thorough study of the biblical terms of sanctification might be helpful in this discussion, but it would require an elaboration for which we have no room. There are convenient sources of information for any who may wish to engage in this study.[7] It will suffice for our own purpose that we treat only such terms as we use to set forth the meaning.

1. *Ceremonial Sanctification.* While the terms of sanctification have a far deeper meaning, as we shall point out, they are sometimes used in the sense of a setting apart from secular to sacred uses, a consecration to God and religion. Here the meaning is the same in application to both things and persons. Thus places, altars, offerings, the tabernacle, and the temple were sanctified. In the same sense there was a sanctification of the priests, and also of the Jewish people. The verb *hagiazō* is thus used (Lev. 8:10-12; Matt. 23:17, 19; 2 Tim. 2:12).

---

6. Cremer, *Biblico-Theological Lexicon of New Testament Greek, hagios.*

7. Lexicons of the Greek Testament, severally by Cremer, Robinson, and Thayer; Lowrey, *The Possibilities of Grace,* 42-66; Beet, *Holiness as Understood by the Writers of the Bible;* Franklin, *Review of Wesleyan Perfection,* part ii.

Even our Lord was thus sanctified (John 10:36). Here, however, all idea of any prior ceremonial impurity is utterly excluded. The word *hagios,* which expresses the result or state of sanctification, is used in like manner; that is, in the sense of a ceremonial sanctification of both things and persons (Matt. 7:6; 24:15; Luke 2:23; Acts 7:33). While such a form of sanctification is without any strictly ethical character, it served a valuable purpose in the Hebraic economy. It was a primary lesson in the divine education of the Hebrew people up to the true idea of holiness.[8]

We may here note the fact that these terms of sanctification are sometimes used in the sense of veneration and reverence. They thus mean a devout and worshipful state of mind respecting God. Here is an instance: "This is it that the Lord spake, saying, I will be sanctified in them that come nigh me" (Lev. 10:3). The *trisagion* of Isaiah—"Holy, holy, holy, is the Lord of hosts" (6:3), is the expression of adoring reverence. The first petition in our Lord's Prayer—"Hallowed be thy name" (Matt. 6:9) . . . is replete with the same spirit. Such too is the meaning of the commandment: "But sanctify the Lord God in your hearts" (1 Pet. 3:15).

Such an adoring reverence is possible only with a deep sense of the divine holiness. There is much in the greatness and majesty of God, much in His mighty works, much in the thought of His infinite knowledge and power, to awaken admiration and awe; much in His justice to inspire fear; much in His love to kindle a grateful love in us; but not without the sense of His absolute holiness can we bow to Him in adoring reverence. This is the spirit of the heavenly worship: "Holy, holy, holy, Lord God Almighty, which was, and is, and is to come" (Rev. 4:8).

2. *Deeper Moral Sense.* The distinction here is between the ceremonial and the moral forms of sanctification. The first is outward and official; the second, inward and of the moral and religious nature.

Regeneration furnishes the best exemplification of this work. In the full extent of it, regeneration is of the nature of sanctification. This was shown in our treatment of that subject. It must be such from the very ground of its necessity, which lies in the depravity or corruption of our moral nature. The removal of this corruption is possible only through an interior purification. Such purification is the work of the Holy Spirit in regeneration, so far as it is therein accomplished.

8. Walker, *Philosophy of the Plan of Salvation,* Chap. 7.

It is hence true that, in the full extent of it, regeneration is of the nature of sanctification; and whatever be the work of sanctification, as distinctively held, it cannot be different in kind. Certainly we have in regeneration the best exemplification of its nature.[9]

3. *Entire Sanctification.* The meaning of entire sanctification is obvious in the light of what has preceded. If regeneration were so thorough as to complete the subjective purification, there could be no place for the special work of sanctification. In case of serious degeneration, as in some instances in the churches of Corinth and Galatia, there would be need of a renewed purification; but it would be accomplished by a renewed work of regeneration, if regeneration were primarily complete sanctification.

REGENERATION INCOMPLETE

The theory, then, is that regeneration is not in its primary work complete sanctification; that it does not immediately produce a fullness of the inner spiritual life. The doctrine is under no necessity of assuming that this is never the case, particularly so far as the subjective state is concerned. We could not affirm that there are no exceptions; and, not only for the reason that we see no doctrinal necessity for it, but also because some, even from the hour of their conversion, give constant proof of a fullness of the spiritual life, if not in its maturity yet in its entirety. Mr. Wesley himself never denied the possibility, nor even the actuality, of such instances, though he thought them rare, even if ever actual. The common fact is that of incompleteness. Hence it is the definite work of entire sanctification to complete the subjective purification. So far the statement is simple and easily made; but a philosophy of the facts is no easy attainment. They will be more fully considered in the next section.

4. *Two Spheres of the Sanctification.* We think it important to observe that there are two spheres of sanctification, as the doctrine is distinctively held: one with the moral nature; the other within the actual Christian life. The two are closely related, the former being the necessary ground of the latter. Only as the nature is sanctified can the life be in holiness. But the perfection or maturity of the Christian graces is not an immediate product of the subjective purification. Hence the importance of distinguishing the two spheres, so that we shall not fall into the error of maintaining the doctrine of an instant attainment of perfection in such graces. Here the law of growth must

9. Cf. Wiley, below, pp. 385-88 (*Christian Theology,* 2:473-76).

be admitted. On the other hand, in the light of this distinction we may see more clearly the possibility of an instant subjective purification.

II. *Sanctification of the Nature*

1. *Incomplete in Regeneration.* The doctrine of an incompleteness of the work of regeneration underlies that of entire sanctification, particularly in its Wesleyan form. Without such incompleteness there could be no place for the definite second-blessing view. That somewhat of depravity remains in the regenerate, or that regeneration does not bring to completeness the inner spiritual life, is a widely accepted doctrine. Indeed, exceptions are so few that the doctrine must be regarded as truly catholic. However, it does not necessarily carry with it the doctrine of entire sanctification as a possible attainment in the present life. Hence many who hold the former deny the latter. On the other hand, the impossibility of such sanctification is no consequence of the incompleteness of regeneration. The grace that therein so largely purifies our nature surely can wholly cleanse it. Hence there is place for the doctrine of entire sanctification as an attainable blessing in the present life.

The question of a remnant of depravity is not without perplexity. As the nature of depravity as a whole is difficult for thought, so that of a remnant, not different in kind from the whole, is difficult. Consequently, there is perplexity in the notion of entire sanctification.[10]

It must not be overlooked that the Scriptures represent the corruption or depravity of human nature in figurative forms, nor that the figures are taken from the physical plane. The same is true of the forms in which the cleansing or purification of the soul is expressed. Thus the subjective state of evil is represented as one of filthiness or uncleanness and, accordingly, the sanctification is represented as a cleansing or washing or purifying (Ps. 51:2, 7; Ezek. 36:25; 1 Cor. 6:11; 2 Cor. 7:1). But for any true conception of either the corruption or the cleansing we must look through the physical imagery and seek to grasp in thought the spiritual realities it represents. Here, however,

---

10. Miley acknowledges that full holiness is not restored in regeneration, but he does not know what to make of this. He gropes for some clear concept of the depravity remaining in the believer, but he never finds it. He does not see the distinction between acquired depravity and inherited sin; nor that the purification of regeneration aims primarily at acquired depravity, not the inherited sin. If he had seen this distinction, he could have said clearly that entire sanctification is needed because the purification of regeneration does not reach inbred sin. Carnality remains to be faced by the regenerate believer, and to be dealt with specifically in God's work of entire sanctification. *Editor.*

is the very point of difficulty—the difficulty of grasping in clear thought the spiritual things that lie back of these physical representations.

If depravity existed in the soul in the form of a substance, as poison exists in a living body, or alien elements in water, or alloy in gold, not only the notion of its nature but also the notion of sanctification, and whether in part or in whole, would be simple. Remove all the poison from the living body, all alien elements from the water, all alloy from the gold, and in each case the purification is complete. In such a sense the removal of all remnants of depravity would be entire sanctification. But the view is purely physical, and hence can afford no clearness of conception. It is too Manichaean for any truly Christian theology.

DEPRAVITY NOT A SUBSTANCE

Depravity is a moral state of the soul, not a substance within it. These facts should not be overlooked in the treatment of entire sanctification. They clearly show that, whatever the certainty of its possibility, or even of its actuality, the nature of it cannot be directly apprehended in thought. The repetitious use of the figurative terms respecting remnants, and roots, and alloys, and sediments cannot exactly define the incompleteness of regeneration; nor can such use of the physical terms of washing and eradication exactly define the purely spiritual work of entire sanctification. It is useless to assume an unattainable clearness of view on these questions; and the proper recognition of such obscurity as we have pointed out might save us from unseemly pretensions, not only to a perfect conception of the inner nature of sanctification but also to an actual presentation of it with perfect clearness both in itself and in its distinction from regeneration. . . .

A MORAL STATE

However, as the truth of native depravity is not conditioned on a capacity in us fully to apprehend it, or clearly to interpret it in thought, so the truth of a remnant of depravity after regeneration is not so conditioned. In each case the inner state may be known through its activities, as manifest in our consciousness. There is another mode of information. By the observation of others, as to their tempers, words, and acts, we gain an insight into their inner nature, and may thus know its characteristic tendencies, whether to the good or the evil. In such manner we may have the proof of a remnant of depravity, whatever its own obscurity for thought. Hence there is no mystery in the distinctive doctrine of entire sanctification that should discredit its reality, just as there is no mystery of regeneration that should discredit the reality of a large measure of sanctification therein.

On the broadest distinction, there is for us the possibility of two lives—two alternatively: one in the flesh; the other in the Spirit. The latter is possible only through the presence of the Spirit as a renewing and purifying power in the soul; the former, inevitable in His absence. This does not mean that the subjective state of all in each class is precisely the same. If we judge the inner state of the unregenerate simply by the outer life, we shall be constrained to admit wide differences therein, or at least the presence of moral forces that in many instances greatly restrain the natural tendencies of such a state. The real truth is that, with the reality of a common native depravity, there are degrees of moral perversity. So if we judge the inner state of the regenerate by the outer life, we must admit the truth of differences therein; that the spiritual life is far deeper in some than in others. There may be such a work of the Spirit within the soul as shall give completeness to the inner spiritual life; but such completeness is rarely the work of regeneration. This is the view that underlies the distinctive doctrine of sanctification.

TWO LIVES ALTERNATIVELY POSSIBLE

If direct proof of an incompleteness of regeneration, such as constitutes a necessity for the distinct work of sanctification, be demanded, what shall we offer? We can hardly pretend to any direct or formal Scripture statement of such a fact.[11] There are very definite statements respecting both the necessity and nature of justification, also respecting the necessity and nature of regeneration. On that latter question we may instance the words of our Lord (John 3:3-5). Here the necessity for regeneration is definitely stated as lying in an inherited depravity of nature; but in all the Scriptures is there any such statement respecting a necessity for sanctification as lying in an incompleteness of regeneration? Certainly the truth of this statement cannot be questioned. What then? Is it a truth that is adverse to the doctrine of sanctification? No, not to the real truth of the doctrine; though it may be adverse to some unwise teaching respecting it. . . .

PROOF OF INCOMPLETENESS

We might adduce the consciousness of the newly regenerate, or even of the regenerate generally, in proof of an incompleteness of

11. Would not our Lord's prayer for the sanctification of regenerate disciples be sufficient evidence of the incompleteness of regeneration? The fact is implied also in Acts 15:9; 20:32; Rom. 5:2 (NASB); 12:1-2; 1 Cor. 3:1-3; 2 Cor. 7:1; Eph. 3:16-19; 5:18, 25, et al. *Editor.*

CONSCIOUSNESS OF INCOMPLETENESS

regeneration. Mostly, such have inner conflicts that accord with such incompleteness and that would be out of accord with a state of entire sanctification. But we have already considered the question whether the Christian consciousness is a source of theology, and found it not to be such; hence we cannot admit it to a place of authority in the case. The Christian consciousness has its value for theology, not, however, as its source, but as confirmatory of its doctrines. It is confirmatory of any doctrine of the Scriptures with which it is in strict accord. But the Scriptures themselves must furnish the doctrine before the accordance can be known or the affirmation be of any doctrinal value. This is a principle that is not always properly observed. We mean no doctrinal dissent from Mr. Wesley if we say that in some instances, as recorded in his *Plain Account of Christian Perfection,* he gave too much doctrinal weight to individual professions of experience. That he so did is manifest in modifications of his own view.

But, while the Scriptures are without any explicit or formal utterance of an incompleteness of regeneration, yet the idea is clearly present in many forms of words respecting the new regenerate life, or even the regenerate life generally; so that the doctrine of such incompleteness may fairly claim for itself a sure basis in the Scriptures. Now, with the doctrine so found in the Scriptures, we may vividly adduce the facts of Christian experience in its affirmation. There is widely in the consciousness of the regenerate a sense of incompleteness in their spiritual life; a sense of the lack of that fullness which is the happy experience of some Christians and which must be the common privilege of believers. The doctrine thus grounded in the Scriptures and affirmed by the common Christian consciousness may easily command the common Christian faith and be accepted as a doctrine of the weightiest practical concern. So far the elements of the doctrine of sanctification are clear and sure.

THE IMPLICIT TRUTH

However, it should not be thought strange that some question the truth of this doctrine, or even oppose it. On the face of the Scriptures not a few things are seemingly against it. Other facts aside, we would most naturally think of regeneration as a complete work of subjective purification. As we are born of the Spirit, so do we receive the impress of His own likeness. "That which is born of the flesh is flesh"—in the sense of depravity; and "that which is born of the Spirit is spirit"—in the sense of holiness (John 3:6). If the likeness is complete in the former case, why not in the latter? "Who can bring a clean thing out of an unclean?" "What is man, that he should be clean? and he which is born of a woman, that he should be righteous?" (Job 14:4; 15:14). We thus prove the native depravity of the race. Conversely, then, why should any uncleanness remain in the soul when it is born of the Holy Spirit? Further, it is clearly true that not a few texts adduced in proof of entire sanctification in some instances express simply the regenerate state; and if they mean a complete work in the one case, why should they mean an incomplete work in the other? Much might be added in the same line.

However, the aim of these remarks is not to support this view, and thus to overthrow what we have before maintained, but rather to show a reason for charity toward such as do not accept it. They can hardly question the possibility of more or less degeneration in the regenerate life, and in such case must admit the need of its renewal. And if, with the completeness of regeneration, they hold, not only the possibility of such degeneration and the need of such renewal but also the common privilege and duty of a wholly sanctified and consecrated life, they hold what is most vital in the doctrine of sanctification, and should be regarded as its friends, not as its enemies.[12]

2. *Completion in Sanctification.* The one distinction of entire sanctification, as compared with regeneration, lies in its completeness. The work of the Holy Spirit, as graciously wrought in the soul, is the same in kind in both. This fact opens the way to a clearer view of entire sanctification. As regeneration is, in the full extent of it, a purification of the nature, or an invigoration of the moral and religious powers, or both, so entire sanctification is a completion of the gracious work.

So far as we may grasp in thought the work of regeneration, we may also grasp that of entire sanctification. As before stated, we have no direct insight into the nature of depravity; but its characteristic tendencies or forms of activity are open to our observation; and so far as such facts are an expression of that nature, we come to know what it is. Much of the natural history of man rests upon such ground. The same is true respecting the natural history of the animal orders. Through the observation of their habits of life we reach a clear notion of the tendencies of their nature. We thus know the ferocity of the

---

12. A more authentic Wesleyan position is that the second work is needed, not because the regenerate believer has begun to backslide, but because he is still beset by the original infestation of carnality. *Editor.*

tiger and the gentleness of the lamb. In like manner we know the subjective state of depravity in man; and so far we may know what must be the work of the Holy Spirit in his purification. Further, while we cannot accompany the Spirit as direct witness of His work within the soul, we may know its nature in the gracious fruits that immediately spring from it, as we observe them in the new life of its subjects. Indeed, we have a far deeper source of knowledge, even that of a conscious experience of the change thus wrought—a change so thorough that old things pass away and all things become new (2 Cor. 5:17). . . . Among men there are innumerable examples of the transforming power of regeneration; indeed, innumerable witnesses of its actual experience.

The facts thus presented are equally applicable to the work of entire sanctification. If somewhat of depravity remains in the regenerate, or there be any lack of thoroughness in the invigoration of the moral and religious powers, there is need of a deeper work, that both the cleansing and invigoration may be complete. The need is the same in kind as in the case of regeneration, and the work of the Holy Spirit the same. As in a very large measure the work is wrought in regeneration, so is it completed in entire sanctification. The clearer spiritual discernment, the easier victory over temptation, the greater strength unto duty, the intenser love, and the closer communion with God, answer to that completion. There are many examples of such a complete work, many witnesses to its attainment.

THE CASE OF ENTIRE SANCTIFICATION

Is the inner work of entire sanctification in the mode of repression or in that of eradication? Such a question is an issue among the friends of the doctrine. Any thorough solution of it would require an insight into the metaphysical nature of depravity, and also into the metaphysical nature of regeneration, which we do not possess and unto which we cannot attain.

MODE OF THE INNER WORK

Bishop Foster clearly holds the view of repression;[13] also Beet.[14] Dr. Whedon is in full agreement with them: "'Washed their robes'—purified their characters. This is a very vivid image of sanctification through the atonement. It illustrates how deep the doctrine of the atonement maintained in the Apoca-

THEORY OF REPRESSION

---

13. *Christian Purity*, 74. (A misapprehension of Foster. *Editor.*)

14. *Holiness as Understood by the Writers of the Bible*, 69.

lypse. But we must look through the intense imagery at the literal fact, and not allow our imagination to be lost in the imagery. There is no literal robe, no literal washing of the robe in blood. What is true is that Christ died for our sins, and through the merit of His atonement the Holy Spirit is bestowed on us, giving us power to resist temptation, to repress our disordered affections, and bring all into obedience to the law of Christ. And that is sanctification."[15] In this characterization of the inner work of sanctification there is no word that means eradication, but there are words that mean repression or subjugation.[16]

On the other hand, Dr. Lowrey maintains the side of eradication. His view is set forth in a criticism of the passage above cited from Dr.

THEORY OF ERADICATION

Whedon: "The first part of the note is a proper caution. But the doctrine of repression brought out in the second part, as definitive of sanctification, we must pronounce extremely erroneous. And to the positive assertion, '*And that is sanctification,*' we have only to say, *And that is not sanctification.* Is power to resist temptation and repress disordered affections all that grace does for us? Then every uncoverted man is sanctified, for he has natural power 'to resist temptation and repress disordered affections.' All codes of criminal laws are founded upon the assumption that every man has such power. And repressive obedience to the law of Christ, in the sense here mentioned, is possible to the natural man. Grace, then, does nothing more for us than resolution and good habits can do. The Greek here, and similar original

15. *Commentary,* Rev. 7:14.

16. Miley's handling of the question, "Is the inner work of entire sanctification in the mode of repression or in that of eradication?" falls short of a full Wesleyan position. He rejects the concept of eradication because he understands it to mean the removal of all "capacity" for "disordered affections." This is a common charge of non-Wesleyans, but we hardly expect such misapprehension from a Wesleyan scholar. No reputable Wesleyan, in the use of the term *eradication,* has ever implied the elimination of one's capacity for sin—in any form.

But the Wesleyan view of the eradication of inbred sin is consistent with the position Miley has already taken, that regeneration and sanctification may both be defined as subjective purification from depravity. Purification, if truly subjective (in the way Miley uses the term), can mean nothing less than elimination of depravity.

But Miley crosses fences by saying that sanctification is "entire when through His [the Holy Spirit's] presence and power the evil tendencies are subdued and the dominance of the spiritual life is complete." The purifying has now become subduing. This is a radical shift, though apparently Miley is not aware of it. Later he returns to the purification term when he says that the issue of entire sanctification is "not the maturity of the Christian life, but the purification of the nature" (369). *Editor.*

words elsewhere, teach that grace penetrates into the texture of our spiritual being, and destroys 'disordered' affections by, as Dr. Chalmers says, 'the expulsive power of a new affection.'"[17]

If the words of Dr. Whedon mean no more than appears in this criticism, he certainly falls far short of the truth of sanctification. But they may fairly mean much more; and it seems to us that he really meant much more in their use. Much of the same criticism might be made, and even more aptly, upon the state of regeneration, as usually maintained. In the doctrine of sanctification, in its truest Wesleyan form, there is conceded to the regenerate a power of repression or subjugation over the remnants of depravity. No other position is more fully maintained by Mr. Wesley himself. But surely this does not level the regenerate state to that of the unregenerate. In the one there is spiritual life; in the other, spiritual death. Further, the repression of subjugation may be so thorough in sanctification that the disorderly affections shall become orderly, or passively yield to the dominance of the higher spiritual life.

The theory of repression certainly does not mean the freedom and full vigor of evil forces that constantly war against the soul. The notable formula of Dr. Chalmers, "the expulsive power of a new affection," is entirely consistent with the theory of repression; indeed more consistent than with that of eradication. The new affection is not from the creation of a new power, but from the development of a capacity all the while latent in the mind; so the expulsion of a prior affection is not an eradication of the power it manifests, but a suppression of its activity. "There is no fear in love; but perfect love casteth out fear" (1 John 4:18). Here is the same principle.

But how does love cast out fear? Certainly not by an eradication of the capacity of fear, but by a suppression of its activity. This is the only mode in which love can cast out fear, or one affection expel another. Every possible affection must have its capacity in our nature. Hence, if in sanctification there is not only a suppression of all disordered affections but also an eradication of all capacity for them, there can be no possible lapse from that state. But nothing could be more contrary than this result to the truly Wesleyan doctrine of sanctification. In a discussion of his own proposition, "sanctification is not the destruction of the passions," Dr. Lowrey seems to us in full accord

17. *Possibilities of Grace*, 55.

with the view of repression, and against that of eradication.[18]

The reality of sanctification concerns us far more deeply than any question respecting the mode of the work within the soul. Sanctification, whether in part or in whole, is in the measure of the incoming and power of the Holy Spirit. It is entire when through His presence and power the evil tendencies are subdued and the dominance of the spiritual life is complete. We know nothing more of the mode of this inner work than we know of the mode of the Spirit in the work of regeneration. It may be a more thorough subjugation of the sensuous and secular tendencies, or in a higher purification and invigoration of the moral and religious power, or in a fuller presence and power of the Holy Spirit, or in all; but whether in one or another, or in all, the sanctification is entire when the spiritual life attains complete dominance. There is the same need of this special work in any incompleteness, whether from a lack of fullness in regeneration, or from deterioration after regeneration, or after entire sanctification. . . .

THE CHIEF QUESTIONS

4. *The Second-Blessing View.* The doctrinal view of the second blessing, as definitely held, consists of two parts, one of which has already been stated, but which may here be restated in connection with the other. The doctrine will thus be presented the more clearly.

Underlying the definite second-blessing view is the doctrine of a common incompleteness of the work of regeneration. Herein the soul is renewed, but not wholly; purified, but not thoroughly. Somewhat of depravity remains that wars against the new spiritual life; not strong enough to bring that life into bondage to itself, yet strong enough to impose a burden upon the work of its maintenance. Such is the first part.

THE NEW EXPERIENCE

The doctrine in the second part is that the regenerate shall come to the consciousness of this incompleteness, and to a deep sense of the need of a fullness of the spiritual life; that these experiences shall be analogous to those that preceded the attainment of regeneration, and be just as deep and thorough. The fullness of sanctification shall be instantly attained on the condition of faith, just as justification is attained; and there shall be a

---

18. Ibid., 219-20. To confuse "destruction of the passions" with eradication of the carnal mind is a further illustration of Miley's incredible misapprehension of the term *eradication*'s true import. *Editor.*

new experience of a great and gracious change, and just as consciously such as the experience in regeneration.

That Mr. Wesley held and taught such views there can be no doubt; though we think it would be a wrong to him to say that he allowed no instances of entire sanctification except in this definite mode. We see no perplexity for faith in the possibility of such an instant subjective purification. Through the divine agency the soul may be as quickly cleansed as the leper, as quickly purified in whole as in part. We admit an instant partial sanctification in regeneration, and therefore may admit the possibility of an instant entire sanctification.

THE VIEW OF WESLEY

Such a view of sanctification does not mean that there need be no preparation for its attainment. The necessity of such a preparation is uniformly held, even by such as hold strongly the second-blessing view. The idea of such a preparation is inseparable from the process of experience through which, according to this view, the regenerate must pass in order to the attainment of entire sanctification.[19]

PROCESS OF PREPARATION

However, this process of preparation need not be chronologically long. No assumption of such a necessity could be true to the soteriology of the Scriptures. Let it be recalled that the question here is, not the maturity of the Christian life, but the purification of the nature. For the attainment of the former there must be growth, and growth requires time. But, while the subjective purification may be progressively wrought, it is not subject to the law of growth; and it is so thoroughly and solely the work of God that it may be quickly wrought. Neither is there any necessity that the mental process of preparation shall be chronologically a long one. Here, as in many other spheres, the mental movement may be very rapid. It is often so in conversion. In many instances the whole mental process has been crowded into an hour, or even less time. Even heathen have been saved, born of the Spirit through faith in Christ, under the first sermon they ever heard. But there is as really a necessary process of preparation for regeneration as for entire sanctification; and such preparation need require no more time in the latter case than in the former.

NEED NOT BE A LONG ONE

That a subjective purification may be attained according to the definite second-blessing view does not limit the possibility to this

---

19. Peck, *The Central Idea of Christianity,* Chap. 5; Lowrey, *Possibilities of Grace,* 137-58, 287-330.

single mode. There is no ground in Scripture for such a limitation. Indeed, the attainableness of sanctification according to this definitely wrought doctrine, as above stated, is a truth that lies in the soteriology of the Scriptures as a whole, and not in any definite teaching on the question. While they are full of the idea of entire sanctification, they are quite empty of any such teaching respecting the mode of its attainment. Hence any insistence upon such a mode as the only possible mode of sanctification must be without definite warrant of Scripture. Further, we think it a serious objection to this view, as thus rigidly held, that it cannot consistently allow any preaching of holiness, or any seeking after it, or any expectation of its attainment, except in this definite mode.

Mr. Wesley held strongly the view of an instant subjective sanctification; and we fully agree with him, not only in its possibility but also in its frequent actuality; but his own illustration of his doctrine points to a possible attainment in a gradual mode. It is given in his answer to the question: "Is this death to sin, and renewal in love, gradual or instantaneous?" His answer is: "A man may be dying for some time, yet he does not, properly speaking, die till the instant the soul is separated from the body, and in that instant he lives the life of eternity. In like manner, he may be dying to sin for some time; yet he is not dead to sin till sin is separated from the soul; and in that instant he lives the full life of love."[20] The instant consummation here emphasized does not exclude the gradual approach to it; so that, according to this illustration, there may be a gradual dying unto sin until the death is complete; a gradual subjective purification until completeness is attained. Such a view is in the fullest accord with the soteriology of the Scriptures.

PREACHING

The privilege of entire sanctification is at once so thoroughly scriptural and Wesleyan that from it there is among us only the rarest dissent. Yet not a few hesitate respecting the sharply defined second-blessing view. We do not share this hesitation, so far as the view represents a possible mode of entire sanctification; though we object to any insistence that such is the only possible mode. Right here is the occasion of unfortunate differences among us. However, much of the evil consequence might easily be avoided . . . through a spirit of mutual forbearance. Let those who hold rigidly the second-blessing view preach sanctification in their own way, but let

---

20. *Plain Account of Christian Perfection,* 80.

them be tolerant of such as preach it in a manner somewhat different; and let such as hesitate respecting that special view be tolerant of those for whom it possesses great interest. All ministers who believe in the privilege of a full salvation can preach it in good faith. Indeed, they are not at liberty to omit this preaching.

Who shall say that the only permissible or profitable preaching of sanctification is that which prescribes an exact mode of its attainment? The doctrine itself, and not any rigid form into which we may cast it, is the real interest; the privilege itself, the great privilege; the actual attainment, the highest aim. And if with one consent, even if without regard to definite modes, we should earnestly preach a full salvation; preach it as a common privilege and duty; preach it as the true aim of every Christian life, surely there would be large gain in a wider spiritual edification, while many would enter into "the fullness of the blessing of the gospel of Christ."

The Life of Holiness[21]

The following excerpts from section III begin with a quotation from Bishop McCabe. In these readings Miley argues for a holiness that is at once complete and at the same time growing; and that such holiness is the common privilege of all believers.

CLEANSING

We add another passage, one with little detail, but intensely forceful in the presentation of the central realities of a life in Christian holiness: "By holiness I mean that state of the soul in which all its alienation from God and all its aversion to a holy life are removed. In this state sin is odious. The more holy any soul, any being is, the more odious sin becomes. To a good man sin is odious; to a holy man it is more odious; to an angel it is far more so still; but to God sin must be inconceivably odious. And therefore it is said that the heavens are not clean in His sight, and that He charged His angels with folly—so insignificant is their holiness when contrasted with the holiness of God. Holiness admits of an infinite number of degrees; and there is set before us an eternal progression in holiness. But that degree of it, or that state of the soul in which temptations to sin leave no damaging moral influence, no tarnish of

21. From sec. III, "The Life of Holiness," 276-79, 382-84.

sin, no pain in the conscience, no corruption of the will, no obscurity or perversion of the spiritual vision—that state in which the all-efficacious blood of Jesus has washed away all the stains of sin, and in which the Holy Spirit constantly presides, rules, and reigns without a rival—is what we call sanctification."[22]

Further appropriate citations could do little more than repeat what has already been well stated, and therefore may be omitted. We add a few words in the form of a definitive statement: With a true and full self-consecration to God; with a trustful resting of the soul in Christ; with a single purpose and earnest endeavor to do His will; with a gracious power through the Spirit against evil and unto a good life; most of all, with the supremacy of love in the soul, the life is in Christian holiness. Such it may be from the hour of the subjective purification, or the thorough invigoration of the moral and religious powers, and while the maturity of the Christian graces is yet wanting. If holiness of life be not possible prior to such maturity, then it must be impossible through all the time necessary to that attainment. In this case holiness of life never can be reached except through a process of growth; and therefore, for a greater or less time, the life in regeneration must be a sinful life. But such is not the Wesleyan doctrine. Mr. Wesley himself maintained the possibility of a holy life in the regenerate state, and from the hour of regeneration. Surely, then, it must be possible from the hour of the subjective sanctification. . . .

THE LIFE OF HOLINESS

HOLINESS BEFORE MATURITY

2. *Grades in Graces.* The life in holiness does not mean an exact equality in the graces of all who so live. Here the element of time must cause wide differences. As these graces acquire strength through trial and reach maturity through a process of growth, so they should be stronger and maturer in those long in the life of holiness than in those who have but recently attained it. There are other laws of difference, particularly in the matter of capacity and temperament. The religious capacity is no more equal in all men than the intellectual capacity. Such being the case, there can be no one grade for all who attain unto a life in holiness. "The point to be maintained is a pure heart, an unsinning life, and a loving service progressively commensurate with our ever-increasing capacity and light. This rule will show a disparity among entirely sanctified persons. Capacity and circumstances will

---

22. McCabe, *Light on the Pathway of Holiness,* 68-70.

make the difference. This fact should caution us not to pronounce all persons unsanctified who do not measure up to the highest standard in our estimation in sanctity of life and propriety of behavior."[23]

The Christian graces of the same person must differ in perfection or strength, whatever the grade of his attainment in holiness. One may excel in one grace; another in another; but none in all. Even in sacred history different persons are examples of preeminence in different graces. Accordingly the faith of Abraham, the patience of Job, the meekness of Moses, the love of John, and the heroism of Paul are familiar ideas. Peculiarities of temperament not only account for such facts but also make them inevitable. It is not in the nature of things, nor according to the worker of divine grace, that anyone should excel in the entire circle of Christian graces.

NONE EXCEL IN ALL GRACES

3. *Law of Perfection.* In an earlier part of this discussion it was shown that a subjective sanctification is the necessary ground of the Christian graces, in all stages of their development; but it was also pointed out that the perfection or maturity of these graces is not achieved in an instant. . . . They must have time for growth; must be tested in the fields of duty and trial; must be strengthened and perfected through the proper exercise. In this manner not a few whose record is in sacred history gained the strength and fullness of their religious character. Such character could not have been gained in any other mode. A glance at the lives of the leading biblical characters will readily discover the truth of these statements. There are many such instances in Christian history.

The men of distinction in Christian character and service have ever reached the perfection of their graces through the fulfillment of trying duty. No endowment of grace ever supersedes this law of perfection. There is a wisdom, a strength, a patience, a courage, a zeal, a self-consecration in the spirit of self-sacrifice that can be won only on the field of duty and trial. Take the instance of St. Paul: with the same recipiency of grace, yet without his many trying experiences, he never could have attained to such a degree of perfection in so many Christian graces. The law thus illustrated by so many notable instances is applicable to every Christian life.

It is not essential to such a life, that it shall be without variations

---

23. Lowrey, *Possibilities of Grace,* 227.

of experience; that no shadow shall fall upon its sunshine, nor sense of sorrow mingle with its joy; that there shall be no moments of temptation or trial, hesitation or doubt. It is true that uniformity of experience is to be regarded as specially characteristic of the life in holiness; but such variations as we have indicated are, as occasional facts, entirely consistent with the truest constancy. In all and through all there may be the unmovable steadfastness of faith and the fullness of love. If it be not so, there is for us no present attainment of a full salvation; none, indeed, in the present life. Whatever the blessedness of this earthly state, it is not the heavenly state. With the fullness of salvation we are still in the body and in the common relations of life. Many infirmities and trials are inseparable from this bodily state—many burdens and sorrows unavoidable in these relations.

VARIATIONS OF EXPERIENCE

The imagination, especially when warmed by the mystical temper, may picture a state of indifference to outward things; a state in which the soul is so lost in God as to be free from all anxiety and care, and even without wish of ease from pain; a state in which sickness and death are indifferent to the calm repose, and even the peril of souls awakens no solicitude; but such a reverie is far more replete with hallucination than with the truth and reality of sanctification. Certainly it is neither Paul-like nor Christlike.

SALVATION IN REGENERATION

The doctrine of sanctification must not be so interpreted as to be made a doctrine of despair to all Christians who have not consciously attained to such an experience, particularly in the definite manner of the second-blessing theory. No such interpretation can be true, because it must deny the salvation of the truly regenerate. The truly regenerate are saved, and in the maintenance of a truly regenerate life must be finally saved. If there is any clear truth of soteriology in the Scriptures, this truth is there. Through faith in Christ they have received the double blessing of justification and regeneration. By the one they are freed from the guilt of sin, and by the other they are born into the kingdom of God and become His children (John 1:12-13; 3:36; Rom. 5:1-2; 8:1). The texts given by reference are replete with the truths just stated, as are many others that might easily be added. Indeed, such is the pervasive sense of the Scriptures. We are redeemed by Christ that we might become the sons of God (Gal. 4:4-5; 1 John 3:1). That sonship is surely attained through regeneration. "And if a son, then an heir of

God through Christ"; "And if children, then heirs; heirs of God, and joint-heirs with Christ" (Gal. 4:7; Rom. 8:17). Wesley taught this doctrine, and so did Fletcher and Watson; and so has every truly Wesleyan representative who has ever written upon the subject.

Is the maintenance of a life in the fullness of sanctification essential to final salvation? Yes, if we are under a dispensation of law; no, if we are under a dispensation of grace. But we are under grace, and not under the law. Such is the doctrine of St. Paul: "For ye are not under the law, but under grace. What then? shall we sin, because we are not under the law, but under grace? God forbid" (Rom. 6:14-15). Our privilege and duty point in the same direction and bid us strive after all the gracious attainment for which we are apprehended by Christ Jesus (Phil. 3:12). Yet with the sense of many shortcomings we may, and we must still cling to Christ and hope in Him. So must we encourage others to do so. Never may we break the bruised reed nor quench the smoking flax. The Master never does (Isa. 42:3; Matt. 12:20). . . .

5. *Sanctification a Common Privilege.* There is a divine side to this question as well as a human side. If we look only at the human, we shall more than doubt the possibility of a full salvation in the present life. In this single view we shall see nothing but the weakness and sinfulness of man. But if we look also on the divine side, we shall see the infinite efficiencies that center in the economy of redemption; efficiencies that work together for our salvation from sin. Let us say, then, that man is corrupt and sinful, and in himself not only weak but utterly helpless; but against all this let us affirm the truth that on the divine side there is a mighty Savior, an all-cleansing blood, and a divine Purifier. In these central truths of our soteriology lies the possibility of a present full salvation. If such a salvation meant a deliverance from the manifold infirmities that are inseparable from the present life, then, indeed, would it be impossible so long as we live; but such infirmities are not sins, and therefore are not inconsistent with a state of full salvation.

AVAILABLE TO ALL CHRISTIANS

Many texts mean the privilege of a life in holiness, a very few of which may here be cited. They so mean because they cannot be properly interpreted without the truth of such a privilege. "Be ye therefore perfect, even as your Father which is in heaven is perfect" (Matt. 5:48). "But as he which hath called you is holy, so be ye holy in all manner of conversation; because it is written, Be ye holy; for I am holy" (1 Pet. 1:15-16). The perfection and holiness here required must be possible in this life. "Thou shalt love the Lord thy God with all thy heart, and with all thy soul, and with all thy mind. This is the first and great commandment. And the second is like unto it, Thou shalt love thy neighbour as thyself. On these two commandments hang all the law and the prophets" (Matt. 22:37-40).

ENTIRE SANCTIFICATION

The meaning is not that such love is literally the fulfillment of every duty, but, rather, that [we are entirely pleasing to God when love in] its fullness is the ruling power of the life. With the possibility and the actuality of such love, the fulfillment of all the other duties must be possible. The life would thus be in holiness. The divine commandment of such love means its possibility. "And the very God of peace sanctify you wholly; and I pray God your whole spirit and soul and body be preserved blameless unto the coming of our Lord Jesus Christ" (1 Thess. 5:23). This prayer means the possibility of the blessings for which the supplication is made. The blessings have respect to both the nature and the life. In the first petition, "sanctify you wholly," the life may be included, but the nature cannot be omitted; and the words of the petition express their own meaning respecting its entire sanctification. The second petition relates to the life, and has the same meaning of entirety: that "your whole spirit and soul and body be preserved blameless unto the coming of our Lord Jesus Christ." A life in which this prayer is fulfilled must be a life in holiness.

THOROUGH CLEANSING

"But if we walk in the light, as he is in the light, we have fellowship one with another, and the blood of Jesus Christ his Son cleanseth us from all sin" (1 John 1:7). The saints in heaven were thus cleansed before their entrance into that holy place: "These are they which came out of great tribulation, and have washed their robes, and made them white in the blood of the Lamb" (Rev. 7:14). The prior text clearly means a cleansing in the present life; for it is while we are walking in the light, and on that condition, that it is promised. Now there can be no question about the completeness of the cleansing of the saints in heaven. The words, "washed their robes, and made them white in the blood of the Lamb," can mean nothing less. But the words, "the blood of Jesus Christ his Son cleanseth us from all sin," are no less full of the idea of completeness. There is still a great difference between the saints in heaven and the saints on earth, in that the former are freed from the manifold infirmities to which the latter are still subject; but infirmities are not sins, and, while they remain, the completeness of the cleansing is still the meaning of the words, "the blood of Jesus Christ his Son cleanseth us from all sin."

PRAYER OF ST. PAUL

The great prayer of St. Paul for the Christians of Ephesus is replete with the ideas of a full salvation in the present life. That it is a prayer involves no uncertainty of the privileges of gracious attainment that its petitions properly mean. In no doctrinal utterance was St. Paul ever more deeply inspired than in this prayer. Hence its petitions have the same doctrinal meaning respecting the privileges of gracious attainment that they could have if cast in the most definite forms of doctrinal expression. Further, these petitions mean for all Christians the same fullness of spiritual blessings that they meant for the Christians at Ephesus, for whom they were directly offered. With these preparatory statements, the prayer shall express its own deep meaning to such as devoutly meditate upon its petitions.

"For this cause I bow my knees unto the Father of our Lord Jesus Christ, of whom the whole family in heaven and earth is named, that he would grant you, according to the riches of his glory, to be strengthened with might by his Spirit in the inner man; that Christ may dwell in your hearts by faith; that ye, being rooted and grounded in love, may be able to comprehend with all saints what is the breadth, and length, and depth, and height; and to know the love of Christ, which passeth knowledge, that ye might be filled with all the fulness of God. Now unto him that is able to do exceeding abundantly above all that we ask or think, according to the power that worketh in us, unto him be glory in the church by Christ Jesus throughout all ages, world without end. Amen" (Eph. 3:14-21).

10

Randolph S. Foster

(1820-1903)

"From Jail to the Episcopal Chair" would be a dramatic title for Foster's biography. The jail, however, was his birthplace, February 22, 1820, in Williamsburg, Ohio, simply because his father was the jailer.

While no demerit attaches to his humble origin, great merit must be granted for the man's gargantuan achievements. His natural endowments were gifts of God, but his disciplined labors in study and ministry were his own. Described as "one of the greatest and most magnetic thinkers in American Methodism," he overcame the handicap of limited formal education to become the first professor of systematic theology of Drew Theological Seminary at 48 years of age. Two years later he became president.

Two years after that he was elected bishop and served in that capacity for 30 years. In 1902, at 82 years of age, he went into semiretirement. During the last few months before his death on May 1, 1903, he concentrated on a monumental 11-volume systematic theology, which he had earlier begun. The fact that he completed 6 large volumes before his death testifies to the native power of the mind, and to its remarkable preservation—even enlargement—in his old age. The theological and philosophical acumen of these volumes do credit to a scholar of any years.

His first widely influential book, *Objections to Calvinism,* was published when he was only 29. But the book having the greatest impact on the holiness movement was *Nature and Bless-*

edness of Christian Purity, 1851 (revised in 1869).[1] This work is marked by evangelistic fervor, eloquent language, clear and vivid perceptions, and a profound and sometimes startling discernment of fine but significant distinctions.

The book is a staunch exposition and defense of second blessing holiness. He maintains (1) the uniqueness of entire sanctification as a work of grace differing from and subsequent to regeneration, and (2) its availability in a moment by faith. The experience is normative for Christian life, not simply a preparation for death. He sought to correct what he interpreted as a belittling of the witness of the Spirit by the Palmerites. On the other hand he pointed out the equal error of some Methodists who erased or at least obscured the difference between regeneration and sanctification.

The Christian's Need[2]

Foster follows Wesley in insisting that believers struggle against a remaining proneness to sin, which impedes spiritual progress and compromises their testimony. When he uses the awkward wording "the merely regenerated believer," he is not downgrading regeneration but means the believer who is not yet entirely sanctified.

In stating that regeneration "is sanctification begun, but not completed," Foster exposes himself to possible misunderstanding. The relation of regeneration to sanctification became a major battleground in Methodism in the last three decades of the 19th century. In the controversy some denied any distinction between regeneration and sanctification. The opposers of this view insisted that sanctification was distinct from regeneration. Peters lists Foster as an advocate of the view that God has provided two distinct works of grace.[3]

---

1. The readings that follow are taken from the original edition of *Nature and Blessedness of Christian Purity,* containing an extensive introduction by Bishop Edmund S. Janes (New York: Carlton & Porter, 1851). In 1869 a revised and expanded edition was copyrighted by Carlton & Lanahan, published in New York by Eaton & Mains and in Cincinnati by Jennings and Pye, with the title, *Christian Purity;* or, *The Heritage of Faith.*

2. This selection is from pp. 72-75.

3. John L. Peters, *Christian Perfection and American Methodism,* 173-76.

Foster's position seems to be that while there is an initial sanctification concomitant with regeneration, and while the new life in regeneration is itself holy, with holy tendencies, regeneration by and of itself does not effect that deeper sin-cleansing needed. For this there must be a second work of grace.

With this experience the teachings of Scripture fully accord. Take a single passage, found in the apostle's letter to the Christians at Corinth: "I, brethren, could not speak unto you as unto spiritual, but as unto carnal, even *as unto babes in Christ.* . . . Ye are yet carnal: for whereas there is among you envying, and strife, and divisions, are ye not carnal?" (1 Cor. 3:1, 3). This passage is precisely in point. It exhibits, upon authority of inspiration, the doctrine above expressed. For first, it is certain that the persons here addressed were believers—justified and regenerated Christians. How else could an apostle address them as brethren; much more, how could he expressly declare them to be "*babes in Christ*"? Is it possible to be a "babe in Christ" without justifying and regenerating grace? Surely no one can think so.

BORN AGAIN YET CARNAL

These persons, then, were in Christ—they were born again. But what next? Were they entirely holy—free from sin, inward as well as outward? Certainly the apostle does not say so: on the contrary, he expressly says they were yet "carnal." He could not speak to them as completely spiritual, but as partly carnal; nay, he specifies what of carnality he found remaining among them, and impairing their spirituality or holiness: "for whereas there is among you envying, and strife, and divisions, are ye not carnal?" Are not these tokens of a sinful nature—"envying, strife"? Indulged, are they not actual sins?—are not the inward dispositions thereto, inward sins? This passage then fully corroborates our expressed views, and it fully authorizes us to say that evils, opposed to complete spirituality, remain in the hearts of persons in the possession of justifying and regenerating grace.

Let it be remembered, we are now speaking particularly of inbred sin—sins of the heart—or, if any prefer it, evils of the heart. We are aware that the believer does not indulge in outward sins—sins of the life—that he does not transgress in this sense: "For whosoever is born of God doth not commit sin" (1 John 3:9). But sin committed, and depravity felt, are very different—the one is an action, the other a state of the affections. The merely regenerated believer is saved from the one; and he has grace to enable him to have the victory over the other: but the dispo-

INNER SIN NOT OUTWARD

sition itself, to some extent, remains . . . still making resistance, and indicating actual presence, and needing to be entirely sanctified.

Regeneration is sanctification begun, but not completed. The foundation thus being laid, we are to "go on unto perfection," to "grow in grace, and in the knowledge of our Lord and Saviour Jesus Christ," "till we all come in the unity of the faith unto a perfect man, unto the measure of the stature of the fulness of Christ" (Heb. 6:1; 2 Pet. 3:18; Eph. 4:13). "Babes" at first, we are to grow until we become "men and women in the Lord." Upon this point Mr. Wesley is very explicit in his sermon, "Sin in Believers," and in various other portions of his writings. Speaking, on one occasion, of justification, he says:

"How naturally do those who experience such a change imagine that all sin is gone; that it is utterly rooted out of their hearts, and has no more place therein. How easily do they draw that inference, 'I feel no sin, therefore I have none; it does not stir, therefore it does not exist; it has no motion, therefore it has no being.' But it is seldom long before they are undeceived, finding sin was only suspended, not destroyed. Temptations return, and sin revives; showing that it was stunned before, not dead. They now feel two principles in themselves, plainly contrary to each other; 'the flesh lusting against the spirit,' nature resisting the grace of God. They cannot deny, that, although they still feel power to believe in Christ, and love God, and although His Spirit still witnesses with their spirits that they are children of God, yet they feel in themselves sometimes pride, self will; sometimes anger or unbelief. They find one or more of these frequently striving in their hearts, though not conquering. . . ."

We do not believe that more upon this point is necessary. It cannot be requisite with the mass of Christians to enter into elaborate argument to convince them, what they so painfully realize to be true, that, after conversion, inward, unsanctified tempers remain to disturb them. How often, how sadly, have they experienced its truth! How, in secret places, have they wept, and poured out their souls before God on account of it! How have they looked, and longed, and struggled for deliverance! How have they desired, and resolved, and prayed to be holy—to have their inward enemies brought forth and slain, and to have Christ, their adorable Savior, reign without a rival! Convince them that they are not sanctified! Alas! they need no conviction—they know it well, and many of them feel it deeply, painfully.

AWARENESS OF NEED

The Nature and Necessity of Consecration[4]

Bishop Foster in discussing consecration wisely distinguishes between consecration and sanctification—a distinction too easily and too frequently blurred. He also objects to the assumption that sanctification has occurred because the consecration is made. This is a probable reference to Phoebe Palmer's teachings, though strictly speaking he is opposing what would more accurately be called a misunderstanding and superficial application of her teachings. At any rate, he deplores any tendency to suppose that a clear witness of the Spirit to entire sanctification can be dispensed with or bypassed.

CONSECRATION

The purpose now being formed, the next point is entire consecration—the giving up of yourself to God—your soul, your body, your time, your talents, your influence, your all; withdrawing all from the world, and from sin, and from self, and giving all in complete sacrifice to God, to be His and His alone forever. Will you do this?

Examine yourself closely in this connection. Are you willing to devote all, entirely, forever, to the Lord? Holiness implies this; if we are not willing to consecrate, we are not willing, and hence not ready for holiness. Here again, you will need grace, to enable you to make the consecration. You cannot do it in your own strength. You will need to pray, and look to God for the assistance of the Spirit. Thus doing, bring forth everything separately—yourself, your family, your reputation, your property; and, with all sincerity, relinquish all claim, and surrender the whole to God, to use and enjoy them only as He directs, and with reference to His glory; never to withdraw again what you thus solemnly covenant away. Will you now do this? Is this your mind?

A word more upon this point: consecration is not sanctification, it is a part of it. Consecration is your work, God giving the requisite grace; when it is entire, sanctification, which is the work of the Holy Spirit, follows, always follows, immediately follows. But more particularly, what is consecration? It is entire dedication to God; in other words, complete acquiescence in His will, and reference to His glory. It does not imply that we retire from the world; that we give ourselves

---

4. This selection is from the chapter "Means for the Obtainment of Holiness," 128-30.

all the time to religious exercises; that we withhold communion with our fellow men; that we give our entire thoughts, affections, and efforts, to technically religious duties: such a thing would be impracticable in this world, would conflict with the expressed will of God, and would be itself therefore sinful. We have business to do, to provide for our households, and to enable us to do good; our thoughts may be given to this: we have families and friends, we may love them—nay, these are a part of our duty.

By consecration to God, therefore, we mean simply, as expressed above, a supreme reference to the will and glory of God, in all things: using and enjoying all, as He wills we should, disclaiming any rights that conflict with His rights; pursuing such business, and in such measure, as from our best light we believe is the will of God; using all the proceeds of our labor, precisely as we believe God directs; loving these objects, and in that degree, which He approves; doing those acts that will be for His glory; living in the world, but living for God.

Whoever does this, consecrates himself to God. He may be in the midst of men, and earnest and industrious; but if he is entire in these respects, he is only the Lord's. His sanctified life, so far as it emanates from him, will be no more than this consecration perpetuated through every minute and every day; so far as it proceeds from God, it will be a perpetual indwelling of God: of such an one it may be said, he lives not, but God liveth in him. His sole reference, as to all things, is the will of God; and with this he never allows his thoughts, affections, *will,* or actions, to conflict. Who will say this is not entire consecration? Who will say it is not duty? Who will say it is not by the grace of God possible?

In this connection there is, in our estimation, unfortunate and injurious advice sometimes given, in some such language as the following:

PREMATURE PROFESSION

"Bring your all and lay it on God's altar; believe it is accepted; and though you may have no direct witness, no special sensible change, do not doubt but it is done; the altar sanctifieth the gift; whatsoever toucheth the altar is holy"—and much more of this kind. I must believe that such instructions tend to delusion, and have been the fruitful source of many spurious, though sincere professions.

It is well, nay, it is indispensable, to make an entire surrender of all to God; and when this is done, God will acknowledge it, by sending the witness of His acceptance; but let no one, at his peril, conclude that he has made this surrender, and is consequently sanctified, without the requisite witness: he will only deceive himself, and receive no benefit. His faith, however strong, being false, will do him no good. It is the Spirit that sanctifies, and He sanctifies through faith, not in any act of ours, but faith in God; and when by faith He sanctifies, He will impart the witness. It is meet, when we have consecrated our all as well as we can, that we should trust in God; not in our act, but in God: not that He has sanctified, because we have consecrated ourselves, but that He will accept the consecration and send us the witness. Until the witness comes, we will not say we are sanctified, we will not even believe we are; we will look to be, and wait in expectation until we are, and then we will rest in God.

The Operation of Faith[5]

Foster raises the question, if faith is the sole condition of sanctification, "How and what are you to believe?" In answering he again presses home the prerequisites of desire, obedience, and consecration, without which effective faith is impossible. Furthermore, faith is what we do, not what God does. Yet he avoids the trap of presenting faith as an assumption that the work is done solely on the basis that we believe it is done. To him the distinction is crucial between saying, "I believe that it is done" (without the witness of the Spirit) and saying, "I believe He is doing it." (Cf. the much more radical position of A. M. Hills and the authorities he quotes, pp. 354-57 below.)

Have you a definite view of holiness? Do you realize your need of it? Are you willing to receive it? Is it your desire and purpose to persevere until you obtain it; and, in order thereto, do you realize a readiness to give up all to God, in entire conscration? If this should be your mind, one thing more and the work will be done; "Believe on the Lord Jesus Christ, and thou shalt be saved" (Acts 16:31).

BY FAITH

Faith, as was remarked in the outset of these advices, is the only condition upon which the blessings of the gospel are offered. "Justification" is by faith—"regeneration" is by faith—"sanctification" is by faith—"glorification" is by faith—by faith as the instrument, and by the blood of Jesus as the merit, and by the Spirit as the agent. Whenever faith is exercised, the work will be done. The pre-

5. The following is from pp. 130-34.

ceding advices are only prescribed as means of assisting—as cooperating with the grace of God to bring the mind up to the point of faith—to prepare us for this saving exercise. And let it not be supposed that a long and tedious process is necessary, in order to this preparation. With diligent application, and by divine assistance, the work may soon be accomplished.

And now we again distinctly repeat, "it is by simple faith." "Believe, and thou shalt be saved." But how and what are you to believe? If the previous advices have been complied with, this is soon and easily answered: but if not, it is vain to talk to you of faith; for, as remarked, without a proper state of mind and the affections, faith is impossible. However directly faith is wrought in the soul, and however sudden the work of sanctification, still intervening is this preparation of mind, which goes before, or if not before, along with faith. But now do you see the prize—"holiness"? Do you feel your need of it? Are you willing to receive it? More, are you desirous to obtain, and resolved not to stop short? Are you enabled to consecrate your all to God—to give up all for this blessing? Is this your feeling? Is it? Are you willing now? Then believe! The work will be done. Believe what? Believe in the Lord Jesus Christ as your Savior. Trust Him to do the work now, just as you are!

STEPS IN BELIEVING

It may be important to be still more explicit at this point. Faith includes the ideas both of "belief and trust," and exists in various stages.

1. A general belief in Christ, as the Savior and Sanctifier.
2. Belief that He is able to sanctify us.
3. Belief that He is willing to do it.
4. Belief that He is able and willing to do it now, not tomorrow.
5. Belief that He has promised to do the work, and that His promise will not fail.
6. Belief that if I now have faith, He will now, this moment, do it.
7. Reliance, or trust in Him now, this moment, to do, accompanied with a belief that He doeth it. Mark, that He now, when I believe according to His promise, doeth it; not a belief that it is done, but, accompanying my faith, it being a sound faith, that He doeth the work.

These, as we believe, are the almost invariable stages, or progressive steps of faith; the mind is thus led along, by easy and regular process, to that reliance—to that taking God at His word, which brings the promised blessing. These various and successive grades of faith may not indeed sensibly take place in the soul; the mind may not detect their existence as elements; but they are, nevertheless, included in the faith that sanctifies.

An error has gained considerable prevalence, and has wrought not a little evil, in relation to this very subject—the faith that brings the sanctifying grace.

It has been indiscreetly said, "We are to believe the work is done, and it will be done." Persons seeking the blessing have been told that they must believe they are sanctified, and they will be sanctified. What a misfortune that so great, so dangerous an error should be taught, in connection with so important a subject! What a manifest absurdity! Making our sanctification to depend upon the belief of an untruth; namely, a belief that it is now wrought, in order that it may be wrought! This is a great delusion. It is not the doctrine of the Bible. It is not, and never was, the doctrine of our church. Some sincere and honest Christians have fallen into this delusion without perceiving its absurdity; and it has gained considerable currency. I trust it will no more find place in the language of the friends of this glorious doctrine. . . .

Let it be remembered that when this exercise of faith takes place, it is not a mere intellectual calculation; it occurs when the soul is travailing for sanctifying power—when it is groaning for deliverance from distressing sinfulness—when it is giving up all to Christ—when it is feeling that "it is worse than death its God to love, and not its God alone"—when it is purposing to claim and obtain holiness, at all hazards. That is the state of the soul: it is now agonizing at God's altar; it is pleading for salvation—looking at the promises; the Holy Spirit is helping, imparting illumination, and strengthening the faltering faith.

Now comes the moment when sanctification is about to be imparted. Now the soul believes it will be done, just now; taking firmer hold of the promises, and looking steadfastly upon the atoning sacrifice—now the intercessor, it believes it is being done; the refining fire touches it, as the coal Isaiah's lips, it yields, it trusts—the work is done; and now the soul, sanctified, believes it is done. The belief that it will be done—that it is being done—is the trust that brings the blessing. The belief that it is done follows after. They are each distinct, though all may occur in the interval of a minute.

One passage of Scripture is sometimes quoted in this connection, which, because of its obvious bearing on the point, ought to be noticed here: "What things soever ye desire, when ye pray, believe that ye receive them, and ye shall have them" (Mark 11:24). The doctrine sometimes supposed to be taught in this passage is precisely that which we have just now condemned as absurd and dangerous. Whatever is its teaching, this it cannot be.

Several commentators have avoided saying anything upon it; among those who have spoken, Mr. Watson's views seem to me most correct. He says, "An ill use has sometimes been made of this passage; as though it meant, that when praying, whatever we believe, that is, persuade ourselves that we receive, we do receive—an absurdity and self contradiction. Here, however, to believe does not signify to persuade ourselves into an opinion, but to trust, or to have faith in God. This trust must necessarily be regulated by God's own *promise* and *warrant*, and it is exercised in order that we may receive.

"The sense therefore is, believe—trust—that ye shall receive them, and ye shall obtain them; that is, all things which God hath expressly promised, and which are, as St. John states, 'according to his will.'" This view of Mr. Watson we believe to be the sober and true view of the passage. It is no more than an encouragement to unwavering confidence and trust in God, which is the best definition of faith. It leads us, when we desire anything that God has promised, to ask Him, without doubting that He will fulfill His own word; meantime, just as confidently expecting to obtain what we ask, as though we already had it in possession.

How Holiness May Be Retained[6]

Bishop Foster reveals a very keen, almost anxious awareness of the tenuous nature of heart holiness. Rather than supposing entire sanctification to be an impervious fixation of the heart—a sort of establishment of holiness in inner concrete—he sees the constant peril of the daily liability to sin. Yet he insists that sinning is not necessary, and shows plainly the way to go forward not only in victory but in progress and growth.

It is not sufficient that we know how to obtain; it is not sufficient that *we have obtained;* we must know, also, how to keep when we have made the acquisition. The secret of its preservation is not less important than the secret of its possession.

6. The full chapter is titled "Holiness—How Retained and Regained," 162-70.

A greater mistake could not be committed, than to suppose that religion, when gained in any of its degrees, will be retained without effort—remain with us, as a thing of course, without care. Character is eminently . . . liable to change; and to be perpetuated in one form, requires nurture and vigilance. Surrounded, as all of us necessarily are in this state, with countercurrents of influence, all acting upon us ceaselessly, with greater or less force, and, in their degree, having a tendency to leave their impression—to impart their tone and coloring, nothing can be more obvious than the absolute importance of constant attention and activity.

These influences need not, indeed, act upon us fatally, but they will act upon us certainly, unless restrained—resisted. A man enters upon the day with unsullied honor; he is tempted; he yields; his honor is in the dust. A Christian goes forth to duty, with a conscience void of offense—with a heart pure: evil presents itself; he is overcome; his purity is marred; his conscience violated. Not a day passes in which there are not some such liabilities. What, under these circumstances, we now particularly inquire, must be done, in order that a sanctified soul may preserve its state and character; that it may be in the evening what it was in the morning; this week, what it was last; this year, what it was the former year? A more interesting practical inquiry could scarcely be started. We will endeavor briefly to answer it.

And we should never, when contemplating the subject of actual salvation, lose sight of the fact that we are coworkers with God; He works, and we work with Him. It is so in the incipient motions, it is so throughout; so in the beginning, so in the progress; so in attaining, and so in maintaining our state. This is so plain as to need no illustration. But the question recurs—What must we do?

COWORKERS WITH GOD

1. We answer, first: we must acquire the habit of constant watching against sin. The tempter is a vigilant and insidious foe, ever on the alert, ever cunning, and full of artifice. We need to be as wakeful and vigilant. There is no place where he may not approach us, no place so sacred that he will not dare to intrude himself. Even in the privacy of the closet, at the communion, in the sanctuary, when alone, when in society, when musing, when conversing, when preaching, when praying, when praising, when engaged in business, when seeking pleasure, when employed, when idle; he ever lurks near us and seeks our ruin.

He often disguises his true character; sometimes appearing to us as an angel of light, using the honeyed tones of friendship, professing love, assuming a meek and suppliant air, consulting our good, wearing the mien of disinterestedness, extremely conscientious, employing plausible agents, not unfrequently using our friends, recommending courses not decidedly sinful, proposing compromises, flattering, that we may become vain, persuading, that we may conciliate, raging, that we may yield, and with a thousand other modes, seeking either to surprise, conciliate, or overwhelm us.

Our only safety is in watching against him; guarding, with sleepless vigilance, the sacred precincts of the soul, that, if he enter, he be not entertained; nay, that he be refused an entrance—repulsed at the portal. This will require watching over our thoughts, that they be not idle, empty, vain, improper—on improper subjects, at improper times, in improper measure; over our motives, that they be not sinful, carnal, selfish, worldly; over our affections, that they do not wander, fix on wrong objects, exist in an inordinate degree, seek sinful indulgence or gratification.

GUARDING OUR THOUGHTS

Let it not be supposed that this would engross one's entire time—that it is requiring too much. By the grace of God, and the *instincts,* if I may employ the term, of a sanctified soul—by which I mean no more than its ready, almost spontaneous effort—it may be done, and done with ease. This is not our rest: and if holiness be worth possessing, it is worthy of the effort requisite to its attainment and preservation; and such effort is neither impracticable, in any state of circumstances, nor excessive.

2. Would you maintain a sanctified state? Then must there be on your part an absolute refusal to comply with temptation, under any circumstances, to *any degree.* The slightest compliance is death. We would impress this deeply upon your minds. It is a very different thing from the watchfulness advised above. A sentinel may be very watchful, but not faithful: he may see the enemy, but not sound the alarm; nay, may make terms with him. You are not only to watch the approach of sin, but absolutely and totally to resist it!

RESIST TEMPTATION

It matters nothing though the temptation be powerful, though the indulgence be venial, you may not yield. You may not parley if the case is unequivocal. You may not go one step even toward apologizing for rudely repelling the unworthy seducer. Treat him with no tenderness when you repulse him; show no pity. Civility encourages him, and kindness begets intimacy. Let the purpose be firmly inflexible, whatever may be the hazard, that you will not go one step—not even look with a desire, toward the path of the transgressor; "avoid it, pass not by it, turn from it and pass away." This is your only safety, if you would maintain your relation to God—the state of your own soul.

If you . . . compromise, if you cannot consent to exercise such firmness of purpose, you need not calculate upon success; it is out of the question. It may require strength. You will have it. As your day is, so your grace will be. God will not leave you to struggle alone. If you use what you have, you shall never lack for whatever more may be needful. Remember this. And be not dismayed though your foes gather upon you like the tempest; though their name be legion; though you seem to be helpless in their hands. Trust in God, be of good courage: greater is He that is for you, than all they that are against you.

EMPLOY ALL MEANS OF GRACE

3. Live in the use of all the ordinary and instituted means of grace. Some who, perhaps, were truly sanctified, have committed a deplorable and fatal error upon this point. Finding themselves greatly sustained and strengthened, they have vainly imagined that they need no longer employ the means. Some have been heard to say, that they found no further occasion for prayer, and other helps, that were indispensable in a merely justified state. However sincere such may have been in the beginning of their experience, they have evidently reached a dreadful state of delusion and fanaticism.

The means of grace, as instituted of God, are undoubtedly essential to spiritual sustenance when they are practicable—that is, when within reach. For, to neglect them is a contempt of God's provision, which must induce His displeasure; and it is a direct violation of His plan, which includes the use of means as a duty. No one has a right to make the experiment; and whoever does will certainly fall into condemnation.

Our own inference would be precisely contrary to the one we have just referred to. While a Christian, in proportion as he is advanced, may discern more clearly the nature of means, and so trust less in them, and more in the great agency they secure, he will, at the same time, be more regular and punctual in their use, honoring them as a divine appointment and deriving profit from them, as aids to communion and growth. We may name as important—

Prayer

We must use all forms of prayer as occasion may require; but particularly closet prayer, which is only another name for inward looking to God, generally performed in secret places. This, with a sanctified soul, will become a habit, a mode; its breath will be prayer, its looking will be to God! This will be a constant, though it may be, and doubtless will be to some extent, an unconscious exercise, or rather a spontaneous state.

Meditation

To preserve this state much meditation and inward looking is useful—the turning of the eye of the soul upon itself and toward its experience. Seasons of serious thoughtfulness of this kind are indispensable to spiritual growth, or even to the continuance of spiritual life. In such retired seasons, the soul takes its reckoning, resolves upon its course, and strengthens its resolution for future contests. We are not, indeed, to go out of the world; not to tear away from business; not to abandon our post: but while we are surrounded with the storm and strife of life, we must often withdraw within ourselves, and ask our souls, what is the interior condition? keep not our attention outside long enough to let disorder obtain within.

Searching the Holy Scriptures

This we will do with a humble, honest, teachable spirit; indeed, if we are sanctified, we will possess no other. This we believe an important means, in proportion as it may be practicable. It will supply the soul with armor, enlarge her powers, provide her for resistance and progress, and strengthen all the elements of her life.

The Sacrament

Perhaps no means will be attended with so great comfort, so much profit as the Holy Communion. Let it therefore never be neglected, and never idly or inconsiderately attended to, but with due preparation, and much prayer, and humiliation, and thanksgiving.

Christian Communion

Conversation and fellowship with those who enjoy, or are seeking, a high spiritual state is of great value. It encourages, strengthens, and corrects. Reading religious biography is of this kind. It is communion with the holy dead, as conversation with the living is communion with them. Holy men of old "spake often one to another, and the Lord hearkened and heard them"; so let us do, and the Lord will hear us also, and when He hears, will bless.

MAINTAINED CONSECRATION

4. Consecutive, or rather perpetual consecration. This to some may seem to be included in the resolute resistance of every approach of sin, and maintenance of the soul in her integrity. However this may be, it does not do away

with the need of the remark we wish to make under this head. Entire consecration, as a means to the attainment of sanctification, has been explained in another connection. What we wish now to say is that it is a means, and an indispensable one, of its preservation. Sanctification cannot exist a moment in its absence. Hence, let it be remembered that the consecration that precedes this state is likewise to continue in the same degree after it is gained, for its perpetuation. It is a constant, uninterrupted, and unending consecration; a point carried on into a full line.

Let it not be inferred that these advices imply so much effort as to be impracticable. It is not so: it requires comparatively no effort for an honest man always to be honest; a benevolent man always to be benevolent. He is so unconsciously. It is so, with respect to this grace, in a measure. The principle implanted will operate with ease; all that we have to do is to be watchful, not so much to keep it active as to prevent its violent interruption. An unconverted sinner thinks it a very hard thing to be even a tolerable Christian; the Christian does not find it so. He meets with some places of difficulty, much of the time he gets along without conscious effort; yet he must use means all the time. It is so with the higher grace of holiness. The absolute necessity that certain means be in constant use does not imply a distressing effort. A man must use means to live, and use them constantly: but he need not always be in distressing effort; he employs them without such labor. It is so with regard to everything pertaining to character; means are in perpetual use.

A LIFE OF FAITH

5. The life of holiness is eminently a life of faith. We have before said it is attained by faith: we now say it cannot continue a moment without faith; faith is its very root and sap. The same faith that at first introduced the principle, preserves it. But we are not therefore to suppose the soul must always be in painful endeavor. Faith in the heart of a Christian operates when he does not think of it, produces fruits without his consciousness. It is obvious that holiness can only coexist with faith. Would you retain the state? Maintain the vital principle; watch against every tincture of unbelief, every approach of infidelity; let the life you live be by the faith of the Son of God. This will keep you in constant union with God; and thus united you can never fail. Not only realize, "Thou God seest me," but ever see Him; keep Him constantly before your mind: and so ever recognizing Him, you will not sin; you will live only in Him; He will become "all in all."

6. Acquire the habit of living by the minute. Learn the secret of that wise counsel, when properly understood, "Be careful for nothing." Not that you are to be careless; but let each minute provide for itself. Let it not be supposed that you are not to act for the future, but act by the minute. Take care of this moment now, while you have it, and the next when it comes; you will not then neglect any. You can live this minute without sin! Is it not so? Do it, then. Never mind what is before you. Do not sin now. When each successive minute comes, do likewise. If you will do this, you will not sin at all. Days are made up of minutes: if each one is sinless, the day will be so. Now try this. Nothing is easier, nothing is more wise. Live by the minute. Carry on your business, trade, labor, study, plan for the future; but in all, act for the present, and do not sin now. Trust in God now; do God's will now; do not offend God now. If you will observe this simple rule, you will not fail to succeed. And now, what more need we add? Surely, if these advices be followed, and they certainly are practicable, you will not come short, you will ever prevail. May heaven prosper you!

MOMENT BY MOMENT

How Holiness May Be Regained[7]

It is the compassionate evangelist exhorting in this stirring section. But the perennial question is not ignored: Can one lose the grace of entire sanctification and retain justification? Foster gives a qualified yes. In treating the question of backsliding and its remedy he concentrates his attention on the two extremes of the spectrum, the profligate backslider and the careless drifter. It is the latter who may still bear a filial relationship with God yet have lost that degree of victory and spiritual-mindedness that mark the entirely sanctified.

But we consider now the question, How may one who has enjoyed the grace of entire sanctification, and lost it, be restored? It is obvious, reference must be had to the extent of his lapse—the condition into which he has fallen. Much more may be necessary for one than for another—a different kind and amount of effort. One has fallen from the summit of

DEGREES OF BACKSLIDING

7. Pages 171-74.

a mountain into a deep gulf at its base; another has just perceptibly declined slightly down its slope: one will need much more to regain the apex than the other.

Has one who was evidently a truly sanctified child of God, fallen entirely away, become sevenfold more the child of the devil than he was before? In addition to the enormity of his sins, has he continued long in this state? How dreadful his condition! One is almost ready to conclude, there is no mercy, no salvation for him; that to renew him again to repentance is impossible. We would not go so far; yet we think the chances are, he never will be restored. Should he, however, in his abyss of sin, ever awake, and think of returning to his injured and dishonored Savior, deep and painful will be his conviction; broken, indeed, will be his heart; his cry will ascend as from the very belly of hell.

The probabilities are, he will find trouble and sorrow. Not because the Savior will be less merciful; but because the man will find it hard to confide in mercy that has been so much abused. Not because the blood of Jesus will be ineffectual to wash away his sins; but because he will find it difficult to avail himself, by faith, of that blood that has been trampled beneath unhallowed feet.

Should one who has fallen so deplorably chance to read this page, we would speak to him in behalf of his abused Lord; and yet, our words shall be kind. See what you have done! How great is your sin! Look back to other days. Call to mind the goodness of God. Behold yourself now! How sad! But what then? Are you overwhelmed?—filled with shame and sorrow? It is well.

RETURN TO THE SAVIOR

Will you return? Will you come back to the arms of your slighted Savior? Do you say, How can I?—there is no mercy. Say, not so. There is mercy, if you have a heart to seek it. Come as first you came. The same Savior can still save, His blood will still be efficacious. You need to commence again at the beginning, to lay again the foundations; but do this, and all will be well. The cup is bitter, but you need to drink it; the path thorny, but you must travel it. It may be your sorrows will be greater than before; you must suffer them. But this one thing remember, and let it sustain you: if you will retrace your steps, if you will make the needful efforts, you may again be happy.

But your case is not that which is described above; the advice does not meet your particular want. You have not entirely forsaken the Savior. You are still a Christian, in the enjoyment of a good hope, outwardly witnessing a good profession, and inwardly enjoying some of the sacred influences of the Spirit; but you are not in the high grace of a former experience.

The love of the world in an undue measure, yielding to the force of some temptation, neglect of some duty, want of watchfulness, has laid waste your confidence. You have departed in some degree from God; your thoughts, or your affection, have been given to an improper object, you have preferred your own will to the will of God in some particular, you have let in vanity or sloth, pride or impatience, uncharitableness or selfishness; you have ceased to be entirely the Lord's; guilt has ensued, condemnation is upon you. You feel it; you are unhappy. You do not doubt your relation, but all is not right within.

Humble yourself before God, confess your fault, return: wherein you have departed in thought, affection, volition, or deed, at once correct the wrong, and expect God to renew you again. There may be times and circumstances when the confession of your departure to the church may be necessary. If your failure has been manifest, it will bring your profession into discredit, and violate your own sense of propriety, should you continue the profession, without an admission of your temporary departure.

WHOLEHEARTED RETURN ESSENTIAL

Soon as you return heartily to God, He will return to you: but it must be a full, hearty, entire return; not a mere desire, not a convulsive effort, not a declaration, not a semisincere and half-earnest thing; you must come as first you came, with an entire offering, and God will accept it. If you find great difficulty, as perhaps you may—it is possible even more than at first, for your reproof—you must overcome, overcome as at first, not in your own strength, but in the strength of God, which will become yours, by the use of the means, with which you are sufficiently acquainted.

TAKE IMMEDIATE ACTION

And should any who have relapsed from this blessed experience, chance to read these pages, we would say to them, Return; retrace your steps. You cannot, whatever other Christians may do, find rest in an inferior state. You know the more excellent way. Duty calls you with a tenfold voice: do not turn away, be not overcome with discouragement, let not self-upbraidings hinder you. You now know the cause of your loss; you may succeed better—try again. Privilege invites, duty points the way, your unsatisfied heart urges, the Spirit moves—do not delay.

Whatever be the extent of your departure, whether of long or short duration, into more grievous or less guilty backslidings; whether you have lost all, or only a part of your religious character—stop now. Go not one step further. Turn at once to your dishonored Savior; bring back your heart, guilty as it may be, and become His again. Think not your case is hopeless. It may be deplorable—dreadful. You may have deeply grieved the Spirit, reproached the Redeemer, insulted the Father: still, if you will return, there is no occasion for despair. See how much is involved, and, as you would not risk your undoing, make haste to find what you have unhappily forfeited.

Look before you. It is high time that you awake out of sleep. What you do must be done now. A moment, and it may be too late. Oh, that we might feel how much and earnestly we are called to work now, and to work diligently, seeing that "the night cometh, in which no man can work!"

11

Daniel Steele

(1824-1914)

Few if any theologians have had a more extensive or enduring influence on the modern holiness movement than Daniel Steele. At 46 years of age, he experienced what he called "the second blessing," and immediately began to devote his great mind to its exposition and promotion. His first book, *Love Enthroned* (1875), was both a personal testimony and a theological defense. Other well-known titles from his prolific pen, still widely read, include *Milestone Papers, Half Hours with St. Paul, Half Hours with St. John's Epistles, The Gospel of the Comforter,* and *A Substitute for Holiness.*

Steele was born in Windham, N.Y., October 5, 1824, and graduated with high honors from Wesleyan University in 1848. He was a member of the New England Conference of the Methodist Episcopal church throughout his long ministry. His wife, Harriet, was the daughter of the famous Amos Binney, author of *Binney's Theological Compend.* One of Steele's own enterprises was to rework his father-in-law's classic and publish it under the title *Binney's Theological Compend Improved.*

Steele was a successful pastor for a total of 20 years (1850-61 and 1878-87), but he was best known as an educator. He taught at Wesleyan University, Genessee College, and New England Deaconess Training School. In 1872 he became the first president of Syracuse University. From 1887 to 1890 he served as acting professor of systematic theology at Boston University, preceding Olin Curtis.

No Wesleyan theologian has more honored the Holy Spirit, or more helpfully described His ministry, than did Daniel Steele, especially in *The Gospel of the Comforter.* Neglect of the Spirit, either topically or experientially, results inevitably in the gradual loss of all orthodoxy. Steele's tracing of the sure steps in theological declension is graphic, accurate, and powerful.

The Spirit's Work in Regeneration[1]

In this chapter Steele makes it clear that the Holy Spirit indwells the believer from the moment of regeneration and is responsible for the believer's progress in sanctification and toward entire sanctification. The presence of the Spirit in the initial work of grace is distinguished from the baptism or fullness of the Spirit received by faith subsequently.

Also, in this chapter the author explains why regeneration, while not defective in itself, is inadequate; but more pointedly, why entire sanctification is not and cannot be consummated simultaneously with regeneration.

Regeneration is the lodgement by the Holy Spirit of the new principle of life. This is love to God, which is the ruling motive of every genuine Christian. There is a radical and an essential difference between those who are born again and the best of those who lay claim to only natural goodness, a beautiful moral character revolving around self as a center. But the great transition from spiritual death to spiritual life does not make the child of God at once complete in holiness. The Holy Spirit in sanctification does not work magically nor mechanically like a washing machine, "but by the influence of grace, in accordance with the essential constitution of man, and in the way of vital process, only by degrees completely renewing the soul."

LIMITATION OF REGENERATION

While the Spirit in the new birth touches the whole nature, the thoughts, the feelings, and the will, so that the man is a new creature, his renewal is not complete in any part. At first he is in spiritual knowledge only a babe. His faith is unsteady and often mingled with distrust, while his love is not usually strong enough to secure uninterrupted victory over tempta-

1. This is the title of Chap. 14 in *The Gospel of the Comforter* (Boston: Christian Witness Co., 1897), 104-17.

tion. The enthronement of love does not immediately render the pleasures of sin unattractive, nor destroy the painfulness of self-denial, nor instantaneously change sinful habits. Such is the state of immature converts to Christ, "the flesh lusting against the Spirit."

The Corinthians were characterized as "carnal, walking as men." John says, "He that has been born of God sinneth not," when he is describing those whom he styles "fathers" or adult believers, just as Paul describes the same class as having crucified the flesh with the passions and lusts. Neither of these apostles is describing an ideal Christian, as some teach who deny the possibility of complete deliverance from depravity in this life. They are describing regeneration at its climax, the glorious possibilities of the birth from above, when it has culminated in perfect holiness.

Bishop Foster sums up the defects of the experience of regeneration in a more comprehensive manner than we remember seeing in any theological treatise. He does not minify the experience of regeneration, but declares it to be a glorious experience. He, however, shows its defects in this manner: "I note, third, that dissatisfiedness of the soul with itself is a common experience of all regenerate souls, varying from intense distress at times to mild regret. Its experiences are not satisfactory. It has a prevailing consciousness of inexcusable defects. It does not reach its ideal. It feels the chiding of the Holy Spirit. It lashes itself with reprovings. It often carries an unhealed wound because of its unfaithfulness or failure to be what it feels it ought to be. There is the abiding consciousness that there is something better for it. Even when it is upheld and sustained in an average experience, and others think well of it, and there is no external failure visible to the eye, it discerns inward poverties which grieve and distress it.

SENSE OF LACK

"It would love more, be more patient, more brave, more trusting, more cheerful, stronger, more robust; it would work more and do more and be more. There are holy yearnings in it after something higher and nobler. There is often a distressing sense of remaining evil in it.

CARNALITY

"I think I am safe in saying this is universal experience, subsequent to the experience of regeneration. This has been called in our theologizing of all the Christian schools, 'the remains of the carnal mind,' 'unextracted roots of inbred sin,' 'the spirit of the flesh,' 'natural corruption,' 'seeds of depravity,' 'the old man,' and by various other semiscriptural names.

"These phrases all point to a fact, but not unfrequently a sensuous meaning is attached to them which leads wide apart from the truth which they aim to represent. They are supposed to represent some sediment or infusion in the soul, or in the body, or in both, which must be washed out. What is meant and what is true is this: when the soul is forgiven and its affections are turned to righteousness, so that it passes from under the dominion of evil, impulses and inclination to evil are not completely eradicated. They still arise and assert themselves. They assail and disturb the peace of the soul. They have a constant tendency to prevail with it. They find support in its old habits and in its native lusts—that is, desires and cravings."[2]

In the above truthful condensation of experience it will be noticed that the bishop teaches that we are not entirely sanctified at conversion—a doctrine often denied in the church today. He teaches, as John Wesley did, that there remains yet that which needs a farther work of the Spirit, which is called, in the language of theology, entire sanctification, which supplements the defects of the soul still remaining after regeneration.

PERIL OF BACKSLIDING

The adverse influences and tendencies that continue after the new birth imperil the very existence of the new principle of love to God by overcoming and choking it, unless it is continually nourished and strengthened by divine grace. Strength is supplied to the believer by the inner presence of the Holy Spirit. His indwelling is by faith. If faith declines, the Spirit's sphere in the soul is narrowed. If confidence in God is "cast away"—a possible act against which we are warned in the Scriptures (Heb. 10:35)—then the Spirit withdraws, or rather, is excluded by unbelief. Then love, the vital spark of the spiritual life, expires.

Hence the question whether the Spirit shall be a merely transient impulse toward purity, or a lasting power, depends on the free will of the regenerate soul. The parable of the sower is exemplified today in the case of those who have no depth of earth. Their love to Christ soon degenerates into a mere sentiment with little or no influence on practical life, and in short time the sentiment itself entirely evaporates, and the soul becomes "twice dead, plucked up by the roots" (Jude 12).

What is the safeguard against such a disaster? It is such an indwelling of the fullness of the Spirit as excludes everything contrary to the divine nature by filling and flooding the soul with a love that is

2. Merrick Lectures, *The Philosophy of Christian Experience.*

ever enlarging the vessel and ever filling it to the brim. Then love is perfect in the sense that it is no longer mixed in kind and so weak in degree as to be unable to encounter the temptation successfully.

Says Prof. Candlish, "The new life of Christianity is a unity, and though, on account of the imperfect and abnormal condition of most Christians, it does not show itself with perfect symmetry, yet it tends toward moral excellence and perfection in every direction, and the more vigorous the central principle of religious life is, the more will particular virtues be developed and increased." This is progress toward entire sanctification by the Holy Spirit and is a necessary condition of that crowning work.

WHY TWO WORKS?

The question is often asked, "Why does not the Spirit entirely sanctify when He regenerates?" We answer, it is because that neither the consecration nor the faith of the penitent sinner is adequate to this complete work. The person then surrenders his bad things, he lays down his arms, quits his rebellion, and sues for pardon. This is all that his faith grasps. But he soon learns that a deeper consecration is requisite, that all his good things, his possessions, his bodily powers, his intellectual faculties must be fully consecrated to Christ. To pour all his money into the treasury of his imperilled country and to give his life by enlisting in her military service is far different from the act of surrender as a prisoner of war.

In the next place, faith for entire sanctification is a far higher act, involving a deeper knowledge of one's spiritual needs and a larger comprehension of the vastness of the supply found in Jesus Christ. This deeper knowledge is not found in the spiritual babe.

Moreover, at the risk of being suspected of predestinarianism, I insist on another reason why the Spirit does not entirely purge the soul at the new birth. The impartation of spiritual life to a dead soul is wrought by the Spirit alone without the soul's cooperation, though it is active in repentance, faith, and turning to the Lord. It is active in conversion, but passive in regeneration. Theologians would call the first a case of synergism and the second an instance of monergism. If our distinction between these works of the Spirit is correct, it affords a sufficient reason why entire sanctification could not be wrought by the Spirit at the time of the new birth.

ONLY THE NEW MAN CAN COOPERATE

The old man cannot be crucified without the cooperation of the new man. He must sign the death warrant of that sin in the flesh which the Son of God by His sacrifice for sin has condemned, in order to make that condemnation effectual for the destruction of "the body of sin" (Rom. 6:6). "In implanting the new life at first, the Holy Spirit has to deal with a soul that is indeed essentially active, but in regard to spirituality insensible or opposed to the call of God. Hence this work is entirely due to divine power; we are His workmanship, created in Christ unto good works. But in the preservation and development of the new life the Spirit has to deal with a soul that is now spiritually alive and able and inclined to work in the same direction as His work."[3]

In sanctification "we are God's fellow workers" (1 Cor. 3:9, Revised Version). Hence the momentous import of the exhortation of Paul, "Carry out with fear and trembling your own salvation. For it is God which worketh in you both to will and to work for his good pleasure."[4] The occasion for fear and trembling arises from the fact that God's work in me may fail to reach perfection because of my failure to work perfectly with Him. It is indeed a solemn and awful thing to be fellow workers with the holy God in the production of the most valuable thing in the universe, a holy character.

In the work of purifying ourselves while God is refining us, how careful should we be lest through lack of faith in His exceedingly great and precious promises, we should mar the work of His Spirit in perfectly conforming us to the image of His Son. As a slight motion may spoil the image that the light is imprinting on the prepared plate [camera film], so a little self-indulgence or heedlessness or wavering of faith may blur the image of Christ that the Spirit is creating in me. I am responsible not only for all I can do toward completed holiness, which is perfect consecration, but I am also responsible for all that the Holy Spirit can do with my cooperation.

The work of the Holy Spirit in the progressive sanctification of the newborn soul is direct: in opening the heart to receive the truth,[5]

---

3. Prof. Candlish.

4. Dean Alford's version of Phil. 2:12-13.

5. "In 2 Thess. 2:13, sanctification of the Spirit is placed in close connection with belief of the truth. And from Acts 26:18 we learn that not only forgiveness of sins, but a lot among the sanctified, is obtained by faith in Christ. This accords with the broad principles asserted in Mark 9:23, 'All things are possible to him who believes'; in Gal. 3:14, 'That we may receive the promise of the Spirit through faith,' and in Acts 15:9, 'By faith having purified their hearts,' and with a great mass of Bible teaching which I have not space to quote and expound. In Rom. 6:11 St. Paul bids us 'Reckon ourselves to be dead to sin, but living for God in Christ Jesus.' This reckoning is the mental process of faith, for it results in assurance resting upon the promise of God."—J. A. Beet, *Holiness as Understood by the Writers of the Bible*, 55.

the instrument of purification; in giving vigor to the spiritual life; in strengthening the will to resist temptation, and in diminishing the power of evil habits. It is repressive of depravity rather than totally destructive.

The entire eradication of the propensity to sin is by the direct and instantaneous act of the Holy Spirit responsive to a special act of faith in Christ claiming the full heritage of the believer. "When we learn that God claims us for His own, and when, after fruitless personal efforts to render Him the devotion He requires, we learn for the first time that God will work in us by the agency of His Spirit and by actual spiritual contact with Christ the devotion He requires, and when we venture to believe . . . we find by happy experience that according to our faith it is done to us. The experience thus gained becomes an era in our spiritual life. We feel that we are then holy in a sense unknown to us before."[6] In reference to this distinctive act of the Sanctifier it is noted by an eminent expositor "that in the New Testament we never read expressly and unmistakably of sanctification as a gradual process." This is said in view of the almost universal use of the aorist tense of the verbs *to sanctify* and *to cleanse.*

INSTANTANEOUS CLEANSING

This distinct and decisive action of the Holy Spirit in the extinction of proneness to sin, brings the believer into the land of rest, in marvellous contrast with his previous wilderness experience, after his regeneration.

There are too many intelligent and trustworthy witnesses to this experience to be lightly passed by as of no account. They assure us that they were truly converted and received the direct witness of the Spirit to their adoption; that they did not backslide, but grew in grace; that they were not conscious of living in willful violations of any known law of God, and that they could testify that there is no condemnation to them who are in Christ Jesus.

MANY WITNESSES

But they solemnly aver that through all their regenerate life, before receiving Christ for their entire sanctification, they were conscious of a strong inward enemy whom they were striving to bind and cast out but always failed. . . . By the study of the Scriptures they found that this rebel within was called "the old man," whom theologians style "original sin." After reading or hearing the testimony of those entirely consecrated souls who had through specific faith and

---

6. J. A. Beet, *Holiness as Understood,* 60.

importunate prayer found complete deliverance, they definitely sought for this distinctive work of the Holy Spirit. And at an ever memorable date they emerged into a blissful consciousness of inward purity and profound peace far beyond all former experiences. This victory many have attested decades and scores of years.

Dr. Asa Mahan's temper in his youth was so ungovernable that his father predicted that in a fit of anger he would kill someone and expiate his crime on the scaffold. Mahan's irascibility in the early years of his Christian ministry was the cause of untold grief, but he testifies to a change wrought by the Holy Spirit so great as to make the last 40 years of his life undisturbed by one gust of irritability, though he often met with insults and other occasions to call it forth if it had been slumbering within. The Sanctifier had cast out this demon and so adorned the place of his former abode with the fruits of the Spirit and so filled it with His own permanent fullness that he could not return though he may have "taken with himself seven other spirits more wicked than himself." The Lord be praised! There is a power that not only cleanses but also keeps. It is to be noted that the witnesses to whom we refer agree in testifying that this entire sanctification was subsequent to regeneration, and that it was accomplished by the Spirit in an instant, and not by the processes of growth.

This negative work of the Spirit in the eradication of inherited proneness to sin is followed by an illimitable development of all the Christian graces. One may reach the point where sin is all destroyed and love become perfect, that is, pure and unmixed, and yet his power of moral discernment and his mental enlargement be capable of increase through time and through eternity. His spiritual development will be commensurate.

Perfection in degree of love is never to be attained. Perfection in kind is the gift of the Holy Ghost to the believer now.

TWO NATURE THEORY

There prevails in certain religious circles the doctrine that in the new birth a new nature is created, while the old nature, or old man, continues till physical death extinguishes his life. It is said that the old nature is nailed to the Cross, but he does not die so long as the human spirit acts through a material organism. Denial of the possibility of entire sanctification in the present life is an obvious inference. Another outcome of this error is that depravity is necessary and that it is beyond the reach of the Holy Spirit in the application of the blood of Christ that cleanses from all sin. Hence the notion of two natures existing in every Christian, however consecrated, so long as he is in the body, the one a new creature and therefore sinless and the other sinful and beyond all hope of change for the better, is exceedingly mischievous, palliating and excusing evil propensities. When we speak of the Holy Spirit as the indwelling Sanctifier we will examine the alleged scriptural proofs of this doctrine.

OFFICE OF THE SPIRIT

We insist that the work of the Spirit in the new creation of the penitent believer in Christ is not the creation of new faculties, but the rectification of those already existing, weakened and marred by sin. He has no need of a new reason, for even after the Fall, reason in man grasps the same self-evident truths that exist in God. In fact, the modern teaching of philosophy is that truths of intuition are the activity of God immanent in the soul of man. His sensibilities, both natural and moral, have been damaged by the fall of Adam, and his will has become enslaved to his perverted affections and depraved desires. It is the office of the Holy Spirit to lift this yoke of bondage and to bring the newborn soul into the glorious liberty of the sons of God. He whom Christ Jesus makes free is free indeed. It is the slave that is emancipated and not a new being just created. Such a being would need no act of emancipation. It is the office of the Spirit to give to the will the gracious ability to make holy choices and to clarify the moral sense or conscience so that its decisions will all harmonize with ethical axioms of immutable morality.

The "new creature" spoken of by Paul is a figure of speech for the vivid presentation of the transforming power of the Holy Spirit in the renewal of a soul badly shattered by sin. Conscience is restored to full activity both in its power to discern and its power to approve or condemn. The human spirit may well be compared to a skylight in the dome of his being through which he was designed to have a vision of spiritual realities. But sin has darkened the windows and intercepted the heavenly vision. The remedy is not in the demolition of the old skylight and the setting of a new one, but in the thorough cleansing of the original windows by One who by taking up His abode in that dome can always keep it transparent by His purifying presence. The process seems to be first to cause the law of God to shine into conscience, the light of forgiveness, then the light of purity, "having no more conscience of sin."

ERROR OF SACRAMENTAL SALVATION

Another error obstructive of the spiritual life of all the so-called sacramentarian churches—more than half of Christendom—

consists in a perversion of the meaning of Christ's words to Nicodemus, "born of water and the Spirit." Those who magnify the sacraments as saving ordinances, and some who do not teach baptismal regeneration, like the Methodist Episcopal church, which uses the Anglican ritual abridged, teach that the words "born of water" refer to water baptism. But others, including the writer, insist that these words have no reference to that ordinance, which was not made obligatory upon believers till after Christ's resurrection, years after His dialogue with Nicodemus.

The identification of water baptism with the new birth has wrought untold harm to myriads of souls, deluding them with a shadow of the requisite for salvation instead of the substance, the impartation of spiritual life and initial sanctification symbolized by water. We sympathize with Weisse, though we cannot use his strong language, that to make regeneration depend upon baptism by water "is little better than blasphemy." We believe with Neander, Calvin, Grotius, and other scholars, that Christ here intends the symbolic import of water, and not water itself, as an agent of cleansing. . . . Thus, "ye must be born of water and the Spirit" for purifying by the Spirit. Desiring to give His distinguished hearer a clear idea of the change which the Spirit must work in the natural heart, He adds the idea of initial cleansing by using the word *water.*

THE CLEANSING OF FIRE

In like manner a more thorough purification is expressed by the words of John the Baptist descriptive of Christ. "He shall baptize you with the Holy Ghost and with fire," an agent of cleansing far more effectual than water in the purification of earthen and metallic utensils. We cannot here, as some do, read *and* as meaning *or,* "with the Holy Ghost or fire," meaning all who do not receive the Holy Spirit's baptism must be baptized with hellfire. We prefer the exegesis of Bishop Hopkins, "those who are baptized with the Holy Spirit are, as it were, plunged into the heavenly flame, whose searching energy devours all their dross, tin, and base alloy."

Here is a promise of a richer blessing, a more thorough sanctification and a far larger equipment for effective service than that which is enjoyed by the average Christian today. "The purification at conversion, comparatively superficial, is only that which may be fitly symbolized by water baptism. But fire searches the inmost springs of life. The baptism of fire must be such a close and intimate contact of the holy

God with the inner man, as to light up its dark secrets and burn out its uncleanness."[7]

Baptism with the Spirit in Relation to Entire Sanctification[8]

It has been claimed that Steele did not link entire sanctification with baptism with the Holy Spirit. The following selection sufficiently puts that misapprehension to rest. In designating the effusion of the Spirit, Steele uses baptism "with," "by," and more commonly "of." When baptism *of* the Spirit is intended as an objective genitive, it means the baptism pertaining to the Spirit and is thus compatible with baptism *in* or *with* the Holy Spirit. Almost all holiness writers of the last century used the phrase baptism *of;* in recent years baptism *with* has become the preferred form.

This reading is taken from Chapter 7, "Metaphorical Representations of Perfect Love." "Baptism" is thus treated as a metaphor. Other metaphors that Steele understands to pertain to the second work of grace are "Anointing" and "Sealing."

Mrs. Harriet Beecher Stowe, in her admirable essay "Primitive Christian Experience," uses the following language:

DEFINITE PRIVILEGES

"The advantages to the Christian Church, in setting before it *distinct points of attainment,* are very nearly the same in result as the advantages of preaching immediate regeneration in preference to indefinite exhortation to men to lead sober, righteous, and godly lives. It has been found, in the course of New England preaching, that pressing men to an immediate and definite point of conversion produced immediate and definite results; and so it has been found among Christians, that pressing them to an immediate and definite point of attainment will, in like manner, result in marked and decided progress. For this reason it is, that, among the Moravian Christians, where the experience by them denominated full assurance of faith was much insisted on, there were more instances of high religious faith than in almost any other denomination."

---

7. Charles Edward Smith, *The Baptism in Fire.*

8. *Love Enthroned: Essays on Evangelical Perfection* (New York: Nelson & Phillips, 1875), 91-106.

Here is sound philosophy, founded on facts corroborated by Mr. Wesley in his wide range of observation: "Wherever the work of sanctification increased, the whole work of God increased in all its branches." In 1765 he found in Bristol 50 less members than he left before. He thus accounts for this decline: "One reason is, that Christian perfection has been little insisted on; and wherever this is not done, be the preacher ever so eloquent, there is little increase either in the numbers or grace of the hearers." When a definite point is presented to the believer as attainable immediately, all the energies of the soul are aroused and concentrated. Prayer is no more at random. There is a target set up to fire at. Faith as an act—a voluntary venture upon the promise—puts forth its highest energies and achieves its greatest victories.

But just here some people find a difficulty. They do not dispute the philosophy, but they question the fact that for believers there is in the New Testament such a distinct point, such a definite line to be crossed. They say that they fail to find in the apostolic Church any instance of such a sudden transition in the spiritual life of the justified soul. It is said that after regeneration there is a gradual development of the new life, with no instantaneous uplifts such as are insisted on by the modern apostles of the higher life. It is the purpose of this chapter to show not only numerous instances of an instantaneous uprising to a higher plane of Christian experience, but that this was the normal development of the spiritual life of primitive Christians. We proceed to show that the baptism of the Holy Spirit is identical with the blessing of perfect love.

St. Paul, in one of his missionary tours, encountered Judaizing teachers who affirmed that those who would be good Christians must be good Jews, obeying all the Levitical law. This question was carried up to Jerusalem to be decided by a council of the apostles and elders. After much discussion, Peter arose and gave an account of his preaching.

"A good while ago God made choice among us that the Gentiles by my mouth should hear the word of the gospel and believe; and God, which knoweth the hearts, bare them witness, giving them the Holy Ghost even as he did unto us; and put no difference between us and them, *purifying their hearts by faith*." Peter refers to his preaching to Cornelius and his staff at his headquarters in Caesarea. On another occasion he declares: "And as I began to speak, the Holy Ghost fell on them *as on us at the beginning*"; that is, on the Day of Pentecost, at the beginning of "the kingdom of the Holy Ghost," as John Fletcher styles it.

The apostles were then *filled,* which is the same as being *baptized,* with the Holy Spirit, for it was the fulfillment of the promise: "But ye shall be baptized with the Holy Ghost not many days hence." The conclusion is inevitable, that the baptism of the Holy Spirit includes the extinction of sin in the believer's soul as its negative and minor part, and the fullness of love shed abroad in the heart as its positive and greater part; in other words, it includes entire sanctification and Christian perfection.

EXTINCTION OF SIN

Let us more clearly trace the successive steps by which we come to this conclusion. Christ promised that when He should be glorified the disciples should receive a blessing they could not receive while His bodily presence remained with them (John 7:38-39). That blessing was not the forgiveness of sins, for Jesus was daily dispensing pardon. It was a blessing of an abiding and aggressive nature, making believers to be as fountains whence should flow forth "rivers of living water." Thus much is determined by this passage, that there is a blessing distinct from pardoning grace, and there is an indefinite interval between them.

DISTINCT FROM PARDON

It remains now to show that this second blessing involves entire sanctification. The proofs are: (1) The account of the fullness of the Holy Spirit on the Day of Pentecost, 10 days after the Lord Jesus ascended to His glorified state (Acts 1 and 2). (2) Peter's declaration (Acts 11:15-16) that the effusion of the Holy Spirit upon Cornelius and his company was the same in character and effect as the outpouring at Pentecost. (3) Peter's incidental remark in Acts 15:9, that the Holy Spirit came to Cornelius and his house in His office of the Sanctifier, "Purifying their hearts by faith." The last text is an incontrovertible demonstration that the fullness of the Spirit is a synonym for entire sanctification. Since there are but two forces that can sway the soul, the flesh and the Spirit, to be completely filled with either is to exclude the other. To be filled with the Spirit is to be completely emancipated from the flesh, or inherent depravity. To be but partially swayed by the Spirit is to afford a foothold in the soul for a contest between these antagonistic powers (Gal. 5:17).

It remains to be proved that Cornelius and his staff, or house, whose hearts "were purified by faith" in the Spirit baptism, were pre-

CORNELIUS JUSTIFIED

viously in a justified state. We have the testimony of the Spirit of inspiration that he was "a *devout* man, and one that *feared God* with *all his house* (military household), which gave much alms to the people, and *prayed* always." Peter, under the inspiration of the Spirit and standing in the presence of Cornelius and his house, asserts, "Of a truth I perceive that God is no respecter of persons; but in every nation he that feareth God and worketh righteousness is accepted with him"—"through Christ, though he knew Him not," says Wesley most truly.

To be *accepted* with God is to be *justified* by God. There was no conviction of sin produced under Peter's discourse in Caesarea, no account that these pious Gentiles "were pricked in their heart," nor was there any outcry, "Men and brethren, what shall we do?" They were ready to receive the Holy Spirit, hence the correctness of the inference made by the Council at Jerusalem: "Then hath God also to the Gentiles granted repentance unto life" (Acts 11:18). The reception of the Holy Spirit in His fullness presupposes their previous repentance unto life.

On the Day of Pentecost so great was the manifestation of spiritual power that the believers in Christ were instantly and completely filled without the instrumentality of preaching, and unbelievers during the sermon of Peter were rapidly transformed into penitent believers, ready to submit to any test of the genuineness of their faith: even to be publicly baptized in the hated name of that Jesus whom they had personally insulted and crucified. The finishing stroke of this rapid transformation was "the gift of the Holy Spirit," with its fruits—unselfishness, oneness of spirit, "gladness and singleness of heart." But generally there was a brief interval between conversion and the baptism of the Spirit.

The people of Samaria were first converted under the preaching of Deacon Philip; "and when they believed, they were baptized, both men and women." Having never been brought into personal contact with Jesus, and having never offered personal insult to Him, water baptism is not made the test of the sincerity of their repentance, so that they were regenerated before that ordinance was used. The successive steps through which they passed were, attention to the word, faith, great joy—implying a change of heart—and baptism with water.[9] Afterward Peter and John

SAMARITAN CONVERTS

9. See Ellicott on Eph. 1:13, and Alford on Gal. 1:16.

were sent down from Jerusalem for the special work of leading the converts on to Christian perfection. They held a special meeting. They prayed with them that they might receive the Holy Spirit, and they laid their hands upon them, and they received the Holy Spirit, not only as the giver of special gifts, but also as a distinct and permanent spiritual endowment. . . .

The apostle Paul found at Ephesus "certain disciples." He asked them a question that seems greatly out of place if there is no distinct work of the Holy Spirit after justification: "Have ye received the Holy Ghost since ye believed?" (Acts 19:2). We admit that there is no word *since* in the Greek text, and that there may be no allusion to time in this passage, which may be rendered: "Have ye believing received the Holy Ghost?" Reading the question even in this form, making the *pisteusantes* a participle of means—"by believing"—and not of time—"since believing," or "having believed" (Ellicott)—there is nothing gained on the part of those who deny a second and distinct work of the Holy Spirit; for there lies plainly on the surface of this question the implication that Christian discipleship is not a proof, prima facie, of "receiving the Holy Ghost." If discipleship implies this blessing, St. Paul asked an absurd question when he thus catechized the 12 justified and baptized Ephesian disciples.

DISCIPLES AT EPHESUS

The question propounded by St. Paul at the very first salutation was probably the interrogatory put to every convert to Christ who had been converted by the instrumentality of some other person. Ignorant of his spiritual state, and fearing that he might not have received "the greatest gift that man can wish or heaven can send," he asks this all-important question: "Have you received the Holy Ghost since you believed?"

Should the great apostle arise from the dead and come into our churches today, we doubt not that this would be his first question. We are not so sure that he would not be more surprised by the answer of multitudes, "We have not so much as heard whether there be any Holy Ghost" as a permanent indweller in the hearts of believers. This despite the fact that they have all their lives heard the apostolic blessing in which the "communion of the Holy Ghost" is the crowning grace of that benediction. This would be because of its not being set forth as a distinct attainment—a prize set before each, to be grasped by faith.

We understand that the baptism, the anointing, the fullness, the abiding, the indwelling, the constant communion, the sealing, the earnest of the Holy Spirit, are equivalent terms, expressive of the state of Christian perfection. Wherever these terms occur, the Spirit of inspiration is pointing to that state of serene rest, that unbroken peace, that repose in the blood of Christ, that unwavering trust in God, that deliverance from fleshly desire, and that eradication of inbred sin, which come from being "filled with all the fullness of God."

DIFFERENT TERMS

This great blessing is the constant theme of the apostle Paul, especially in his later Epistles. He exhorts all to be filled with the Spirit; he prays for believers that they "may know the love of Christ which passeth knowledge; that Christ may dwell in their hearts." St. Paul was a practical man, and never wasted his time urging the impracticable, or inciting to the unattainable. According to Meyer the ordinary sequence of blessings is, *(a)* Hearing; *(b)* Faith, implying preventing [preparatory] and saving grace; *(c)* Baptism; *(d)* Communication of the Holy Spirit. Compare Acts 2:37-38 *(a, c, d);* 8:6, 12, 17 *(a, b, c, d);* 19:5-6 *(c, d).*

SEQUENCE OF BLESSINGS

Acts 10:44 *(d, c),* and *perhaps* 9:17, are exceptional cases. The reason for the seeming blending of the baptism of the Holy Spirit with regeneration in exceptional instances in the Acts of the Apostles is to be attributed to the fact that the regenerate were urged to the immediate attainment of this great blessing, so that they did attain it with the interval of only a brief period. A similar experience was that of Rev. John Fletcher, who seems to have been born into the kingdom with such a grasp of faith that he apprehended Jesus Christ as his complete Savior a very few days afterward.

TIME FACTOR

In the days of John Wesley, where this privilege was held up to the young convert by the preachers, and exemplified by many believers, there are instances of the attainment of perfect love within a day or two after justification. "The next morning I spoke severally with those who believed they were sanctified. There were fifty-one in all—twenty-one men, twenty-one widows or married women, and nine young women or children. In one of these the change was wrought three weeks after she was justified; in three, seven days after it; in one, five days; and in S. L., aged fourteen, two days only" (*Wesley's Journal,* August 4, 1762).

Please observe how minute and searching Wesley was in his investigation into this subject. No naturalist in pursuit of a scientific truth could be more patient and painstaking in the collection of facts from which to make his induction. . . .

Again, two days afterward, he says of another Society, "Many believed that the blood of Jesus Christ had cleansed them from all sin. I spoke to these, forty in all, one by one. Some of them said they received the blessing ten days, some seven, some four, some three days after they found peace with God, and two of them the next day. What marvel, since one day is with God as a thousand years!"

To our position that the baptism of the Spirit is identical with entire sanctification, it may be objected that there was no need of the

JESUS' ANOINTING

purification of Jesus Christ, and yet He, the sinless man, was baptized with the Holy Spirit. Our reply to this is, that entire sanctification is a negative work—the destruction of sin; the positive work, the constructive part, is much the greater—it is the subsidizing of all the faculties, filling all the capacities with divine life and power. A sinless soul may need the positive when it has no need of the negative part of the work wrought by the Holy Spirit. We believe that Jesus was baptized of the Holy Spirit because that baptism, at a certain stage of spiritual development, is the normal method of advancement necessary to the perfect unfolding of the spiritual life of every soul.[10] Because many people are greatly puzzled by Christ's baptism by the Holy Spirit, as if it were a strange and abnormal thing, we will endeavor to divest the subject of some of its difficulties.

All orthodox believers admit that two distinct natures are so blended in Jesus Christ as to constitute one personality. The human nature was not changed by its union with the divine. By Christ's human nature we mean His perfect human soul and body. This nature was subject to the limitations and laws of universal humanity. The body grew in stature, the intellect in strength, the moral and spiritual susceptibilities in capacity and beauty. "He grew in favour with God and man." To this end He made diligent use of all the means of grace, read the law, the psalms, and the prophets, prayed much in secret, fasted on important occasions, and gathered with the worshipers in the synagogues and in the temple.

As a man, these means of grace were as necessary as to any other Jew who would retain the favor of God. He did not, as the Son of God, need such means for retaining His love to the Father. As equal

---

10. H. Orton Wiley denies the propriety of calling the descent of the Spirit upon Jesus (Matt. 3:16) a baptism. See below, p. 382 (*Christian Theology*, 2:324). *Editor.*

with the Holy Spirit He did not need any endowment of the Spirit, for the Christian church, both papal and Protestant, believe . . . that the Holy Spirit proceeds from the Father *and the Son.* But although the Son of God is the channel through which the Holy Spirit flows down to the world from the Father . . . yet nevertheless Jesus, the Son of man, receives Him in the way appointed for all believers—an instantaneous effusion, received by faith in the promise of the Father. In this Jesus Christ is our pattern as much as in prayer and praise. The form of the dove, and the voice from heaven, and the coincidence[11] of the Spirit baptism with water baptism, were peculiarities of this blessing in the case of our Lord that are not essential to it.

What a revolution would be wrought in the church—what a resurrection to spiritual life—what a girding with power, if preachers insisted on the duty of all believers imitating their Master in the Spirit baptism as in the water baptism, in the reality as in the shadow, in the thing signified as in the symbol!

O blessed Jesus, hasten that day—the day of power in Thy Church, as it was when it was the first inquiry of the preacher, "Have ye received the Holy Ghost since ye believed?" Then would he who writes these words for Thy glory, O adorable Savior, joyfully drop his pen, and exclaim with good old Simeon, Nunc Dimittis, "now lettest thou thy servant depart in peace!"

Christ Our Sanctification[12]

The author explains the distinction between Christ as our sanctification *provisionally* and the Holy Spirit as our Sanctifier *effectually.* He also discusses the paradox of the two receptions of the Spirit, the first in regeneration, the second in entire sanctification. He points to two similar mysteries that, while not understood, are normally accepted without question: first, the *presence* of the Spirit in the world from creation versus His *coming* at Pentecost; and second, the presence of the Spirit in Jesus from conception and birth versus His coming upon Jesus following His baptism.

---

11. Obviously this is not the correct word here. They were closely associated, but not coincident. *Editor.*

12. The following reading is a portion of Chap. 15 in *The Gospel of the Comforter,* 118-24.

The work of each of the three Persons of the Trinity in the scheme of salvation is quite definitely stated in the Holy Scriptures. The Father originated the plan, the Son by His atoning death provided the means, the blood of sprinkling, and the Holy Spirit conditionally applies it for the soul's purification. But sometimes the work of the Spirit is ascribed to the Son. This seeming confusion perplexes the student of the Bible, till he learns that when the Son is spoken of as sanctifying, it is always in a different sense from the Spirit's work of purification. In the interest of clearness of thought and of saving truth set forth as the cloudless noonday sun, let us note in what sense the sanctification ascribed to Christ in several texts differs from that internal work wrought by the Comforter.

When Christ is spoken of as our sanctification, it is meant, not that He enters into the hearts of believers and cleanses them but that He provides the purifying medium, His own shed blood, and the sanctifying agent, the Holy Spirit. The Son's work is external, the Spirit's is internal; or in philosophic terms, the work of the one is objective, that of the other is subjective; the one sanctifies provisionally and the other effectually.

CHRIST PROVIDES CONDITIONAL SANCTIFICATION

Now let us carry this distinction into Paul's letters to the Corinthians. In 1 Cor. 1:2 they are addressed as "sanctified in Christ Jesus," but in 3:1, Paul "cannot speak unto them as spiritual, but as unto carnal, even as unto babes in Christ." How are these apparent contradictions harmonized? It will not do to say that Paul, to say nothing of the Spirit who inspired him, flatly contradicts himself. In the light of the distinction between provisional sanctification in Christ and actual sanctification by the Holy Spirit, a very beautiful harmony emerges. Through faith the Corinthians had been born from above, and had become "babes in Christ," and were now entitled to all the privileges He had purchased for believers, among which was conditional sanctification.

But since they had failed to appropriate their heritage by the exercise of faith, they were still strongly carnal in their leanings, as evidenced by their "envying, strife and divisions." They were provisionally sanctified in Christ; they were not [yet] actually sanctified by the Holy Spirit. The contradiction disappears. In the same way the contradiction between the statement that "Jesus Christ is the Saviour of all men" and His sentence of a part of them in the last day to eternal punishment disappears in the consideration that Christ is the conditional Savior of all the human race, but the real Savior of believers only.

In 1 Cor. 1:30 Christ "is made unto us wisdom, and righteousness, and sanctification, and redemption." This He is to everyone who does by faith appropriate Him and become wise by believing divine revelation personified in Christ, the truth, and justified through faith in Him. In Him also one is sanctified through the reception of the Spirit in His office as Sanctifier, and redeemed, soul and body reunited and glorified, through persevering faith in Him who shall change the body of our "humiliation," that it may be fashioned like unto His glorious body. This distinction between provisional sanctification in Christ and sanctification inwrought by the Holy Spirit secured by faith utterly excludes the doctrine of holiness imputed to persons whose hearts are still filled with depravity. One may die for another, but one cannot be holy for another. Sin and holiness are personal, and not transferable.

Alford calls attention to the double conjunction in 1 Cor. 1:30, between "righteousness, the source of our justification before God, and sanctification by His Spirit, implying that the Christian life is complete, the negative side and positive side are so joined as to form one whole." The piety of the Corinthians lacked the positive side. They were forgiven, but not cleansed. They had appropriated part of their heritage in Christ, justification, but they had not by an appropriating faith claimed sanctification. The Corinthian type of Christians has not become obsolete. In every age, with here and there an exception, it has been the prevailing type. This accounts for its failure to conquer the world. When the possible in Christian character shall have become the actual in the whole Church, the world's evangelization will be speedily accomplished. That generation will see the glorious consummation.

In Heb. 2:11 "he that sanctifieth" is Christ, regarded as the Author of the provision of salvation and of the agency of the purifying Spirit, who applies to those who are "being sanctified" the cleansing efficacy of the Atonement on the condition of their faith in Christ.

HOLINESS POSSIBLE TO ALL

In Heb. 10:10 is another instance of sanctification by Christ provisionally, "through the oblation of the body of Jesus Christ once for all." That inward holiness, which the altar ritual of the Hebrews with their interminable repetitions was unable to produce, has been rendered possible to every believer through the offering of the body of the adorable God-man once for all. While the Atonement sanctified no one, it renders possible the entire sanctification of every offspring of Adam who will trust in Christ for this purchased blessing.

Verse 14 has often been misunderstood as teaching that Christ brought to perfection the work of our inward sanctification 1,800 years before we were born: "For by one oblation hath he perfected forever them that are being sanctified" (Alford). The sanctification that Christ thus perfected is provisional. As such it is eternally efficacious and incapable of improvement. It stands ready from age to age to be applied by the Holy Spirit to the inward cleansing of every believer. Nothing is lacking but the outstretching of an empty hand to grasp the pearl of great price. Under the Atonement "all things are possible to him that believeth."

Verse 15 does not teach the witness of the Holy Spirit to the actual, inward work of entire sanctification, as some erroneously teach, but His testimony in the Old Testament to the coming of the days when the provisions for the inner purification will be complete, when the law will no longer be a galling yoke on the neck, but a joyful song in the heart. It is true that this inner change will be through the agency of the Holy Spirit, who, by shining on His own work, is a witness to its genuineness. But this is not a proof text of such a witness.

Well says Delitzsch: "The Holy Ghost is the Spirit of prophecy, and from Him comes the whole God-inspired written Word. He also in that Word is the witness that with Christ's return to the Father all is accomplished, and nothing remains to be done to procure for us inward perfecting and a complete restoration to communion with God." Man's relation to God is no longer merely legal, but inward, evangelical and spiritual. He ceases from outward, compensative works, but concentrates his view upon the sanctifying and endowing grace already procured, and seeks to enter in and lay hold of it. This once-for-all provisional grace for justification and entire sanctification, according to Jeremiah (23:6), is the basis of the new covenant.

TWO INCOMINGS OF THE SPIRIT

Many good Christians find it difficult to accept the doctrine of a definite and instantaneous work of the Holy Spirit subsequent to regeneration, because they cannot draw a sharply defined line between the incoming of the Spirit, the Lord of life, to impart life, and His second incoming to impart the more abundant life by the removal of all antagonisms thereto. When told that there is a difference between being free and being "free indeed," between the work of the Spirit in inspiring love and in perfecting love, they are still unable to construe to themselves satisfactorily this distinction. Hence they are inclined to reject the doctrine as an untenable theory.

But in the face of so much Scripture exhorting to holiness and commanding perfection and the fullness of the Spirit, and of so many promises and prayers relating to the same blessing as immediately attainable, is it not the wiser course to bind up this difficulty with two others pertaining to the Holy Spirit, which every evangelical mind believes, but none understands?

The first mystery is involved in the question how the Holy Spirit was always in the world as the inspirer of all true piety in human hearts, from Abel to John the Baptist, and yet at a definite moment, on the Day of Pentecost, the same Spirit came down from heaven into the world. Here is an enigma that orthodoxy universally fails to explain, and yet universally believes. For orthodoxy receives the doctrine of the Trinity, which implies the eternity and the omnipresence of the Holy Spirit, while the Bible asserts His agency in creation and His activity in human hearts in all the pre-Christian ages.

Faith accepts this mystery, which is too high for the grasp of reason. In a similar manner faith answers another question, how the Holy Spirit was in the heart of the man Jesus Christ, inspiring, illumining, and guiding Him all His life up to the hour of His baptism, when the Holy Ghost descended upon Him and abode in Him. How could He be in Him 30 years, and then enter into Him at a definite moment?

Here is a question that reason cannot answer. Yet every believer in the New Testament assents to these unharmonized facts in the relation of the Holy Spirit to the humanity of Jesus Christ. If the Bible teaches that entire sanctification through the Holy Spirit is a crisis in Christian experience, subsequent to the new birth by the same divine agent, and if reason cannot draw an accurate boundary line between these two works of the Spirit, why should we not bind up this mystery in the same bundle with the two we have just described, and relegate this difficulty to the domain of faith?

The first immediate effect would be the cessation of the debate that exists even in Wesleyan circles, there being no more occasion for a theological controversy on this third question than there is in the case of either of the other two.

The second effect would be that multitudes of earnest believers, having now emerged from the foggy metaphysics environing the subject of entire sanctification into the clear atmosphere of faith, would aspire with all the energy of their being to enter into the full spiritual heritage of the children of God, now clearly set before the eye of faith.

A third effect would be: "He that is feeble among them at that day shall be as David; and the house of David shall be as God, as the angel of the Lord," in efficiency to resist sin and to sway unbelievers to bow to Christ. There would be a spiritual revolution in the church, and vigor would supersede supineness, spiritual hunger would take the place of satisfied worldliness, harmony would succeed discord, and unity displace all tendencies to schism.

The Holy Spirit and Conscience[13]

Steele is addressing the question of the so-called collective conscience (without using that term) and the proper attitude of individual Christians toward it. He also recognizes the complexity possible in debatable questions, wherein difference of opinion may occur even among the sanctified. He calls this area "mutable morality." He sees the conscience quickened and guided by the Spirit, without being made infallible.

Among the unregenerate, conscience "is the activity of the Spirit of God, on the plane of nature, as Creator and Preserver." But in regeneration and entire sanctification the "Spirit works on the plane of grace, as the Reconstructor aiming to restore what sin had defiled."

Steele closes with some very practical directions for the proper understanding of the Spirit's guidance in matters of conscience, and for the prevention of fanaticism.

The question of worldly amusements has for centuries been before the court of conscience, and no final decision has been reached. But it is quickly decided by the arbiter which the gospel has called to the judgment seat, "the peace of Christ." All truly spiritual minds all down the Christian ages present a consensus on the deadening spiritual effect of the dance, the card table, and the theater. Because this consensus has been formulated into a rule of life for the benefit of inexperience, a great outcry has recently been made by some who seem to have forgotten that Christian character consists in something

13. This selection from *The Gospel of the Comforter* breaks into the third page of Chap. 19, "The Holy Spirit and Conscience," 166-73.

more than good morals, and that its essential principle is spiritual life imparted by the Holy Spirit and sustained by converse with the skies. What all truly spiritual minds have found detrimental to the life of Christ in the soul should be avoided by all who aspire to dwell on what Joseph Cook has recently called "spiritual uplands."

There are two classes of Christians. One class asks, "Is this amusement or indulgence forbidden? If it is not, I will embrace it." The other asks, "Is it obstructive of cloudless communion with the Father and the Son through the Paraclete? If it is, I will discard it." The one aims at innocence, the other at spirituality. The party of higher aim, even though it should be in the minority in any church, should prevail. Their standard should become universal. Thus will the unity of the Body of Christ be promoted, as is implied in the words of St. Paul: "Let the peace of Christ arbitrate in your hearts, to the which also ye were called *in one body.*"

TWO CLASSES

Paul asserts his love for the Hebrew nation, his "kinsmen according to the flesh," declaring that his conscience was "bearing him witness in the Holy Ghost." This strong asseveration implies an intimate relation between the Spirit and conscience. We may not be able to give a full and accurate statement of this relation. Among the self-evident truths with which the human mind is originally furnished is the distinction between right and wrong. The power to discover this distinction inheres in every sane mind. On questions relating to immutable morality, all such minds agree in their decisions. Such questions are few, and theoretical rather than practical. They are not modified by circumstances. They are such as these: Is it right to hate a benefactor? Is it right to punish the innocent? Is it right to reward the guilty? Is it right to intend injustice to a fellowman? Is it right to violate my own sense of right? to dishonor a parent? to commit adultery? There can be but one answer to these questions. They are addressed to the intuitive sense of right and not to the understanding or practical judgment that modifies the decision.

But when we ask the question, Is this accused man worthy of punishment? we have now to exercise our judgment and go through a course of reasoning before we can decide, and two perfectly conscientious persons may disagree in their verdict, because we are now in the region of mutable morality. Most of the moral questions in daily life are of this character. It is not enough to know that one man has killed another. I must take into account the circumstances, whether it was in self-defense when at-

MUTABLE MORALITY

tacked by a robber; or a burglar by night was shot in the act of breaking into the dwelling. This sufficiently illustrates mutable morality.

THE SPIRIT-QUICKENED CONSCIENCE

I can but think that the philosophy of Lotze and others is true, that all the self-evident truths are in the last analysis the activity of the immanent God in the human spirit. Hence the moral intuitions, immutable and invariable, are the voice of the divine Spirit immanent in all men, irrespective of regeneration and the gracious indwelling of the Spirit. There is a sense in which the Spirit of God is upholding nature. Men are not conscious of this immanent substratum of their being. But when the Holy Spirit, as a gracious gift, is bestowed upon the believer, he is conscious of His presence within as was Paul. The effect is manifest not so much in the increase of the power of moral discrimination, though it does clarify the moral perceptions, as in the marvellous addition to the power that impels toward righteousness. For the conscience has a threefold power—discrimination, impulse toward the right, and, after the act, approval or disapproval, according as the act is right or wrong. The gracious work of the Holy Spirit intensifies each of these functions, the second more manifestly than the first, and the third more than the second.

What effect does the fullness of the Spirit have in the decisions of practical questions in the province of mutable morality? We answer, it does not prevent errors in judgment and fallacies in logic. The Holy Spirit renders no one infallible in such matters. Yet He indirectly helps us by delivering us from the dominance of appetites and passions inimical to clearness of intellect and calmness of judgment. By inspiring in our hearts love to our neighbor as to ourselves, He strongly incites us to do perfect justice to him in our decision of questions involving his rights. Still the best of men and women who love God with all their hearts, and their neighbors as themselves, may go astray in judgment without a loss of love. . . .

KEEPING A GOOD CONSCIENCE

We do not teach that error is as good as truth in the production of holy character. . . . However, salvation consists in a vital union with Christ and not in opinions about Him. The maintenance of a good conscience toward God from day to day is essential to the life of faith. The believer must aim at, must be satisfied with nothing less than this. It is within his reach. Even the Old Testament saints had the witness that they pleased God. By a good conscience we mean an unaccusing conscience, not the assurance that we are exempt from errors in practice arising from misjudgments but the consciousness that our intentions and aims are unselfish and holy.

True spirituality cannot exist unless accompanied by scrupulous conscientiousness, the purpose to do right at any cost. If believers live as they should, they will find as the Christian life progresses, the testimony of conscience and the voice of the Holy Spirit becoming identical. As we have before intimated, the conscience is the activity of the Spirit of God, on the plane of nature, as Creator and Preserver. In regeneration and sanctification the Spirit works on the plane of grace, as the Reconstructor aiming to restore what sin had defiled.

It is interesting and instructive to note the relation of the Holy Spirit to conscience in the work of regeneration and sanctification. If man was created to be a temple of God, his spirit must be the holy of holies in which God dwells, and his conscience must be the ark of the covenant, which carries God's law. Sin defiled that sacred ark and rendered it offensive to the holy God. The scheme of redemption must have direct reference to the purification of the conscience.

The writer to the Hebrews intimates that Mosaism "could not make him that did the service perfect, as pertaining to the conscience" (Heb. 9:9), and he exhorts the believer to "draw near . . . having his heart sprinkled from an evil [guilty] conscience" (10:22). The conscience, relieved of guilt through faith in the atonement made by Christ, and ever after prompting to a life of obedience, is the spiritual organ in which the Holy Spirit evermore dwells, keeping watchful guard over the living law in the heart and constantly witnessing to the persevering believer that he is a child of God. Peace, the fruit of the Spirit, can dwell only with a "conscience void of offence." Holiness, the work of the Spirit, is also attested by conscience. "For our glorying is this, the testimony of our conscience that in holiness we behaved ourselves" (2 Cor. 1:12, Revised Version).

This is the place to set safety guards against the danger of a fanatical conscience, which is sometimes associated with extreme and erroneous views respecting the guidance of the Spirit. We lay down the following principles.

1. The Holy Spirit dwelling in the heart does not supersede the activity of our own reason, judgment, and moral sense in the decision of practical questions.

HOW THE SPIRIT GUIDES

2. While the Holy Spirit's testimony to the fact of adoption, including pardon, is direct and infallible when corroborated by the fruit of the Spirit, His guidance in the conduct of

life is not designed to be sole and infallible, but in connection with the inspired Word, our own common sense, divine providences, and the godly judgment of Christian people.

3. No guidance is of the Holy Spirit that collides with the Bible inspired by the Spirit. In such collision the Holy Scriptures must be followed in preference to the supposed leading of the Spirit.

4. The *Holy* Spirit, so named because it is His office to create and conserve holiness, never leads into sin, nor to doctrines that belittle sin by denying its exceeding sinfulness and its desert of eternal punishment, or by weakening the motives to repentance.

5. It being the office of the Spirit to glorify Christ, no teaching that disparages His divinity as the only Savior can come from the Spirit.

6. It being the work of the Spirit to regenerate and to sanctify, the declaration of any substitute for the new birth and holiness cannot be approved by the Spirit of truth, much less can it be inspired by Him.

7. In practical matters, the province of mutable morality, where fallible intellectual processes are involved and erroneous conclusions are possible, it is a species of fanaticism to ascribe each conclusion to the Holy Spirit.

8. There are two classes of people with whom pastors of churches have difficulty. The first consists of those who consider conscience as infallible beyond the sphere of motives, dispositions, and principles, and insist on infallibility in all practical questions, the realm of mutable ethics. They demand that the decisions of the intellect in respect to all moral subjects should be regarded as always right and clothed with the authority of intuitive judgments. Just here is found a fruitful source of most dangerous self-deception and of fanaticism in its various forms and degrees.

The second class includes those who make an analogous mistake in respect to the Holy Spirit. They insist that His infallibility, evinced in His direct witness to adoption, be carried into all questions of everyday life, questions involving intellectual research and the practical reason.

These erroneous claims respecting conscience and the Holy Spirit put these two classes beyond the reach of argument, persuasion, and advice. If members of the church, they inevitably become dictatorial, censorious, and divisive.

12

Olin A. Curtis
(1850-1918)

The simple facts of Professor Curtis' life are plain enough. Born in Frankfort, Maine, December 10, 1850, he forever displayed the rock-ribbed sturdiness of his New England upbringing. His basic education was obtained at Lawrence University (A.B., A.M., and S.T.D.); later he earned the B.D. at Boston University School of Theology, and still later he studied at various times at Leipzig, Erlangen, Marburg, and Edinburgh universities in Europe.

He first entered the Methodist ministry in Wisconsin, where he served at Janesville, Milwaukee, and Summerfield. After two years in Europe he settled into a happy pastorate in Chicago, determining to become a strong doctrinal preacher.

But his dreams of a pulpit ministry were shattered when, at 38 years of age, he was notified by telegram of his election to the chair of systematic theology at Boston University. His reluctance was overcome by the persuasive argument of Bishop Merrill, who reasoned: "It is, as you say, important to preach; but our preachers need the right kind of a message; and such a message you can, I think, give to them. As to this Chicago pulpit, it can be filled much more easily than we can find a suitable man for the Boston chair."

After seven years at Boston, Curtis accepted the position as professor of systematic theology at Drew Seminary, succeeding John Miley. John Peters claims that the transfer was in part because the liberal trends at Boston made the atmosphere increasingly uncongenial to Curtis.

Whether in the classroom or in the pulpit Curtis was the epitome of truth on fire. His passion for full Christological orthodoxy expressed with flaming eloquence and razor sharp logic galvanized the minds and souls of hundreds of students.

He was personally dissatisfied with the contours of a theological system that while orthodox seemed sterile. It was while studying a few months in Marburg, Germany, in 1904, that "the theological vision" came to him, he believed in answer to prayer. This vision was his racial concept of the Atonement (see Wiley, *Christian Theology,* 2:268). In it he preserved what he believed to be true in the three major theories—satisfaction, governmental, and moral—but with a greater stress on the holiness of God and the corresponding necessity of holiness in man. Christ, the Second Adam, was the progenitor of literally a new race, made Christlike not just outwardly but internally by both regeneration and total remaking. The new race was destined to completely displace the old and live in an environment equally remade.

Out of this vision his teaching was revolutionized and electrified. Out of it also was born his best-known work, *The Christian Faith.*

As an original and profoundly perceptive thinker, Curtis has few peers. His approach is anthropological, that is, he begins with man, including an analysis of personality, morality, and freedom. A chief cornerstone of his theology is free agency, without which there can be no basis for either sin or redemption and without which the goal of sainthood has no meaning. The cornerstone of redemption with Curtis is Christ—His incarnation, atonement, and unmodified deity. Because of this, Wiley classified his methodology as Christological (*Christian Theology,* 1:57).

Yet it can be claimed, with equal ground, that Curtis' method is psychological. His thinking moves consistently on the level of the inner working of personality, both in God and in man. His psychological grasp is impressive, revealing a dimension of understanding altogether unique for his day.

So basic is the fundament of moral concern in Curtis' theology that it shapes his views of God, of Christian experience, and of eternal destiny, requiring him to concede the possibility of eternal lostness. Man's will is finally determinative of personal destiny, both because of and in spite of the Atonement. It is the Atonement that makes fallen man's new choice possible. But the

Atonement is not causative in its power; God leaves the will free to accept or reject its provisions and requirements.

The following selections are taken from the original edition of *The Christian Faith,* 1905, reprinted in 1956 by Kregel Publications, Grand Rapids.

Generic Sin, Personal Sin, and Depravity[1]

Sin, generically conceived, includes legal defects as well as moral. When sin is thus given its broadest possible meaning, blameworthiness and innocence are undifferentiated. But *personal* sin is "responsible violation of God's law."

Personal sin cannot be inherited, Curtis says, but depravity can. To understand Curtis here, one must grasp his distinction between the individual and the person. An infant is an individual but not yet a person, for it has not yet reached the stage of "the power of self conscious decision." Moral character is the product of those self-conscious choices that personalize the cluster of traits and capacities that constitute the individuality—received by inheritance from one's progenitors. It is a *person* who sins because only a person is capable of living as a sinner or becoming a saint. Therefore, evil character, created by sinning, cannot be inherited or transmitted.

The kind of depravity that *can* be inherited Curtis defines as the inorganic condition of the self under moral law, a condition marking every individual of Adam's race. By "inorganic" Curtis means disorganized and incoherent; or, in his own words, "the individuality is out of harmony with the ideal of the moral person" (382). No person can successfully organize his own character into wholeness and holiness, because fear, the only motive available to man since the Fall, is not an organizing motive. Love alone will suffice, but it is available in dynamic measure only in Christ.

The term *sin* is used in so many ways that it is, in systematic theology, especially important to secure a more rigid classification of phases under the general term. The underlying idea of any kind of sin is that of lawlessness, or *anomia.* In the widest sense a sinner is anyone

1. The following is Chap. 15, "The Doctrine of Sin," 199-206.

who does not measure up to God's perfect law. Taken in this generic meaning, the Westminster definition is perfect: "Any want of conformity unto or transgression of the law of God."

Personal Sin. But when John Wesley said that sin is "a voluntary transgression of a known law" he was not thinking of sin in this sweeping manner, he was thinking of a *responsible* violation of God's law. For such violation it is evident there must be knowledge of what the law is, and a personal intention to break it. Why may we not say, then, that under generic sin there is personal sin, or that sin for which the moral person is accountable? Precisely analyzed, in relation to ethics, there are three features in all personal sin, namely: (1) A moral standard; (2) This standard in actual grasp by the personal judgment as to right and wrong; (3) Personal intention.

Surely you can see that this personal sin cannot be inherited. No man can inherit another man's personal bearing toward moral judgment. In fact, no personal act, or activity, or experience, can be inherited. Strictly speaking, nothing personal can ever be passed from being to being. And inasmuch as the personal deed, or attitude, cannot be inherited, it is inconceivable that the personal responsibility for such deed or attitude can be inherited. The theological conception of "an inherited guilt" results from a full failure to understand what personal life is, on the one hand, and what moral life is, on the other hand. With a few verbal changes, I would adopt Bishop Foster's words: "Sin is something which the individual man does; it is an act. There is no sin where there is not a sinner; and there is no sinner where there is not an act committed by him which constitutes him a sinner."

NONINHERITABLE

Individual Depravity. In considering depravity we need to bring up again the distinction made in this work between the individual and the person. Under the fact that man is a person is the fact that he is an individual being with body and soul. Before a babe comes to self-consciousness he has a fundament of being with a complex of characteristics, which are some of them physical and some of them psychical. The sum total of such characteristics I call the individuality of the child. This individuality is developed, and even modified, as the child grows. Indeed, the whole complex of native characteristics is at last treated from the standpoint of self-consciousness. And the ultimate man is, as I have said before, the individual *personalized* by self-decisive rejection and endorsement of original traits.

By depravity we mean that this basal individual life of a man is *inorganic.* The native characteristics are a clutter of items as unrelated as the odds and ends one finds in an attic. The term *total depravity* is one of those unfortunate phrases with which the scholastic theologian is fond of weakening his message; but there is a profound sense in which a man is, as he comes into the world, totally depraved. The point . . . is this: No man can organize his individual life under the demand of conscience. He is totally unable to start an organism. And the greater his development in moral personality the greater the impossibility of that adjustment which secures wholeness and peace in manhood. It is this inorganic condition of a man's fundamental, individual being that I understand to be depravity.

INHERITABLE DEPRAVITY

Every man comes inorganic into the world. Concerning this inorganic condition of depravity, there are two things so patent that they require no proof whatever: This first is the fact that depravity is *universal.* No organic man is ever born. The second thing is that depravity is *inherited.* Each person is a new creation, personality is never repeated, no man receives ability for self-consciousness and self-decision from his ancestors. But the individual has his complex of traits under the law of heredity. In other words, individuality is a racial matter and personality is not. Thus, inorganic individuality is inherited.

UNIVERSAL DEPRAVITY

This, though, only raises a larger question: "Why is it that the free moral person cannot organize his individual being under his moral ideal?" This question, you will remember, we answered thus: The natural moral life is one of fear, and fear is not an organizing motive; the man needs to have for organization the motive of moral love. In a simple word, no man can be complete unless he actually loves the holy God. Now we must push the discussion into a further recess. Why does man have this fear under moral authority? Because, I say, man now lives under the dominion of conscience *alone,* and he was not made so to live. Conscience itself is a ragged, unfinished item.

A COMPLETE MAN MUST LOVE GOD

Man was planned to live in constant personal intimacy with God, and to have his moral life perfectly saturated with that blessed holy fellowship. Just as one of our children is born into a home, and gradually, as the little human life opens into personality, comes to the personal grasp and regard for the father and mother, so it was intended that a man should be at home with God.

But now man is an outcast from the personal vision and intimacy with God. No wonder he is afraid, all alone out there under that vast, vague, ever-growing, absolutely pitiless moral demand. "So he drove out the man; and he placed at the east of the garden of Eden Cherubims, and a flaming sword which turned every way, to keep the way of the tree of life." This, then, is my understanding of depravity: Man's entire individual being is inorganic in its relation to the moral person. It is thus inorganic because the moral person lives under moral fear. And he lives under fear because he has been banished from the divine fellowship and is but a lonely slave under moral law.

The Broken Brotherhood. In the Arminian sense (responsible transgression) there can be no such thing as racial sin; but the race can be racially *anomia,* it can be out of joint with its under plan, it can be a failure. This is what we should mean by racial sin. Let us urge the meaning for a moment. The human race was designed to be an organic brotherhood of moral persons, in which every member would fit into the life of all, and minister to the progress and joy of all, and receive stimulus and social companionship and positive supplement from all.

But this great plan has been defeated by sin. Precisely as the individual man is inorganic, so the race is inorganic. The brotherhood is broken. Here and there we have a pathetic group of men trying to help each other, but often a large part of their effort is sheer waste. Of course, it is easy enough to contribute to the surface comfort of men; but to enter their real life, to understand them, profoundly to enlarge them and bless them, is an extremely difficult matter. Now think of doing this for all men, and you will begin to realize the awful extent of our racial failure! The cause of this racial failure is twofold: First, every individual member of the race is born depraved, and many members of the race are living in personal sin. Thus, the racial members are not capable of racial coalescence.

Second, the race has lost its center of organism. That center was to be God in immediate personal companionship with all men. To say

THE SUPREME LAW

that the race now exists only through the omnipresence of God is to miss the point altogether. The point is not that God is needed as a present power but that God is needed as a present personal companion. Men need to enjoy the actual vision of God as their supreme Friend. And all aims should begin in this vision, and all activities should feel the warmth of this vision even as in a cloudless day every growing thing feels the warmth of the sun. This conception is so sublime that we are timid before it, but we must dare to seize it. Never can we understand the work of our Lord until we can see that the original purpose was to have a brotherhood of men made complete by fellowship with God.

God's Hatred of Sin. When we try to explain this recession of the divine personal companionship from the race and the individual man there are several halfway things that can be said in the spirit of euphemism; but it is much more wholesome to state at once, and with plainness, the final fact. The recession is due to God's hatred of sin. But this hatred must be carefully related to our sentiment; for this is one of those places where the Christian feeling is fully as important as the Christian idea. We must not go to the one extreme of holding that the divine hatred is arbitrary, is a thing merely of God's naked and unrelated will. We must not feel that "God *could* have a different attitude toward sin, if He only *would*." We must realize that God could not be God, that He could not exist at all, without hating sin.

But we must not go to the other extreme of holding that this divine hatred is but an intense smiting by an impersonal law, and that there is no personality involved. If in any way you drop the personal element out of the hatred, you will lose, altogether or in part, its mighty ethical stroke. In the deepest sense, no impersonal bearing or performance can be ethical. No, we are to think of the law of God's holiness (and then to feel it) as plunging eternally into His absolutely exhaustive self-consciousness, and there furnishing motive for an active personal hatred of all sin as a violation of that fundamental holiness. Thus, God not only hates sin but *He means to hate it.*

This divine hatred of sin is expressed not only in depravity and the broken brotherhood but also in the natural world. I have said several partial things about nature, but it is now necessary to give a thoroughly Christian view. The reason why nature is such a bewildering jumble—now declaring the glory of God, and then becoming as voiceless as the sphinx; now as gentle as a mother, and then as cruel as a monster; now suggesting the most noble mood, and then actually violating every known moral principle—the reason for this bewildering jumble is that nature also is a broken organism. In a low sense, it is an organism still, it is organic as a physical system, and it appeals to the individual. But the world of nature is no longer competent for man as a moral person. God has not withdrawn from the cosmos as its cause, its present force, its life, its beauty; but as a divine revelation, as a word from the Infinite, Moral, Personal Being, the universe has been cast aside. Just as the individual man and the whole race are broken, so the home of man and the race is broken. Consequently the cosmos is to be finally destroyed. There is to be not only a new man and a new race but also a new universe. Redemption is to cover the person, the race, and their perfect home.

DEATH

Even now we have not exhausted the expressions of God's hatred of sin. There is one more expression and that the most dreadful of all—*death*. In relation to the death of Christ it will be necessary to bring out the full Christian interpretation of death; but here a general, tentative word should be spoken in this connection. A most striking evidence of the success with which science has eaten into the very vitals of Christian opinion is seen in the typical modern Christian view of death, and even of the death of Christ. If one ever could die of a broken heart, he might, I think, be justified in doing so after reading some of those popular poems and sermons and books that try to show that death is almost, if not quite, the most useful and most beautiful event in human experience. But if I understand, even in the smallest measure, the substance of the Christian faith, death should be to the Christian consciousness an abnormal event, a monstrous action of physical law against man, to express in every movement of its loathsome and appalling process God's boundless hatred of sin.

A NEW RACE

The race is a failure, and therefore it is to be destroyed. Beyond the grave there will be no Adamic race, but a new race in which our Lord will take the place of Adam. This racial destruction is by the method of death. The body, the old racial nexus, is to be torn from the man, and then to be made the starting point for another body, a new and a glorious social nexus. The entire divine bearing in death and depravity can, I think, be expressed in this way: God so loves man that He will himself pay the most costly price for man's salvation; but He so hates sin that He must secure, at every step of the way, a most extraordinary and even abnormal expression of His holy hatred. Man can be saved, because God loves him, but the path of salvation must be one violently out of course. Thus, we may say that depravity, and the broken race, and the wrench in nature, and the death of men—culminating in the death of our Lord—all manifest God's hatred of sin, but they manifest that hatred as an awful background from which stands out the infinite love of God toward men.

The Peril of Sin. Depravity in and of itself has no peril. As related to the work of the Holy Spirit, all depravity can ever do is to change

EVERLASTING MORAL DEATH

the form of the conflict of the moral person. Nor is the peril of sin in a habit of vice. Vice is really a superficial thing, and, at its worst, but an expression of depravity or of personal sin. The peril of sin lies in the fascination of personal sin, in that extreme self-assertion that is selfishness.

In the very nature of the case, every untested, every unsubdued person wants his own way. And if you place this untested person under a moral law, he will have instant interest in breaking the law. Personality itself must be chastened by free choice into the enjoyment of lawfulness. But let the free person once break the law, once get the taste of lawlessness, once have wildly throbbing in consciousness the experience of an immoral freebooter, and the untrammeled self-assertion is endlessly fascinating. And just here lies the dreadful peril. For this personal bearing in selfishness will soon stiffen into personal habit; to endure any moral restraint will become more and more irksome; until finally there will be no motive to submit to moral demand. This means, indeed, that the moral demand itself has been emptied of all urgency. And that means nothing less than everlasting moral death.

Personal Holiness—Old and New Formulations[2]

Curtis (1) summarizes Wesley's teaching, (2) evaluates its biblical support, and (3) offers his own psychological understanding.

It would be difficult to find a more simple, compact, and on the whole more accurate exposition of John Wesley's doctrine of Christian perfection than is found here, at least in such a brief compass. Before analyzing the teaching Curtis briefly reviews Wesley's personal spiritual pilgrimage. He gives his reasons for believing that Wesley's Snowsfields experience, December 23-25, 1744, was the time of his entry into the experience that he preached.

Curtis faults Wesley for his so-called crude realism, or "slavery to the lump" (which is certainly a misunderstanding of Wesley). Curtis acknowledges, however, the reality of what Wesley describes. He obviously understands Wesley's intent, as is evident in his illustration of the jealous preacher.

---

2. From Chap. 27, "Personal Holiness," 373-93.

As a regenerate man, the preacher fights his jealousy "to a standstill," but when made perfect in love *never feels it at all.* Curtis goes to the heart of the matter when he says, "As our preacher grows what does his growth in grace accomplish? According to Wesley, the growth does not affect the inherent disposition of jealousy at all. But it does bring the regenerate man himself to a more potent attitude, both of intolerance toward the disposition and of trust towards Jesus Christ. With this strengthened personal attitude the man dares to believe that his Lord can and will take that jealousy, and every wrong disposition, out of his life. In full, simple faith he asks Christ to do it; and, precisely as when he was converted, *it is all done at one stroke.*"[3] Though Curtis himself would not endorse the word *eradication*—because out of step with his psychology—what he describes as being Wesley's view obviously is compatible with the eradication model.

In discussing whether or not Wesley's teaching is biblical, Curtis advances strong affirmative evidence. However, he insists that to demand full systematic chapter and verse proof is not fair. "The Bible," he says, "is the *normative* authority on Christian doctrine; but we must also provide for the larger and larger interpretations by the developing Christian consciousness. . . . If we can make it indubitable that the Bible itself never allows the great saints to rest until they hold and experience this doctrine of supreme love, we will have secured quite as good a basis for the doctrine as could be secured by any amount of precise scriptural proof."[4]

Curtis' exposition of holiness from the standpoint of his personal psychology is both helpful and disappointing. For him the focus of personal holiness is "self consciousness and self determination." This relates to the awareness of one's motives and to the handling of those motives. Loyalty to God in the regenerate person is prompted by two motives, that of love and that of duty, with duty usually predominating. This fact explains the lackluster Christian life so common among the unsanctified; acting out of duty does not produce joy and exuberance. But in "personal holiness this motive of loyalty is transformed into the simple motive of pure love. . . . The 'whip of the ought' is gone. The holy person

---

3. Ibid., 384.
4. Ibid., 385.

does not do things because it is his duty to do them, but *because he loves to do them.*" In this single-minded motive of love, all "wrong motives are exhausted." The greater power of the love motive bleeds other motives of their urgency, in effect, enervating them if not displacing them utterly.

At this point Curtis' Wesleyanism wavers. He affirms the *usual* need for a crisis experience for the establishment of love in full supremacy. But he leaves the door open for the possibility that a man on his own may so cultivate the love motive as to gradually reach his goal of perfect love. Such growth is not growing *in* holiness, but growing *into* the experience. This position seems to minimize the radical cleansing of the Holy Spirit as an absolute, universal requirement.

Psychologically this doctrine belongs to the general subject of conversion, for holiness is really the completion of regeneration; but there are practical reasons for a separate discussion and formal emphasis.

BACK TO WESLEY

Our wisest course is to avoid the many controversies, and go back to John Wesley himself. We could not fairly deal with the controversies without making use of certain books that, while very penetrating and suggestive, manifest a spirit so narrow and ungenerous as to create an atmosphere unworthy of the theme. Of all the places in Christian discussion, this is the one place where it is more wholesome to have a weak argument than to have a vitiating atmosphere. And, further, there are three positive reasons why it is of the larger importance to go back to Wesley.

First, Wesley was the central point of Christian consciousness in a special doctrinal epoch. Historically, Wesley had almost the same epochal relation to the doctrinal emphasis upon holiness that Luther had to the doctrinal emphasis upon justification by faith, or that Athanasius had to the doctrinal emphasis upon the deity of our Lord.

Second, because Wesley was the leader in such an epochal movement, he had at hand *quantity in data.* The flaw in some of the modern discussions of Christian perfection is not so much in the reasoning as in the want of sufficient data to reason upon. The author is like a botanist giving out a *dictum* about a rare plant that he has cultivated in a hothouse. Every word he says is the truth, but it is not the *typical truth.* There is sometimes a genuine Christian experience that is so individualistic as to be almost worthless for theology.

Third, quantity of data, however, is of small worth unless there be surety in Christian discrimination. There are several recent scientific studies of Christian experience that would be almost priceless in value had the authors only known the difference between reality and imitation. It is possible to obtain a thousand answers to a list of set questions and have only a hundred of them with any real Christian meaning. It is just at this point that John Wesley was a master in Israel. He did almost no fundamental thinking, not merely because he was ceaselessly occupied with practical affairs, but mainly because his mind, like that of Gladstone, was receptive and not creative. But Wesley had such extraordinary spiritual insight, and such sanity in judgment, that often his most casual statement, especially in his *Journal,* is more illuminating than many a profound monograph in theology.

The Wesleyan Doctrine of Christian Perfection

Wesley's Own Experience. John Wesley was always loath to reveal the deepest things of his Christian life. He freely gives you his opinions and delights to talk about his work; but it is only now and then that you can catch any glimpse of "the inner chamber of introspection." And yet, by careful search, we can discover a few very significant points of self-revelation.

1. It is significant that Wesley was greatly impressed by Jeremy Taylor's discussion of *purity of intention.* Forty years afterward, in his *Journal,* May 14, 1765, Wesley writes: "I was struck particularly with the chapter upon *intention,* and felt a fixed intention 'to give myself up to God.'" For a young man 22 years of age, and having Wesley's ecclesiastical surroundings, to lift this one idea of intention into potent emphasis is not only remarkable but also momentous. It is, indeed, Wesley's prophetic start.

PURITY OF INTENTION

2. About five years later we find another significant point. He has now become "a man of one Book," and he perceives that love is the key to the full Christian life. In his *Journal,* same date as already quoted, he says: "I then saw, in a stronger light than ever before, that only one thing is needful, even faith that worketh by the love of God and man, all inward and outward holiness; and I groaned to love God with all my heart, and to serve Him with all my strength." Let us now note precisely what Wesley has: He has a clear idea that the person's central purpose is an important feature of the Christian life; but he perceives that it is not enough to hold passively this purpose, it must be positively expressed in a faith that works

LOVE THE KEY

by love. Further, he has a craving both for a supreme love toward God and for a life giving out that love in the largest service.

HIS SNOWSFIELDS EXPERIENCE

3. But did Wesley actually reach the experience for which he yearned? In his *Journal,* December 23-25, 1744, we read this: "I was unusually lifeless and heavy, till the love feast in the evening; when, just as I was constraining myself to speak, I was stopped, whether I would or no; for the blood gushed out of both my nostrils, so that I could not add another word: but in a few minutes it stayed, and all our hearts and mouths were opened to praise God. Yet the next day I was again as a dead man; but in the evening, while I was reading prayers at Snowsfields, I found such light and strength as I never remember to have had before. I saw every thought as well as every action or word just as it was rising in my heart; and whether it was right before God, or tainted with pride or selfishness. I never knew before (I mean not as at this time) what it was 'to be still before God.'

"*Tuesday, 25.* I waked, by the grace of God, in the same spirit; and about eight, being with two or three that believed in Jesus, I felt such an awe and tender sense of the presence of God as greatly confirmed me therein, so that God was before me all the day long. I sought and found Him in every place, and could truly say, when I lay down at night, 'Now I have lived a day.'"

To anyone familiar with John Wesley's careful, realistic manner of speech, it is evident that we have here the same sort of testimony to the experience of holiness that we have in his *Journal,* May 24, 1738, to the experience of conversion. If the one is not quite so near a full definition as the other, it surely is just as expressive of the fact. I find it almost impossible to read Wesley's words in the light of all his later utterance about the doctrine of Christian perfection, and not consider this date, December 24, 1744, as the probable time when he began to love God supremely.

THE WAY OF FAITH

4. In a letter from London,[5] June 19, 1771, there is another important reference to Wesley's own experience: "Many years since I saw that 'without holiness no man shall see the Lord,' I began following after it, and inciting all with whom I had any intercourse to do the same. Ten years after, God gave me a clearer view than I had before of the way to attain this, namely, by faith in the Son of God. And immediately I declared to all, 'We are saved

5. Letter No. 353.

from sin, we are made holy, by faith.' This I testified in private, in public, in print; and God confirmed it by a thousand witnesses. I have continued to declare this for above thirty years; and God hath continued to confirm the word of His grace."

By using this passage as a supplement to all we had before, I think it would be possible to make out quite a probable history of Wesley's movement in grace from the point where he was impressed so deeply by Jeremy Taylor on to his own actual experience of holiness; but such a history is not what I am really after. I want these references by John Wesley to his own experience simply to prepare the way for our better understanding of his teaching, and for our better appreciation of the quiet intensity and certainty manifest in his demand that Christian people should be holy.

Wesley's Teaching Analyzed

1. *The Name.* It is to be noted, first of all, that Wesley called the experience of holiness "*Christian* perfection, or *scriptural* perfection." (See especially Letter 351.)

2. *As to Conduct.* Such perfection does not mean perfection in conduct. "But these souls dwell in a shattered, corruptible body, and are so pressed down thereby that they cannot exert their love as they would, by always thinking, speaking, and acting precisely right. For want of better bodily organs, they sometimes inevitably think, speak, or act wrong" (Letter 186; also see Letter 229).

NOT PERFECT IN CONDUCT

3. *As to Individual Character.* The imperfection is deeper than conduct and belongs even to the individual character itself. "These very persons feel more than ever their own ignorance, littleness of grace, coming short of the full mind that was in Christ, and walking less accurately than they might have done after their divine Pattern; and are more convinced of the insufficiency of all they are, or do, to bear the eye of God without a Mediator; are more penetrated with the sense of the want of Him than ever they were before" (Letter 351).

4. *As to Temptation.* Nor does Christian perfection secure freedom from actual temptation. In a letter to the Bishop of London (8:484) Wesley says, "There is no such perfection in this life as implies an entire deliverance from manifold temptations." And in commenting on the *Journal* of Elizabeth Harper (9:278) Wesley says, "She was exceedingly tempted, after she

NOT BEYOND TEMPTATION

believed God had cleansed her from inbred sin." (Also see *Plain Account,* sec. 25, question 14.)

5. *As to Sinless Perfection.* Wesley himself avoided the phrase *sinless perfection,* because, in a generic sense, sin is any want of individual conformity to the law of God. But Wesley's own final definition of sin was strictly personal. In a letter (402) he writes, "Nothing is sin, strictly speaking, but a voluntary transgression of a known law of God." But I have found no way of harmonizing all of Wesley's statements at this point; and I am inclined to think that he never entirely cleared up his own thinking concerning the nature and scope of sin. At first I believed that a path out of his seeming inconsistency might be found by means of an exact chronology, but a more severe examination of all his writings forced me to give up even that hope.

6. *As to love.* While again and again Wesley makes much of personal intention, this intention of the person is not enough; the intention must be gathered up into a positive fullness of love. To be a perfect Christian is nothing other than being perfect in love toward God and man. In his *Journal,* August 27, 1768, Wesley writes: "I mean, 'loving God with all our heart, and our neighbor as ourselves.' I pin all its opposers to this definition of it. No evasion! No shifting of the question!" And the same statement, in slightly varying words, can be found all through Wesley's writings.

POSITIVE FULLNESS OF LOVE

7. *As to Time.* In *Brief Thoughts* (January 27, 1767) Wesley says: "As to time, I believe this instant is generally the instant of death, the moment before the soul leaves the body. But I believe it may be ten, twenty, or forty years before. I believe it is usually many years after justification; but that it may be within five years or five months after it, I know no conclusive argument to the contrary." In another place (not taken from the London edition) Wesley says that "some of the most unquestionable witnesses of sanctifying grace were sanctified within a few days after they were justified."

In his *Journal,* September 7, 1765, there is an account of what Wesley deems a most remarkable case—"a person convinced of sin, converted to God, and renewed in love, within twelve hours." And Wesley adds, "Yet it is by no means incredible, seeing one day is with God as a thousand years." I have found no testimony in Wesley's writings that justification and entire sanctification ever take place at the same time; but it is plain enough that in his last years he was unwilling to set any limit. As his experience with men widened, and his pastoral intuitions deepened, he became

PROCESS AND CRISIS

less conservative on all questions of divine grace—was more open to new and astonishing results in the work of the Holy Spirit.

8. *As to Growth.* On the surface there seems to be a contradiction in Wesley's teaching at this point. At times, apparently, he teaches that a regenerated man can actually grow into Christian perfection. In Sermon 107, on God's Vineyard, we read: "And as, in natural birth, a man is born at once, and then grows larger and stronger by degrees; so, in spiritual birth, a man is born at once and then gradually increases in spiritual stature and strength. The new birth, therefore, is the first point of sanctification, which may increase more and more unto the perfect day." There are a number of passages to the same effect.

To harmonize this view of growth with Wesley's other statements, some have said that he believed Christian perfection is obtained either by growth or by instant and crucial faith; but the truth, I think, is that Wesley regarded the *decisive stroke* in attainment as always instantaneous, growth being but a preparation for the stroke, or an after work in utilization and enlargement. In the *Minutes of Several Conversations,* Wesley says, "The substance, then, is settled, but, as to the circumstance, is the change gradual or instantaneous? It is both the one and the other. From the moment we are justified, there may be a gradual sanctification, a growing in grace, a daily advance in the knowledge and love of God. And if sin cease before death there must, in the nature of the thing, be an instantaneous change; there must be a last moment wherein it does exist, and a first moment wherein it does not" (8:328). . . .

Again in *Brief Thoughts,* Wesley touches upon the method of attainment: "I believe this perfection is always wrought in the soul by a simple act of faith; consequently, in an instant. But I believe there is a gradual work, both preceding and following that instant" (11:446).

9. *As to Assurance.* In the *Plain Account,* sec. 25, question 16: "How do you know that you are sanctified, saved from your inbred corruption?" Answer: "I can know it no otherwise than I know that I am justified. . . . We know it by the witness and by the fruit of the Spirit. And, first, by the witness. As, when we were justified, the Spirit bore witness with our spirit that our sins were forgiven; so, when we were sanctified, He bore witness that they were taken away. Indeed, the witness of sanctification is not always clear at first (as neither is that of justification); neither is it afterwards always the same, but, like that of justification, sometimes stronger, and some-

HOW KNOWN

times fainter. Yea, and sometimes it is withdrawn. Yet, in general, the latter testimony of the Spirit is both as clear and as steady as the former."

10. *As to Losing the Experience.* At first Wesley believed that the experience of Christian perfection could not be lost, but finally he was convinced that it could be. In a letter to his brother (No. 67, London, February 12, 1767) Wesley writes: "Can one who has attained it fall? Formerly I thought not; but you (with Thomas Walsh and John Jones) convinced me of my mistake." In the month before (January 27) Wesley had said: "By perfection I mean the humble, gentle, patient love of God and our neighbor, ruling our tempers, words, and actions. I do not include an impossibility of falling from it, either in part or in whole. Therefore, I retract several expressions in our hymns which partly express, partly imply, such an impossibility."

In his *Journal* (July 25, 1774) Wesley writes: "I went on to Sheffield and on Tuesday met the Select Society. But it was reduced from sixty to twenty; and but half of these retained all that they received. What a grievous error to think those that are saved from sin cannot lose what they have gained! It is a miracle, if they do not; seeing all earth and hell are so enraged against them; while, meantime, so very few, even of the children of God, skillfully endeavor to strengthen their hands."

11. *As to the Primary Compromise.* "From long experience and observation, I am inclined to think that whoever finds redemption in the blood of Jesus, whoever is justified, has then the choice of walking in the higher or the lower path. I believe the Holy Spirit at that time sets before him the 'more excellent way,' and incites him to walk therein, to choose the narrowest path in the narrow way, to aspire after the heights and depths of holiness—after the entire image of God. But if he does not accept this offer he insensibly declines into the lower order of Christians. He still goes on in what may be called a good way, serving God in his degree, and finds mercy in the close of life through the blood of the covenant" (Sermon 89, "The More Excellent Way").[6]

---

6. That many Christians drift into a low level of Christian experience because they know nothing better, is undoubtedly true. But to teach that entire sanctification is a personal option is dangerous (Wesley notwithstanding). When once confronted with clear light, and a personal conviction of need, deliberate rejection is disobedience, and disobedience is sin. Continued disobedience is fatal. Such a person may continue in the church and retain a form of godliness but will need to be restored before eligible for

12. *Personal Conclusion.* By constant association with an author we may come to have a conception of his real meaning in spite of all his inconsistencies. For our conception has been gradually formed by a number of features in a complex combination—by his peculiar silences; by his spontaneous repetitions; by the way a certain paragraph closes, or a certain discussion culminates; by the instant and eager answer to an unexpected question; and even by his choice of phrase in a crucial situation. My view of John Wesley's meaning is of this indefensible sort. I am sure of his doctrine of Christian perfection, as sure of its essential import as I am that I walk the earth; but I am unable to relate my view, in an exact way, to all of his statements, or even to all of his very important statements.

I will give my own personal conception without quotation and without defense. According to John Wesley, a sinner has three things the matter with him: First, he is *guilty;* second, he is morally *powerless;* and, third, his inherent and inherited *disposition is wrong.* Or, as I would say, the individuality is out of harmony with the ideal of the moral person. When a sinner is justified, the guilt is canceled. When he is regenerated he receives a nucleus of power, not enough to exterminate his wrong disposition, but enough "to fight it to a standstill." In Christian perfection, there is no such fight with the disposition, "no civil war at all," for the wrong impulse never enters the consciousness as motive.

Now, when you ask, "What becomes of the wrong disposition?" Wesley can give no fundamental answer, for the simple reason that he was all mixed up in his psychology. I am not one of those courageous men who dare to say that John Wesley had at the bottom of his thinking a consistent psychology. My opinion rather is that he was a very crude realist, but usually restless under that unspeakable curse, and trying to break away, without ever being fully able to accomplish his purpose. This "slavery of man to the lump" is not surprising in Wesley's time. . . . Many of the recent Christian books, and many more of the modern scientific books, have been written with an underlying realism so gross that any serious thinker should have been unwilling to grant it toleration at any time since the death of Immanuel Kant; and I almost said at any time since the death of Plato.

---

heaven. The deathbed experience of many (sometimes believed to be conversion and at other times called sanctification) is often precisely such a restoration to the justifying favor of God. The "blood of the covenant" does not automatically cover a lifetime of walking against light (1 John 1:7). *Editor.*

But Wesley does this much for us: he holds that the civil war in the perfect Christian is rendered impossible by love, supreme love toward God and man. Whether the natural disposition is extirpated or only overwhelmed, it does not appear in a consciousness full to the brim of pure love.

It will help us all, probably, if I can give a concrete illustration of Wesley's view. Here is a man, a Christian preacher now, who has from infancy been naturally jealous. He is not only converted, but is a noble Christian man, ready to sacrifice for his Lord, and equally ready to serve his brethren. But he is still jealous in disposition. Yesterday he heard another preacher's sermon receive large commendation, and, like an uprush of mercury in the heat, that old feeling of jealousy rose into consciousness. His volition, his personality, had no more to do with it than his will had to do with the coming on of night. But the moment our preacher realizes that he is jealous he makes Christian battle, and forces the disposition back, back into its cave.

WESLEY'S DOCTRINE ILLUSTRATED

Now, we have here an exceedingly strange psychological situation, for the man's struggle is plainly Christian in its revelation of the moral ideal, and yet the struggle reveals a motive life that no Christian ought to have, at all. Or, we can say this: The victory is truly that of a Christian man—but as a Christian man he should have been without the possibility of that kind of battle.

Now comes a pivotal inquiry. As our preacher grows, what does his growth in grace accomplish? According to Wesley, the growth does not affect the inherent disposition of jealousy at all; but it does bring the regenerate man himself to a more potent attitude, both of intolerance toward the disposition and of trust toward Jesus Christ. With this more potent personal attitude the man dares to believe that his Lord can and will take that jealousy, and every wrong disposition, out of his life. In full, simple faith he asks Christ to do it; and, precisely as when he was converted, *it is all done at one stroke.*

Now what is the man's condition? On the one hand, he never is conscious of jealousy. Rather does he spontaneously rejoice in another man's success. On the other hand, he never comes to self-consciousness without being filled, like the prodigality of a freshet, with the love of God. This, as I understand him, is what John Wesley means by the conquest of inbred sin through supreme love. And if there is one man here to whom Wesley's view of inbred sin suggests no reality, no point in kindred experience, he most surely is to be regarded as extremely fortunate.

Christian Perfection and Biblical Theology

Is there, though, for this Wesleyan doctrine of Christian perfection any support in biblical theology? In Wesley's day there was such an arbitrary and fragmentary and superficial use of Scripture, even by the finest scholars, that many students have gained the impression, if not the belief, that the scriptural argument for Christian perfection cannot endure the test of our modern method of studying the Bible. I am certain that the test can be endured; but, before taking up that matter, I wish to enter a protest against the prevailing notion that before we can accept a Christian doctrine every feature of it must have exact scripture proof.

THE BIBLE NORMATIVE

The Bible is not to be used in that hard and fast manner. The Bible is the *normative* authority on Christian doctrine; but we must also provide for the larger and larger interpretations by the developing Christian consciousness. For example, it would be enough to show that Christian perfection is not in contradiction of any Scripture, but harmonizes with the *trend of emphasis* in the New Testament upon moral love; and is the loftiest ideal belonging to the most normal and most thoroughly developed Christian consciousness. If we can make it indubitable that the Bible itself never allows the great saints to rest until they hold and experience this doctrine of supreme love, we will have secured quite as good a basis for the doctrine as could be secured by any amount of precise scriptural proof.

St. John's Doctrine of Love. The essence of the message of St. John to the Christian man is in this glowing message (1 John 4:16 to 5:5): "God is love; and he that abideth in love abideth in God, and God abideth in him. Herein is love made perfect with us, that we may have boldness in the day of judgment: because as he is, even so are we in this world. There is no fear in love: but perfect love casteth out fear: because fear hath punishment. He that feareth is not made perfect in love. We love, because he first loved us. If a man say, I love God, and hateth his brother, he is a liar: for he that loveth not his brother whom he hath seen, cannot love God whom he hath not seen. And this commandment have we from him, that he who loveth God love his brother also.

"Whosoever believeth that Jesus is the Christ is begotten of God: and whosoever loveth him that begat loveth him also that is begotten of him. Hereby we know that we love the children of God, when we love God and do his commandments. For this is the love of God, that we keep his commandments: and his commandments are not grievous. For whatsoever is begotten of God overcometh the world: and this is the victory that hath overcome the world, even our faith. And who is he that overcometh the world, but he that believeth that Jesus is the Son of God?"

When we separate the real message of this passage from its rhetorical mannerism, we find the connected points to be these: First, in St. John's conception of God the finality is love. Second, we make entrance into this love of God by being "begotten of God," and this takes place when we believe "that Jesus is the Christ." Third, we are prepared for the day of judgment by having this love of God made perfect in us; and this perfection of love can be achieved in this life—"because as he is, even so are we in this world." Fourth, the marks of the perfect love are that it "casteth out fear," that it makes a man "love his brother also," and that it enables him to "do his commandments," and to have that perfect faith which "overcometh the world."

St. Paul's Teaching. In coming to St. Paul's teaching, I wish to be sure of avoiding not only all personal bias but also all Methodist bias, so I will make use of Professor Bartlet, Mansfield College, Oxford. In his article on Sanctification in the *Hastings Dictionary of the Bible,* Professor Bartlet writes of St. Paul's teaching as follows:

"There is a state possible to Christians, corresponding to the ideal of their calling, in which they can be described as 'unblamable in holiness' *(amemptous en hagiōsunē),* and into which they may be brought by the grace of God in this life. Therein they stand hallowed through and through *(holoteleis),* every part of their being *(holoklēron humōn to pneuma kai hē psuchē kai to sōma)* abiding by grace in a condition fit to bear the scrutiny of their Lord's presence without rebuke *(amemptōs en tē parousia tou kuriou hēmōn Iēsou Christou tērētheiē).* Such is the teaching of 1 Thess. 3:13 and 5:23.

"The fidelity of God to His purpose in calling men to be Christians is pledged to this achievement (1 Thess. 5:24), though there is no definite time, as measured from the initial hallowing of the Spirit in conversion, at which it must needs be accomplished. God, who begins the good work in the soul, also continues to work at its perfecting *(epitelein)* right up to the day of Jesus Christ (Phil. 1:6); and yet, ere that day dawns, Christians may become already 'pure in purpose' (*eilikrineis* = Christ's *katharoi tē kardia,* Matt. 5:8) and 'void of offense,' and so remain 'until the day of Christ' (Phil. 1:10).

"It is this state of realized sanctification of conduct, or 'walk,' so as to 'please God,' that Saint Paul has constantly in view in exhorting his converts to holy living (for example, 1 Thess. 4:1). This is what he means, at times, by his use of *hagiasmos.* But the conception needs to be carefully guarded and explained by other aspects of his thought. Thus (1) it represents a growth *in* holiness rather than *into* holiness out of something else; (2) it is conceived as realizable by a definite act of faith—claiming and appropriating its rightful experience by an act of will informed by the living energy of the Holy Spirit—rather than as the cumulative result of a slow, instinctive process after conversion; (3) it is not the same as absolute moral perfection or consummation *(teleiousthai),* but is rather the prerequisite to its more rapid and steady realization."

Our Lord's Injunction. "Jesus said unto him, Thou shalt love the Lord thy God with all thy heart, and with all thy soul, and with all thy mind. This is the first and great commandment. And a second is like unto it, Thou shalt love thy neighbour as thyself. On these two commandments hang all the law and the prophets" (Matt. 22:37-40).

This one passage should forever settle the entire controversy as to both the ideal and the possible achievement in the Christian life. From the Old Testament (Deut. 6:5 and Lev. 19:18) our Lord takes the two items of supreme moment and lifts them into a Christian primacy of injunction. It has been said that our Savior did not intend to give an actual injunction, but only to suggest a Christian ideal. But I do not understand how anyone can hold such a view; for a study of the Savior's life will show that love toward God and love toward man were the two tests He used in determining all religious values. And the fact is that today the Christian consciousness anywhere grasps the Master's words as injunction, and responds to them as such, making them the final test of life.

Every Christian deed *is* Christian, every Christian thought *is* Christian, every Christian feeling *is* Christian, precisely to the extent that it expresses this supreme love. Ignatius clearly apprehended the whole thing when he said: "The beginning of life is faith, and the end is love. And these two being separately connected together, do perfect the man of God; while all other things which are requisite to a holy life follow after them. No man making a profession of faith ought to sin, nor one possessed of love to hate his brother. For He that said, Thou shalt love the Lord thy God, said also, And thy neighbor as thyself."

A Psychology of Personal Holiness

With my conception of a perfect Christian very much more is required than perfection in motive, and so I prefer the expression *personal holiness.* The holiness is *personal* because it is holiness exactly from the standpoint of self-consciousness and self-determination. What you have is holiness in personality.

The Transformed Motive. As we have seen, the motive life of a regenerate man is organized about the motive of *loyalty to Christ.* This motive of loyalty is not a simple motive, but is made up of two elements, one of love and the other of duty. At rare moments these two elements are in self-consciousness with equal force, but usually the sense of duty is paramount. The regenerate man, in any typical situation, is seeking to do his duty. His common remark is: "I will be true; I will not deny my Lord."

LOVE AND DUTY

This loyalty is very different from the loyalty of the moralist; and for two reasons, namely, it is loyalty to a Person, and it is rooted in the enthusiasm of a positive personal affection. And yet the Christian loyalty has some of the same psychological weakness that renders morality so ineffective. Duty always implies a conflict, a civil war. The sense of the ought is, like a bugle, intended to call the person into battle. And while this moral battle is great, it is less than the highest mood. You will see what I mean if you think of a home where husband, wife, parents, children are ever trying to do their duty by each other. What a dreadful home that would be! Not one day with the simple, rejoicing impulse of dominant love.

Now we can quickly uncover the fundamental flaw in the condition of the regenerate man. In his life of struggle to do his duty he cannot organize his inner personal life. He has the beginning, the ground plan, so to speak, of an organism, but he cannot carry out the plan. And the reason of this failure is that when duty is paramount in consciousness, even though it be the most noble sense of duty, the personal task is done under fear; and fear is never an organizing motive.

In personal holiness this motive of loyalty is transformed into the simple motive of pure love. There remains all the ethical quality of duty, for the new supreme love is a moral love; but "the whip of the ought" is gone. The holy person

HOLINESS IS PURE LOVE

does not do things because it is his duty to do them, but *because he loves to do them.* But note this closely, the important thing here, psychologically, is not the *vastness* of love (that is a matter of endless growth), but simply that the love *entirely occupies the self-conscious mood.* Whenever the person comes to self-consciousness it is crammed with love to the very edges. Thus, there is a perfect personal organism, because all the man's motivity is nothing but love in a variety of shapes. In the man's personal life there is no antagonism, no civil war whatever. He may be tempted, as we shall see, but he cannot be tempted by his own inorganic condition, by his own depravity.

The Exhaustion of Wrong Motive. The old question, "Suppression or eradication?" I cannot fairly consider; for my psychological point of view is different from that of the combatants about that question. But if you will recall my early discussion of motivity, you can see what I think takes place when the motive of loyalty is transformed. The new motive of pure love is not used in a negative conflict, but is used positively; and by this positive use the wrong motives are exhausted. There is no longer any heart-interest in them. They are mere ideas empty of all urgency toward the will. It is not that they are *for the time being* shut out from consciousness; no, the work is profounder than all that; they cease to have any existence as motives. The full use of pure love has exhausted them.[7]

The Question of Growth. Is this experience of personal holiness obtained by growth? First of all, the practical concern in the matter leads me to say that the very word *growth* is a word that should be used, in this discussion, only with extreme care. For to many people growth means a natural, an unurged development from an implanted germ. Now, there is no such unurged development in the Christian life. The whole thing is personally strenuous from conversion until death. But is personal holiness obtained gradually by earnest endeavor? Looking at it in the most comprehensive way, our answer should be in the affirmative; for the crisis itself is profoundly involved in all that has led up to it. Some of the evangelists to the contrary notwithstanding, no man can arbitrarily leap into that faith which is the condition of the divine gift of supreme love. It may, now and then, look like such a leap, but psychologically

GROWTH NOT SPONTANEOUS

---

7. Whether the terms *suppression* and *eradication* are in his view relevant to his concepts or not, what Curtis is describing, in his unique psychological way, is what competent eradicationists would mean by their use of the term. *Editor.*

it is not so. You can leap into self-assertive presumption but never into real faith.

And yet John Wesley's emphasis upon the ultimate stroke is exceedingly important. For there is a great difference between the last phase of the regenerate life and the first phase of the life of supreme love. As it is only in the latter case that the motive of loyalty *entirely* loses the note of duty; only in the latter case that love absolutely fills self-consciousness to its rim; so only in the latter case that all the wrong motives of disposition are exhausted.

But the question has been asked, "Why, on the principle of your discussion of motivity, may a regenerate man, with his motive of loyalty, not simply fight his way into personal holiness?" My answer is this: To exhaust all wrong motive by a sheer negative fight would require more time than belongs to our earthly life; and even if there were time enough the victory would exalt the element of duty and not the element of love in the motive of loyalty. What we are after is so to escape sin as to escape the bondage of conscience itself, and, like God himself, live the life of moral love.

But I have yet one suggestion to offer. I can conceive of another way of obtaining Christian perfection in love. It is, anyway, a theoretical possibility that a man might at the beginning of his Christian life lay hold of the under element of love in his loyalty, and *emphasize that.* He might by self-sacrifice express his love for Christ in the most complete manner. He might in prayer cultivate the mood of love for Christ. And so on and on until his love for the Savior absolutely filled his consciousness, and his entire service was one of rejoicing love and not one of moral obligation.[8] There are a few of the saints whose experience is at least a hint of this kind of earnest growth into the fullness of love.

Falling Away from Personal Holiness. If it be true that the wrong motives of our depraved, inorganic individuality are thoroughly exhausted of their urgency, then the question arises, How is it possible to fall away from personal holiness? I answer: No Christian who is perfect in love can fall in the same way that a regenerate man may fall, by yielding to a motive that springs out of individuality into consciousness in antagonism to the moral ideal. But this higher life itself, as strange as it may seem at first, is a life of the most extreme self-

8. Self-cultivation of the "mood of love for Christ" would prove a fruitless endeavor without the decisive liberating and enabling action of the Holy Spirit (Rom. 5:5). *Editor.*

assertion. It is *spiritual* self-assertion, but it is fundamental self-assertion, all the same.

PERILS OF THE SANCTIFIED

Out of this spiritual self-assertion there may come three motives, any one of which may bring on struggle, and with the struggle the possibility of personal defeat. These three motives are: First, spiritual discouragement. A saint in this world, in situations where Christ is not triumphant, can have a sort of discouragement that actually grows out of his supreme love for his Lord; and there is very great peril in such a mood. Second, spiritual pride. There is no experience so lofty in this life to a moral person as entirely to protect him from spiritual pride. In studying the temptations of our Savior, you see the whole method of its approach. A regenerate man is not half so likely to have this temptation as is the saint who is filled with love. Third, spiritual ambition. A holy man may have an ambition to be a great leader in the church, or a great preacher, or a great evangelist; and his ambition may have been created by his love for Jesus Christ; and yet there may come such a turn in his affairs that he must choose between his ambition and his Master. That is, his ambition is so interesting to the man now that it stands over against the very love that created it.

I am inclined also to think that sometimes this supreme love has created a subordinate love for some human person, which has grown and grown, until at last, in an abnormal crisis, the saint was obliged to make a choice between his human friend and his Savior. But beyond all our psychological theorizing we positively know that there are peculiar temptations that are characteristic of the life of personal holiness; and, such temptations once in force, there is ever the possibility of falling away from the experience. The Christian battle is not over until through death we pass into the intermediate state.

13

Wilson Thomas Hogue

(1852-1920)

Bishop Hogue, of the Free Methodist church, was born March 6, 1852, in Lyndon, N.Y. After attending the Ten Broeck Free Academy for three years, he entered the Free Methodist ministry at 21 years of age. After he had completed the four-year course of study, he was ordained by Bishop E. P. Hart in 1877.

Following several successful pastorates Hogue was invited to become the founding president of Greenville College, Greenville, Ill., in 1892. From 1893 to 1894 he doubled as bishop, filling out the term of B. T. Roberts who had died.

In 1894 Hogue was elected editor of the *Free Methodist,* which position he held along with his college responsibilities for eight years. In 1903 he was elected bishop and held the office until his death February 13, 1920.

The sturdy discipline and great capacity of the man are seen in that during the years of his busy presidency, he earned the Ph.B., A.M., and Ph.D. degrees from Illinois Wesleyan University.

Bishop Hogue was a shaping force and guiding star in every facet of the development of the young denomination, including its educational program, music, foreign missions, and Sunday School polity and literature. He was the author of nine books, including the well-known *Hogue's Homiletics and Pastoral Theology* (1887); *History of the Free Methodist Church in North America* (1915); and *The Holy Spirit: a Study* (1916).

Hogue was a man of titanic caliber—a rare saint, an able administrator, and certainly a deep and sound Wesleyan thinker.

His influence has been felt far beyond the limits of his own church.

Throughout his entire ministry his commitment was strong and unequivocal to the Wesleyan doctrine of entire sanctification—in testimony, in sermon, and by pen. It sprang from an inner drive and conviction. Perhaps this commitment can best be explained by his own testimony that he "received the baptism with the Spirit soon after being licensed to preach."

The Holy Spirit in Sanctification[1]

Bishop Hogue's major work, *The Holy Spirit: a Study,* is less than a systematic theology but much more than an ABC introduction. It is the rich culmination of 30 years of study in the field. The scope is as broad as the specialized nature of the topic allows. In 28 chapters the author deals with every aspect of first, the person and nature of the Holy Spirit, and second, the nature of His soteriological functions. The treatment is traditional, yet there is in the book a very stimulating freshness and originality. As the heading indicates, the concentration of this chapter is on the direct ministry of the Spirit in effecting the entire sanctification of believers.

The Holy Spirit is "the Spirit of holiness," the Sanctifier of God's people. It is His province to sanctify the Church, that it may be presented "as a chaste virgin unto Christ" at His coming, "not having spot, or wrinkle, or any such thing; but that it should be holy and without blemish" (Eph. 5:27).

The Church can be made holy, however, only through the sanctification of the individual members composing it. Hence, in order that He may be the Sanctifier of the Church, the Holy Spirit is the Sanctifier of individual believers in Christ. Every true believer on the Son of God is "elect according to the foreknowledge of God the Father, through sanctification of the Spirit, unto obedience and sprinkling of the blood of Jesus Christ" (1 Pet. 1:2).

Holiness is indeed "the central idea of Christianity." It is the golden thread that runs through the whole Bible, binding all its separate parts into one harmonious and glorious whole. Dr. Randolph S.

---

1. The following is Chap. 22, "The Holy Spirit in Sanctification"; it includes pp. 264-81. The volume was published in Chicago, 1916, and printed by William B. Rose, Agent.

HOLINESS CENTRAL

Foster (later Bishop), in his admirable book on *Christian Purity*, aptly says, "It breathes in the prophecy, thunders in the law, murmurs in the narrative, whispers in the promises, supplicates in the prayers, sparkles in the poetry, resounds in the songs, speaks in the types, glows in the imagery, voices in the language, and burns in the spirit of the whole scheme (of redemption), from its alpha to its omega, from its beginning to its end. Holiness needed. Holiness required. Holiness offered. Holiness attainable. Holiness a present duty, a present privilege, a present enjoyment, is the process and completeness of its wondrous theme. It is the truth glowing all over, webbing all through revelation; the glorious truth that sparkles, and whispers, and sings, and shouts in all its history and biography, and poetry and prophecy, and precepts, and promises and prayers; the great central truth of the system. The wonder is that all do not see, that any rise up to question a truth so conspicuous, so glorious, so full of comfort."

The Bible is a holy Book. It is the Word of an infinitely holy God, revealing to man the true nature of holiness, its absolute necessity, its transcendent and eternal benefits, the divine provision made for its attainment by the children of men, the way into this gracious experience, the excellent fruits by which the experience is evidenced, the glorious destiny to which it leads, and the irreparable doom of neglecting such a great salvation. It presents the incarnation, death, resurrection, and ascension of Jesus Christ as having been comprehended in the divine method of providing complete redemption for sinful men, and the Holy Spirit as having been given in His Pentecostal effusion as a result of Christ's finished work, and as the omnipresent and omnipotent Agent in the application of redemption to believers for their uttermost salvation. It is the Spirit's work to quicken from the death of sin; to regenerate man's moral and spiritual nature; to assure him of the forgiveness of sins, and of his acceptance with God through Christ; to be his Teacher, Guide, Strengthener, Comforter, and the Perfecter of his life in Christ.

Sanctification Begun in Regeneration

The Holy Spirit's work of sanctification is begun and in goodly degree accomplished in regeneration. In this experience a new life is begotten in the soul, a life of holy love, which thenceforth takes the ascendency over all the carnal tendencies of human nature, bringing them into habitual

INITIAL SANCTIFICATION

subjugation to the law of Christ; so that, as Wesley says, "Even babes in Christ are so far saved as not to commit sin." "He that is born of God doth not commit sin," St. John says, "for his seed remaineth in him: and he cannot sin, because he is born of God." Every one who becomes an experimental Christian ceases to practice sin and begins to practice holiness as the rule of his life. Holy principles are begotten in his heart, and thenceforth have the mastery in his life. Hence it is that all Christians are designated in Scripture as "holy brethren." They are so far sanctified, by virtue of their conversion, that the power of sin over them is broken, and the power of a new and holy life in Christ is set up in its stead. Holiness is the predominating character of every person justly entitled to be regarded as a Christian. We cannot insist too strongly on the fact that sanctification has its beginning in the work of regeneration.

REMAINING SIN

But while the Holy Spirit begins the work of sanctification by the regeneration of the heart and life, it does not follow, nor is it true, that the work of sanctification is completed at the time of regeneration. The power of sin is broken, but its presence, in the form of sinful principles and propensities, is still within, and is a constant source of danger. It is like inflammable material in the basement of one's house, where it is likely at any moment to come in contact with fire and result in explosion, or conflagration, or both. It is a foe that lurks within the citadel awaiting the opportunity to betray it to its final overthrow, and which, when detected and resisted, struggles mightily for the mastery. "The flesh lusteth against the Spirit, and the Spirit against the flesh: and these are contrary the one to the other: so that ye cannot do the things that ye would" (Gal. 5:17). Both the Scriptures and the common experience of Christians, the world over, alike declare the falsity of Count Zinzendorf's teaching, that sanctification is complete at the time of regeneration; or, that "all true believers are not only saved from the *dominion* of sin, but from the *being* of inward as well as outward sin, so that it no longer *remains* in them" (Wesley).

Entire Sanctification Defined

But what is complete sanctification? and wherein does it differ from the experience of regeneration? Entire sanctification is deliverance from all inward sin—from evil thoughts and evil tempers. It is a state in which no wrong tempers, dispositions, or affections remain in the soul; but in which all the thoughts, words, and actions are governed by pure love. Regeneration is a work of grace within the heart that effects a change of our moral state and character, emancipating us from the dominion and love of sin, planting the principle of obedience in the heart, and restoring the soul to the image of God. As to the difference between this experience and that of entire sanctification, the late Rev. William McDonald has well expressed it as follows:

1. In regeneration, sin does not *reign;* in sanctification, it does not *exist.*

2. In regeneration, sin is *suspended;* in sanctification, it is *destroyed.*

3. In regeneration, irregular desires—anger, pride, unbelief, envy, etc.—are *subdued;* in sanctification, they are *removed.*

4. Regeneration is salvation from the voluntary *commission of sin;* sanctification from the *being of sin.*

5. Regeneration is the old man *bound;* sanctification is the old man *cast out* and *spoiled of his goods.*

6. Regeneration is sanctification *begun;* entire sanctification is the work *completed.*

The Holy Spirit Convicts Believers of the Need of Holiness

The Spirit of God enlightens believers as to their *need* of being sanctified as a means of leading them into the experience. He convicts them of inbred sin, makes them feel and loathe the plague within, and leads them to humble themselves and cry mightily to God for deliverance. Conviction for sanctification is not conviction of guilt for wrong done or for duty neglected. It is not in any sense a conviction of having backslidden from God. On the other hand it presupposes present consciousness of walking in the light and enjoying full justification from all past offenses and failures, through faith in the atoning merits of Jesus Christ. But the conviction of which we speak is a painful consciousness that, while we are fully justified from all past transgressions and derelictions, there is a *principle* of sin *within* us, which clings to our very thoughts, tempers, and desires, evermore seeking the ascendency in outward conduct, defiling the inward man in every part, and from which we should and must be *cleansed* before we can fully glorify God and enjoy uninterrupted communion with Him.

HOW THE SPIRIT CONVICTS

This conviction is accomplished by the Spirit in two ways: first, by those inward operations through which He sheds light upon the soul and reveals to it its own corruptions, still remaining since the work of regeneration has been effected; and second, by so illuminating the Scriptures to the understanding as to make these reveal to him the necessity and privilege of being made altogether holy. Sometimes the disclosures thus made of inbred sin are well-nigh overwhelming and cause the soul to doubt for the time being whether it can be possible that he has ever been truly converted. "How can one be a true child of God," he asks himself, "in whom there is so much moral impurity and such a painful sense of unlikeness to the moral character of God?" To be led from the raptures of a sense of reconciliation with God into such a humiliating and painful consciousness of inward unfitness for His holy presence, is, for the time being, a melancholy experience; but by this experience the Holy Spirit is seeking to lead the soul, not to disparage the work already accomplished in its regeneration, but to aspire for and definitely seek after that "higher life" in Christ, that full conformity to the character and will of God that is attainable through faith in the blood of Jesus.

Reveals the Possibility

The Holy Spirit not only shows the believer the need of this higher work, but in doing so He likewise reveals the assured possibility of receiving it. He so illuminates the commands, precepts, prayers, promises, and provisions of the Scriptures bearing upon this very point that the conviction of its glorious possibility becomes not only assured, but a mighty incentive to seek it at every cost, and a mighty uplift and inspiration to the faith that is necessary to its attainment. Thus assured, uplifted, and inspired with a vision of the glorious possibility, the soul advances to the realization of the desired object, saying,

The thing surpasses all my thought,
But faithful is the Lord;
Through unbelief I stagger not,
For God has spoke the word.

Faith, mighty faith the promise sees,
And looks to that alone;
Laughs at impossibilities,
And cries, "It shall be done!"

Obedient faith that waits on Thee,
Thou never wilt reprove;
But Thou wilt form Thy Son in me,
And perfect me in love.

Blessed be God! the Comforter who convinces of the *necessity* of this work points us also to the *possibility* of its enjoyment. Our blessed Savior in His intercessory prayer says, "Sanctify them through thy truth: thy word is truth" (John 17:17). So the Holy Spirit who inspired the Word brings to mind the promises and assurances, and reveals the rich provisions of infinite love. Does the child of God groan over his impurities and corruptions? He is pointed to the fountain over which is written, "The blood of Jesus Christ his Son cleanseth us from all sin" (1 John 1:7). Does he sigh over his want of conformity to God? He is assured that, beholding with open face as in a glass the glory of the Lord, he shall be changed (metamorphosed) into the same image, from glory to glory, even as by the Lord the Spirit (2 Cor. 3:18). Does he doubt whether this is his great privilege? Again the Spirit speaks in His Word, "Faithful is he that calleth you, who also will do it." He is thus led to see that such is the amplitude of the provision, such is the all-cleansing power of the blood of Christ, such is the almightiness of the Eternal Spirit, that no matter what he may be, the work can be done; and whenever, at any stage of the believer's experience, his faith lays hold of these great promises and provisions, the work will be done. According to his faith will it be done unto him.[2]

Leads Toward Perfection by Promoting Growth in Grace

The Holy Spirit also leads the believer on toward perfection or entire sanctification through promoting his growth in grace. There is a growth in grace before one is sanctified, and a more rapid and healthful growth in grace after sanctification is experienced. All growth in grace preceding the experience of sanctification is a gradual approach to the point where sanctification will be complete. "Are we to understand, then, that entire sanctification is finally reached by a gradual process?" someone may inquire.

CRISIS AND PROCESS

No. That is not the idea. To use Mr. Wesley's figure, death is reached through a process of dying, which may be longer or shorter in its continuance; but the man is never dead until the *process* has ended, and a *crisis* has occurred. So that we may say of death it is both a process and a crisis. However long the process may be continued, the crisis must be reached wherein death is complete. That crisis in case of a man dying must of necessity be

2. Dunn, *Mission of the Spirit,* 184-85.

instantaneous. Just so with a soul seeking holiness. Under the quickening, illuminating, prompting, and guidance of the Holy Spirit, he is led more and more to "mortify the deeds of the flesh," or continually to die to sin, which is a process comparable to the gradual approach of physical death. "For if ye live after the flesh, ye shall die: but if ye through the Spirit do mortify the deeds of the body, ye shall live" (Rom. 8:13).

But as sure as the gradual process of dying physically leads to an instantaneous crisis in which physical death is complete, just so surely will constant growth in grace and the corresponding process of dying to sin bring one at last to that spiritual crisis where he is "dead indeed unto sin" in the deepest meaning of the term, "and alive unto God through Jesus Christ." Moreover, the crisis will be instantaneous in this case, as well as in the former one.

CONVICTION FOR CARNALITY

In the meantime, however, it is the work of the Holy Spirit to lead the soul more and more to that self-judgment of his own inbred sin and to that outward purification of himself in the new light shed upon him, which will bring him nearer to God and into deeper fellowship with Him, and which will beget within him deeper loathing of his own impurity and intense hungering and thirsting after "all the fulness of God." Without this he cannot attain unto that deep and abiding rest of soul that he sees to be his privilege in Christ. This is one of the ways in which the Spirit promotes growth in grace on the part of believers.

Then, too, He broadens, deepens, and clarifies the vision of the soul regarding the Scriptures and the things of the kingdom of God. He also brings before it the numberless incentives to utter self-abandonment and to following on to know the Lord in the fullness of His saving power, as well as revealing to him in ever deeper measure the disastrous consequence of allowing the light that is in him to become darkness; and thereby He both lures and spurs the soul on in exercising itself unto godliness and seeking to be perfect, even as its Father in heaven is perfect. "As many as are (thus) led by the Spirit of God, they are the sons of God" (Rom. 8:14). While led by the Spirit, they continually fulfill the precept, "Grow in grace, and in the knowledge of our Lord and Saviour Jesus Christ"; and this growth involves increasing sanctification, and brings them constantly toward the point where the crisis will be reached in which their sanctification will be complete. There is a sense in which such souls can truly say, "I die daily."

Leads to Final and Permanent Self-consecration

The Spirit of God likewise leads the believer to that final and permanent act of self-consecration to God that his increased light upon the character and claims of the Almighty shows him is required as a prerequisite to being sanctified wholly. In order to sanctify us wholly, God must have us wholly. In other words, we must yield ourselves to Him in utter self-abandonment, passive in His hands as clay in the hands of the potter, before it is at all possible for Him to consummate the work within us. "I beseech you therefore, brethren, by the mercies of God, that ye present your bodies (including your entire manhood) a living sacrifice, holy, acceptable unto God, which is your reasonable service. And be not conformed to this world: but be ye transformed by the renewing of your mind, that ye may prove what is that good, and acceptable, and perfect, will of God" (Rom. 12:1-2). The Spirit of God alone can enable us to present such a sacrifice to God; but when once it is made, through the power of the Spirit, we shall quickly prove the will of God to be in all things "good, and acceptable, and perfect." Such a consecration is a condition of knowing the will of God, and also being brought into full and perfect harmony therewith.

TOTAL YIELDING

Consecration, in the sense of separation and dedication unto God, is our part of sanctification; but it is very far from being the whole of the experience. Hence those who are taught to consecrate themselves to God, and then to rest in that act of consecration, on the supposition that they have put themselves upon the altar, and that "the altar sanctifieth the gift" (which is not true in this sense, although it is in another sense), are being misled and are apt to rest in their own doing instead of resting alone on the atoning blood of Jesus Christ. Our own consecration no more saves us than any other work in which we might trust. But when full and complete it brings us to where, and to the only point where, it is at all possible to exercise that appropriating faith in Jesus that will bring the realization that His part of the work is done as well as ours, and that we are now cleansed from all sin, or wholly sanctified.

Author of the Faith That Sanctifies

But *faith* is the final and absolute condition of our sanctification; and the Spirit of God develops in fully surrendered hearts that faith which lays hold upon the promises, appropriates them, and realizes their fulfillment. "When he, the Spirit of truth, is come, he shall guide

FAITH THE FINAL CONDITION

you into all truth." "He shall glorify me," the Master said; "for he shall receive of mine, and shall show it unto you." "He shall teach you all things." "He shall bring all things to your remembrance, whatsoever I have said unto you." By this work of teaching, guiding, quickening the memory regarding Christ's words, and revealing the things of Christ, the Spirit gives us strong ground for our faith to stand upon; sets the object of faith before us in the most transparent light; and enables us to grasp and hold that object unwaveringly in the face of whatever would occasion our staggering or failure. The Holy Spirit stimulates, strengthens, steadies us in our attitude of faith in God, through Jesus Christ, as we yield ourselves to Him in *willing* and *trustful* surrender. Thus our faith grows strong, and we are finally enabled to say:

Bold I approach the eternal throne,
And claim the crown through Christ my own.

The last thing we can do to bring a realization of the blessing as in actual possession is to *close in with God by faith.* "Believe on the Lord Jesus Christ, and thou shalt be saved." The heavens and the earth may fail, but this Word of Jehovah can never fail. It is true yesterday, and today, and forever. There may have been failure on our part, but it is impossible on God's part. Nor can the prayer prompted by the Holy Spirit and offered in true faith ever be in vain, whatever suggestions to the contrary may assail us.

Unanswered yet? Faith cannot be unanswered;
Her feet are firmly planted on the Rock;
Amid the wildest storms she stands undaunted,
Nor quails before the loudest thunder shock.
She knows Omnipotence has heard her prayer,
And cries, "It shall be done, sometime, somewhere."

But our faith must get beyond saying, "It shall be done, *sometime, somewhere,*" and must be emboldened to claim the blessing *now,* before the experience can be realized.

"But what is the faith by which we are sanctified?" it may be asked. No better answer can be given to this question than that which

FAITH APPROPRIATES NOW

Mr. Wesley has furnished. Speaking of "the faith by which we are sanctified, saved from sin, and perfected in love," he says:

This faith is a divine evidence or conviction

1. That God hath *promised* this sanctification in the Holy Scriptures.

2. It is a divine evidence or conviction that what God hath promised He is *able* to perform.
3. It is a divine evidence or conviction that He is *able* and *willing* to do it *now.*
4. To this confidence that God is *able* and *willing* to do it *now,* there needs to be one thing more—a divine evidence or conviction that He *doeth* it.

The Author of Assurance

Such a faith will inevitably result in assurance. "He that believeth hath the witness in himself." It will bring a blessed consciousness of the incoming and infilling of the Holy Spirit, the divine Comforter, the Almighty Sanctifier; and He is the witness to His own accomplished work. "As it is written, Eye hath not seen, nor ear heard, neither have entered into the heart of man, the things which God hath prepared for them that love him. But God hath revealed them unto us by his Spirit: for the Spirit searcheth all things, yea, the deep things of God. For what man knoweth the things of a man, save the spirit of man which is in him? even so the things of God knoweth no man, but the Spirit of God. Now we have received, not the spirit of the world, but the spirit which is of God; that we might know the things that are freely given to us of God" (1 Cor. 2:9-12).

The various experiences of divine grace are among the things that are freely given to us of God, and therefore are among the things that we *know* by the revealing of the Holy Spirit. One may know when he is sanctified as certainly and as satisfactorily as when he is justified. Every seeker of this grace should claim it by faith, and hold steadfast in this faith, until his faith is sealed with assurance that the Comforter has come and has finished His gracious work. Then he can sing exultingly, from a deep consciousness that his heart is made pure,

'Tis done! Thou dost this moment save,
With full salvation bless;
Redemption through Thy blood I have,
And spotless love and peace.

Some Things Sanctification Will Not Do

But there are some things that the experience of entire sanctification will not do for those who receive it. First, it will not render them

STILL FALLIBLE

perfect in the sense of being infallible. The fully sanctified do not attain unto absolute perfection, which belongs to God alone; nor to the perfection of angels, who were created pure, spiritual beings, and have a perfection of sinlessness and intelligence that we cannot attain unto while in the flesh; nor to the perfection of the unfallen Adam in his paradisaical estate; nor to any state of human perfection such as exempts from error in judgment and consequent errors in practice, from numberless infirmities of mind and body, from subtle and powerful assaults of temptation, or from fallibility of any kind and the possibility of backsliding. Satan will contend every inch of the ground from the place where one is sanctified until he is safely within the gates of the celestial city. It will be our only safety to "watch, and fight, and pray," mustering all the faith and courage we can command at all times. The character of the assaults upon the faith and love and patience of the sanctified may be changed, but they will never be very long without something of the kind occasioning the necessity for vigilance, wisdom, courage, and strength.

Second, the experience of holiness will not supersede the possibility and necessity of growth in grace. Some have urged as an objection to this doctrine that if one were fully sanctified he could no longer grow in grace. How absurd! As well might one caution a lady against getting all the weeds out of her flower bed, because if she gets all the weeds out, the flowers can grow no more. She would suspect such a man of having escaped from a lunatic asylum; and, unless she regarded him as dangerous, would proceed with her work in the calm assurance that the more free she could make the flower bed from weeds, the more rapidly and healthily the flowers would grow.

GROWTH IS NEEDED

"After a soul is cleansed from all sin, it is then fully prepared to grow in grace." Moreover, it is not only possible to grow in grace after one has been sanctified, but it is absolutely necessary, in order to maintain the ground already occupied, and retain the experience already received. The rule in the kingdom of Christ is, "To him that hath shall be given, and he shall have abundance; but from him that hath not shall be taken away even that which he hath." This was spoken by our Lord regarding the matter of improving or failing to improve upon the talents entrusted to the servants during their lord's absence. Is it not equally pertinent here? The lesson should be laid diligently to heart by all.

Third, the experience of entire sanctification in no sense excludes the need of a Mediator on the part of those who receive it. It has been ignorantly objected to the doctrine that, if it be true that men may be sanctified wholly in the present life, such an experience would place them beyond further need of the mediation of Christ. Such an objection is wholly without foundation. Entire sanctification is derived only through the mediation of Christ, and the experience is continuously dependent upon faith in that mediation. All spiritual blessings are perpetually conditioned upon our relation to Christ as Mediator, "who of God is made unto us wisdom, and righteousness, and sanctification, and redemption" (1 Cor. 1:30). Even the redeemed before the throne of God stand there only through the mediation of the Son of God (Rev. 7:15).

CHRIST STILL NEEDED

I ask them whence their vict'ry came;
They, with united breath,
Ascribe their conquest to the Lamb,
Their triumph to His death.

The holiest souls are the most deeply conscious of their need of the Atonement. The holy life is ever a "life of faith in the Son of God." All the fruits of Christian holiness are conditioned upon our abiding in Christ, the living Vine. The sanctified believer rejoices in Christ Jesus (Phil. 3:3); walks in Christ Jesus (Col. 2:6); glories in His cross (Gal. 6:14); does all things in His name (Col. 3:17); constantly looks and longs for His appearing to claim the Kingdom for himself and for His Bride (Titus 2:13; Rev. 22:20). His is the life that is "hid with Christ in God" (Col. 3:3); "and never does he so fully comprehend the preciousness of Jesus as when he has put away the evil and bitter thing which Christ hateth."

The Holy Spirit Produces Holy Fruit

The Holy Spirit invariably produces the *fruit* of holiness in all who are truly sanctified. Vain, and positively damaging and wicked, is all profession of holiness that is unaccompanied by corresponding fruit. "Either make the tree good and his fruit good, or else make the tree corrupt and his fruit corrupt." Nothing is surer than that the tree is known by its fruit. "But now being made free from sin, and become servants to God, ye have your fruit unto holiness, and the end everlasting life" (Rom. 6:22). "The fruit of the Spirit is love, joy, peace, longsuffering, gentleness, goodness,

THE SPIRIT'S FRUIT

faith, meekness, temperance: against such there is no law" (Gal. 5:22-23). The one fruit of holy character that comprehends all others is LOVE. "He that dwelleth in love dwelleth in God, and God in him. Herein is our love made perfect, that we may have boldness in the day of judgment: because as he is, so are we in this world. There is no fear in love; because perfect love casteth out fear: because fear hath torment. He that feareth is not made perfect in love" (1 John 4:16-18).

To love God with all the heart, soul, mind, and strength, and to love one's neighbor as himself, is to manifest the fruit of sanctification or holiness. This is the sum total of Christian perfection.

14

Solomon Jacob Gamertsfelder
(1851-1925)

Hundreds of pastors now in the United Methodist church and the Evangelical Church of North America, as well as related groups, cut their teeth on Gamertsfelder's *Systematic Theology*. He was by far the dominant theological influence in the branch of the Evangelical United Brethren Church known as the Evangelical Association, or, the Evangelical Church—a German Methodist group dating from the early 1800s.

Converted at 10 years of age, Gamertsfelder lived consistently thereafter as a thoughtful and studious Christian, devoting his entire life to the message and work of his church. By temperament he had a philosophical as well as a theological cast of mind. It shaped his sermons, his teaching, and his writing. His personal warmth and steadfastness were shared by his wife, Emma, and his five children. But also hundreds of students confided in him their most personal problems, and they learned to rely on the soundness of his practical and theological judgment.

Gamertsfelder was educated at North-Western College, Harvard and Chicago universities; he received the Ph.D. degree from the University of Wooster, in Wooster, Ohio (1903). Before his election to the faculty of the Evangelical Theological Seminary in Naperville, Ill., he taught in the public schools and enjoyed several successful pastorates in the Ohio Conference of the Evangelical Association.

For 28 years (1895-1923) Gamertsfelder taught at the seminary in Naperville (now merged with Garrett, Evanston, Ill.). For some years he also served as the seminary's president. His *Systematic Theology*, first published in 1921, was reprinted in 1938. The teacher's influence not only lives on, but through his writings has become even wider since his death, August 4, 1925.

Sanctification[1]

In discussing entire sanctification S. J. Gamertsfelder is strong at some points where weakness is sometimes found in others. He writes, "The essential element of entire sanctification is the removal of certain carnal remains that occasionally becloud the consciousness of being a child of God, or weaken the disposition of holy love implanted in regeneration." He also argues for the rationality of two natures coexisting in the believer; but protects himself from misunderstanding by defining nature as "an order or form of activity." He says that he is meaning moral natures, not material substances, for both the carnal nature and the regenerate nature.

Gamertsfelder explains the cleansing of the carnal nature in terms of Thomas Chalmers' "expulsive power of a new affection." Holy love therefore is the "instrumental cause of entire sanctification." There is some ambiguity, however, in relating the Holy Spirit as the efficient Agent to the Word and to divine love, both of which he calls the instrumental agents. Careful analysis seems to yield something like this: The truth, or Word of God, convinces us of our carnal state and provokes seeking; the Holy Spirit floods us with love, which in turn eradicates the carnal mind by counteraction.

In discussing the terms *suppression* and *eradication*, Gamertsfelder opts for eradication. He writes, when suppression means "only that evil tendencies arising in consciousness are not expressed outwardly, then there is at least a manifestation of the carnal nature within the self, and there can be no claim to entire sanctification whatever. Any term that expresses the idea that carnal remains are not found in consciousness may be used, but eradication is unequivocal and the strongest term that can be employed."

1. S. J. Gamertsfelder, *Systematic Theology* (Harrisburg, Pa.: Evangelical Publishing House, 1921; reprint, 1938). Part VII, Chap. 7, "Entire Sanctification," 529-44.

Entire Sanctification

The subject of entire sanctification is not without its difficulties. It is difficult to formulate a definition that will meet with general approval. It is difficult to state clearly the relation of entire sanctification to regeneration, on the one hand, and to Christian maturity, on the other. It seems difficult for some to keep in mind the distinction between sanctification in the general sense, and entire sanctification. These difficulties, however, will not be so formidable if we avoid ambiguous terms and hold ourselves strictly to the accepted significance of the terms we use.

Much of the opposition we encounter in defending this sacred doctrine will be avoided if we practice Christian forbearance toward those who do not apprehend the Christian life in precisely the same form as we do. It will be especially advantageous to us in discussing this subject with an opponent to be clothed with the spirit that prompted the great logician Paul when he said: If eating meat make my brother to offend, I will eat no meat while the world stands.

1. Biblical Terminology

It is very desirable that our terminology be biblical. The term *second blessing* is not biblical; there is no warrant for its use in the Bible, and moreover, it has no rational ground to support it. The fact that a few leaders of some parts of the church have used this term is no reason why we should use it. If by using the term we give offense, we have special reason to avoid it. There is really no occasion for defending the use of this term, because other better terms are in common use.[2]

The terms *entire sanctification* and *perfect love* are best adapted to express our doctrine on this subject. The former expression has

NAMES

biblical warrant in the words of St. Paul when he prays for the church at Thessalonica that they might be wholly sanctified (1 Thess. 5:23). The words "sanctify you wholly," or as Carl Weizsaecker translates Paul, "sanctify you through and through," give biblical warrant for our term. Moreover, the fact that the term *entire sanctification* is used in the doctrinal standards of the Evangelical

2. The author's distaste for the term *second blessing* is puzzling, in view of the fact that he argues for the possibility and major importance of entire sanctification to be experienced by believers after conversion. Would that not be a second blessing? *Editor.*

Association commends it to our use. The term appears in our Discipline and also in our Catechism. Bishop J. J. Esher uses equivalent German terms in his *Christian Theology.* He uses the term *Völlige Erneuerung,* and *Völlige Heiligung.* These terms of Bishop Esher are literally equivalent to expressions used by Dr. H. C. Sheldon. He says, "As the first decisive stage of sanctification is identical with regeneration or the initiation of sonship, so complete sanctification signifies perfected sonship—the state of one so truly a child of God as to have naught of the unfilial remaining in himself."[3]

It will be necessary to use the modifying term *entire,* so as to distinguish this subject from progressive sanctification. The term *perfect love* is appropriate and very significant. This term is St. John's favorite, as appears from the following: "Herein is our love made perfect, that we may have boldness in the day of judgment: because as he is, so are we in this world. There is no fear in love; but perfect love casteth out fear, because fear hath torment. He that feareth is not made perfect in love" (1 John 4:17-18). This is the most definite term.

Other formulas are also used to express this stage of Christian experience, such as holiness, Christian perfection, heart purity, love enthroned, the higher Christian life, and perfect consecration. There is no valid objection to the use of these terms, except perhaps the thought that they are not sufficiently definite for doctrinal discussion. But to determine a suitable terminology is scarcely more than the antechamber of this subject. The burden of the task before us is to set forth the real import of the stage of Christian experience indicated by the term *entire sanctification.*

Under the preceding subject we have endeavored to set forth the Christian life as progressing from regeneration to the end of natural life. Entire sanctification must not be thought of as simply identical with, nor the acme of, progressive sanctification. But we should rather look on entire sanctification as a definite stage of Christian experience, a stage that has been preceded by a progressive Christian life, and that continues simultaneous with other new attainments in the divine life of the soul.

2. The Essential Element of Entire Sanctification

By essential we mean that particular constituent ingredient, or form of activity, without which the attainment, whatever it may be,

3. *System of Christian Doctrine,* 464.

cannot be properly called entire sanctification. Like all other stages of the Christian life, entire sanctification, or perfect love, cannot be bounded as to details by the same lines for all believers. In regeneration the vigor of the spiritual life imparted to one may vary greatly from the vigor imparted to another, although the persons may have been brought up in the same environment and under the same religious instruction. So also in the experience of perfect love; the higher Christian life of one person may differ widely from that of another as to details. Notwithstanding all this diversity, there is a unity in essential element that justifies a doctrinal statement of this stage of Christian experience. The essential element of entire sanctification is the removal of certain carnal remains that occasionally becloud the consciousness of being a child of God or weaken the disposition of holy love implanted in regeneration.

(1) Remains of the carnal nature appear after regeneration. John Wesley designated these remains sin in the believer. The expression is not well chosen, because of the broad sense in which the word *sin* may be used. In regeneration we are made partakers of the divine nature by being raised up from the death of sin. When we are born again a new nature is imparted that counteracts the old nature, but the old nature is not thereby necessarily ejected in its entirety. The disposition of holy love is the dominant power in the soul, but it does not reign undisturbed. Let us bear in mind that the term *nature* here stands for an order or form of activity. The depraved nature in man is nothing more or less than an order of evil and sinful activity. The divine nature imparted at the new birth is identical with an order of holy activity. The elements of this nature are righteousness, peace, and joy in the Holy Spirit. We are speaking of moral natures and not of material substance.

It is a common occurrence in the physical world that two natures are found in the same organism. One branch of a tree may be dead while others are living. In the dead branch an order of activity called death reigns alone and works for dissolution. In the living branches an order of activity called life prevails, and these branches live. A gnawing worm may be destroying the sap of a tree, and yet the living forces of the tree keep it alive. Two opposing natures may operate in a tree weakened by a gnawing worm for some time without killing the tree. The only question is which nature will gain the victory over the other.

A similar conflict between two natures may be discovered in man's physical life. Disease fastens itself upon the body. The forces of life at once rush in to reinvigorate the diseased members, and to throw off the disease; but for the time being both natures are active in the same body. If disease gains the ascendency, physical death follows; but if the disease is cast out, or at least kept under by the forces of life, physical life continues. These illustrations are a positive demonstration of the fact that two opposing natures may be active simultaneously in the same physical organism.

We do not hesitate to affirm that two opposing natures may be active simultaneously in the same moral organism. A believer may be annoyed and weakened by the remains of the depraved nature in him. We may not be able to comprehend fully the metaphysics of this moral phenomenon, but it is not more mysterious than its analogue in the physical realm. We can know a nature only by its activities. This principle of epistemology applies to the physical, mental, and moral realms alike. By their fruits we know them. If there be a good nature in man, it can be known only by activities of good proceeding from him. If an evil nature is alive, it will, in the course of time, manifest itself by evil deeds.

TWO NATURES

That there are remains of the carnal nature in the believer ordinarily after he has experienced the new birth, can be determined first of all by an appeal to his own consciousness. Anyone who honestly inquires concerning the source of the evil tendencies he feels rising occasionally from within, will be forced to admit that his experience agrees with the doctrine of carnal remains after conversion. This appeal, however, is valid in theology only if it is in accord with the teaching of God's Word. The Word of God is our ultimate authority.

CARNAL NATURE

There are many exhortations in the Word of God, addressed to believers, to put away the remains of the carnal nature. The apostle Paul says in writing to the Church at Ephesus: "Put off concerning the former conversation the old man, which is corrupt according to the deceitful lusts; and be renewed in the spirit of your mind" (Eph. 4:22-23). In his letter to the Colossians he says, "Mortify therefore your members which are upon the earth; fornication, uncleanness, inordinate affection, evil concupiscence, and covetousness, which is idolatry" (Col. 3:5). A similar exhortation is sent forth by the apostle Peter to the strangers scattered in various parts of Asia Minor, "Wherefore laying aside all malice, and all guile, and hypocrisies, and envies, and all evil speakings, as newborn babes, desire the sincere milk of the word, that ye may grow thereby" (1 Pet. 2:1-2).

SCRIPTURAL

In these words newborn babes are admonished to lay aside all malice, and guile, and envy. The apostle John also says, "Every one that hath this hope in him purifieth himself, even as he is pure" (1 John 3:3).

The fact that the Holy Spirit, speaking through the inspired apostles, admonishes believers to lay aside and put off these remaining manifestations of the carnal nature, is proof in itself that some activities of the carnal nature remain after conversion. The apostles found it necessary to exhort believers to continue in the work of cleansing from sin and to go on unto perfection; yea, that it was the duty of everyone to purify himself after the pattern of Jesus.

The Evangelical Association is perfectly in accord with the Scriptures in her doctrine on entire sanctification and Christian perfection. In our Discipline we define Christian perfection as being nothing else than a "total deliverance from all sin, in the proper sense of the word, which is accomplished by means of the love of God being perfected in the heart."[4] The state here described is the same as that which we have designated perfect love. In our Catechism we say, "Entire sanctification consists in purification from all sin or eradication of all *evil* affections and desires."[5]

In this definition the remains of the carnal nature are designated "evil affections and desires." We require of all candidates for admission into our ministry that they have, or earnestly seek to have "the love of God shed abroad in the heart by the Holy Spirit in such a measure that they have complete victory over every sin inwardly and outwardly."[6] We also say that it is the Christian's privilege to "be redeemed from all sin long before he die; that is from all evil affections and desires."[7]

AWARENESS OF NEED

We gather, then, from the reading of the Scriptures and the doctrinal standards of the church, that the remains of the carnal nature in the believer, to be removed in entire sanctification, consist of malice, envy, self-will, lack of resignation to the will of God, yielding either voluntarily or negligently to the tempter, evil affections and desires, uncleanness, and covetousness. These and other terms are used to describe the carnal nature. Christian consciousness, when enlightened by the Holy Spirit, will lead to the dis-

4. Discipline of the Evangelical Association, Sec. 29.
5. Catechism of the Evangelical Association, Question 302.
6. Discipline of the Evangelical Association, Sec. 110.
7. Ibid., Sec. 30.

covery of the evil tendencies and desires that should be removed by the grace of God. This teaching of carnal remains in the believer after conversion is corroborated by the experience of everyone who seeks in all sincerity to walk in fellowship with God by putting on the Lord Jesus Christ.

CLEANSING

(2) Ample provision is made to remove the remains of the carnal nature. If we were to look to human strength alone, we should have no hope of perfect deliverance in this life. But our help cometh from the Lord, the Almighty God, who has provided a perfect redemption for His saints. It is in the provision of grace made by the shedding of Christ's blood that all uncleanness may be washed away. This is the plain teaching of God's Word. It was said by the angel concerning the promised Messiah, "Thou shalt call his name Jesus: for he shall save his people from their sins" (Matt. 1:21). We find here no limitations as to God's purpose to save. When Jesus was about to finish His work of redemption on the earth, He said: "I have declared unto them thy name, and will declare it: that the love wherewith thou hast loved me may be in them, and I in them" (John 17:26). The believer shall be made the recipient of God's love as freely and fully as Jesus himself.

Then also that classic passage of St. John, giving in one sentence the whole plan of salvation by grace, teaches us that ample provision is made for our cleansing: "If we walk in the light, as he is in the light, we have fellowship one with another, and the blood of Jesus Christ his Son cleanseth us from all sin" (1 John 1:7). He who has said, "Be ye holy; for I am holy," and "Be ye perfect, as your Father which is in heaven is perfect," cannot consistently fail to make provision for the attainment of the goal He sets before us.

The author of our salvation has opened a fountain in the house of David for sin and uncleanness. The stream of salvation proceeding from the throne of God is a river broad and deep, a river that cannot be passed over, waters to swim in. It should never be thought a thing impossible or incredible that God, who is absolutely holy and omnipotent, should provide a full and free salvation for all mankind. This is the teaching of the inspired author who writes to them that are sanctified by God the Father and preserved in Jesus Christ, saying, "Now unto him that is able to keep you from falling, and present you faultless before the presence of his glory with exceeding joy, to the only wise God our Saviour, be glory and majesty, dominion and power, both now and ever" (Jude 24-25).

(3) God himself has appointed means and agencies to lead believers into the experience of entire sanctification. We do not get a full view of the essential element of entire sanctification until we form some conception of the causal forces employed to remove the remains of the carnal nature. In a deep sense the source of all holiness and the power that makes for righteousness is found in God alone. However, He is pleased to work through agencies and to call man to voluntary cooperation with himself.

ATONEMENT

The meritorious cause of entire sanctification is the precious blood of Jesus. The shed blood stands for the death of Christ, and the death of Christ is the supreme expression of God's saving grace. The sinner cannot merit pardon, neither can anyone merit entire sanctification by growth in grace or by the deeds of the law. The power that cleanses is not in man, but in God and must be graciously applied. Of His fullness have we all received and grace for grace. The import of the inspired dictum, the blood of Jesus Christ cleanses from all sin, is, that God by His love and free grace, revealed in Christ Jesus, washes away the stains of sin from the souls of men. There is no new provision made for this specific stage of Christian experience. The one healing stream that flowed from Calvary is sufficient to heal the malady of sin perfectly. There is no stain of sin, either actual or original, that cannot be washed away by the blood of Jesus. His blood, His saving grace alone, can make the soul whiter than the snow. The meritorious cause is not limited to the use of any sacramental means. Baptism and the Lord's Supper may serve to prepare the heart to apprehend the free grace of God, but they have no meritorious power in themselves.

HOLY SPIRIT

The efficient or working agent of entire sanctification is the Holy Spirit. We are saved by the bath of regeneration and the renewing of the Holy Spirit (Titus 3:5). We are elect through the sanctification of the Spirit (1 Pet. 1:2). We are chosen to salvation through sanctification of the Spirit and belief of the truth (2 Thess. 2:13). These biblical citations bear on the subject of sanctification in general and not on entire sanctification in particular. But just as there is no special blood shed for the grace of entire sanctification, so also there is no special agency appointed to effect this stage of Christian experience. The eternal, all-pervading Spirit of God is the executive of the Godhead operating equally effectively in all parts of the kingdom of grace. The eternal Spirit, who gives life and soul and mind and spirit to man, and upholds all the moral forces in the world, is the efficient agent that cleanses from all sin.

The instrumental cause of entire sanctification is holy love. The apostle John states this truth very plainly when he says, "There is no fear in love; but perfect love casteth out fear: because fear hath torment. He that feareth is not made perfect in love" (1 John 4:18). The summary of all that God requires is comprehended in the one word *love.* "Thou shalt love the Lord thy God with all thy heart, and with all thy soul, and with all thy strength, and with all thy mind" (Luke 10:27). This is the same requirement that was made of God's people in a former dispensation. It will never be abrogated, and it can never be improved. It is a perfect means of fellowship with God.

Why should holy love be called the instrumental cause of entire sanctification? It is very fittingly called the instrument because it is that form of human activity that God employs to drive out the remains of the carnal nature from the believer's heart. We have now come to the crucial point of this important subject. How can a man get rid of the remains of his carnal nature that annoy him more or less in his Christian life? What can remove the deep-seated corruption of both actual and original sin? The biblical answer is supported by reason. It can be done only by the expulsive power of a superior force; Dr. Thomas Chalmers calls this superior force a new affection.

EXPULSIVE POWER OF LOVE

Dr. Chalmers, the founder of the Free Church of Scotland, whom all the churches of Scotland unite to honor, is competent to speak with authority on such an important phase of the Christian life. . . . As he examined more deeply the doctrines of Christianity, his whole soul was set on fire and his culture was now put under contribution to show that God's truth was a saving power, namely, the expulsive power of a new affection.

The carnality that must be removed in entire sanctification is not material substance. It cannot be weighed nor measured, nor handled with hands nor moved with a derrick. It is some form of moral or ethical activity; it is evil tendencies and desires. The only way to eradicate these evil tendencies and desires is to fill the soul with good tendencies and desires. When these new affections completely fill the soul and engage all its powers, there will be no room for any evil affection to arise in the mind. That degree of holy love that is sufficiently strong in present and enduring force to

SELFISHNESS ERADICATED

drive out all evil tendencies and desires, is perfect love. When that disposition of holy love which became the dominant power at the new birth, has been made sufficiently strong by the Holy Spirit to drive out all evil tendencies and desires, then the soul is made perfect in love. One who has attained such an experience has the victory over every sin inwardly and outwardly and is so firmly rooted and grounded in God that all selfishness is eradicated, and he is perfectly resigned to the will of God.

The Holy Spirit inspires perfect love in the heart of the believer as His instrument to work entire sanctification by means of the truth. It is the truth that makes us free from the carnal nature. The Savior prayed that God might sanctify His disciples by means of the truth. The truth energized by the Holy Spirit reveals the corruption of the carnal nature, begets an urgent longing for cleansing, and leads the soul to the open fountain for cleansing from all sin.

3. Human Condition for the Attainment of Entire Sanctification

Since entire sanctification is an integral part of the Christian life and a definite stage in Christian experience, it is evident that the condition for its attainment cannot be essentially different from

FAITH

the common requirement of walking in the way of life. All of the human condition is included in the one word, *faith* in the Lord Jesus Christ. "By grace are ye saved through faith; and that not of yourselves: it is the gift of God" (Eph. 2:8). The apostle Peter voiced the teaching of the primitive Church when at the great Jerusalem Council, speaking of the Gentiles, he said, "And put no difference between us and them, purifying their hearts by faith" (Acts 15:9). The faith that appropriates the blessing of entire sanctification is that perfect response of the soul to the call of God that issues in complete surrender to God and in perfect trust in Christ and His power to cleanse from all sin. The faith that sanctifies wholly is based solely on the promise of God wrought in the soul by the Holy Spirit in response to earnest prayer and full surrender to God.

Directions for seeking this state of grace are tersely given us in our Catechism where in answer to the question, "How does this faith of the child of God approve itself unto sanctification?" we say, "By our walking in the light and denying all ungodliness and worldly lusts; by childlike fidelity toward God and resignation to His will; by an ardent desire for the fulness of salvation in Christ, and a confident appropriation of the same to ourselves."[8] If these directions are conscientiously followed, a soul will soon be enabled to appropriate the offers of divine mercy and grace to the removal of all carnal tendencies and evil desires.

4. Various Questions Answered

Special advocates of the doctrine of entire sanctification have raised the question whether the mode of casting out the remains of the carnal nature is by suppression or by eradication. The word *repression* is at times used instead of *suppression.* Bishop Foster[9] and Dr. Whedon have said, by suppression; Dr. Lowrey said, by eradication. The main question is, Are the remains of the carnal nature removed? This is a spiritual attainment, and there is no material substance either pressed down or rooted out. Carnal remains are only forms of activity arising out of the carnal nature, and when they do not manifest themselves in consciousness, we have no evidence that a carnal nature exists. When by the grace of God, anger does not arise under provocation, it is not in the soul, and it matters not whether we say it is kept out by repression, suppression, or eradication. When, however, suppression means only that evil tendencies, arising in consciousness, are not expressed outwardly, then there is at least a manifestation of the carnal nature [within the] self, and there can be no claim to entire sanctification whatever. Any term that expresses the idea that carnal remains are not found in consciousness may be used, but eradication is unequivocal and the strongest term that can be employed.

SUPPRESSION OR ERADICATION

Another question of greater practical bearing than the preceding should be considered, namely, How soon after conversion should a soul be urged to seek entire sanctification? Every believer is pledged to walk in the light of God from the moment his sins are pardoned. Without a purpose of righteousness, no one can be saved nor continue long in a state of justification. As soon as the consciousness of carnality arises in the believer's heart, he should flee to the fountain for cleansing. And as soon as he knows that he needs more grace to prevent the uprising of evil within, he should seek definitely and perseveringly the complete renewal of his soul; he

THE TIME ELEMENT

8. Catechism of the Evangelical Association, Question 304.

9. The author is echoing Miley here, who misinterprets Foster.

should seek perfect love, the expulsive power of a superior affection; he should seek with all his heart entire sanctification.

WHEN HOLINESS IS LOST

If there is a lapse from the state of entire sanctification, does the fall carry with it the loss of justification and childship? There is no consensus of teaching on this subject. Bishop J. J. Esher says, the state of grace is one, but a state with different stages, which are inseparably connected with each other. Then he adds emphatically, "None is lost without the others."[10] We must demur against this opinion. We hold that it is possible for a believer to lose the experience of entire sanctification without necessarily losing his childship or justification. We may consistently pray daily, Forgive us our sins, without implying thereby that we daily need to be born again. If we hold that a Christian may, on account of infirmity or negligence, fall into sin without thereby losing his regeneration, then it is consistent to hold that one may decline from the high experience of perfect love without losing immediately his standing as a child of grace. Regeneration and entire sanctification may be separated in experience.

ASSURANCE

Is there any direct witness of the Holy Spirit on the attainment of entire sanctification? We gladly quote Bishop Esher with approval on this subject. "While the Holy Scriptures teach the immediate witness of the Holy Spirit on the childship of one born of God, they say positively nothing concerning such a witness on entire sanctification."[11] Although we may not have the direct and immediate witness of the Spirit on any particular stage of Christian experience, we may, nevertheless, have full assurance of the grace given to us of God. Perfect love is a blessed conscious experience; it is a state wrought in Christian consciousness. The very essence of the experience consists of the removal of carnal remains after conversion. The consciousness of the absence of carnality is the witness of our spirit wrought by the indirect operation of the Holy Spirit. So we teach that a believer may be fully assured of having attained the grace of perfect love. In the absence of carnality, that is, *evil* tendencies and desires, and in the enjoyment of greater joy and unsullied love to God and our fellow men, there comes the evidence of having attained entire sanctification.

Should the believer be encouraged to make a public profession of entire sanctification? Because of erroneous views and culpable fanat-

---

10. *Christian Theology,* 2:500.

11. Ibid., 502.

WITNESSING

icism, this question is beset with difficulties. It is a general Christian principle that we should testify to the saving grace of our Lord Jesus Christ. If a believer has the assurance that by the grace of God he has complete victory over every sin inwardly and outwardly, he should be encouraged, on proper occasions, to testify to this fact. Whenever we have an opportunity to glorify our Savior by giving testimony of complete deliverance from sin, we should do so; but pearls should not be cast before swine. In every public profession the aim must be to glorify Christ and not to boast of superior attainments. One thing is positive, that there is no biblical ground for holding that no one is a child of grace or an heir of heaven unless he make a profession of entire sanctification.

PREACHING

It behooves us to teach the doctrine of entire sanctification, because it is taught in the New Testament. We should preach it, because it is a doctrine of the Evangelical Association. We should preach a full and perfect salvation, because it is the privilege of every child of grace to enjoy this blessing. We should teach it and preach it and enjoy it, because it is to the glory of God, and it affords a powerful impetus to the evangelization of the world.

16

Aaron M. Hills
(1848-1935)

The 87 years of A. M. Hills' life spanned the most vigorous days of the holiness movement in America, reaching back to the time of Charles G. Finney and Asa Mahan down to the days of the holiness denominations.

He first became a seeker for heart holiness as a student at Oberlin, but did not succeed in his quest until 24 years later. Soon thereafter he became a central figure in the burgeoning full salvation movement, and he remained so until his death. The famous Holiness General Assembly, held in Chicago in 1901, was opened with an address declaring the doctrinal position of the assembly. This document carries the name of A. M. Hills, as a coauthor, along with Bishop Hogue, E. F. Walker, Hiram Ackers, M. L. Haney, L. B. Kent, and W. E. Shepard.

From his original goal of law, Hills surrendered to a long-haunting call to ministry. He was for at least 16 years a successful pastor in Congregational churches. Educated in Oberlin and Yale, he possessed a first-rate mind, together with thorough orthodoxy and a deeply serious piety. Naturally a careful scholar, he became after his own "Jordan crossing" one of the holiness movement's most able and articulate exponents. As one of its most effective educators he trained such leaders as J. B. Chapman and R. T. Williams, Sr.

The classic most commonly associated with Hills' name is *Holiness and Power.* It was originally published by Martin Wells Knapp in 1897, though written in 1896, the year following Hills' own Canaan experience, December 7, 1895. In readership and influence the book swept the country and is still in print. Written in only 14 weeks during hectic travels as a busy evangelist, the book is perhaps the most comprehensive collection of arguments, exposition, and documentation produced during that time. With great skill Hills organized a massive array of material to create an irresistible avalanche of argument. The book reflected the months of arduous research on the subject before December 7, as well as Hills' wide reading after coming into the experience.

The breadth of the man's interests is indicated by the scope of his Christian writings, from theology to homiletics and evangelism. He also developed a special ministry to children, represented by his widely used book, *Food for Lambs.* As an educator he was the pioneer president of three holiness colleges, and spent some time teaching and evangelizing in the British Isles. For the last 16 years of his active life he was professor of theology at Pasadena College, Pasadena, Calif.

Hills' other books include *Pentecost Rejected* and *Whosoever Gospel.* His largest works and in some respects the climactic achievement of his long life were written in his 70s and 80s: *Homiletics and Pastoral Theology,* and a two-volume work, *Fundamental Christian Theology,* published by C. J. Kinne, 1931.

A. M. Hills is a sharp, clear thinker and a gripping writer. Even his theology is marked by simplicity and clarity. His special interest is holiness doctrine, though not narrowly conceived. To Hills holiness doctrine is rooted in every branch of theology; therefore he does battle with his razor-edged verbal sword on every theological front. His special antipathy is toward Calvinism because of its antiholiness implications. As a polemist he is a formidable foe, at times drawing blood when balm might have been better. However, this weakness should not be exaggerated or permitted to spoil the student's appreciation for an outstanding thinker and excellent writer. While there is rigor and sharpness, there is also warmth, intense devotion, and love of people.

Primitive Holiness and Probation[1]

A foundation stone of scriptural holiness is a proper under-

1. Hills' discussion is from Chap. 5 of Part III, 1:376-80 of *Fundamental Christian Theology.*

standing of primitive holiness, that is, the holiness that Adam and Eve possessed at their creation. To understand primitive holiness in relation to ethical holiness is to be able to understand its obverse: the relation of inbred sin (which could be called primitive sin) to ethical or actual sin.

Original sin is analogous to original or primitive holiness. Both are predispositional, nonvoluntary qualities of moral nature derived, in the one case from God at creation, in the other case from Adam through racial descent. Both are subethical in the sense that they have not yet either been confirmed or repudiated by a self-conscious moral choice, which is the sine qua non of personal character.

God intended that the primitive holiness of Adam should have become ethical holiness; but Adam's wrong willing prevented such a sequence of moral development. In the case of infants now coming into the world, not with primitive holiness but with primitive sinfulness, the inherited bent constitutes a powerful push toward voluntary acts of sin at the age of accountability. These voluntary sins turn nonaccountable sinfulness into accountable sinning. A depraved person becomes an evil person.

Hills grasps these issues firmly but moves in a more traditional framework of terminology than Curtis, whom we studied in Chapter 12. Hills defines primitive holiness as a spontaneous inclination or disposition toward fulfillment of the claims of God (379). Quickly, however, he adds, "There was a second element, or addition to it, viz., the presence and help of the Holy Spirit." The native inclination combined with a living communion with the Holy Spirit constituted a powerful force for righteousness, making its perpetuation easily possible and its destruction doubly heinous. (Cf. Watson, supra, pp. 37-38.)

The unique value, therefore, of Hills' discussion of primitive holiness is in clarifying the distinction between primitive holiness and ethical holiness. This distinction is essential to a proper understanding of inherited sinfulness that needs to be cleansed by God in entire sanctification, and personal sinfulness that God forgives when we are converted.

We have seen, in our previous discussions, what are the essential elements or attributes of a moral being, viz., intellect, sensibility, and free will. We must have these to be *moral persons,* accountable beings, creatures of moral obligation and accountability. In the possession of these faculties consists our likeness to God, as His children.

But we are not holy, save as we have been made so by a special work of grace. This is the moral consciousness of the race. And our present was not our original condition. We were created in the moral image and likeness of God. God looked upon man as he came fresh from His creating hand and pronounced him "very good"—superlative praise for superlative wisdom to bestow. There was nothing abnormal in his moral nature then—no moral derangement, as there is now.

I. What, Then, Was the Nature of Adamic Holiness?

We are now discussing the primitive *quality* of it, prior to any moral action. It must have been void of any ethical element; for that comes by personal faculties—intellect, sensibility, and free will. The question is, what was the state of Adam's nature before he had made any character by the use of his faculties? Wherein did it differ from the nature of man as he is now born? In a true godly life, such as Paul lived, there is personal holiness, the holiness of character, with the ethical qualities of righteous action. This is, in a way, quite different from a primitive holiness, divinely created and all unused. Adam's holiness must have consisted simply in *a natural disposition in perfect harmony with moral duty.* It was, in other words, a *subjective state in harmony with his moral relations.* It took time for Adam to know all his duties, and to choose the right; but he came into being with a *subjective moral tendency to the good.* It was "a created moral excellence, perfect in its kind but wholly unmeritorious." And so, Adam's nature was holy, that is, correct; but a holy character had yet to be made, by a right use of his will. There was no merit due to Adam for it, he was created so, just as he was created with eyes and ears, and two feet.

RIGHT TENDENCY

Such holiness is clearly possible before moral action. If not it is forever impossible; for holiness is the work of God anyway; and if He cannot produce a right trend to the nature by creation, how can He do it by grace? Whatever nature might become by good conduct and redeeming grace, that it might be constituted in original creation. Constantly bear in mind that it is the primitive *nature* of Adam that we are discussing, not his character. Character is made, and as yet he had no character. But we are saying that his *nature* was in harmony with the nature of his Creator. All his aptitudes, all of his fixed and strong desires, were toward the right, just as we may suppose is the case with the holy angels.

The spontaneous tendencies grow out of the NATURE, and Adam's nature was holy because free from all wayward lawless tendencies. It was natural for him to do right, as it is natural for an apple tree to bear apples. The quality of a tree is shown by the quality of its fruit. Likewise the deeds of men correspond to their nature. The need of regeneration depends on this truth. The transformation of the life that attends regeneration is produced by the renewal of the moral nature. "Thus," says Miley, "it appears that the question of primitive holiness, is not a merely speculative one, but one which vitally concerns the deepest truth and reality of regeneration. If there be no moral quality of our nature, then regeneration loses its meaning for the Christian life. Hence Adam as newly created could be holy in *his nature*" (1:413).

II. Proofs of Primitive Holiness

1. *From the Nature of God*

Man is a moral being and was made so at the beginning. That means that he was endowed with moral faculties necessary to moral personality—intellect, sensibility, and free will. Without such a moral nature man is not a man.

Now God is holy. We cannot suppose that a holy God would have created an unholy race with natural propensities going out spontaneously to the evil instead of the good. The new Adam was precisely what God made him; consequently his spontaneous tendencies, expressive of his innermost nature, must have been pleasing to God, and in harmony with divine goodness. His moral inclination must naturally have been to the good in preference to the evil, and this is the real nature of holiness.

2. *From the Scriptures*

"And God saw every thing that he had made, and, behold, it was very good" (Gen. 1:31). This is said immediately after the creation of man. It does violence to the text, to say that it has no reference to man's moral nature, as some do, in the interest of their speculations.

"Lo, this have I found, that God hath made man upright; but they have sought out many inventions" (Eccles. 7:29). The only natural meaning of the word *upright* here is *rectitude of moral nature* with its spontaneous tendencies.

"And that ye put on the new man, which after God is created in righteousness and true holiness" (Eph. 4:24).

"And have put on the new man, which is renewed in knowledge *after the image of him that created him*" (Col. 3:10). The central truth of these texts is the transformation of man from an evil to a good life. The old man that must be put off is a corrupt nature with vicious practices; and the new man that must be put on is a holy nature and a good life. This purification wrought by the Holy Spirit is a renewal of the soul in the image of God in which man was originally created. Hence in that image there is the truth of a primitive holiness.

3. *Errors of Augustine and Pelagius*

Here we quote a very critical worthy passage from Miley—abbreviating somewhat. "In the great contention between Augustine and Pelagius each went to an extreme; the former in the maintenance of original sin in the sense of native demerit; the latter in the denial of native depravity. Both failed to make the proper distinction between moral character from personal conduct, and the subjective moral state (or nature).

"With an omission of the proper analysis, native depravity was with Augustine native sin and demerit. On the other hand, Pelagius, equally overlooking that distinction, and holding the impossibility of demerit without one's own personal conduct, denied the *truth of native depravity.* With the proper analysis, Augustine might have maintained the whole truth of native depravity, without the element of sinful demerit; while Pelagius might have held the same truth of depravity and yet have maintained his fundamental principle, that *free personal conduct absolutely conditions all sinful demerit.* We thus point out the opposite extreme and the opposite errors of the two parties.

"Other errors logically followed. If all men might be sinners with the desert of punishment by virtue of an inherited depravity, Adam could have the moral worth and rewardableness of an eminent saint simply by virtue of an original creation. This is the tendency of Augustine's anthropology. On the other hand, the denial of primitive holiness on the part of Pelagius was logically consequent to his denial of Augustine's doctrine of original sin. His denial of native sin carried with it the denial of native depravity. On such a principle there can be no moral quality of a nature, and therefore, no primitive holiness" (1:416-17).

The thoughtful student will notice that both these combatants were partly right and partly wrong. Neither had the full truth. Augustine fathered Calvinism; Pelagius helped to produce modern liberalism. The truth lies between the two, as held by the best Methodism. Pelagius denied all change in the moral state or nature of the race, as the result of Adam's fall.

It will be seen, then, that the denial of primitive holiness is not a merely speculative error, but one that carries with it momentous consequences. It carries with it the denial of the Adamic fall, and the depravity of the race, and therefore leaves no place for an evangelical, scriptural theology. There is no longer any need of an atonement, or regeneration, or justification by faith, or sanctification, or a new life in Christ. The *tap-root of all sound theology is the sin question,* and goes back to the garden of Eden and the fall of man from *primitive holiness.* A theology that is weak here is weak everywhere, and worse than worthless.

III. ELEMENTS OF PRIMITIVE HOLINESS

1. The Romish church teaches that "*original righteousness is not a natural, but a supernatural endowment*"

2. *The Elements of the True Doctrine*

The first element of primitive holiness was the *moral rectitude of the Adamic nature* as newly created. The nature was so constituted as to be responsive to the claims of God in the sense of a SPONTANEOUS INCLINATION OR DISPOSITION toward fulfillment. This is all that we can properly mean by primitive holiness.

There was a second element, or addition to it, viz., the presence and help of the Holy Spirit. The Adamic nature was holy in itself, yet needed the help of the Spirit. Man was made for the society of God, and Adam had it freely. The life-energizing presence and power of the Spirit is what Jesus promised to His children, as the supreme grace this side of heaven. We may well believe that this was lost by the Fall. So the peculiarly precious constant presence and keeping influence of the Holy Spirit was lost. Depravation of nature and deprivation of the Spirit consummated man's ruin.

We might represent this to the eye somewhat as follows:

Before the Fall	*After the Fall*
man had	man has
25% Conscience	15% Conscience
25% Reason	15% Reason

25% Sensibility	55% Sensibility
25% Willpower	15% Willpower
+ The Holy Spirit	– The Holy Spirit

RESULT OF THE FALL

Before the Fall there was a keen conscience, a clear-eyed reason, a dominant willpower, and correct, submissive sensibilities—a harmonious balance of faculties, aided and guided by the Holy Spirit. After the Fall, conscience was less keen; the vision of reason to see duty was not so clear; the power of will was less kingly and supreme; the sensibilities were abnormally developed, unsubmissive to reason and will, and clamoring for self-indulgence. And, saddest of all, the blessed communion and intimate companionship of the Holy Spirit was lost.

Holiness Doctrine Encapsulated[2]

This chapter constitutes the core of the book *Holiness and Power*. In a sense it could stand alone as a summary of the doctrine. The chapter is typical in its extensive use of quotations; the major ones documented, but a few brief items undocumented. In this chapter as well as throughout the book Hills relies heavily on Asa Mahan, especially his *Autobiography*. Yet he also quotes other holiness stalwarts: Daniel Steele, A. B. Earle, Henry Cowles, Luther Lee, John Wesley, Isaiah Reed, W. McDonald, Bishop Merrill, Beverly Carradine, and A. B. Simpson.

In contrast to those who tend to think of sanctification as merely the extension and perfecting of regeneration, the writers quoted in this chapter see sanctification as distinct *in kind* from regeneration.

Very vigorous claims are made respecting the thoroughness of God's cure for depravity, making the term *eradication* virtually inevitable. Yet to ascribe to Hills and the school he represents the teaching that one filled with the Spirit "cannot sin"[3] is quite inexcusable. Even a casual reading of this chapter, to say nothing of the book in its entirety, would prevent such a misconstruction.

---

2. The selection is from *Holiness and Power*, 82-100, and is titled "Sanctification the Cure of Depravity."

3. Harold Lindsell, *The Holy Spirit in the Latter Days*, 140.

PART II—THE REMEDY

The careful reader has already observed that the author holds, with the many authorities he has quoted, that the word *sin* is used in the Bible with at least two very distinct meanings. It is also so used in theological literature generally. This may be a misfortune; but if so, we cannot help it. We have been born too late in the history of the world to correct the language of St. Paul and St. John, and the theologians of the Christian ages. We do not invent language usually; we use it as we find it ready-made.

TWO MEANINGS OF SIN

The word *sin* designates: (1) Actual transgressions, willful acts of disobedience to a known law of God. "Sin is the transgression of the law." It is very frequently used in the plural, as "sins," "iniquities," "transgressions." It is for this kind of sin that every man's conscience holds him directly responsible.

The word *sin* is often used, without any adjective and, as scholars who have studied the subject most carefully tell us, always in the singular number, to designate a sinful STATE, not an act. This second use of the word refers to that sinful state of our moral nature brought upon each of us by our connection with a sinful race. It is that natural lack of conformity of our whole being to the moral law.

A small Greek lexicon of the New Testament lies before me. The first three definitions of a common Greek word for sin are "error, offense, sin," but the next three definitions are, "A principle or cause of sin; proneness to sin; sinful propensity." These two sets of definitions of a Greek noun in an unbiased dictionary prove that this double use of the word *sin* in the New Testament is no fanciful notion of the author, but the actual Bible usage. The apostle John used the word in the first sense when he wrote: "If we confess our sins he is faithful and righteous to forgive us our sins" (1 John 1:9, Revised Version). He used the word in the second sense when he wrote: "All unrighteousness is sin" (1 John 5:17). The same Greek word is used in both passages. St. Paul used the word in this second sense when he wrote of the "sin that dwelleth in me" (Rom. 7:17).

A CURE NEEDED

Now this corruption of our moral nature, this disordered state of our faculties, this abnormal condition of our being, needs to be rectified. It is a perpetual source of temptation to *acts* of sin, which in turn react upon the innate corruption and intensify it. We are not primarily responsible for this diseased condition of our moral nature. It was born in us through no fault of ours. As Dr. Steele writes, "Under the remedial system, it involves no guilt till approved by the free agent and its remedy is rejected" (*Love Enthroned,* 11). A man may not be blamed for taking involuntarily a contagious disease; but he is to blame if he keeps it by willfully rejecting a known remedy.

BIBLE TERMS FOR INBRED SIN

Though a gracious God does not hold us responsible primarily for the evils of the Fall that have perverted our beings, yet He cannot be pleased with the fact that His children, designed to be perfect images of himself, are morally diseased, infested with "sin that dwelleth in us," "the body of sin," "the old man" of corruption, "the law of sin and death," "the lusts which war in the members." These striking expressions all mean the same thing and constitute what is called "depravity" or "indwelling sin" or "inbred sin." It makes us unlovely in the eyes of a pure and holy God. So He has made a provision of grace for us, "that the body of sin might be destroyed," that "our old man might be [is] crucified with him." He "condemned [to destruction] sin in the flesh," that He might "take the heart of stone out of your flesh and give you an heart of flesh."

FRUIT OF INBRED SIN

This inbred sin produces a sad harvest of unlovely fruit—pride, anger, self-will, jealousy, covetousness, peevishness, hatred, variance, emulations, strife, envyings, unbelief, and such like. These do not *reign* in the justified believer, but they keep up an incessant warfare against the holiest purpose of his soul. The thoughts and feelings and cravings and appetites are unclean and displeasing to God.

The conduct and inner life of the *disciples* grieved Jesus. They were converted men, ordained preachers, with power to work miracles and cast out devils. Jesus said of them in His intercessory prayer: "Thou gavest them me," "and the world hath hated them, because they are not of the world, even as I am not of the world." Jesus also said to the disciples, "Rejoice that your names are written in heaven" . . . And yet the Savior had found it necessary to reprove them for unbelief, instability, selfishness, a worldly, secular spirit, a retaliating spirit, a cowardly and vacillating spirit, and repeated feelings of jealousy.

These manifestations of the "indwelling sin"—the carnal nature—troubled the Master, and He prayed for them that they might be sanctified. When the Holy Spirit came upon them that "old man" of

CHANGE IN THE DISCIPLES

sin was crucified, and they were sanctified. He took the cowardice out of Peter, and the unbelief out of Thomas, and the overgrown ambitions out of James and John. The "Son of Thunder" became the "Apostle of Love." And right here we touch the meaning of SANCTIFICATION. It is the work of the Holy Spirit—the act of God's grace, by which "our old man is crucified" and the moral nature is cleansed of all "unrighteousness"—*unrightness,* "proneness to sin," "sinful propensity."

NAMES

Sanctified souls have called this experience by different names. The apostle Paul, filled with ecstatic rapture, called it "the fulness of God." John Wesley, following the apostle John, called it "perfect love." Mrs. Jonathan Edwards, with doubts forever slain and looking with steadfast gaze upon her Savior, "whose presence was so near and real" that she "was scarcely conscious of anything else," called it "the full assurance of faith." A. B. Earle, the great Baptist evangelist, was so conscious of a deep, sweet resting in Christ, after his painful struggles for holiness, that he called it "the rest of faith." President Mahan, filled and thrilled by "the refining and sin-killing Spirit," chose Pentecostal language and called it "the baptism of the Holy Ghost." Prof. Henry Cowles, heart aglow with the conception of a Church some day purified and walking with God, called it the "holiness of Christians." President Finney, with a floodtide of rapture flowing over his soul, used the language of Christ and called it "entire sanctification."

But the work, by whatever name called, is essentially the same. It is God's act of cleansing the soul.

ASA MAHAN

When he was 82 years old, the venerable Mahan wrote, "Facts of experience of the most palpable character, and of every variety of form, absolutely evince that in the renewing of the Holy Ghost believers are fully cleansed from *indwelling* as well as from actual sin. Tens of thousands of eminent and most trustworthy believers testify to being as conscious of permanent changes and removals of evil appetites, tempers, and dispositions, of the longest standing and dominion, as they are of their own existence. Nothing can be verified by testimony if the fact of such changes cannot be. Those who deny that such changes are among the possibilities of faith render impossible . . . their own 'deliverance from the body of this death.' 'If ye will not believe ye shall not be established'" (*Autobiography,* 345).

In another passage he wrote, "My inner life, as I came unto God by Jesus Christ, not only for pardon, but for heart purification, was taking a surprisingly new form. Old habits, evil tempers, and sinward propensities which had been the bane of my impenitent career, and the cause of the groaning servitude of my primal Christian life, had suddenly lost all power and control. I became distinctly conscious to myself of being no longer carnal, 'sold under sin,' but the Lord's free man, emancipated from former enslavement, and now a divinely inaugurated sovereign over those propensities" (326). . . .

NO LONGER CARNAL

We are now ready for some formal definitions of sanctification.

Rev. Luther Lee, president of Leoni Theological Institute, defined sanctification thus: "Sanctification is that renewal of our fallen nature by the Holy Spirit received through faith in Jesus Christ, whose blood of atonement has power to cleanse from all sin; whereby we are not only delivered from the guilt of sin, which is justification, but are washed entirely from its pollution, freed from its power, and are enabled, through grace, to love God with all our *hearts,* and to walk in His holy commandments blameless" (*Elements of Theology,* 211).

DEFINITIONS OF SANCTIFICATION

Wesley, in his *Plain Account of Christian Perfection,* says, "It is the loving God with all our heart, soul, mind, and strength. This implies that no wrong temper—none contrary to love—remains in the soul; and that all the thoughts, words, and actions are governed by pure love." "By one that is perfect, we mean one in whom is 'the mind which was in Christ,' who so 'walketh as Christ also walked,' who is cleansed 'from all filthiness of flesh and spirit,' in whom is 'no occasion of stumbling,' who accordingly 'does not commit sin,' one in whom God hath fulfilled His faithful word, 'From all your filthiness and from all your idols will I cleanse you; I will also save you from all your uncleanness.'"

Rev. Isaiah Reid, an exceedingly clear writer on this subject, says, in *The Holy Way* (10-11): "Doctrinally, holiness may be defined as that secondary work of grace by which the depravity of the soul is remedied. . . . Holiness or entire sanctification is the application of redemption to the depraved, corrupt nature in which we were born. It is that feature of salvation which lies back of pardon—which is for an act—and back of justification, which refers to our adjusted relations: it relates to our depravity. For this inheritance of our depravity we are not responsible. We never committed the sin that produced it, and cannot repent of being so born, nor seek pardon for it.

"God's remedy is CLEANSING, called 'entire sanctification,' 'holiness,' 'perfect love.' On the side of man it is through consecration and faith. On the part of God it is the application of the cleansing blood. Entire sanctification makes us morally *pure* from our inherited depravity. It destroys the old man of sin, the carnal mind. The [sanctified man] is *perfect* as to the kind of . . . Christianity . . . yet not in such a way that the measure of it cannot be increased. He is *holy* in the sense that he is morally pure. He is *sinless* in the sense that his past sinful acts have all been pardoned, and his corrupt nature cleansed. He is *blameless* in the sense that God sees in his pardoned and cleansed soul nothing condemned by the gospel law. As to his *love,* it is perfect in the sense that he loves with all the heart, mind, soul, and strength, and in the sense that 'love is the fulfilling of the law.' As to *progress,* he is growing *in* it. 'His soul made in kind heavenly, now *matures* in degree, and ripens for glorification.'

"Holiness is properly the name for the state of a soul sanctified wholly, and denotes (1) the absence of depravity, (2) the possession of perfect love. A heart emptied and a heart refilled."

If such an experience is possible in this life, then there is a blessed privilege offered to every child of God.

President Mahan gives this definition: "Sanctification is exclusively the work, not of the creature but of God, a work wrought in us by the eternal Spirit, on the condition that 'God be inquired of by us to do it for us.' Entire sanctification implies 'salvation to the uttermost' from sin in all its forms as God sees it, and perfect moral purity as He requires it" (*Autobiography,* 375). "By the state under consideration I do not understand mere separation from *actual* sin, and full *actual* obedience. I understand more than this, namely: a renewal of the *spirit,* and *temper,* and *dispositions* of the mind, and [a cleansing] of the *tendencies* and *habits* which impel to sin, and prompt to disobedience to the divine will. A fully sanctified believer is not only *voluntarily* separate from sin, and in the will of God, but is in this state with the full assent of every department of his moral and spiritual nature. He not only 'feareth God and escheweth evil,' but *loves* righteousness and *hates* iniquity" (322).

Dr. W. McDonald, of Boston, defines as follows: "It is to be cleansed from all *actual* sin and *original* depravity. Sin exists in the soul after two modes or forms, actual and original, the sins we have committed, and the depraved or sinful nature inherited, which was ours before we were conscious of sinning. . . . A fully saved heart can look up into the face of Jesus, and without mental reservation say, 'Thy will be done,' while the whole nature responds, 'Amen.' This is entire holiness. . . . But if depravity remain, it will rebel and refuse to yield.

"But to be saved from all sin, and made perfect in love is to have:

A heart in every thought renewed,
And full of love divine;
Perfect, and right, and pure, and good—
A copy, Lord, of Thine!

"A soul in possession of such a blessing can sing,

Thou art the sea of love,
Where all my pleasures roll,
The circle where my passions move,
And center of my soul.

"There is no longer a conflict between the inclinations and the judgment. The desires are no longer at war with the will. The seat of war has been mainly changed. Formerly we not only contended with outward foes—the world and Satan—but with inward enemies—our own unholy desires and tempers. Now the citadel is purged, the heart made pure, the enemies are without, and the fort royal is all friendly to the king" (*Saved to the Uttermost,* 25-32).

The *Methodist Catechism* says, "Sanctification is that act of divine grace whereby we are made holy."

Dr. Steele says, "The act is that of removing impurity existing in the nature of one already born of the Spirit—the deliverance from sin as a tendency born with us." . . .

To make the subject still more clear we will define negatively, and show what sanctification is not, and what it does not do in us and for us.

WHAT SANCTIFICATION IS NOT

1. It does not bring us to ideal or *absolute* perfection. God only is absolute. "God charges His angels with folly; with errors in judgment, but not with sin." In this sense, "there is none good but one, that is God."

2. It does not bring us *angelic* perfection. With their freedom from all inherited infirmities, and their superior knowledge, judgment, and discernment, they have a degree of perfection that no grace of God makes possible to mortals in this life.

3. It does not bring us to the perfection of our own glorified state, in the after-resurrection life. St. Paul disclaimed that celestial

perfection in Phil. 3:12 while he did claim the perfection of a sanctified man in 3:15.

4. It does not bring a "sinless perfection," in the sense that it makes it *impossible* for one to sin and fall. The angels fell and Adam fell, though they were once holy.

5. Entire sanctification does not imply or involve *infallibility* of knowledge or judgment or memory..There is still room for innocent mistakes; the heart may be right while the judgment is wrong.

6. It does not secure us from temptation; only the tempters and temptations are not reinforced by traitors within the citadel of the soul. Jesus himself was tempted; but He said, "Satan cometh and findeth nothing *in me.*"

7. Sanctification does not end Christian growth; but, cleansing the heart of its vileness, makes the growth of all graces possible and certain. Eleven months after the recorded date of her sanctification, Frances Ridley Havergal wrote:

Like a river glorious
Is God's perfect peace,
Over all victorious
In its bright increase.
Perfect, yet it floweth
Fuller every day;
Perfect, yet it groweth
Deeper all the way.

Thus does the tide of divine life deepen and widen in the soul when the cleansing has come, and the proneness to evil no longer vexes the heart.

8. This blessing of sanctification does not obviate the need of constant dependence upon the atoning work of Christ. No other class of believers so constantly trust in Jesus, or so feel their utter dependence upon Him, and so live in Him moment by moment. Miss Havergal thus stated the method of holiness, "I would distinctly state that it is only as and while a soul is under the full power of the blood of Christ that it can be cleansed from all sin; that one moment's withdrawal from that power, and it is again actively, because really sinning; and that it is only as and while kept by the power of God himself that we are not sinning against Him. One instant of standing alone is certain fall!" (*Forty Witnesses,* 240).

In this chapter it may be well to observe that in current discussions both the terms *regeneration* and *sanctification* are sometimes used in two senses. Dr. Daniel Steele, in an address before the Boston ministers' meeting, following Arminius and the early writings of John Wesley, spoke of regeneration first as *"the instantaneous impartation of the divine life"*; second, as the *"perfect recovery of the moral image of God which sin has effaced."* In this latter sense, regeneration is not a single act but "a *process* implying steps and intervals, and entire sanctification is one of these steps, and the preceding interval was a period of progressive sanctification." . . . "After a man is born of the Spirit he needs an interval for a heart knowledge of Christ, through the light of the Holy Spirit, as the basis of that supreme act of faith in him as the Sanctifier."

Bishop Merrill, in *Christian Experience,* speaks of sanctification first as *initial sanctification,* which, though entirely distinct from regeneration, is concurrent with it, beginning with the cleansing of the soul. "In its fullest signification, sanctification relates to a process of cleansing which goes on and on through all the experience of growth, maturity and perfection" (188).

Second, he speaks of it as the *act of entire sanctification.* "In the *primal* act of sanctification, at the time of the new birth, the heart is washed from the defilements of old sins; but neither Scripture nor experience will justify the assertion that all the impurities of thought and the evil tendencies of nature, which are impurities in God's sight, are entirely purged till the new life has expanded and the indwelling Spirit has revealed to the enlightened conscience the enormity of inbred depravity.

"The 'filthiness of the flesh and spirit' must be loathed before it can be washed away. Hence the general experience is that the full cleansing follows a season of deep self-abasement. The provision for this *entire sanctification* is ample, and the Spirit of God is always ready to respond to a longing desire for it. As soon as the soul feels the need of this great deliverance and takes hold of the atonement as efficacious to this end, the merit of the cleansing blood is applied, and the Spirit reveals the result as suddenly as faith will apprehend the evidence given" (194).

We may close this chapter by meeting an objection raised in some quarters, that those who advocate holiness as a special, second experience belittle justification to make room for sanctification. It is a mistake. I find nothing of the kind in . . . 40 volumes on the subject of holiness. Three quotations will suffice to show the sentiment of all.

Wesley says, "But even babes in Christ are so far perfect as not to commit sin." Luther Lee says, "No man can believe with the heart unto righteousness, or so as to obtain justification, while living in the practice of any known sin, or in the neglect of any known duty. . . . The moment he does what he knows to be a sin, or neglects what he knows to be a duty, faith, by which he is justified, loses its hold upon God, and he loses his justification" (191).

Dr. McDonald writes, "Freedom from sin belongs to the justified believer. No man can retain his justification and commit sin. Entire sanctification is far in advance of mere freedom from the voluntary commission of sin. This is too low a standard for entire sanctification. . . . Conversion is no inferior work. It is a change so great as to be called a 'new creation.' If it be genuine, it will stop men from committing sin, and free them from the condemning power of the law, and make them obedient to all of God's commands. Do not call this entire sanctification; it is far below that exalted state. . . .

"Some place Christian holiness too low and make a profession of sanctification, when, as Mr. Fletcher very justly says, 'They have not so much as attained the mental serenity of a philosopher, or the candor of a good natured, conscientious heathen'" (*Saved to the Uttermost,* 22-24).

Jesus said, "That they may receive remission of sins, and an inheritance among them which are sanctified by faith that is in me" (Acts 26:18).

"The great salvation is twofold: 'Forgiveness of sins, and . . . sanctified by faith that is in me.' The forgiveness of sins is a perfect work; but a perfect forgiveness is a very different thing from entire sanctification. Forgiveness refers to one hemisphere of your moral nature, and entire sanctification to another. There is a hemisphere of voluntary wrong-doing and a hemisphere of unintentional evil dispositions; there are things people do that they know are wrong, and there are yearnings that do not come to the surface; they lie beneath and do not come to the will power; it lies behind the will.

"The hemisphere of what a man is responsible for is covered by pardon. When God forgives your sins He forgives every sin you were ever responsible for; but complete sanctification goes into bed rock in the moral nature. There are evil dispositions way down that we grieve over; sanctification proposes to give us relief in the 'basement story' of our moral nature. And this is by faith, not by growth; grace can grow, but cleansing can't grow. Cleansing prepares the way for grace and puts grace where it can grow" (*Love Enthroned,* 28). [Daniel Steele]

The difference between the justified and the sanctified state of the believer is not inaptly set forth in the following lines by Dr. A. B. Simpson:

CHRIST HIMSELF

Once it was the blessing, now it is the Lord;
Once it was the feeling, now it is His Word;
Once His gifts I wanted, now the Giver own;
Once I sought for healing, now himself alone.

Once 'twas painful trying, now 'tis perfect trust;
Once a half-salvation, now the uttermost:
Once 'twas ceaseless holding, now He holds me fast;
Once 'twas constant drifting, now my anchor's cast.

Once 'twas busy planning, now 'tis trustful prayer;
Once 'twas anxious caring, now He has the care;
Once 'twas what I wanted, now what Jesus says;
Once 'twas constant asking, now 'tis ceaseless praise.

Once it was my working, His it hence shall be;
Once I tried to use Him, now He uses me;
Once the power I wanted, now the Mighty One;
Once to self I labored, now for Him alone.

How to Be Sanctified Wholly[4]

Hills here draws on F. B. Meyer, Wilbur Chapman, William and Catherine Booth, Andrew Murray, and Samuel Keene, among others. The position taken in this chapter is that there must be a definite, deliberate act of appropriating faith for the heart cleansing and the fullness of the Spirit, before the witness of the Spirit can be reasonably expected.

1. *Believe It Is God's Will*

Do you, reader, believe that what God says is true? He says, "The promise [of the Spirit] is unto *you* and to your children, and to all, even as many as the Lord our God shall call." He says your sanctifica-

4. Chap. 16 of *Holiness and Power,* "Entering In," 281-96.

tion by the Holy Spirit is His will. Do you believe it? He says He hath *called* you to sanctification. Do you believe it? Do you hear the call of the Holy Spirit in your heart now? Will you respond to Him and rise up and claim the blessing? Is this inestimable blessing for one man out of thousands—for Edwards, and Finney, and Moody, Fletcher, Bishop Simpson, and a few other favored souls, or is it for every regenerated child of God, and so for you? . . .

I wish the readers of these lines would pause a moment and think. Don't hurry. Can you solemnly say with a prayerful heart, "My God, I believe this baptism with the Holy Spirit is for me?"

2. *Be Willing That God's Blessed Will Should Be Done in You—to Your Sanctification and Holiness*

Are you *willing* to pray the Lord's prayer and mean it? "Thy kingdom come (in my heart), thy will be done in earth (in *me,* and by my *will*), as it is in heaven (by the angels of God)." Or are you "willing to be made willing about everything," as F. B. Meyer puts it, "at any cost to yourself?" . . .

3. Said an evangelist: "*We should be willing to forsake every sin that we know, and also the sin that we do not know.* . . .

"No matter what it may be, if there is a touch of sin about it, will you abandon it now? As God searches your heart, if He shall show you anything sinful and impure will you make this pledge to Him, as though you stood in the white light of the judgment, that you will give it up? Can you, reader, say, 'I will'?"

4. *We Should Be Willing to Give All Our Good Things to God*

A soul winner said, "I believe a man may forsake every known sin, and pledge himself to give up every unknown sin as well, and still not be qualified for the filling of the Holy Spirit. Oh, so many fail here. There are what we call the neutral things—the *friends,* and the *ambitions,* and the *money,* and the *time,* and the *talents*—all to be turned over to God. Here many fail. When God calls to bring out Isaac, there they hesitate. Let us bring out the last good thing and lay it on the altar of God.

"I preached six years before I was willing to consecrate the things that were good. Are you willing to do it—to give Him the known things and the unknown? the things that are good—the *money* and the *time,* the *talents* and the *friends,* the *husband* or *wife* or *child,* the *wisdom* and the *ignorance,* the *wealth* and the *poverty,* the *strength* and the *weakness,* all that you know or may know, all that you *have* or *may* have, and say, 'Lord God, it is mine no longer.'"

General Booth says, "Thus consecration has in it the nature of a REAL SACRIFICE. It is the presentation or giving away of all we have to God; a ceasing any longer to own anything which we have hitherto called our own, but all going over into God's hands for Him to order and arrange, and our taking simply the place of servants, to receive back again just what He chooses. This is no easy task, and can only be done in the might of the Holy Spirit; but, when it is done, when all is laid on the altar—body, soul, spirit, goods, reputation, all, *all,* ALL—then the fire descends and burns up all the dross and defilement of sin, and fills the soul with burning zeal and love and power. Consecration is being crucified with Christ; it means dying to all those pleasures and gratifications which flow from the undue love of self, the admiration of the world, the ownership of goods, and the inordinate love of kindred and friends which go together to make up the life and joy of the natural man. This may be painful, but we must be crucified with Christ if we are to live with Him."

DISOBEDIENCE BLOCKS FAITH

Mrs. Catherine Booth said in an address on "Hindrances to Holiness," "A lady a short time ago was brought to the very edge of this blessing, but there was something she felt she ought to do. She had a sum of money which she felt ought to be given up to a certain object. She prayed and struggled and attended prayer meetings, and prayed long into the night; but, no, she would not face the difficulty. She said, 'Oh! no; I am not satisfied in my own mind. How do I know God wants it for that purpose?' She might have struggled till now if she had not made up her mind to obey; but, the moment she did, alone, up in her bedroom, the blessing came.

"A gentleman came to the penitent form after one of my West-end services, last season, and told me: 'I am a preacher; I have been laboring in the gospel for eight years, but I know I am utterly destitute of this power.'

"'Do you want it?' I asked.

"'Oh,' he said, 'I do,' and he looked as though he were sincere.

"'Then,' I said, 'what is it? There is a hindrance. It is not God's fault. He wants you to have it. He is as willing to give you the Spirit as He was [to sanctify] Peter or Paul, and you want to have it. Now *will you have it?* Have you understood the conditions?'

"'Ah!' he said, '*that* is the point.'

"'Now you know I should be a false comforter if I were to try to make you believe you were right when you had not yielded that point.'

"'Well,' he said, 'you see, it would be cutting loose from one's entire circle.'

"Ah! he was led, you see, by Christian friends. I said, 'Did not the Lord Jesus cut loose from His circle to save you? And, if your Christian friends are such that to live a holy life you must cut loose from them, what are you going to do—stop in that circle, ruin your soul and help to ruin them, or cut loose and help to save them? Oh! there is no profounder philosophy in any text in the Bible than that—"How can ye believe who receive honor one of another, and seek not the honor that cometh from God only?" You will have to come to God not caring what anybody thinks'" (*Godliness,* 147).

Are you, who read these lines, willing thus to consecrate all to belong to God? Can you say, from the depths of your soul, to God in prayer, "I will make the sacrifice"?

5. *There Is Just One Thing More*

The Lord says, "Ye receive the Spirit through faith." "I believe," said one to the great convention, "if we have been honest with God in these acts, every one of us has a right to rise up and say, 'I am going out now as one filled with the Holy Spirit.' 'Lord, I do receive the Spirit now.'"

Reader, will you say in faith, "Yes, Lord, I do receive the Holy Spirit for my sanctification now?" Do not turn away from this blessing and make yourself a legalist and say, "I will be sanctified by WORKS AT SOME FUTURE TIME WHEN I HAVE MADE MYSELF BETTER." God would have you say, "I will be sanctified"; nay, He would have you say in faith, "I AM SANCTIFIED BY MY SANCTIFYING SAVIOR AND HOLY SPIRIT, NOW, AS I AM."

President Mahan says, "The Scripture reveals Christ as an 'uttermost Savior,' who has made provision for our complete 'redemption from all iniquity,' and our perfect moral and spiritual cleansing. Sanctification, complete and entire, therefore, is the object of rational faith and prayer and hope. Both blessings, justification and entire sanctification, stand distinctly revealed in the Word of God as available on the same condition, and as, for the same identical reasons, objects of faith and expectation, and the individual who professes to have received the one blessing makes a no more incredible profession, than he who professes to have received the other.

"Through faith it is the revealed privilege and duty of every believer to be 'saved unto the uttermost,' 'sanctified wholly,' and in 'his spirit and soul and body be preserved blameless.' After regeneration there awaits the faith of the believer, 'the promise of the Father,' for which he is to tarry in prayer and supplication until he is 'filled with the Holy Spirit.'" By faith, dear reader, be filled NOW.

FAITH WITHOUT FEELING

F. B. Meyer says, "As once you obtained forgiveness and salvation by faith, so *now* claim and receive the Spirit's fullness. Fulfill the conditions already named, wait quietly but definitely before God in prayer; for He gives the Holy Spirit to them that ask Him: then reverently appropriate this glorious gift, and rise from your knees, and go on your way reckoning that God has kept His word, and that you *are filled* with the Spirit. Trust Him day by day to fill you and keep you filled. There may not be at first the sound of rushing wind, or the coronet of fire, or the sensible feeling of His presence. Do not look for these, any more than the young convert should look for feeling as an evidence of acceptance. But BELIEVE *in spite of feeling* that YOU ARE FILLED. Say over and over, 'I thank thee, O my God, that thou hast kept thy word with me, though as yet I am not aware of any special change.' And the feeling will sooner or later break in upon your consciousness, and you will rejoice with exceeding joy, and all the fruits of the Spirit will begin to show themselves."

A Testimony to Entire Sanctification

HILLS' OWN TESTIMONY

This is a fair description of the author's experience, and so he might as well take the witness stand and testify here. As far back as when I was a student in Oberlin College, my beloved classmate, the now well-known faith missionary in Bulgaria, Mrs. Anna V. Mumford, had received the baptism with the Spirit and urged me to seek it. She presented me a volume of President Mahan's *Baptism of the Holy Ghost.* The book has inspired many another to seek and find the blessing, but somehow it did not make the matter plain to me *how* to take the blessing in simple faith. I went to President Finney, who tenderly prayed with me, but gave me no light. I was thoroughly persuaded that there was such a blessing for men. Indeed, all these years I have felt that a dozen unanswerable arguments could be made that would satisfy any logical mind of the attainability of holiness.

I soon after went to Yale Seminary to study theology, and there, I confess it now with shame and sorrow, like many another theological student does, I suffered a decline in spirituality and lost much of the heart-hunger for holiness. I have deserved all I have received, and much more, of sorrow and disappointment at the hands of a grieved and patient God, who lovingly chastised His child that he might become a partaker of the divine nature.

God gave me revival after revival in my pastorates, gracious harvests of souls, and I had more calls to help pastors in revival work outside of my own pulpit than I could fill. But I was a slow, dull pupil of grace, and God permitted my pride to be wounded, and my ambitions to be crushed, till I cried out in agony, "Oh, my Father, dost Thou not care for Thy child?" But through it all, He was bringing me to himself, driving me, I might say, by a whip of love, to His very bosom, and awaking again the deep and abiding heart-hunger for holiness and Spirit-power.

After two long pastorates, lasting 16 years, followed by two short pastorates—short, as a doctor of divinity kindly wrote me, through no fault of mine—and nearly 2 years' service as state evangelist of Michigan, I moved to Oberlin to enter general evangelistic work, with my humbled soul hungering for God. My constant reading, outside of the busy work of preaching 15 times a week and writing *The Life and Labors of Mary A. Woodbridge,* was all on the precious theme of the Holy Spirit.

In such a frame of mind I was invited to lead a revival in Oberlin in January of 1895. I preached in the afternoon meetings a full salvation; I dared not preach anything else. Months afterward the leader of the holiness band of Oberlin . . . loaned me some books of Wood and Garrison and Steele and Mahan that fed all the more the consuming flame of my soul.

I was providentially invited to assist Rev. G. S. Butler of Three Rivers, Mass., who with his wife had received the baptism with the Spirit, and who had much literature on the subject in his library. Among other things I there found an address by Brother Torrey, of Chicago, and the address of another man already referred to. I took down the outlines of them in my note book. On the famous hilltop back of the parsonage, overlooking 11 cities and villages, under a tree I knelt in prayer and gave myself away to God anew for the baptism with the Spirit, and wrote in my book, "Oh, my God, Savior, sanctifying Spirit, I receive Thee. Come in now and fill my soul. A. M. Hills, May 29, 1895."

The influence of that act was a refreshing blessing to my soul all the summer through, and had I then believed with all my heart, I might have received the blessing at once; but I retained a lingering doubt. However, in the month of December in that same dear parsonage, I read an address of Varley on "The Sin of Unbelief," that went to my heart. I determined not to be shut out of the blessing any more by a wicked unbelief so cruel and so dishonoring to Jesus. I went to the Thursday evening meeting and publicly confessed my sin, and declared I would take God for a full salvation.

I had read previously in Keene's *Faith Papers:* "Are you a child of God seeking FULL SALVATION? Seize upon some declaration of God's Word, such as 'The blood of Jesus Christ his Son cleanseth from *all* sin'; apply it to your heart; confess to yourself, to Satan, and to God, that it is true to *you,* because the Lord hath spoken it; refuse to listen to the lying voice of Satan that it is not so. Let no inward feeling or outward sign dissuade you from your voluntary choice to count God's Word true to yourself. And according to such a faith it shall be done unto you. Have you given all to Christ? Are you now longing to be *fully* saved? Are you persuaded that

> *''Tis the promise of God full salvation to give*
> *Unto him who on Jesus, His Son, will believe'?*

You may at once begin to sing:

> *'I CAN, I WILL, I DO, believe,*
> *That Jesus saves me now.'"*

The next day I said over and over again, "I will believe; I will believe." At night I walked the park in the darkness, saying:

> *I CAN, I WILL, I DO believe,*
> *That Jesus saves me NOW.*

With such a persistent determination of faith I retired. The next morning (December 7) before I rose it occurred to me to thank God for the blessing as a thing received, just as F. B. Meyer advises. I began to do it, when speedily the Spirit came to bring the witness that God is true. A tide of joy swept into my soul, and I cried out, "O bless the Lord! praise the Lord! He does come and fill my spirit!" From that hour my life has been consciously changed.

O that Christians would learn this simple lesson of *believing,* of simply taking God at His word without evidence! We should soon have "the oil of joy for mourning; the garment of praise for the spirit of heaviness," and the Church, no longer bowed down in weakness and sorrow and doubt and sin, would "arise and shine, her light having come, and the glory of the Lord having risen upon her."

"The method of faith," says Dr. Keene,[5] "is for the soul to recognize that *it can believe* God's word, then *choose to believe* it, which always carries it over to the consciousness: '*I do believe.*' Believing is our part, and is antecedent; saving is God's part, and is consequent. All the blessed effects of faith—pardon, adoption, entire sanctification—are the Lord's doings, and are marvelous in our eyes; and they are all possible to him that believes on the Son of God."

Dear reader, as you lay down this paper, say: "Lord, I believe."

Thou dost this moment save,
With full salvation bless.

5. *Faith Papers,* 41.

16

Albert Frederick Gray

(1886-1969)

Born in a North Dakota prairie sod house March 18, 1886, the youngest of six children, Albert Gray became his denomination's (Church of God, Anderson, Ind.) leading administrator, educator, and theologian. His active and exceedingly productive ministry spanned half a century, from his ordination at 23 years of age to his retirement at 73 from the presidency of Warner Pacific College, Portland, Oreg., in 1957.

In his early ministry he served several churches as pastor, including the prestigious Park Place Church, Anderson, Ind. In 1937 he founded a struggling school for ministers in Spokane, Wash. (commuting from his Seattle pastorate). Three years later he led in the school's relocation to Portland, where it now thrives as Warner Pacific College, an accredited four-year liberal arts college.

In addition to teaching and school administration Dr. Gray traveled worldwide and served his church in nearly every major capacity. He was a member of the Publications Committee of Warner Press, and for 40 years a contributing editor to *The Gospel Trumpet* (now *Vital Christianity*). For 35 years he served on the Missionary Board, and for 16 years held the denomination's highest position as chairman of the General Ministerial Assembly.

Among Gray's many writings the best known is a two-volume *Christian Theology*, published by The Warner Press, Anderson, Ind., 1946. It was written for undergraduate classroom use, but its

simplicity of outline and clarity of language make it superb for lay use as well. It has been widely used and translated.

The Holy Spirit Baptism[1]

The chapter begins with a brief survey of the identity and work of the Holy Spirit. The author then proceeds to a discussion of the baptism with the Spirit. He reviews the promises of such a baptism and seeks to prove that it is a second experience. In the rite of confirmation Gray sees a historical link with true experiential Spirit baptism, and hence a support for its original secondness. This is significant for a writer in the mid-'40s, because the same hypothesis has been seriously advanced by several scholars more recently. Gray identifies the Spirit baptism with entire sanctification, which he sees as both consecration and cleansing.

Inasmuch as the personality and deity of the Holy Spirit were discussed in the chapter on the Trinity in Volume I there is no need to repeat that discussion at this point. It will be profitable, however, to seek a further acquaintance with the Spirit and His works before entering directly into the discussion of the Holy Spirit baptism.

I. His Identity and Works

1. **The Spirit's Identity.** There are many Christians who, though believing in the doctrine of the Trinity, become confused as to the identity of the Spirit. He has been confused with His influences and His activities. And because various names are used, some have become confused as to His identity.

(1) *The term "spirit" is used impersonally.* It is a common practice to use "spirit" in an impersonal sense. We speak of one having a good spirit, a generous spirit, or perhaps a contentious spirit. Such use is also found in the Bible, which speaks of a haughty spirit, a humble spirit, or a spirit of fear. In such usage the reference is to one's attitudes. We also speak of one as manifesting a Christian spirit, or the spirit of Christ, meaning that he shows a Christlike attitude. Such an attitude may be evidence of one's Christian experience, though there are people who show a very splendid attitude who are not Christians.

---

1. This is the author's own title of Chap. 5, 2:77-92.

Again, the term *spiritual* is used loosely to mean immaterial, animated, emotional, enthusiastic, or mystical. It may be used also to mean the state of the soul resulting from the operations of the Spirit of God.

(2) *Various names are applied to the Spirit.* When a strictly personal sense is intended, applying to the Third Person of the Trinity, various names are used. These include the Holy Spirit, the Spirit of God, the Spirit of the Lord, the Spirit of Truth, the Spirit, and the Comforter. These various names do not represent different personalities; they are all used of the one and only Holy Spirit. One does not receive the Spirit of God at one time and the Holy Spirit at another time. It is the same Spirit, but the operations may be different.

2. **Works of the Spirit.** There are various works of the Spirit apart from the baptism, which will be discussed later.

(1) *His work in creation.* We are told in Gen. 1:2 that "the Spirit of God moved upon the face of the waters." Hence the Spirit had His part in the work of creation. In what manner and to what extent the Holy Spirit now directs the universe we may never know. The immanence of God in the universe may involve more of such operations than we think.

(2) *As the Spirit of Prophecy.* God has given a revelation of himself and His will to man through the operations of the Holy Spirit. The prophet was God's spokesman, but before speaking he must receive a message from God. Such revelation, and the inspiration for delivering it, was the work of the Spirit. "Men spake from God, being moved by the Holy Spirit" (2 Pet. 1:21). This very important work under the old dispensation found its culmination in John the Baptist, who was filled from birth with the Holy Spirit. It was through the work of the Holy Spirit that the inspired Scriptures were prepared for us.

(3) *His work with men.* God said, "My Spirit shall not strive with man for ever" (Gen. 6:3). It was the work of the Spirit to strive with the antediluvians for a period of time. It is now His work to "convict the world in respect of sin, and of righteousness, and of judgment" (John 16:8). Such work may apply to society as a whole and also to the individual sinner. The Spirit convicts the sinner and invites him to Christ. He encourages the penitent to yield to Christ and to accept mercy. When we have fully surrendered, it is the same Spirit who brings assurance of acceptance; by Him we are born again and at the same time inducted into the Body of Christ. All this is the work of the

one and selfsame Spirit of whom Jesus said, "He abideth with you, and shall be in you" (John 14:17).

II. The Baptism

1. **Promises of the Baptism.** The best-known prediction of the baptism with the Spirit is one quoted by Peter at Pentecost: "And it shall come to pass afterward, that I will pour out my Spirit upon all flesh; and your sons and your daughters shall prophesy, your old men shall dream dreams, your young men shall see visions; and also upon the servants and upon the handmaids in those days will I pour out my Spirit" (Joel 2:28-29). Isaiah also had prophesied of the pouring out of the Spirit.

John the Baptist, himself filled with the Holy Spirit, said of Christ, "He shall baptize you in the Holy Spirit." Jesus assures us of our privilege to receive the Holy Spirit: "If ye then, being evil, know how to give good gifts unto your children: how much more shall your heavenly Father give the Holy Spirit to them that ask him?" (Luke 11:13). In His last discourse with His disciples before His death, Jesus assured them repeatedly of the coming of the Holy Spirit. At the time of His ascension He instructed them to remain in Jerusalem till they should receive the fulfillment of His promise, which they did. On the Day of Pentecost Peter assured his hearers that the gift of the Holy Spirit was for them and us: "For to you is the promise, and to your children, and to all that are afar off, even as many as the Lord our God shall call unto him" (Acts 2:39).

The question Paul asked the Ephesian brethren, "Did ye receive the Holy Spirit when ye believed?" (Acts 19:2), indicates the privilege of receiving Him. The recorded instances of those who did receive the Spirit since Pentecost indicate that the promise is still for the people of God.

2. **The Baptism a Second Experience.** Many people who speak freely of the baptism with the Spirit associate this experience with conversion. They do not distinguish between being born of the Spirit and being baptized with the Spirit. There are definite scriptural evidences that distinguish the two experiences.

(1) *The disciples were converted before Pentecost.* It seems scarcely necessary to prove that the disciples were already converted men before Pentecost. They had left the world to follow Jesus, who sent them forth to preach, heal, raise the dead, and cast out devils. They were commended by Christ as not of the world, having believed

in Him, obeyed the word, and belonged to the Father. Before Pentecost they met for prayer and worship and conducted important church business.

If during His ministry Jesus forgave sin, delivered from the power of sin, and made people new, it would be strange indeed if He had not done as much for His chosen apostles.

(2) *People since Pentecost receive a second experience.* There are those who allow that the disciples were converted before Pentecost and that they received the Holy Spirit after conversion for the reason that the Holy Spirit had not been given earlier and was not available. These people assume that since Pentecost all receive the baptism with the Spirit at the time of conversion. An examination of the experiences recorded in Acts will show the error of this view.

A great many Samaritans were converted through the preaching of Philip and were baptized by him. The whole city was stirred by his preaching. Later, when Peter and John came to Samaria they laid their hands on these converts that they might receive the Holy Spirit; "For as yet it was fallen upon none of them: only they had been baptized into the name of the Lord Jesus" (Acts 8:16). This was not a ceremony; these people received a definite experience so convincing that Simon, wishing he might have power to bestow the Spirit, sought to buy the power.

The 12 men at Ephesus furnish another example. Some people contend that these men were not converted when Paul found them. Even if that were true they were converted before Paul baptized them, for Paul did not baptize unconverted sinners. After they had been baptized in water they received the Holy Spirit. "And when Paul had laid his hands upon them, the Holy Spirit came on them; and they spake with tongues, and prophesied" (Acts 19:6).

The experiences recorded in Acts uniformly describe the receiving of the Holy Spirit baptism as subsequent to conversion. In no instance does it appear that sinners were converted and baptized with the Spirit at the same time. It is true that this fact does not prove that such never did happen or never could happen. These experiences recorded in Acts do not of themselves establish a positive doctrine of a second experience, but they are found to be fully in accord with that doctrine. In the absence of contrary evidence they may be accepted as normal Christian experience. It remains for those who profess to "get it all at once" to find scriptural support for their doctrine and to demonstrate the experience.

(3) *Church ritual testifies to a second experience.* The sacrament of confirmation, observed by certain churches, is a substitute for the Holy Spirit baptism. In this ceremony the candidate is supposed to receive the Holy Spirit. Though this ceremony is but an empty form, it does testify to the fact that throughout the ages the Church has regarded the receiving of the Holy Spirit as subsequent to conversion. It is a monument erected to what was once a living reality in the Church. As in some churches baptism has become a substitute for regeneration, so confirmation, coming later, is a substitute for the Holy Spirit baptism.

SACRAMENT OF CONFIRMATION

III. Sanctification Through the Spirit

A most important work of the Holy Spirit is that of sanctifying the people of God. Paul declares that he is "a minister of Christ Jesus unto the Gentiles, ministering the gospel of God, that the offering up of the Gentiles might be made acceptable, being sanctified by the Holy Spirit" (Rom. 15:16). Under the old covenant the Gentiles were excluded from God's altar. They were regarded as unclean and unacceptable. Such was the attitude of Peter toward them before he received the vision in which he was told, "What God hath cleansed, make not thou common" (Acts 10:15). The Gentiles are no longer to be regarded as unclean, but have the same privileges as Jews. With some hesitation Peter went to the home of Cornelius and there learned the secret of purification. The Gentiles were not cleansed ceremonially, or reputed to be clean, but received the actual cleansing of their hearts. All, both Jews and Gentiles, who are thus sanctified by the Holy Spirit are really holy. This is a special work of the Holy Spirit.

1. **The Meaning of Sanctification.** To sanctify means to make holy, hence sanctification and holiness are synonyms. Both dedication to God and purification are included in the general idea of sanctification. Both of these ideas are to be included. In Old Testament usage the term is applied to both persons and things dedicated to God, accompanied with a ceremonial cleansing. In Christian usage sanctification usually refers to a moral cleansing. It may be applied to any cleansing wrought by the Spirit. It is so used in the Bible and in works of theology. But it is used widely also in reference to the specific cleansing wrought at the time of the Holy Spirit baptism. The two principal meanings of the term are these:

TO MAKE HOLY

(1) *Sanctification is consecration and dedication.* It is quite clear from Old Testament usage that sanctified things were dedicated to

God for His exclusive use. It was an act of sacrilege to use such holy things for secular purposes. The same idea of complete dedication and consecration to God is found in the New Testament. Paul wrote: "I beseech you therefore, brethren, by the mercies of God, to present your bodies a living sacrifice, holy, acceptable to God, which is your spiritual service" (Rom. 12:1). God sanctified Jesus and sent Him into the world; likewise, Jesus sanctified himself. This was a setting apart of himself for His work of redemption. In His case no cleansing was needed.

Although man must offer himself in dedication to God, such consecration on man's part is by no means the whole of sanctification. The offering must be accepted by God. When Solomon dedicated the Temple and had prayed his prayer of dedication, the glory of God filled the house. Thus God accepted the offering. Nothing is really sanctified till God has accepted it, for sanctification involves both a consecration to God and an acceptance by Him. Sanctification in its highest Christian sense is something that God does.

(2) *Sanctification is a moral cleansing.* Under the old dispensation it was required that any offering presented to God be perfect. No defective offering could be accepted. Rites of cleansing were employed to remove any ceremonial uncleanness. This was typical of the moral purity required in the new dispensation, for in the Christian meaning of sanctification of moral beings moral purity is required. And since man of himself is not morally pure, God must purify him that he may be sanctified. "Christ also loved the church, and gave himself up for it; that he might sanctify it, having cleansed it by the washing of water with the word" (Eph. 5:25-26). Paul insisted on purity: "This is the will of God, even your sanctification, that ye abstain from fornication; that each one of you know how to possess himself of his own vessel in sanctification and honor" (1 Thess. 4:3-4). "If a man therefore purge himself from these, he shall be a vessel unto honor, sanctified, meet for the master's use, prepared unto every good work" (2 Tim. 2:21).

Here purity of life is insisted upon, but an inward purity is required also: "Having therefore these promises, beloved, let us cleanse ourselves from all defilement of flesh and spirit, perfecting holiness in the fear of God" (2 Cor. 7:1). "The God of peace himself sanctify you wholly; and may your spirit and soul and body be preserved entire, without blame" (1 Thess. 5:23).

2. **Sanctification Is for Believers.** The foregoing promises and exhortations are addressed to believers, which shows that the experience of sanctification is for them. Christ prayed for the sanctification of His disciples who were already converted.

(1) *Further cleansing is needed.* In observing the lives of the disciples before Pentecost, we find serious character defects that indicate the need of a deeper experience. There were manifestations of selfish ambition, jealousy, retaliation, cowardice, and other defects. These men were poorly equipped to carry on the work when Jesus should leave them.

Many modern Christians have felt keenly the need of a deeper grace to qualify them for the service of the Lord. Many will testify to receiving such grace in a second experience at the time of the Holy Spirit baptism.

(2) *The church was sanctified.* Christ gave himself for the church "that he might sanctify it, having cleansed it by the washing of water with the word" (Eph. 5:26). The church in Jerusalem numbered about 120 people. These were filled with the Holy Spirit on the Day of Pentecost, and thus were sanctified, as is evident from the words of Peter who, in describing the experience at Caesarea, said, "And God, who knoweth the heart, bare them witness, giving them the Holy Spirit, even as he did unto us; and he made no distinction between us and them, cleansing their hearts by faith" (Acts 15:8-9). Thus it is evident that a purification of the heart accompanies the baptism with the Spirit.

3. **Progressive Work of the Spirit.** Though the baptism with the Holy Spirit is a most wonderful experience, the total of His work is not performed in an instant. He comes, and He abides. He remains with and in the believer to comfort, guide, enlighten, and teach. His work began before the baptism and continues after. The presence of the Spirit makes one holy, but he will grow in holiness in the development of a more holy character. The Christian life is a growth in grace as well as in knowledge. There is a sense in which there is a progressive sanctification. One cannot grow *into* sanctification, but he must grow *in* it. The Spirit-filled life is one of constant increase in power and of continued improvement.

4. **Sanctification and Regeneration Compared.** Regeneration includes a change of heart, with a purifying of the conscience and change of attitudes, which cleanses from all such base affections and

lusts as incur guilt. The regenerated man is freed from hatred and lust and the love of the world. Sanctification as a subsequent cleansing has to do with tendencies that, though not incurring guilt and to which the will does not give consent, incline toward sin. In regeneration we are saved from sin in word, thought, and deed. We no longer give the consent of the mind to attitudes that are sinful. Full sanctification cleanses from the involuntary tendencies toward sin.

Sanctification does not destroy human nature, but purifies it. Depravity may be compared to a bodily disease. In sanctification the disease is cured. But as a well person is susceptible to disease, so a sanctified person may be tempted and may sin. Sanctification does not remove the possibility of sinning, but the probability of sinning has been reduced greatly; for strength to overcome is provided.

5. **The Means of Sanctification.** Since sanctification is God's will for His people, it is evident that He will place no unnecessary obstacle in the way of its reception. Long, frenzied seeking is not necessary if one will but meet the necessary conditions.

(1) *The divinely provided means.* Three things are named as the means of sanctification—the Word of God, the blood of Christ, and the Holy Spirit. The Word provides the instruction and the promise. The blood has been shed for cleansing. "Wherefore Jesus also, that he might sanctify the people through his own blood, suffered without the gate" (Heb. 13:12). The Holy Spirit is the active agent, cleansing and empowering. All the necessary means have been provided.

(2) *The effort required.* That he may be sanctified one must consecrate, or dedicate, himself to God. This is something God cannot do for us; each person must do it for himself. We are sanctified by faith. Such faith is more than a mental effort to believe. It is a commitment of oneself in full trust to God and complete reliance upon Him, and an acceptance of His gracious favor. It is more than an immediate act; it is a constant state of the soul. Such faith brings the reward.

IV. Spiritual Gifts

The promise of Christ, "Ye shall receive power, when the Holy Spirit is come upon you" (Acts 1:8), finds a part of its fulfillment in the spiritual gifts that are given to God's children. Every child of God receives power for testimony. The manifestations of the Spirit through spiritual gifts greatly strengthen that testimony.

1. **The Nature of Spiritual Gifts.** Our information concerning spiritual gifts must be found in the New Testament. The most extended discussion is found in 1 Corinthians 12 to 14. Elsewhere gifts are mentioned also and evidences of their use are found in several places.

(1) *Gifts distinguished from graces.* The graces, or fruits of the Spirit, are to be distinguished from spiritual gifts. This is not to say that they are to be segregated in actual practice or that a person can be filled with one and have none of the other. They are closely related; for instance, the gift of faith works by the grace of love. But for the sake of analysis they are considered separately. A list of the fruits of the Spirit is found in Galatians 5.

(2) *They are not natural abilities.* Many people are gifted with unusual abilities. When these are consecrated to God the Spirit will use them to His glory. They are of great value in the work of the Lord. However, these abilities are a part of one's personality and can be used for self as well as for God. They differ from spiritual gifts in that they are a natural inheritance, or development, quite apart from any special work of the Spirit.

(3) *They are supernatural enduements of power.* Spiritual gifts are supernatural powers bestowed by the Spirit upon individuals to be exercised for the glory of God in the interests of the whole church. They are special qualifications for service. Although these gifts are under the rational control of the possessor, he cannot exercise them wholly at his own will, but only in cooperation with the Spirit.

2. **A List of the Gifts.** A list of nine gifts is given in 1 Corinthians 12 and a few others are named in Romans 12. It is not claimed that these lists include all the actual or possible gifts of the Spirit. Only a few of the gifts will be considered here.

(1) *The gift of prophecy.* The gift of prophecy, though it may make one eloquent, is not to be confused with natural eloquence and certainly not with elocution. The prophet is God's spokesman. The gift of prophecy makes one a prophet. It is that spiritual endowment which brings one into close union with the mind of God, enabling him to understand spiritual things and giving him power to proclaim them. One may speak well on various themes without the gift of prophecy. Likewise, he may have keen insight in social and political problems. But the Holy Spirit operating through the gift of prophecy enables the prophet to see spiritual things in their true light.

(2) *The gift of discernment.* The gift of discernment enables the possessor to discern spiritual things. He has a special insight into the operation of spiritual forces and is keen to detect evil spirits. A humble exercise of this gift is a protection to the church, but it must be distinguished clearly from suspicion, which is the cause of much trouble. Not all who imagine they were set in the body as an "eye" have the gift of discernment. This is a rather rare gift and is exercised only by the humble.

(3) *Miracles and healing.* Though God hears the prayers of all His children, there are some who possess the gift of miracles or of healing. Such persons are used in a remarkable way, particularly in the healing of the sick. Miracles can be wrought only by the Spirit, and the gift of miracles cannot be used at will by the possessor. This gift is such an evident manifestation of divine power that it is clearly distinguished from any mere mental power.

(4) *The gift of tongues.* This gift is declared to be the least valuable of all. It is the power given by the Spirit to speak in a language not previously known. It has no practical value except as a sign to unbelievers. So far as we have record, it was never used in preaching. The gift of tongues is not to be confused with the meaningless, hysterical utterances that are sometimes substituted for it.

3. **The Receiving of Gifts.** It is clear from the record that spiritual gifts are received in connection with the baptism with the Spirit. Such was the case on the Day of Pentecost and on other occasions. However, it appears that gifts may be received at other times also. They are distributed as the Spirit wills, and hence are not to be sought for at the wish of the individual. It is not to be expected that any one person will possess all the gifts and neither is there any one gift possessed by everyone. The assumption that the gift of tongues is given to all as the evidence of the baptism with the Holy Spirit is without foundation and is contrary to Paul's express statement that not all have the gift of tongues.

4. **Permanency of the Gifts.** It is the opinion of some people that the gifts of the Spirit were placed in the church for the first generation only and that they are no longer needed. The words of Paul are quoted: "Whether there be prophecies, they shall be done away; whether there be tongues, they shall cease; whether there be knowledge, it shall be done away" (1 Cor. 13:8). It is assumed that these (except knowledge) have been done away, while love remains. Since it

does not appear that "that which is perfect" has come yet, it would seem gifts may be remaining also.

However, we must recognize the right of the Spirit to give gifts as He pleases, and it may be He does not give every gift in every congregation in every age. A conclusive proof that gifts have not ceased is that they are now found in the church. If some of the gifts, such as tongues, are seldom manifested, this is because the Spirit does not see fit to bestow them. We must recognize in the Spirit the right of freedom of action. He may give such gifts as He wishes, withholding, if He will, some gifts mentioned in the Bible and possibly giving some not mentioned therein. It is for us to accept what He gives and to use them for God's glory and the profiting of the church.

17

H. Orton Wiley
(1877-1961)

This diminutive giant began life in Marquette, Nebr., November 15, 1877, but grew up in Oregon and California. Though he majored in education at Ashland State Normal, Ashland, Oreg. (1897-98), he became, not a teacher, but a licensed pharmacist. After dispensing prescriptions for six years he responded to a call to preach and became a licensed minister in the United Brethren Church. Soon thereafter he transferred to the Church of the Nazarene and was ordained by Dr. Phineas F. Bresee in 1906. For several years he pastored Berkeley and San Jose Nazarene churches, combining pastoral labors with academic pursuits.

He earned the A.B. in philosophy from the College of the Pacific, San Jose, Calif., and the B.D., S.T.M., and S.T.D. degrees from Pacific School of Religion, Berkeley, Calif. While president of Northwest Nazarene College at Nampa, Idaho, he was honored with the D.D. degree by Pasadena College (now Point Loma Nazarene College).

Dr. Wiley's entire professional career from 1905 onward was within the structure of the Church of the Nazarene, serving as educator, editor, and versatile, indefatigable churchman. He was twice president of Pasadena College, Pasadena, Calif., and for 10 years president of Northwest Nazarene College. For eight years he served as editor of the *Herald of Holiness.*

Small in stature and modest, even shy in manner, Dr. Wiley's first impression on people belied his hidden strength as a leader and administrator. He was no ivory-tower hermit hidden behind his books, but deeply involved in molding the shape and polity of a fledgling denomination. His judgment in ecclesiastical and interpersonal matters was far-seeing and sound.

Yet without doubt Wiley's greatest service to the holiness movement was as a theologian. Spiritually and intellectually, he "stood head and shoulders above other men" (W. T. Purkiser). His major work, the three-volume *Christian Theology,* is highly respected throughout the evangelical world and still used widely not only by Wesleyans but also by non-Wesleyans. This is due to its breadth of scholarship and its irenic, ecumenical tone.

While eminently fair with divergent viewpoints, the work is an unequivocal statement of Wesleyan-Arminian theology at its best. In its free use of previous theologians, *Christian Theology* gathers up the wisdom of the past but organizes and synthesizes it with Wiley's own great heart and mind.

It is not easy reading; it was not designed to be. But it provides a comprehensive theological education for those who are willing to study—a gold mine of knowledge not apt to be equalled or superseded in this century. Critics can find flaws in organization and documentation, but the flaws do not detract from the overall stature of the accomplishment.

Other major works were a commentary, *The Epistle to the Hebrews,* and, in collaboration with Dr. Paul T. Culbertson, *Introduction to Christian Theology.*

While Dr. Wiley's extensive footnotes in *Christian Theology* added immeasurably to the resource value of the work, they are not repeated (with one exception) in the following selections.

The Dispensation of the Holy Spirit[1]

In this chapter Wiley gives a remarkably clear overview of the entire sweep of holiness doctrine as it relates to the Holy Spirit. The selection below begins with some introductory comments on the nature of the church dispensation, and the nature of the Spirit's present ministry in relation to the other members of the Trinity. The discussion proceeds with an analysis of Pentecost,

1. This reading is from Wiley's *Christian Theology,* 2:310-28. The entire chapter (25) is titled "The Person and Work of the Holy Spirit."

then a study of the Offices of the Holy Spirit, as Gift and Giver. Here are presented the Gifts and Graces of the Spirit.

Then, without a separate heading—which there should have been—the author expounds the Spirit's salvation ministry in (1) the Birth of the Spirit, (2) the Baptism with the Spirit, (3) the Anointing, and (4) Sealing. In the subsection called "The Holy Spirit and the Individual" (326), we have a profound and pivotal résumé of human nature as defaced by sin and redeemed in Christ. This section is a check on those who would settle for a solely relational view of holiness.

Wiley's identification of entire sanctification and the baptism with the Holy Spirit is pervasive and consistent, not only in this chapter but throughout his three-volume work.

The Spirit as Gift and Giver

Pentecost marks a new dispensation of grace—that of the Holy Spirit. This new economy, however, must not be understood as in any sense superseding the work of Christ, but as ministering to and completing it. The New Testament does not sanction the thought of an economy of the Spirit apart from that of the Father and the Son except in this sense—that it is the revelation of the Person and work of the Holy Spirit, and therefore the final revelation of the Holy Trinity. Here, too, the economical aspect of the Trinity is the more prominent as emphasizing the distinction in offices. *All things that the Father hath are mine: therefore said I, that he shall take of mine, and shall shew it unto you* (John 16:15). As the Son revealed the Father, so the Spirit reveals the Son and glorifies Him. *No man can say that Jesus is the Lord, but by the Holy Ghost* (1 Cor. 12:3).

The mediatorial Trinity, one in essence and distinct in office, affords the true explanation of the dispensation of the Holy Spirit. His work as the Third Person of the Trinity is therefore in connection with His offices as the Representative of the Savior. He is the Agent of Christ, representing Him in the salvation of the individual soul, in the formation of the Church, and in the witnessing power of the Church to the world.

But He is not the Representative of an absentee Savior. He is our Lord's ever-present other Self. This is the meaning of the promise, *I will not leave you comfortless: I will come to you* (John 14:18). It is through the Spirit, therefore, that our Lord enters upon His higher ministry—a ministry of the Spirit and not merely of the letter. For this reason He said, *It is expedient for you that I go away; for if I go not away, the Comforter will not come unto you* (16:7). In the Old Testament God used history to teach spiritual truth by means of divinely given symbols; in Christ as the historical Person, this truth was actualized in human experience; in the New Testament the fullness of grace and truth revealed in Christ is through the Holy Spirit universalized and made available to the Church.

The Inaugural Signs

Pentecost was the inauguration day of the Holy Spirit. As in the Old Testament the Passover marked the deliverance of Israel from Egyptian bondage, and Pentecost celebrated the giving of the law 50 days later; so in the New Testament Christ our Passover was sacrificed for us, and the Pentecost that followed marked the ushering in of a dispensation of inward law (Heb. 8:10; 10:16).

THE GIFT OF A PERSON

The Pentecostal Gift was the gift of a Person—the Paraclete or Comforter. This Gift Jesus promised to His disciples as the Agent through whom He would continue His office and work in a new and more effective manner. As the Advent of Christ was attended by miraculous signs, so also the inauguration of the Holy Spirit was attended by signs indicative of His Person and work. These signs were three, *first,* the sound as of a rushing mighty wind; *second,* the cloven tongues like as of fire resting upon the disciples; and *third,* the gift of other tongues. We may say, then, that the first sign was the harbinger of His coming; the second indicated His arrival; and the third marked at once the assumption of His office as Administrator, and the beginning of His operation.

The first inaugural sign was that of the *rushing mighty wind* that filled all the house where they were sitting (Acts 2:2). While the account is brief, we may draw the following conclusions from the data at hand: (1) The sound came suddenly, not as winds ordinarily arise by increased intensity, but was at its height immediately. (2) The sound came from heaven . . . heard not only by the disciples but throughout the city. The Revised Version reads as follows: *When the sound was heard, the multitude came together* (v. 6), indicating that it was the sound that attracted them and not the reports of the disciples as is sometimes urged. This sign is indicative of the inner, mysterious, spiritual power of the Holy Spirit that was to characterize His administration in the Church and in the world. There is another rendering of this text that brings out added

THE SOUND OF WIND

beauties of the Spirit of grace. It may be translated, *the sound of a mighty wind, rushing along,* conveying the thought of an intense eagerness on the part of the Spirit, to carry into effect the great salvation purchased by the blood of Christ.

TONGUES OF FIRE

The second inaugural sign was the appearance of *cloven tongues like as of fire,* which sat upon each of them (Acts 2:3). From the use of the singular pronoun, it has been argued that the holy fire like a living flame hovered over the entire company, parting or cleaving into tongues that reached out to each of the waiting company. The generally accepted position, however, is that a cloven or forked tongue sat independently upon each of the disciples. These tongues "like as of fire" were glowing, lambent, and quivering flames that gleamed like a corona above the heads of the spiritual Israel, recalling the signs at Mount Sinai, when the Lord descended in fire and the whole mount quaked greatly (Exod. 19:18).

The significance of this symbol is to be found in the purifying, penetrating, energizing, and transforming effect of the Spirit's administration; while the cloven tongues signify the different gifts communicated by the one Spirit to the different members of the mystical Body of Christ.

MIRACLE OF LANGUAGE

The third inaugural sign occupies a unique position in the events of the day. It must be regarded not only as a sign of the Spirit's coming, but in some sense also as the actual beginning of the Spirit's operations. It is described as follows: *And they were all filled with the Holy Ghost, and began to speak with other tongues as the Spirit gave them utterance* (Acts 2:4). It is a significant fact that the words *heterais glossais* or "other tongues" appear only in this scripture, which describes the phenomena of Pentecost. In the account of the gift of the Spirit to the Gentiles in Caesarea, 10 years after Pentecost (10:46); and to the Ephesians, about 23 years after Pentecost (19:6), the word *heterais* does not appear.

In the Greek language, the word *glotta,* or tongue, always stands in strong contrast with the word *logos* or reason. Hence the contrast between the *logos* and the *glotta,* is the difference between that which a man thinks with the mind, and that which he utters with the vocal organs. Ordinarily, of course, the *glotta* follows the *logos;* but at Pentecost the Holy Spirit by a miraculous operation enabled the disciples to declare the wondrous works of God in such a manner that the representatives of the nations heard them in their own languages. As the word *logos* connotes the idea of reason or intelligence, so the word *glotta* connotes the idea of rational utterance or an intelligible language. It may and often does signify an ecstatic utterance, but never a mere jargon of sounds without coherence or intelligibility. The Church has always maintained that the true interpretation of the phenomena of Pentecost is that the "other tongues" referred to the miraculous gift of "divers languages."

The Offices of the Holy Spirit

The Holy Spirit is both Gift and Giver. He is the Gift of the glorified Christ to the Church, and abides within it as a creating and energizing Presence. This center of Life and Light and Love is the Paraclete or the abiding Comforter. Following His inauguration at Pentecost, the Holy Spirit became the Executive of the Godhead on earth. While He abides perpetually in the Church, this does not imply that He is not still in eternal communion with the Father and the Son in heaven. As we have previously pointed out, arrival in one place does not with God necessitate the withdrawal from another. It does mean, however, that the Holy Spirit is now the Agent of both the Father and the Son, in whom they hold residence (John 14:23), and through whom men have access to God. There is therefore a twofold intercession. As the Son is the Advocate at the right hand of the Father, so the Holy Spirit is the Advocate within the Church; and as the Son was incarnate in human flesh, so the Spirit of God becomes incarnate in the Church—but with this difference; in Christ the divine and human natures were immediately conjoined, while in the Church as the Body of Christ, they are mediated through the Living Head. Christ is the "only begotten" Son of God; men are sons by the adoption of Jesus Christ to himself (Eph. 1:5-6).

EXECUTIVE OF THE GODHEAD

The Holy Spirit as the *Giver* or Administrator of redemption, ministers in two distinct though related fields—that of the fruit of the Spirit and that of the gifts of the Spirit. In his enumeration of the graces and gifts, St. Paul catalogs nine graces (Gal. 5:22-23) and nine gifts (1 Cor. 12:8-10), the former referring to character and the latter to personal endowments for specific vocations.

The fruit of the Spirit is the communication to the individual of the graces flowing from the divine nature and has its issue in character rather than in qualifications for service. It is the outflow of divine life, which follows as a necessary consequence of the Spirit's abiding presence. The apostle may have had in mind the parting parable of our Lord concerning the vine and

FRUIT OF THE SPIRIT

the branches. *I am the true vine, and my Father is the husbandman. Every branch in me that beareth not fruit he taketh away: and every branch that beareth fruit, he purgeth it, that it may bring forth more fruit . . . I am the vine, ye are the branches. He that abideth in me, and I in him, the same bringeth forth much fruit: for without me ye can do nothing* (John 15:1-5).

Here the Spirit is not mentioned but is assumed as the life of the vine, giving character and quality to the fruit. That which obstructs the free flow of life affects the fruit; hence there must be a purging in order to an increased fruitage. This fruit is not named, but St. Paul catalogs nine graces—a trinity of trinities as follows: (1) in relation to God, love, joy, and peace; (2) in relation to others, longsuffering, gentleness, and goodness; and (3) in relation to ourselves, faithfulness, meekness, and temperance (or self-control). These qualities the apostle sets in strong contrast with the *works* of the flesh (Gal. 5:19-23). Fruit grows by cultivation. It receives its life from the vine and takes its character from that life. Works are the result of effort and human striving; fruit is the consequence of the Spirit's abiding. It is not of man's producing, it grows by the life that is in the Vine.

GIFTS OF THE SPIRIT

The gifts of the Spirit are known in Scripture as *charismata* or gifts of grace. Hence there is an internal connection between the graces and the gifts in the administration of the Spirit. The gifts are the divinely ordained means and power with which Christ endows His Church in order to enable it to properly perform its task on earth. Paul summarizes the teachings of the Scriptures concerning spiritual gifts as follows: *Now there are diversities of gifts, but the same Spirit. And there are differences of administrations, but the same Lord. And there are diversities of operations, but it is the same God which worketh all in all. But the manifestation of the Spirit is given to every man to profit withal. For to one is given by the Spirit the word of wisdom; to another the word of knowledge by the same Spirit; to another faith by the same Spirit; to another the gifts of healing by the same Spirit; to another the working of miracles; to another prophecy; to another discerning of spirits; to another divers kinds of tongues; to another the interpretation of tongues: but all these worketh that one and the selfsame Spirit, dividing to every man severally as he will* (1 Cor. 12:4-11).

There are two other scriptures from the same writer that refer to the gifts of the Spirit in a more official capacity. The first is found in the Epistle to the Ephesians and is concerned with the general order of the ministry. *And he gave some, apostles; and some, prophets; and some, evangelists; and some, pastors and teachers* (Eph. 4:11).

The second is concerned with the gifts that attach to the ordinary service of the Church. *Having then gifts differing according to the grace that is given unto us, whether prophecy, let us prophesy according to the proportion of faith; or ministry, let us wait on our ministering: or he that teacheth, on teaching; or he that exhorteth, on exhortation: he that giveth, let him do it with simplicity; he that ruleth, with diligence; he that sheweth mercy, with cheerfulness* (Rom. 12:6-8).

The gifts of the Spirit, then, are supernatural endowments for service and are determined by the character of the ministry to be fulfilled. Without the proper functioning of these gifts, it is impossible for the Church to succeed in her spiritual mission. Hence the subject is of great importance, not only to theology but also to Christian experience and work. It will, however, be impossible to deal adequately with the subject here, and hence we can give only a brief summary of the more important truths concerning spiritual gifts.

(1) The gifts of the Spirit must be distinguished from natural gifts or endowments, although there is, admittedly, a close relation between them. While they transcend the gifts of nature, yet they function through them. Grace quickens the powers of the mind, purifies the affections, and enables the will to energize with new strength; and yet the gifts of the Spirit transcend even sanctified human powers. The strength of the Church is not in the sanctified hearts of its members, but in Him who dwells in the hearts of the sanctified. It is the indwelling Spirit who divides to every man severally as He will, and then pours His own energy through the organism He has created.

(2) There is a diversity of gifts in the Church. Not all members are similarly endowed. Hence in a series of rhetorical questions St. Paul asks, *Are all apostles? are all prophets? are all teachers? are all workers of miracles?* (1 Cor. 12:29). Nine such gifts are mentioned—wisdom, knowledge, faith, miracles, healing, prophecy, discernment of spirits, tongues, interpretation of tongues (vv. 7-11). Doubtless the Spirit takes into account the ability of sanctified nature, and its capacity to receive and function spiritually, but the energizing power is not the natural spirit alone, it is *the power that worketh in us* (Eph. 1:19).

(3) The gifts of the Spirit take their character from the positions that the various individual members occupy in the mystical Body of Christ. St. Paul compares the Church as a spiritual organism to the natural human body with its many and varied members. As the func-

tions of the several members of the body are determined by the nature of the organs—the eye for seeing and the ear for hearing, so it is in the Body of Christ. The Spirit who creates the spiritual body, of necessity creates the members that compose that body, *for the body is not one member, but many* (1 Cor. 12:14). God has set the members in the natural body as it has pleased Him (v. 18); so also the Spirit divides to every man severally as He will in the spiritual body (v. 11). The gifts of the Spirit, therefore, are those divine bestowments upon individual members that determine their functions in the Body of Christ. Consequently *the eye cannot say unto the hand, I have no need of thee: nor again the head to the feet, I have no need of you . . . that there should be no schism in the body; but that the members should have the same care one for another* (vv. 21, 25).

(4) The gifts of the Spirit are exercised in conjunction with, and not apart from, the Body of Christ. The human body cannot function through maimed and lifeless members, nor can members separated from the body exist, much less perform their natural functions. So, also, God does not bestow extraordinary gifts upon men to be administered through mere human volition, and for self-glory and aggrandizement. The true gifts of the Spirit are exercised as functions of the one Body, and under the administration of the one Lord.

(5) The gifts of the Spirit are essential to the spiritual progress of the Church. As physical ends can be accomplished only by physical means, or intellectual attainments by mental effort, so the spiritual mission of the Church can be carried forward only by spiritual means. From this it is evident that the gifts of the Spirit are always latent in the Church. They did not cease with the apostles but are available to the Church in every age.

Salvation Functions of the Spirit[2]

LORD AND GIVER OF LIFE

In addition to the gifts and graces of the Spirit, there are certain other acts or functions of His administrative work that demand brief attention before taking up more directly His work as related to the individual, the Church, and the world. These pertain especially to the work of salvation and may be classified broadly under two general heads—the Holy Spirit as "the Lord and Giver of Life," and the Holy Spirit as "a sanctifying Presence." To the former belongs the "birth of the Spirit" or the initial

2. This heading added by the editor.

experience of salvation; to the latter, the "baptism with the Spirit"—a subsequent work by which the soul is made holy. This is known as entire sanctification, which as our creed states "is wrought by the baptism with the Holy Spirit, and comprehends in one experience the cleansing of the heart from sin and the abiding, indwelling presence of the Holy Spirit, empowering the believer for life and service."[3]

Analyzing this state of holiness from the viewpoint of the Agent rather than the work wrought, we notice a threefold operation of the Spirit in the one experience of the believer: the *baptism,* which in its restricted sense refers to the act of purifying, or making holy; the *anointing,* or the indwelling Spirit in His office work of empowering for life and service; and the *sealing,* or the same indwelling Presence in His witness-bearing capacity. When, therefore, we speak of the birth, the baptism, the anointing, and the sealing, as four administrative acts or functions of the Spirit, we are referring only to the two works of grace, but are considering the latter under a threefold aspect.

We are to be understood as referring (1) to the birth of the Spirit as the bestowment of life in the initial experience of salvation—an experience that will be considered later under the head of regeneration and its concomitants, justification and adoption. We shall then consider the subsequent work of the Spirit as sanctifier, under the threefold aspect of (2) the baptism; (3) the anointing; and (4) the sealing—an experience that we shall treat later under the head of "Christian Perfection" or "Entire Sanctification."[4]

NEW LIFE

1. *The Birth of the Spirit* is the impartation of divine life to the soul. It is not merely a reconstruction or working over of the old life; it is the impartation to the soul, or the implantation within the soul, of the new life of the Spirit. It is therefore a "birth from above." As the natural birth is a transition from fetal life to a life fully individualized, so the Holy Spirit infuses life into souls dead in trespasses and sins, and thereby sets them up as distinct individuals in the spiritual realm. These individuals are children of God. To them is given the Spirit of adoption by which they are constituted heirs of God and joint-heirs with Christ (Rom. 8:15-17). The apostle defines specifically the nature of this inheritance. It is the blessing of Abra-

3. *Manual, Church of the Nazarene,* Article 10.

4. While the baptism with the Spirit is usually considered as the act by which regenerated men are made holy, it is sometimes used also in the broader sense of the state of holiness flowing from that act. The former appears to be the more exact position (Wiley, 2:322, n.).

ham, which God gave to him by promise, that is, the promise of the Spirit, through faith (Gal. 3:14-18).

While the child of God as an individual possesses life in Christ, there is in him also the "carnal mind" or inbred sin, and this prevents him from entering fully into his New Testament privileges in Christ. Jesus as the "Lamb of God" came to take away "the *sin* of the world." There must therefore be a purification from sin. Until then he *differeth nothing from a servant, though he be lord of all; but is under tutors and governors until the time appointed of the father* (Gal. 4:1-2). He is an heir, but he has not yet entered into his inheritance. The time appointed of the Father is the hour of submission to the baptism of Jesus—the baptism with the Holy Spirit that purifies the heart from all sin. With the cleansing of the heart from inbred sin, the son is inducted into the full privileges of the New Covenant; through that baptism he enters into *the fulness of the blessing of the gospel of Christ* (Rom. 15:29).

BAPTISM WITH THE SPIRIT

2. *The Baptism with the Spirit,* as we have indicated, is the induction of newborn individuals into the full privileges of the New Covenant. *This is the covenant that I will make with them after those days, saith the Lord, I will put my laws into their hearts, and in their minds will I write them; and their sins and iniquities will I remember no more. Now where remission of these is, there is no more offering for sin* (Heb. 10:16-18). Both the individual and social aspects of personality are involved. As by the natural birth each individual comes into possession of a nature common to others, and thereby becomes a member of a race of interrelated persons; so also the individual born of the Spirit has a new nature that demands a new spiritual organism as the ground of holy fellowship.

The old racial nature cannot serve in this capacity, for it is "corrupt according to the deceitful lusts" (Eph. 4:22). The new nature of Christ, "created in righteousness and true holiness" (v. 24), can alone supply this spiritual nexus. Hence we are commanded to "put off the old man" and to "put on the new man." The baptism with the Spirit, therefore, must be considered under a twofold aspect; *first,* as a death to the carnal nature; and *second,* as the fullness of life in the Spirit. Since entire sanctification is effected by the baptism with the Spirit, it likewise has a twofold aspect—the cleansing from sin and full devotement to God.

3. *The Anointing with the Spirit* is a further aspect of this second work of grace—that which regards it as a conferring of authority and power. It refers, therefore, not to the negative aspect of cleansing but to the positive phase of the indwelling Spirit as "empowering the believer for life and service." Prophets, priests, and kings were in the Old Testament dispensation, inducted into office by an anointing with specially prepared oil. This administrative act of the Spirit, therefore, bears an official as well as a personal relation to Christ. As previously indicated, purification from sin is in order to the full devotement of the soul to God. But this devotement is not merely human energy exercised toward God. It is the inwrought power of the Holy Spirit—the operation of the abiding Comforter who dwells within the holy heart. Hence we read, that *God anointed Jesus of Nazareth with the Holy Ghost and with power: who went about doing good, and healing all that were oppressed of the devil; for God was with him* (Acts 10:38).

JESUS NOT BAPTIZED WITH THE SPIRIT

While it is recorded that Jesus was baptized with water by John, it is not stated that He was baptized with the Holy Spirit. This is significant. The reason is plain: baptism implies cleansing, and Jesus had no sin from which to be cleansed; neither could He in this sense be filled with the Spirit, for the Spirit already dwelt in Him without measure. But He was anointed with the Spirit at the time of His baptism by John, and thereby inducted into the office and work of the Messiah or Christ. As we become sons of God by faith in Jesus Christ, so also, because we are sons, God gives us the Holy Spirit as a sanctifying and empowering Presence. This Spirit, our Lord tells us, the world cannot receive, because *it seeth him not, neither knoweth him* (John 14:17). St. John further declares that this anointing abides in us as the personal Paraclete or Comforter, and consequently is ever present to confer authority and to supply the needed power for the accomplishment of every divinely appointed task.

4. *The Sealing with the Spirit* is a further aspect of this second work of grace. The seal to which St. Paul refers in his letter to Timothy, had two inscriptions—*The Lord knoweth them that are his*, or ownership; and *let every one that nameth the name of Christ depart from iniquity*, or holiness (2 Tim. 2:19). The Pentecostal gift of the Holy Spirit, under one aspect is the baptism that purifies the heart; and under another, the anointing that empowers for life and service. Under still another aspect, it is the seal of God's ownership and approval. This approval is not only a claim upon the service of the sanc-

tified as involved in ownership, but the seal of approval upon that service as rendered through the Holy Spirit.

The seal is also the guaranty of full redemption in the future. Hence St. Paul says that after *ye believed, ye were sealed with that holy Spirit of promise, which is the earnest of our inheritance until the redemption of the purchased possession, unto the praise of his glory* (Eph. 1:13-14). Here the Spirit is not only the promised Gift but the gift of promise, which in connection with the earnest is the guaranty of future perfection. The "earnest" was a portion of the inheritance given in advance as a sample and guaranty of that which later was to be had in its perfection—*for if the firstfruit be holy, the lump is also holy* (Rom. 11:16).

The earnest of the Spirit, then, is given to us for our present enjoyment until the end of the age and is the seal of assurance that the purchased possession will then be fully redeemed—all of which shall redound to the praise of His glory.

In this connection, also, it may be well to note the close relation that the work of the Spirit bears to that of Christ. These four administrative acts belong at once to Christ and the Spirit. It is Christ who quickens dead souls into life by the Spirit; it is Christ who baptizes men and women with the Holy Spirit; and it is Christ, also, who both anoints and seals His people with the Spirit.

The Holy Spirit and the Individual

As the Spirit formed the body of the incarnate Christ and took up His abode in the new nature thus formed, so He thereby becomes the Intermediary between Christ and the human soul. There are therefore two sources of life in Christ—the fullness of the Spirit, and the redeemed human nature through which the Spirit is mediated, and by means of which He unites himself to the individual soul.

This will appear more evident, if we take into consideration the fact that while Christ was free from sin in both nature and act, yet this new Man appeared in the midst of a sinful race, and dwelt in the likeness of sinful flesh (Rom. 8:3). He that had no sin, by His birth into a fallen race, thereby took upon himself the penalty due its sin, and died without the camp that He might sanctify the people with His own blood (Heb. 13:12; cf. Titus 2:14). Only by death could He be freed from the old race into which He was born; and by the resurrection from the dead could He establish a new, unique, and spiritual people. He was, therefore, the "first begotten from the dead," uniting in himself as did the first Adam, both the individual and the race.

If now we refer briefly to the question of original sin . . . we may note that the sin of Adam not only brought penalty but entailed consequences, both for himself and for his posterity. Two effects followed the first transgression—a criminal act and a subjective change.

RACIAL SIN

When man consented to sin, God withdrew the fellowship of His presence through the Spirit. Deprived of life, only corruption and impurity remained. This fallen nature is continued in the posterity of Adam as "inbred sin" or "inherited depravity," an element utterly foreign to the original character and life of man. Sin therefore exists in a twofold manner, as an act and as a state or condition back of that act; and while guilt does not attach to the latter, it is nevertheless of the nature of sin. In Adam depravity followed as a consequence of sin; in his posterity sin exists as a nature before it issues in sin as an act.

As a state or quality that is the racial inheritance of every man born into the world, sin is the root or essence of all spiritual impurity and corruption. It is the primal cause of every transgression and the fountain of all unholy activities; but it must not be confused with these activities, or with any one of them. It is the nature back of the act, the generic or racial idea of sin, to which St. John refers when he says, *All unrighteousness is sin* (1 John 5:17); and again, *The blood of Jesus Christ his Son cleanseth us from all sin* (1:7). It is this to which John the Baptist referred when he cried out and said, *Behold the Lamb of God, which taketh away the sin of the world* (John 1:29). St. Paul uses the word in the same sense when he says, *Likewise reckon ye also yourselves to be dead indeed unto sin, but alive unto God through Jesus Christ our Lord* (Rom. 6:11); and he refers to the same elementary antagonism to holiness when he uses the terms "the body of sin," the "old man," or the "carnal mind."

SIN AS CONDITION AND ACT

We must hold firmly to the fact that in the teaching of Christ there is a moral condition antecedent to the act of sin. *A good tree cannot bring forth evil fruit, neither can a corrupt tree bring forth good fruit* (Matt. 7:18). There is therefore not only human personality as a free and responsible agent, but there is a nature or character that attaches to this agent, which in thought at least is distinguishable from it—that is, the person may be either good or bad, may exist in the state of holiness or in the state of sin. If we may be permitted to use the technical terms applied usually only to the Trinity, we may say that as in the Godhead the Three Persons subsist in one divine nature and as angels subsist in angelic nature, so also human beings are persons who subsist in human nature. Previous to the Fall, man subsisted in holy human nature; since that time he subsists in a fallen and depraved human nature.

As persons, each human being is by the very nature of personality forever separate and distinct from every other; as members of a common race each individual possesses a nature in common with every other individual, and this furnishes the common bond of racial union. *What man knoweth the things of a man, save the spirit of man which is in him? even so the things of God knoweth no man, but the Spirit of God* (1 Cor. 2:11). It is evident, then, that Christ as the theanthropic Person furnishes the source of life for both the person and the race. Since in Him human nature was conjoined in vital union with the divine, this new life becomes in the administration of the Holy Spirit the principle of regeneration in respect to the person; and since Christ not only died for sin but unto sin, His shed blood becomes the principle of sanctification as it respects the sinful nature inherited from Adam.

Regeneration and Sanctification[5]

The careful reader of this anthology will have noticed that some Wesleyans have been more successful than others in defining sanctification in relation to regeneration. Some, as Miley and Curtis for instance, have tended to see sanctification as merely the extension and perfection of regeneration.

Wiley, however, insists that the definitive weight in regeneration should be on the creation of spiritual life. The definitive weight in sanctification should be on cleansing of sin. In regeneration the sin of *acquired depravity* is cleansed. The primal essence of entire sanctification is the cleansing of inbred sin, or *native depravity.*

There are adjuncts and overtones in regeneration, and also in entire sanctification; but these concomitant elements should not be so stressed as to obscure the fundamental notes.

5. *Christian Theology,* 2:471-76.

The relation existing between regeneration and sanctification is set forth in an able and unique manner by Bishop Jesse T. Peck in his *Central Idea of Christianity.* He says,

"Now two things so entirely distinct as the fact of spiritual life and the moral state of the spiritually alive ought to have different names. Regeneration designates the former, sanctification the latter. . . . The word sanctification just as appropriately denotes certain treatment of the soul, which God has brought to life, as regeneration does the fact of bringing it to life. Sanctify is from *sanctus,* holy, and *facio,* to make. Sanctification is literally the act of making holy, and this is its essential meaning in systematic divinity.

"Now here are two things totally distinct from each other . . . and here are two terms, of entirely different import, completely adapted to represent these two things respectively—regeneration, the production of spiritual life; sanctification, the treatment of the soul spiritually alive—neither of which can, without violence to the laws of language, perform the office of the other. We humbly submit, therefore, that they ought not to be used interchangeably, and that attempts to so use them have caused nearly all the confusion which has embarrassed these great points in theology" (Peck, *Central Idea of Christianity,* 15-17).

Concerning Sin in the Regenerate

It has been the uniform belief of the church, that original sin "continues to exist with the new life of the regenerate, until eradicated by the baptism with the Holy Spirit" (Creed, Art. 5).[6] As stated in the Thirty-nine Articles, "this infection of nature doth remain, yea, in them that are regenerated; whereby the lust of the flesh, called in Greek *phronēma sarkos,* is not subject to the law of God. And although there is no condemnation for them that believe, yet this lust hath of itself the nature of sin" (Art. 9). "By sin," says Mr. Wesley, "I here understand inward sin; any sinful temper, passion, or affection; such as pride, self will, love of the world, in any kind or degree; such as lust, anger, peevishness; any disposition contrary to the mind which was in Christ" *(Sermon: Sin in Believers).*

The condition of the regenerate, therefore, previous to entire sanctification, is in a modified sense, a mixed state. There is within the heart of the believer, both grace and inbred sin, but there is not, nor

6. *Manual, Church of the Nazarene.*

can there be any commingling or blending of these antagonistic elements. They exist in the heart without admixture or composition. Otherwise we should have an adulterated holiness.

A MIXED STATE

Those who hold to the erroneous idea of regeneration as a making over of the old life, instead of an impartation of the new, find difficulty in accounting for a second work of grace.

Entire Sanctification as Subsequent to Regeneration

Theologians of the Wesleyan type frequently speak of the incompleteness of regeneration and of the necessity of entire sanctification in order to complete or perfect the redemptive process. Thus Dr. Miley states that "the doctrine of an incompleteness of the work of regeneration underlies entire sanctification, particularly in its Wesleyan form" (Miley, *Systematic Theology,* 2:357). There is a sense in which this is true, but the form of the statement is unfortunate.

Regeneration considered in itself is not an imperfect work. It is the bestowal of divine life, and as an operation of the Spirit, is complete in itself. But regeneration is only a part of the grace embraced in the New Covenant, and in this sense only may be said to be incomplete—incomplete as not in itself representing the totality of New Covenant blessings.

REGENERATION BRINGS SPIRITUAL LIFE

Again, regeneration is frequently represented in Wesleyan theology, as the beginning of sanctification—a work that comes to its perfection in entire sanctification. Here, also, discriminating thought is necessary. Regeneration is the beginning of sanctification in this sense only, that the life bestowed in the new birth is a holy life. This new life, being one of "holy love," may be said to be the beginning of holiness. But we are not to infer from this that the expanding of this new life by growth, or the increase and development of this love, will bring the soul to entire sanctification. Failure to discriminate here leads inevitably to the "growth theory" of sanctification. Sanctification is an act of cleansing, and unless inbred sin be removed, there can be no fullness of life, no perfection in love. In a strict sense, regeneration is not purification. Initial sanctification accompanies regeneration, as do also justification and adoption, but regeneration is the impartation of life, and initial sanctification is the cleansing from guilt and from acquired depravity.

Closely related to both of the foregoing is another statement that needs to be qualified also. We refer to the expression that sanctification is not something new, but a perfecting of that which we already possess. It is indeed true

TWO WORKS SEPARATE AND DISTINCT

that there is a *substratum* that is common to both regeneration and entire sanctification, that is, a life of moral love. But regeneration is the impartation of this life of love, and entire sanctification is such a purification of the heart as makes love sole and supreme in experience. The two works are separate and distinct, and consequently the latter is something more than the mere finishing touches of the former.

The Divinely Appointed Means and Agencies[7]

To say in one sermon that we are sanctified by the blood of Christ, and in another that we are sanctified by faith, can be confusing to the untrained listener. The preacher needs to virtually memorize the following distinctions and explain these relationships frequently.

We find it impossible to properly appreciate the nature of entire sanctification, without taking into account the means and agencies that God employs to stamp His image anew upon the hearts of men. Sanctification is said to be by blood, by the Spirit, by faith, and through the truth.

(1) The originating cause is the love of God. *Herein is love, not that we loved God, but that he loved us, and sent his Son to be the propitiation for our sins* (1 John 4:10).

(2) The meritorious or procuring cause is the blood of Jesus Christ. *If we walk in the light, as he is in the light, we have fellowship one with another, and the blood of Jesus Christ his Son cleanseth us from all sin* (1 John 1:7).

(3) The efficient cause or agency is the Holy Spirit. We are saved *by the washing of regeneration, and the renewing of the Holy Ghost* (Titus 3:5); we are said to be elected *through sanctification of the Spirit* (1 Pet. 1:2); and again, that we are chosen to salvation *through sanctification of the Spirit and belief of the truth* (2 Thess. 2:13).

(4) The instrumental cause is truth. Frequently faith is regarded also as the instrumental cause, since faith is conditioned on truth. We prefer, however, to regard truth as the instrumental cause and faith as the conditional or proximate cause. Our Lord himself, in His high

---

7. *Christian Theology*, 2:478-79.

priestly prayer, used the words *Sanctify them through thy truth: thy word is truth* (John 17:17). The Holy Spirit is the Spirit of truth and acts through its instrumentality. Hence St. Peter says, *Ye have purified your souls in obeying the truth* (1 Pet. 1:22); and St. John declares that *whoso keepeth his word, in him verily is the love of God perfected: hereby know we that we are in him* (1 John 2:5).

(5) The conditional cause is faith. *And put no difference between us and them, purifying their hearts by faith* (Acts 15:9); *that they may receive forgiveness of sins, and inheritance among them which are sanctified by faith, that is in me* (Acts 26:18).

When, therefore, we speak of sanctification as being wrought by the Father, or by the Son, or by the Holy Spirit; whether we speak of it as by the blood, or through the truth, or by faith, we are referring merely to the different causes that enter in to this great experience.

Progressive Sanctification[8]

Human nature being what it is, the tendency is to swing like a pendulum from one extreme to another. Those who see only the crisis of entire sanctification, and emphasize the experience as a second, definite, instantaneous work of grace, tend to leave little room for growth. On the other hand, those among us who react to that extreme and wish to stress holiness as a process and progress, tend equally to drift into what in the end becomes a purely Calvinistic view of gradual sanctification.

Why can we never find the "golden mean"? The following selection from Wiley will help. Sanctification, both initial and entire, must be viewed (and experienced) in a moment of time. Sanctification considered as preparatory growth before, and continued growth after the crisis, is progressive. In conquering weaknesses and faults, developing strength of character, and conforming the entire being to mature Christlikeness, a lifetime is needed.

But should the expression *progressive sanctification* ever be used? Wiley points out:

The term *progressive* as used in connection with sanctification must be clearly defined. As used in the Wesleyan sense, it means sim-

8. *Christian Theology,* 2:479-86.

ply the temporal aspect of the work of grace in the heart, as it takes place in successive stages. Each of these stages is marked by a gradual approach and an instantaneous consummation in experience, and the stages together mark the full scope of sanctifying grace. Thus "in His administration of sanctifying grace the Holy Spirit proceeds by degrees. Terms of progress are applied to each department of that work in the saint; or, in other words, the goal of entire sanctification is represented as the end of a process in which the Spirit requires the cooperation of the believer. This cooperation, however, is only the condition on which is suspended what is the work of divine grace alone" (Pope, *Compendium of Christian Theology,* 3:36).

There is here a great truth that no student of theology can afford to overlook, and failure to emphasize this point leads to confusion concerning the experience itself. But this point was not sufficiently guarded by Methodist theologians, and as a consequence, the emphasis came gradually to be placed upon the aspect of growth and development, rather than upon the crises that marked the different stages in personal experience. Later writers on this subject have more carefully guarded this point. They have emphasized the instantaneousness of sanctification as an act, and thereby preserved the truth of progressive sanctification without falling into the error of the growth theory. Three subjects must be considered in this division, as follows: (1) Sanctification as partial and entire; (2) sanctification as gradual and instantaneous; and (3) sanctification as instantaneous and continuous.

Sanctification as Partial and Entire

The concomitant blessings that make up conversion as a first work of grace are: (1) justification as an act of forgiveness in the mind of God; (2) regeneration as the impartation of a new nature; and (3) adoption as an assurance of the privileges of heirship. To these there must be added another concomitant known as (4) "initial" sanctification. Defilement attaches to sinful acts, and so also does guilt, which is the consciousness of sin as our own. There must be, therefore, this initial cleansing, concomitant with the other blessings of the first work of grace, if this guilt and acquired depravity are to be removed from the sinner. Since that which removes pollution and makes holy is properly called "sanctification," this first or initial cleansing is "partial" sanctification.

But the term is not an indefinite one, referring to the cleansing away of more or less of the sinner's defilement. It is a definite term and is limited strictly to that guilt and acquired depravity attaching to actual sins, for which the sinner is himself responsible. It does not refer to the cleansing from original sin or inherited depravity, for which the sinner is not responsible. We may say then that initial or partial sanctification includes in its scope all that acquired pollution that attaches to the sinner's own acts; while entire sanctification includes the cleansing from original sin or inherited depravity. Since sin is twofold—an act, and a state or condition—sanctification must be twofold. There is and can be but two stages in the process of sanctification—initial and entire—the full consummation of the process being rightly known as glorification.

Sanctification as Gradual and Instantaneous

Mr. Wesley taught that there is a gradual work, both preceding and following the act of God by which we are sanctified wholly. This is true of justification as well as of sanctification. To overlook the preparation of the Spirit in the hearts of men is to undervalue the prophetic work of Christ in relation to His priesthood and to minimize the importance of prevenient grace.

THE TIME ELEMENT

God neither justifies a sinner nor entirely sanctifies a believer except by grace through faith. This grace operates only on the plane of self-abnegation and godly sorrow for sin, apart from any merit in the seeker himself. And this godly sorrow for sin, or this renunciation of inbred sin, this loathing of the carnal mind with its "depths of pride, self-will and hell," is never found, either in the sinner or the child of God, apart from the illuminating, convincing power of the Holy Spirit. Thus the progressive element is seen to be fundamental to the synergistic positions of Arminian theology. This gradual, preparatory work may be cut short in righteousness. When the sinner perfectly submits to the righteousness of Christ, and believes the promises of God, that moment he is justified and the Spirit imparts new life to his soul. When, also, the child of God through the Spirit fully renounces inbred sin and trusts the blood of cleansing, that moment he may, by simple faith in Christ, be sanctified wholly.

The classic passage in support of this position is found in *A Plain Account of Christian Perfection* (51). The question is asked, "Is this death to sin and renewal in love gradual or instantaneous?" The answer is, "A man may be dying for some time; yet he does not, properly speaking, die until the instant the soul is separated from the body; and that instant he lives the life of eternity. In like manner he may be dying to sin for some time; yet he is not dead to sin until sin is separated from his soul; and in that instant he lives the full life of love."

The Scriptures bear out the thought of the gradual preparation and instantaneous completion of entire sanctification so clearly stated by Mr. Wesley. Perhaps the most familiar passage is that which represents inbred sin as under the doom of death. *Our old man,* says St. Paul, *is crucified with him, that the body of sin might be destroyed, that henceforth we should not serve sin* (Rom. 6:6). Crucifixion as a manner of death is a gradual process, disqualifying the body from serving any master, but certainly tending to death and having its final issue in death. The same writer in another epistle exhorts us to *make not provision for the flesh, to fulfil the lusts thereof* (13:14). Here, again, the apostle speaks of the renunciation of the carnal mind, which he portrays under the strong figure of a crucifixion, or a nailing to the cross; and he commands that no provision be made for the fulfilling of the inordinate desires of the flesh. The "old man" must be kept on the cross until he dies; and when sin expires, in that moment the soul is entirely sanctified and lives the full life of perfect love.

THE "OLD MAN"

Entire Sanctification as Instantaneous and Continuous

While there is a gradual approach to sanctification, and a gradual growth in grace following it, the sanctifying act by which we are made holy must of necessity be instantaneous. In the words of Bishop Hamline, "It is gradually approached, but instantaneously bestowed." Dr. Adam Clarke states that "in no part of the Scriptures are we directed to seek holiness *gradatim.* We are to come to God for an instantaneous and complete purification from all sin, as for instantaneous pardon. Neither the seriatim pardon, nor the *gradatim* purification, exists in the Bible" (Clarke, *Christian Theology,* 208).

But entire sanctification is not only a definite and completed act; it is also a completed and continuous act. We mean by this that we are cleansed from all sin, only as through faith, we are brought into a right relation to the atoning blood of Jesus Christ; and only as there is a continuous relation to atoning blood by faith, will there be a continuous cleansing, in the sense of a preservation in purity and holiness. In this connection we refer again to Dr. Adam Clarke, who says, "The meritorious efficacy of His passion and death has purged our conscience from dead works; and cleanseth us *(katharizei hēmas)*—continues to cleanse us; that is, to keep clean what He has made clean; for it requires the same merit and energy to preserve holiness in the soul of man, as to produce it" (Clarke, *Commentary,* 1 John 1:7).

Both the instantaneous and continuous aspects of sanctification are set forth by the apostle John as follows: *But if we walk in the light, as he is in the light, we have fellowship one with another, and the blood of Jesus Christ his Son cleanseth us from all sin* (1 John 1:7). Here there is (1) a definite and instantaneous act of sanctification by which the soul is cleansed from all sin; (2) a progressive sanctification whereby those who walk in the light are the recipients of the continuous merits of the atoning blood. Viewed from the standpoint of the Spirit, those who are sanctified by His agency as an instantaneous act are through the indwelling of the Spirit made the recipients of His continuously sanctifying grace. There is a remarkable degree of harmony between this text and that found in 1 Pet. 1:2: *Elect according to the foreknowledge of God the Father, through sanctification of the Spirit, unto obedience and sprinkling of the blood of Jesus Christ.*

Here it is clear (1) that salvation is through the sanctification of the Spirit;

(2) that sanctification, as an instantaneous act, cleanses from all sin and brings the believer to a place of obedience, internally and externally;

(3) that walking in this obedience, the elect dwell constantly under the sprinkling of the all-atoning and sanctifying blood. Sanctification, as an instantaneous act, cleanses us from all sin and brings us to a place of obedience; walking in the light of obedience we are the recipients of a progressive or continuous sanctification, which renders even our obedience acceptable to God.

ONGOING CONDITIONALITY

It is important to bear in mind, therefore, that we are cleansed by the atoning blood, only as we are (1) brought into right relation to Jesus Christ; and (2) we are continuously cleansed, or kept clean, and only as these right relations are continued. We are sanctified by Christ, not separate from, but in and with himself; not only by the blood of cleansing, but under the sprinkling of that blood. Faith is the vital bond of union with Christ, and the pure in heart abide in Him only by a continuous faith. If this connection be severed, spiritual life ceases immediately.

If now, we analyze this position carefully, we shall see that as in justification there was a judicial or declarative act which set the soul in right relation to God, and concomitant with it in experience, though logically following it, an inward cleansing by the Spirit from guilt and acquired depravity; so also in entire sanctification there is a *judicial* sanctification or a declarative act that pronounces the soul holy, attended by the concomitant grace of the Spirit that cleanses from all sin.

This act is sometimes known as *positional,* or *imputed* holiness, in the same sense that justification is regarded as imputed righteousness. But to maintain that it is possible for a soul to be positionally holy, apart from the inner work of the Spirit, which makes it actually holy, is one of the errors of imputationism. All the damaging errors that underlie imputation as dissevered from impartation in regard to justification or Christian righteousness, attach likewise to entire sanctification or Christian holiness.

IMPUTED AND IMPARTED HOLINESS

Christian Perfection[9]

Earlier in this volume Benjamin Field discussed objections to the doctrine of Christian perfection, and Curtis traces John Wesley's teaching on the subject. The following selection from Wiley, however, is a systematic exposition of holiness under the rubric of Christian perfection. Naturally there is overlapping with his discussion in the previous chapter, because he sees Christian perfection as including entire sanctification; but he also sees perfection as a much broader concept, a concept that embraces the full panoply of Christian graces.

Wiley makes a careful distinction between that relative adulthood that marks the attainment of perfection in the sense of entire sanctification, and that adulthood that is to be conceived as maturity in distinction from purity. His distinction between purity and maturity, and also his treatment of perfection in relation to infirmities and temptation, are especially helpful.

Christian perfection in the critical sense represents the more positive aspect of the one experience, known theologically either as entire sanctification or Christian perfection. Entire sanctification, however, is a term that applies more to the aspect of a cleansing from sin, or the making holy; while Christian perfection emphasizes especially the standard of privilege secured to the believer by the atoning work of Jesus Christ. "We give the name of Christian perfection," says Mr.

---

9. *Christian Theology,* 2:496-517.

Fletcher, "to that maturity of grace and holiness which established adult believers attain to under the Christian dispensation; and thus we distinguish that maturity of grace, from both the ripeness of grace which belongs to the dispensation of the Jews below us, and from the ripeness of glory which belongs to departed saints above us. Hence it appears that by Christian perfection, we mean nothing but the cluster and maturity of graces which compose the Christian character in the Church militant. In other words, Christian perfection is a spiritual constellation, made up of these gracious stars: perfect repentance, perfect faith, perfect humility, perfect meekness, perfect self-denial, perfect resignation, perfect hope, perfect charity for our visible enemies, as well as our earthly relations; and, above all, perfect love for our invisible God, through the explicit knowledge of our Mediator, Jesus Christ. And as this last star is always accompanied by all the others, as Jupiter is by his satellites, we frequently use, as St. John, the phrase 'perfect love' instead of the word 'perfection'; understanding by it the pure love of God shed abroad in all the hearts of established believers by the Holy Ghost, which is abundantly given them under the fullness of the Christian dispensation."

PERFECT IN QUALITY

Here the word *perfection,* used in connection with the graces of the Spirit, must be understood to refer solely to their *quality,* as being pure and unmixed, not to their *quantity,* as precluding further growth and development.

Misconceptions of Christian Perfection

There are numerous misconceptions concerning Christian perfection that must be cleared away before there can be a right understanding or a proper appreciation of this work of the Holy Spirit. The term seems to connote a standard of excellence that those who are rightly informed never claim for it. It is well, therefore, when using the word in this connection, to always accompany it with its guardian adjectives, such as *Christian* or *evangelical* perfection. Rightly understood, there can be no objection, either to the doctrine or the experience.

(1) Christian perfection is not *absolute* perfection. This belongs to God only. In this sense, *there is none good but one, that is, God* (Matt. 19:17). All other goodness is derived. So, also, God alone is perfect; but His creatures are also perfect in a relative sense, according to their nature and kind. (2) It is not *angelic* perfection. The holy angels are unfallen beings, and, therefore, retain their native faculties unimpaired. They are not liable to mistake, as is man in his present

state of weakness and infirmity, and, therefore, have a perfection impossible to mankind. (3) It is not *Adamic* perfection. Man was made a little lower than the angels, and doubtless in his pristine state, possessed a perfection unknown to man in his present state of existence. (4) It is not a perfection in *knowledge.* Not only was man's will perverted, and his affections alienated by the Fall, but his intellect was darkened. Hence from this defective understanding may flow erroneous opinions concerning many matters, and these may in turn lead to false judgments and a wrong bias in the affections. (5) It is not immunity from temptation or the susceptibility to sin. These are essential to a probationary state. Our Lord was tempted in all points as we are, and yet He was without sin.

Implications of the Doctrine

Before considering the scriptural meaning of Christian perfection, it will be well also to give attention to some of the implications of the doctrine. (1) This perfection is *evangelical* as opposed to a legal perfection. *The law made nothing perfect, but the bringing in of a better hope did* (Heb. 7:19). Christian perfection, therefore, is of grace, in that Jesus Christ brings His people to completion or perfection under the present economy. The term *sinless perfection* was one that Wesley never used because of its ambiguity. Those who are justified are saved from their sins; those who are sanctified wholly are cleansed from all sin; but those who are thus justified and sanctified still belong to a race under the doom of original sin and will bear the consequences of this sin to the end of the age. The term *perfection,* however, is a proper one, in that *the righteousness of God without the law is manifested. . . . Even the righteousness of God which is by faith of Jesus Christ unto all and upon all them that believe* (Rom. 3:21-22). This righteousness is forensic, but correlative with it, sin is purged from the soul, and the perfect love of God shed abroad in the heart by the Holy Spirit. This, too, is a completed or perfected act, although the love thus imparted is capable of eternal increase. Again, perfection is a proper term, because we are conformed to the image of His Son, that is, we are made sons by a completed act, and as sons may be purged from all spiritual disease. The consequence of this is a state of gracious or evangelical perfection.

EVANGELICAL PERFECTION

(2) Christian perfection is a *relative* term. Those who use the term are frequently charged with lowering the meaning of the word in order to make it conform to the experience of those who profess the

blessing. That it is a lowering of the standard we deny, although we freely admit that it is an "accommodation," to use Dr. Pope's term, an accommodation that bears the impress of the condescension and lovingkindness of God. It is a perfection that, when viewed in relation to the absolute perfection of God, may never be reached, either in this life or that to come; but when viewed in relation to the present economy, marks a finality, in that it is the deliverance of the spiritual nature from the defilement of sin. It is true that this redeemed and perfected spirit dwells in a body that is a member of a sinful race, but man's spirit may be lifted from darkness to light while his body remains the same "muddy vesture of decay" that it was before his spirit was redeemed. Consequently it is still beclouded with weakness, in that the soul is under the influence of material things, and will be until the creature itself shall have put on incorruption and immortality.

(3) Christian perfection is *probationary.* It is a state that is always under ethical law, and hence must be guarded by constant watchfulness and maintained by divine grace. While we remain in this life, however deep our devotion or fervent our religious life, there are sources of danger within us. In our nature, and as essential elements of it, there are appetites, affections, and passions, without which we should be unfitted for this present state of existence. These are innocent in themselves but must ever be kept under control by reason, conscience, and divine grace.

The original temptation was a skillful appeal to human elements that were not depraved but were fresh from the hand of God. The desire for pleasant food is not sinful in itself, nor is the artistic taste, which delights in beautiful form and color. Neither can we condemn the desire for intellectual development or the acquisition of knowledge. These are original and essential elements of human nature, and had they not existed before the Fall, there could have been no temptation. The evil lay in the perversion of God-given faculties to wrong ends. To argue, therefore, that Christian perfection will destroy or eradicate essential elements of human nature; or that a man or woman may not enjoy perfection of spirit while these elements remain, is to misapprehend entirely the nature of this experience. What Christian perfection does is to give grace to regulate these tendencies, affections, and passions, and bring them into subjection to the higher laws of human nature.

(4) One thing further remains—this perfection is *mediated.* It is not a triumph of human effort, but a work wrought in the heart by the

Holy Spirit, in answer to simple faith in the blood of Jesus. We are kept by His abiding intercession. *I pray not that thou shouldest take them out of the world, but that thou shouldest keep them from the evil* (John 17:15).

The Fundamental Concept of Christian Perfection

The aspect of the Christian's full privilege in Christ is estimated according to the New Testament standard of love as fulfilling the law (Matt. 22:40; Gal. 5:14). This can be understood only in relation to the New Covenant. Viewed from the human standpoint, wherein Christ is regarded as the "surety of the covenant," it is said, *This is the covenant that I will make with the house of Israel after those days, saith the Lord; I will put my laws into their mind, and write them in their hearts: and I will be to them a God, and they shall be to me a people* (Heb. 8:10). Viewed from the divine standpoint, in which Christ is regarded as the "minister of the sanctuary," it is said, *This is the covenant that I will make with them after those days, saith the Lord, I will put my laws into their hearts, and in their minds will I write them; and their sins and iniquities will I remember no more. Now where remission of these is, there is no more offering for sin* (Heb. 10:16-18).

CHANGED ATTITUDES

Two things stand out clearly in these texts: (1) The Security of the Covenant. The two immutable things mentioned here, in which it is impossible for God to lie, signify the minister of the sanctuary on the one hand and the surety of the covenant on the other; and hence both the divine and human aspects center in the one theanthropic being. This gives security to the New Covenant. (2) The Nature of the Covenant. This is the full life of love, made perfect in the heart by the agency of the Holy Spirit. Pure love reigns supreme without the antagonisms of sin. Love is the spring of every activity. The believer having entered into the fullness of the New Covenant does by nature the things contained in the law, and hence, the law is said to be written upon his heart. *Herein is our love made perfect, that we may have boldness in the day of judgment: because as he is, so are we in this world. There is no fear in love; but perfect love casteth out fear: because fear hath torment. He that feareth is not made perfect in love* (1 John 4:17-18).

St. Paul uses an illustration that bears directly upon this subject. *Now I say, That the heir, as long as he is a child, differeth nothing from a servant, though he be lord of all; but is under tutors and governors until the time appointed of the father* (Gal 4:1-2). We must distinguish here, between two things, (1) the growth and development of the child, by which he is brought to a relative degree of maturity; and (2) a legal enactment, declaring him to have officially entered into his inheritance. To have made this declaration without a proper period of preparation would have been to dissipate the inheritance; to have omitted the declaration would have left the legal status indefinite and uncertain.

It is not the mere fact of growth that gives a youth the full rights of citizenship. A relative degree of maturity, which in the natural realm can come only through physical and mental growth, may underlie the judicial act, but he becomes of age, or ceases to be a minor and attains his majority, only at an appointed time in conformity to law. At that time he comes legally to manhood, with all the rights and privileges of full citizenship in the commonwealth. So also in the spiritual realm, there is a period of growth following regeneration, which precedes his coming to full age; and there will be even more rapid growth following it, but growth does not lead to Christian perfection. This is accomplished by a judicial pronouncement. It is a declarative act, wrought by the Spirit through faith. As in justification there is a judicial act in the mind of God accompanied by the work of the Spirit imparting life to the soul; so in Christian perfection there is likewise a declarative act accompanied by the purifying work of the Holy Spirit.[10]

THE TIME FACTOR

What, then, is the appointed time of the Father—the time when the son becomes of age, when he ceases to be a minor and attains his majority? It is the hour of submission to the baptism with the Holy Spirit (Matt. 3:11-12; Acts 1:5), which purifies the heart from sin (Acts 15:9) and fills it with divine love (Rom. 5:5). There is no need here for an extended lapse of time. It is sufficient only that the believer come to feel his need and see his privileges in Christ Jesus.

Through the exercise of his senses, we are told (Heb. 5:12-14), he comes to discern both good and evil, and thereby finds within himself the carnal mind warring against the new life in his soul. He finds, also, that God has promised a cleansing from all sin through the blood of Jesus. He lays hold of the promises of God, and in a moment, the Holy Spirit purifies his heart by faith. In that instant he lives the full life of love. In him love is made perfect, and the conditions of the New

---

10. Similar to the "declarative act" of Jesus on the leper: "I will; be thou clean. And immediately his leprosy was cleansed" (Matt. 8:3). *Editor.*

Covenant are, therefore, perfectly fulfilled in him. The law of God is written upon his heart. No longer is his spiritual status that of a child but of an adult; no longer a minor but of full age—a *teleiōn,* or one of the "perfect ones."

Here perfection "refers especially to the fullness of spiritual knowledge manifesting itself in the Christian profession as the antithesis of babyhood." The Greek adjective used here signifies adulthood. Hence the writer follows immediately with an exhortation: *Therefore leaving the principles of the doctrine of Christ, let us go on unto perfection* (Heb. 6:1). Here the word *teleiotēta* is the noun of the word used in Heb. 5:14, and is "represented not as something realized by the lapse of time, or by unconscious growth, and least of all, attainable only at death. . . . For the Greek preposition 'unto' here embraces both motion to a place and rest in it, and cannot mean an unattainable ideal" (Steele, *Half Hours with St. Paul,* 113). The verb *pherōmetha* meaning to press on is used with *epi,* unto, as the goal to be attained; and as Delitzsch indicates, "combines the notion of an impulse from without with that of an eager and onward pressing haste."

PERFECTION AS ADULTHOOD

We may conclude, then, that nothing is clearer from the Scriptures than that there is a perfection which may be attained in this life; that this perfection consists solely in a life of perfect love, or the loving God with all the heart, soul, mind, and strength; that this perfection of love has no reference to the degree or quantity of love, but to its purity or quality; that this state of perfect love is a consequence of the purification of the heart from all sin, so that love remains in soleness and supremacy; that this purification is accomplished instantaneously by the baptism with the Holy Spirit; that the resultant state of perfect love is regarded as adulthood in grace, in that the believer enters into the fullness of privilege under the New Covenant; and last, in that love is the fulfilling of the law, this state of pure or perfect love, is known as Christian perfection.

PERFECT LOVE

Important Distinctions

It is necessary in this connection to emphasize a few important distinctions in order to preserve the doctrine of Christian perfection from some of the popular errors that militate against it.

PURITY AND MATURITY

1. Purity and maturity must be carefully distinguished from each other. Failure to do this lies at the base of practically every objection to entire sanctification. Purity is the result of a cleansing from the pollution of sin; maturity is due to

growth in grace. Purity is accomplished by an instantaneous act; maturity is gradual and progressive and is always indefinite and relative. When, therefore, we speak of perfect love, we have reference solely to its quality as being unmixed with sin, never to its degree or quantity. As to the latter, the Scriptures teach that love and all the graces of the Spirit are to increase and abound more and more. We have previously indicated that Christian perfection is to be regarded as adulthood, in contrast with spiritual childhood; but this is true only in the sense of having been cleansed from all sin and thereby brought into the fullness of the new covenant of love. From the standpoint of growth in grace and spiritual understanding there are "babes" and "young men" in the state of entire sanctification, as well as those of more mature experience. A clear comprehension of the difference between purity and maturity will prevent confusion, both as to the doctrine and experience of Christian perfection.

SIN AND INFIRMITIES

2. Infirmities must be distinguished from sins. Sin in the sense used here is a voluntary transgression of a known law. Infirmities, on the other hand, are involuntary transgressions of the divine law, known or unknown, which are consequent on the ignorance and weakness of fallen men. These are inseparable from mortality. Perfect love does not bring perfection in knowledge and hence is compatible with mistakes in both judgment and practice. There seems to be no remedy for this until the body is redeemed from the consequences of sin, and glorified. Infirmities bring humiliation and regret, but not guilt and condemnation. These latter attach to sin only. Both, however, need the blood of sprinkling. The careful student of the Levitical rites of purification will have noticed that the errors and infirmities of the individual Hebrew were put away solely by the sprinkling of blood (Heb. 9:7); while sin always demanded a special offering. It is for this reason we maintain that there is not only a definite act of cleansing from sin, but that there is also a continuous blood of sprinkling for our involuntary transgressions. The Scriptures as well as the testimony of human experience, take into account this distinction between sins and infirmities. St. Jude says, *Now unto him that is able to keep you from falling* [or exempt from falling. The Vulgate reads, *sine peccato,* without sin] *and to present* [*stēsai,* to place in the presence of His glory] *you faultless* [*amōmous,* without blemish, faultless, unblamable] *before the presence of his glory with exceeding joy* (Jude 24). We may be kept from sin in this life, we shall be presented faultless only in our glorified state.

3. Temptation is reconcilable with the highest degree of evangelical perfection. Jesus was holy, harmless, undefiled, and separate from sinners but was tempted in all points as we are, yet without sin. Temptation seems to be necessarily involved in the idea of probation. No temptation or evil suggestion becomes sin, however, until it is tolerated or cherished by the mind. As long as the soul maintains its integrity, it remains unharmed, however protracted or severe the temptation may be.

TEMPTATION

Several questions arise in this connection. (1) When does temptation become sin? To this most difficult question Bishop Foster replies, "Sin begins whenever the temptation begins to find inward sympathy, if known to be a solicitation to sin. So long as it is promptly, and with full and hearty concurrence of the soul, repelled, there is no indication of inward sympathy, there is no sin" (Foster, *Christian Purity,* 55).

(2) What is the difference between the temptations of those who are entirely sanctified, and those who are not? The difference lies in this, that in the latter, temptation stirs up the natural corruption of the heart with its bias toward sin; while in the former, the temptation is met with uniform resistance.

(3) But how may I distinguish the temptations of the enemy, from the carnal mind or corruption of my own heart? Mr. Wesley admits that sometimes "it is impossible to distinguish, without the direct witness of the Spirit." In general, however, there need be no confusion. In this sanctified soul there is a fullness of love, humility, and all the graces of the Spirit, so that a temptation to pride, anger, or any of the works of the flesh is met with the instant recoil of the whole being. Holiness in man, as in Christ, is found in that fundamental ethical nature that loves righteousness and hates iniquity.

Temptation and trial may appear to be evils, but in reality they are God's method of establishing the believer in holiness and preparing him for the life to come. By them, God empties the appeals of the world of their urgency, and strengthens the motives of faithfulness in the kingdom of God. *Blessed is the man that endureth temptation: for when he is tried, he shall receive the crown of life, which the Lord hath promised to them that love him* (James 1:12; Heb. 12:11).

Christian Perfection a Present Experience

Christian perfection, as we have shown, is nothing more and nothing less than a heart emptied of all sin and filled with pure love to God and man. As such, it is a state, not only attainable in this life, but is the normal experience of all those who live in the fullness of the new covenant. It is the result of a divine operation of the Holy Spirit, promised in the Old Testament, and fulfilled in the New Testament by the gift of the Spirit as a Paraclete or Comforter. *And the Lord thy God will circumcise thine heart and the heart of thy seed, to love the Lord thy God with all thine heart, and with all thy soul, that thou mayest live* (Deut. 30:6). *I indeed baptize you with water,* declared the forerunner of Jesus, but *he shall baptize you with the Holy Ghost, and with fire: whose fan is in his hand, and he will throughly purge his floor, and gather his wheat into the garner; but he will burn up the chaff with unquenchable fire* (Matt. 3:11-12). That these passages of scripture refer to a spiritual cleansing is confirmed by St. Peter in these words, *And put no difference between us and them, purifying their hearts by faith* (Acts 15:9).

OBTAINED BY FAITH

As to the manner in which this work is wrought, the Scriptures are clear—it is always wrought by simple faith in the atoning blood of Jesus Christ; this blood of atonement being not only the ground of what Christ has purchased for us but the occasion of that which His Spirit works within us. Nor do the Scriptures teach that a higher degree of faith is demanded for sanctification than for justification. It is not so much the strength of the faith as its purity that is required in any operation of grace. Furthermore, there is no specific degree of conviction demanded as a prerequisite to this faith—all that is essential is a firm belief that this grace is needed and that God has promised it. In every case of evangelical perfection, three things are clearly discernible: (1) A consciousness of inbred sin and a hungering and thirsting for full conformity to the image of Christ. (2) A firm conviction in the light of the scriptural provisions that it is not only a privilege but also a duty to be cleansed from all sin. (3) There must be perfect submission of the soul to God, commonly known as consecration, followed by an act of simple faith in Christ—a sure trust in Him for the promised blessing.

"The voice of God to your soul is, Believe and be saved. Faith is the condition, and the only condition, of sanctification, exactly as it is in justification. No man is sanctified till he believes; and every man when he believes is sanctified" (Wesley, *Works,* 2:224). "But what is that faith whereby we are sanctified, saved from sin, and perfected in love? This faith is a divine evidence or conviction: (1) That God hath promised this sanctification in the Holy Scriptures. (2) It is a divine evidence or conviction that what God hath promised He is able to perform. (3) It is a divine evidence or conviction that He is able and willing to do it now. (4) To this confidence that God is able and willing to sanctify us now, there needs to be added one thing more—a divine evidence or conviction that He doeth it" (Wesley, *Sermons,* 1:390). The older theologians defined faith as the *assent* of the mind, the *consent* of the will, and *recumbency,* or reclining with undoubting confidence in the atoning merits of Jesus Christ. Thus as we have previously indicated, faith is incomplete without the element of trust.

Evidences of Christian Perfection

It is the uniform testimony of those who believe and teach the Wesleyan doctrine of Christian perfection, that the Spirit bears witness to this work of grace in the heart, exactly as He bears witness to Christian sonship. "None, therefore, ought to believe that the work is done," says Mr. Wesley, "till there is added the testimony of the Spirit witnessing his entire sanctification as clearly as his justification." "We know it by the witness and by the fruit of the Spirit" (Wesley, *Plain Account,* 79, 118).

WITNESS OF THE SPIRIT

Dr. J. Glenn Gould says that "this inner assurance is made up of three distinct phases. That is, they are logically distinct, though the sinner's experience of them may seem to be instantaneous. They are (1) the witness of the seeker's own heart; (2) the witness of God's Word; and (3) the inner illumination of the Holy Spirit" (Gould, *The Spirit's Ministry,* 8). The sanctified soul may know by the testimony of his own spirit, and the witness of the Holy Spirit, that the blood of Jesus Christ has cleansed him from all sin. Here we have the testimony of consciousness, which we can no more doubt than our own existence. And in addition to this, there is the direct and positive testimony of the witnessing Spirit.

To the scriptural evidences already cited, we may add aso, those personal examples that confirm the doctrine of evangelical perfection. *Noah was a just man and perfect in his generations* (Gen. 6:9). Job was *perfect and upright, and one that feared God, and eschewed evil* (Job 1:1). Zacharias and Elisabeth *were both righteous before God, walking in all the commandments and ordinances of the Lord blameless* (Luke 1:6). Our Lord said of Nathanael, *Behold an Israelite indeed, in whom is no guile!* (John 1:47). St. Paul also speaks of those in the apostolic church who were evangelically perfect. *Howbeit we speak wisdom among them that are perfect* (1 Cor. 2:6); and *Let us therefore, as many as be perfect, be thus minded* (Phil. 3:15).

Were we to attempt to present here, the testimonies of those men and women who have enjoyed the experience of perfect love, our task would be too great. Inspiring as they are, we cannot include them. "A study of the biographies of Christian leaders," says Dr. D. Shelby Corlett, "reveals the facts that with few exceptions they all had a second crisis experience. While it is true all would not interpret this experience in terms of Wesley's 'second blessing properly so-called'; it is also true that this second experience made a distinct change in their lives and ministry. Universally unbiased Christians long for and seek a deeper experience than that which they obtain in regeneration. Thousands have enjoyed a 'second blessing' without being instructed in the truth as taught by believers in the Wesleyan emphasis on the doctrine of entire sanctification" (Dr. D. Shelby Corlett, *Herald of Holiness,* Vol. 27, No. 11).

We close this chapter on "Christian Perfection" or "Entire Sanctification" with what we regard as the clearest statement of the doctrine and experience ever written, aside from divine inspiration. This is the definition given by Arvid Gradin to John Wesley in 1738. On his return from America, Mr. Wesley says, "I had a long conversation with Arvid Gradin, in Germany. After he had given me an account of his experience, I desired him to give me, in writing, a definition of 'the full assurance of faith.'" The definition was given in Latin, and both the Latin statement and the English translation are included in Mr. Wesley's *Plain Account of Christian Perfection.* . . .

"Repose in the blood of Christ; a firm confidence in God, and persuasion of His favor; the highest tranquility, serenity, and peace of mind, with a deliverance from every fleshly desire, and a cessation of all, even inward sins."

"This," says Mr. Wesley, "is the first account I ever heard from any living man, of what I had before learned myself from the oracles of God, and had been praying for (with the little company of my friends), and expecting, for several years" (Wesley, *Plain Account of Christian Perfection,* 8).

18

J. Paul Taylor

(1885-1973)

Jesse Paul Taylor was born in Mount Vernon, Ill., April 1, 1885. Though reared in the Free Methodist denomination, and converted early, he did not enter the ministry until about 30 years of age. He was ordained by the Central Illinois Free Methodist Conference in 1919.

After successful pastorates from 1914 to 1940, including one year in the evangelistic field, he was elected superintendent of the Genesee and Buffalo districts. From there he moved to the Olean and Chatauqua districts for two years, before returning to his first superintendency. From this position he was elected as bishop of the Free Methodist church in June 1947. After serving his church 17 years in this office he retired as bishop emeritus in 1964. He died July 2, 1973.

Bishop Taylor was known as an eloquent preacher, an able administrator, and above all as a powerful defender and exponent of Wesleyan doctrine. He wrote *A Goodly Heritage,* a historical survey of the theological characteristics and backgrounds of the Free Methodist church; and also a larger volume, *Holiness, the Finished Foundation.* This is an exposition and defense of his denomination's creedal statement on entire sanctification.

According to Bishop Donald Bastian, Taylor was one of the most "widely read men of his times." His literary style is vivid and flowing, and he draws on varied fields of learning with intimate familiarity.

Entire Sanctification a Cleansing[1]

In Wiley we have seen the sober, restrained, no-nonsense prose that most readers expect in theological writing. It is difficult for some to believe that any other style can at the same time be good theology. But in Taylor we have sound thinking coupled with exciting literary flourish, marked by vivid metaphors and brilliant epigrams.

The structure of Bishop Taylor's book *Holiness, the Finished Foundation* is very simple. He takes the creedal statement on entire sanctification in the Free Methodist discipline and devotes a chapter to the exposition and defense of each phrase. The selection that follows is based on the line from the *Discipline* "is cleansed in that moment from all inward sin."

It is fitting that once again we be reminded that cleansing is the central note of New Testament sanctification, as the only means whereby sanctification as consecration can be authentic. Even in the Old Testament we should have learned that unclean or blemished offerings are not acceptable to God. Furthermore, normal growth in believers is impossible in the presence of the carnal mind. Just as it is folly to expect a free flow of water through a pipe partially blocked by an obstruction, so it is equally foolish to presume to promote spiritual progress without urging upon believers the necessity of facing up to their need of a radical cleansing.

It is an old saying that "cleanliness is next to godliness." In the spiritual world cleanliness is godliness. To be pure "even as Christ is pure," through the cleansing blood, is to be under the canopy of the highest beatitude, "Blessed are the pure in heart, for they shall see God." Sin is the great defiler, and we need a great cleansing. Entire sanctification is the cleansing that goes as deep as the stain has gone.

NOT COVERED BUT CLEANSED

Therefore, sin is not merely covered by the imputed righteousness of Christ. John recognized a host of people who had "washed *their* robes and made them white in the blood of the Lamb," but there is no suggestion that Christ exchanged *His* white *robe* for their filthy garments, much

1. From *Holiness, the Finished Foundation* (Winona Lake, Ind.: Light and Life Press, 1963), Chap. 4, 65-81.

less that He put His spotless robe on them to cover their spotted garments. Character is nontransferable. The whole doctrine of imputed righteousness and imputed holiness assigns to the infinitely holy One the role of a juggler of accounts, and a creator of fictions by which He imposes on himself. He who pronounces a curse upon the man who covers his sin is represented as covering it for the man, instead of cleansing it away.

The holiness of Christ is as of little benefit to a man as the holiness of a fellow Christian, so far as heart conditions are concerned. It is not by confounding the believer with Christ that God secures his salvation, but by cleansing him into a personal correspondence with Christ, changing him "into the same image." A borrowed mask is not an image or likeness of another. The garment of holiness is not some abstract, impersonal thing taken from a celestial wardrobe, furnished by the merits of Christ, and put on us by imputation. It is Christ in us, showing out through us. Moral qualities cannot be wrapped in a package and delivered to us. Moral qualities are inherent in persons.

It is a terrible reflection upon the perfections of God to hold that He will cover man's evil nature with the righteousness of Christ and make him eternally secure, regardless of his character or conduct, because he has become a favorite of God by an easy act of believing. The believer, or rather, believing sinner, on this theory, has an immunity that the ordinary sinner does not have, and God is made a respecter of persons. If the theory were true, then when Paul exulted over the fact that he and other believers were "more than conquerors through him that loved [them]," and enumerated a list of adverse things and conditions that could not separate them from the love of God, he should have added "or sin."

Fletcher, in his usually incisive and vivid manner, answered the imputationists of all time in these words: "If they insinuate by their language, that we need not, cannot be perfect, by an inherent conformity to God's holiness, because Christ is thus perfect for us, we are bound to oppose it. Or should they mean, that we are perfect in Him, just . . . as the sick in a hospital are perfectly healthy in the physician that gives them his attendance; as the blind man enjoyed perfect sight in Christ when he saw walking men like moving trees; as the filthy leper was perfectly clean in our Lord, before he had felt the power of Christ's gracious words, 'I will, be thou clean'; or, as hungry Lazarus was perfectly fed in the

FLETCHER ON IMPUTATION

person of the rich man, at whose gate he lay starving—should this, I say, be your meaning, we are bound, in conscience, to oppose it."

Again he quotes the words of Jesus, "Be ye therefore perfect, even as your Father in heaven is perfect," and comments, "Who can read these words and not see that the perfection which Christ preaches, is a perfection of holy dispositions, productive of holy actions in all His followers? And that, of consequence, it is a personal perfection, as much inherent in us, and yet as much derived from Him, and dependent upon Him, as is the perfection of our bodily health? The chief difference consisting in this; that the perfection of our health comes to us from God in Christ, as the God of nature; whereas our Christian perfection comes to us from God in Christ, as the God of grace."

Those who lie down in the fancied robe of Christ's righteousness and sleep in a carnal security that they call "eternal security" are due for a rude awakening when they face the holy God who hates all fictions, and their imaginary robes disappear as a dream. Holy men do not parade in rented or borrowed robes, for they are not acting a part in a theatrical play. Holiness is their uniform, worn day and night, for it is a part of themselves. It is not a theft of Christ's righteousness but a gift of personal holiness. Christ *within* them, and not merely *for* them, clothes them with a garment of pure light.

CURBING CARNALITY INADEQUATE

If sin is not merely covered by imputed righteousness, neither is it merely curbed and controlled by the power of the Spirit, and one may live "the victorious life," so-called. If indwelling sin is curbed but not cured, controlled but not cleansed away by the coming of the Holy Spirit in His fullness, then logically we are driven to believe one of three things: either God has no purpose to cleanse us, thus belying His own promises; or He controls sin so that it might be harnessed for good ends; or He does not have the power to cast out the strong man He has bound, robbed of his armor, and stripped of his goods. He can wound, stun, or cripple depravity, but cannot destroy it. The conclusion must be that there was an inability on the part of the great Physician properly to diagnose the disease of sin, or a miscalculation as to the virtue of the remedy provided. It strikes a blow at all the divine perfections.

Some talk about inbred sin being counteracted by the lovely graces of the Spirit and the stench of inner pollution being neutralized by the fragrance of the new life. It is true that in the regenerate man, the sin nature is controlled and counteracted by grace, but the man is painfully conscious at times that remaining sin counteracts the work of the indwelling Spirit, so he is crippled, hampered, and muzzled, more or less, and his spiritual life is not satisfactory. Regenerating grace may smother sin, but it cannot smother sin to death. The cleansing of the heart alone will remove the hindering element.

One of the labors of Hercules, in fable, was to cleanse the Augean stables that were full of the accumulated filth of years. He did not bring tons of snow from the mountaintop to *cover* the filth. He did not *control* the filth by laying a polished floor over it. He did not *counteract* its foul stench by filling the stables with fragrant flowers. He turned the current of two rivers through the unclean habitations, and the uncleanness was swept away in the flood. Behold a greater than Hercules is here. The Holy Spirit comes as a pure river of water of life from the throne of God and of the Lamb, "a lamb as it had been slain," and that stream, crimson with the blood of Christ, washes and makes whiter than snow. At the sight of this, the soul, sensible of its pollution, cries,

Let the water and the blood,
From Thy wounded side which flowed,
Be of sin the double cure,
Save from wrath and make me pure.

In this world Christ is preparing a bride to dwell with Him in a holy heaven forever. He does not prepare her by providing a white facial cream of imputed righteousness to cover her moral spots and blemishes and wrinkles. He does not provide the cosmetics of lovely graces to counteract them. But "Christ . . . loved the church, and gave himself for [her], that he might sanctify and cleanse [her] with the washing of water by the word, that he might present [her] to himself a glorious church, not having spot, or wrinkle, or any such thing; but that [she] should be holy and without blemish" (Eph. 5:25-27). He purges out the disease, giving perfect moral health, and with the going of the disease and the coming of health, the spots and wrinkles and blemishes disappear.

CLEANSED FROM ALL SIN

"Cleansed from *all* sin." Note the italicized word *all.* All sin must be removed because it cannot be utilized and worked into the plan of God. It is enmity against God, a contradiction to all goodness and a threat to all peace. It is an utterly discordant element in the universe. One modern secular writer holds that sin "is at most the failure, the blundering of the pupil in the first stages of a new discipline; his ugly hut, his first miserable crop in that new territory, which in all its vastness of resources is destined to become his own." If this were true, we could dismiss the whole moral case with a sigh of regret that God did not give man a better start. But sin is not a hut that may become a temple by the discipline of experience. It is the defilement of a human temple and the prostituting of it to the sacrilegious uses of a den of thieves until its primal glory is lost.

It is not the "first miserable crop" of stunted wheat, but the tares sown in the field of human character by an enemy to God and man. The defilement is not a part of the original temple. The tares are not a species of wheat. The defilement must be removed and the tares uprooted. "What concord hath Christ with Belial? or . . . what agreement hath the temple of God with idols?" None. Belial must be dethroned. The idols must be pulverized as the golden calf was, in Moses' time, and washed away by the stream that flows from Calvary. In no kind or degree is sin usable. It puts on the mask of virtue and masquerades as a blessing, but it is the offspring of him who came "to steal, and kill and destroy." The pleaders for sin would make it an ugly, yet necessary, servant in the household of the heart, instead of a robber of spiritual wealth.

Sin is not needed to exercise our patience and watchfulness. It is an opiate that dulls the senses. It is a spy within the city of Mansoul that would betray the city into the hands of the adversary. It is said that we need some sin in the heart to keep us humble. The very taproot of sin is pride, and can the root of pride produce the fruit of humility? Sin may humiliate, but it cannot make one humble. Pride is all the more enraged when one is humiliated. It has been often said that we need indwelling sin as a spur to drive us on.

Fletcher answered this teaching long ago.

"Is not indwelling sin a clog rather than a spur to the heavenly racers? If sin is of such service to us to make us run the career of holy longing after heavenly rest, why does the apostle exhort us to 'set aside every weight, and the sin which does so easily beset us'? If we want a spur to mend our pace; need we keep the spur, indwelling sin? Is it not more likely to spur us to hell? If we have thousands of sinless spurs, what need have we of keeping that to drive us to heaven, which drove Adam behind the trees of the garden; not to say, out of his native paradise?" Have not all regenerate men realized that indwelling sin was often a curb-bit holding them back from service through the doubt and fear it inspired? In some cases it has been a knife to cut the tendons of activity while the Christian slept. Paul wrote to the Galatians, "Ye *did* run well; who did hinder you?" (5:7). Is not the answer in the same chapter, verse 17, "For the flesh [the sin principle in you] lusteth against the Spirit, and the Spirit against the flesh . . . so that ye cannot do the things that ye would"? It hinders; it does not help.

Men have harbored inbred sin with the sanction of wrested Scriptures. In the case of Holiness versus Sin that has been tried ever since the Fall, John the beloved disciple took the stand in his old age and witnessed as clearly as any inspired man could, in defense of holiness. In every generation a battery of self-appointed, uninspired, prosecuting attorneys, frequently wearing clerical garb, have appeared in court to plead against holiness and for sin, as if holiness were public enemy number one, and sin the world's great benefactor. Our day has its full quota of such self-appointed attorneys. They prosecute the case and make their plea to the jury in such a manner that one would think their brief had been prepared by the first sinner, Satan, "the accuser of the brethren."

WRESTED SCRIPTURE

They call the beloved disciple to the stand, and twist his words to make it appear he is the chief witness for sin. They undertake to persuade the jury he is speaking of the same people when he says, "If we confess our sins, he is faithful and just to forgive us our sins, and to cleanse us from all unrighteousness. . . . If we walk in the light, as he is in the light, we have fellowship one with another, and the blood of Jesus Christ [God's] Son cleanseth us from all sin," and, when he says, "If we say that we have not sinned, we make him a liar," and "If we say that we have no sin, we deceive ourselves."

1 JOHN 1:7-10

It is perfectly clear that he is speaking about two different classes of people. Those who confess they have sinned are forgiven, and when they go on to confess they "have sin" as an indwelling principle, they are cleansed from all sin. Those, on the other hand, who deny they have any sins to be forgiven and no sin to be cleansed away, make God a liar and deceive themselves.

Undoubtedly the latter class were the Gnostics of John's day who denied they had any sin to be dealt with. The modern antinomians confess they have sin but deny that any deliverance from it is possible, and in self-defense they pervert the words of John to mean that God has no purpose to cleanse men from all sin. So they become pleaders for sin and claim the holy apostle as their witness and advocate. John does not charge those with being liars who profess to be cleansed from all sin, but those who say they have no sin to be cleansed from.

Their position would make John the arch liar, for he says, "our love is made perfect—and as Christ is so are we in this world," being made "pure even as he is pure." The man who said "no lie is of the truth" is made a perjurer before earth and heaven. The Christ of holiness has thus been crucified afresh in the house of His professed friends, the Barabbas of unholiness has been released, and the multitude of spectators have gone out of the courtroom to put darkness for light and light for darkness, because the verdict is in harmony with their own sinful tendencies. But the verdict will be reversed by the Supreme Court of heaven before "the great white throne."

CHRIST CLEANSES CARNALITY

Thousands can witness to complete deliverance from sin. Pirates, in the form of sinful inclinations, were aboard the craft of their personality when it was launched upon the seas of life. The carnal nature was at the helm, wearing the mask of an angel of light, persuading them that their course would take them to the sea of glass before God's throne. But under conviction they got their bearings and sensed that they were sailing toward the lake of fire. They cried for help and Christ came aboard, and put the pirates with their father, the helmsman, in chains, under hatches. But while the usurpers could no longer control, they could disturb. One day in weariness of soul over the disturbing elements, saved men pled for deliverance, and their cry was heard. Christ, the Captain of the vessel, executed the criminal pirates, and now gives orders without dissenting voices within trying to shout Him down. The Holy Spirit is the infallible helmsman, and He steers them through the crystal sea of peace toward their heavenly home, the only place that would welcome them, for it is the only place with which they are in full harmony.

Bunyan, in *The Holy War,* represents a "stiff old man" by the name of Mr. Loath-to-stoop, as pleading with Emmanuel to allow his master, Diabolus, a little place in the city, as a term of his surrender. Emmanuel replied that he should have "not a hoof nor a hair . . . no, not the least corner . . . all, and all manner of Diabolonians that now are or that at any time shall be found in Mansoul, shall not only lose their lands and liberties, but also their lives. . . . I shall not admit of, or consent, that there should be the least scrap, shred, or dust of Diabolus left behind." So Mr. Loath-to-stoop reported to Diabolus "how Emmanuel would not admit, no, not by any means, that he, when he was once gone out, should forever have anything more to do either in or with any that are of the town of Mansoul."

Wesley asks, "Had not the good old man forgot himself? Did not the force of truth so prevail over him as utterly to overturn his own system?—to assert perfection in the clearest manner? For if this is not salvation from sin, I cannot tell what it is." Bunyan's purging of Mansoul is the negative side of the experience set forth in its positive aspect in his lovely Beulah land picture. Holiness is being emptied of all *sin* and filled with love.

SIN IN THE HEART

"Cleansed from all *inward* sin." Note again, the emphasized word. Sin is rooted in the heart. It is an internal defilement and disorder. It is not resident in the body. To those who held that "surely we cannot be saved from sin, while we dwell in a sinful body," Wesley answered by saying, "A *sinful body?* I pray observe, how deeply ambiguous, how equivocal this expression is. But there is no authority for it in Scripture: the word, *sinful body,* is never found there. And as it is totally unscriptural, so it is palpably absurd. For no *body* or matter of any kind, can be *sinful:* spirits alone are capable of sin." The members of the body may be "instruments of unrighteousness unto," or in behalf of "sin," as Paul indicated, but the sin is not in the members. The greatest and oldest sinners in the universe never had bodies, rather, they are *unclean spirits.* The inner man is the *sinful* man, the outer man is the *sinning* man controlled by the *sinful* man within.

Internal righteousness is our great need. Much of the world's religion is an external thing, whitewash on a sepulchre that is full of dead men's bones and all uncleanness. Thousands regard religion as a terrible necessity. They are prisoners, painfully keeping up the lockstep of outward obedience to church orders. Their duties are doled out. Some of them follow a rigorous regimen of imposed righteousness. They are ethical ritualists, going through the motions of outward obedience when their hearts are elsewhere.

LEGALISM

It is to be feared that the holiness ranks have sometimes been invaded by both rude and refined legalism in the name of superior spirituality. Men professing the highest state of grace often become legalistic detectives engaged in a microscopic search for harmless bacteria, and when they find them, they are magnified many times by the legalistic microscope until they look like devouring monsters. It is Aesop in reverse; the mouse labors and brings forth a mountain. The discoverer of the mouse-mountain is wrought into great excitement, for he is convinced he is ordained to rectify the matter even if he wrecks the church in the process. It is a righteousness that does not exceed the righteousness of Pharisees, for both are external. The Pharisees could strain out gnats and swallow camels coming from Egypt, carrying the heavy freight of malice and unkindness. When they could not find divine laws to put themselves on a strain, in their effort to excel others religiously, they invented prohibitions and demands.

While some have tried to broaden the narrow gate of the Kingdom in order that anyone might take the world with him through it, others have placed barbed wire entanglements before the gate and made demands that God never made upon those who would enter. Fletcher warned, "Beward of stiff singularity in things barely indifferent—it is self in disguise; and it is so much the more dangerous, as it comes recommended by a serious, self-denying, religious appearance." The hypocrite is no more difficult to deal with than is the sincere fanatic. The fanatic's vision is out of focus, and he gets everything out of place and out of proportion. He can take a very incidental thing involving no moral principle, and out of it whittle a rod that he fancies is the axis on which the whole world of religion revolves, and if you disagree with him, he will use the rod to give you a beating.

FANATICISM

The Bible speaks of "the beauty of holiness." When holiness reigns in the heart and goes forth in queenly beauty in the life, men are attracted. But when anyone undertakes to produce a homemade holiness out of a few dry sticks and dyed rags of legalism, it becomes a scarecrow that drives people from the vicinity of the ugly thing, falsely labeled "holiness." No amount of conformity to the law of outward holiness will work toward the center and purify the heart.

We have heard much about radical preaching from those who have no clear conception of what radical means. The word comes from a Latin word meaning "having roots." Preaching is radical only when it lays the ax to the root of the tree and deals with heart sin. Clubbing off fruit or cutting off limbs is very surface work. And it is surface work of the worst kind when energy is spent brushing off things that have accidentally caught on the tree, and are no part of the tree. No doubt this kind of external work is preferred by some because it is so much easier to take *off* a coat than it is to take *out* an appendix.

TRUE RADICALISM

There are external things and conditions that have a most important connection with internal religion, but even here, we must begin at the heart and work outward. Peter saw this connection clearly when he said to the wives, "Whose adorning let it not be that outward adorning of plaiting the hair, and of wearing of gold, or of putting on of apparel; but let it be the hidden man of the heart, in that which is not corruptible, even the ornament of a meek and quiet spirit, which is in the sight of God of great price." The "let it not be" is as obligatory as the "let it be," but you may strip one of outward ornaments and leave him without the inward adorning. Give the hidden man of the heart the "ornament of a meek and quiet spirit," and interest in outward adorning will end. Take away the outward adorning without giving the "ornament of a meek and quiet spirit" to a man, and at best he will be an empty soul robbed of the riches of both worlds, and at worst he will be what Fletcher called "a perfect Christian Pharisee."

Pride in its most religious guise occupies the stage, for one can show off what he has taken off or put on, but the "*hidden* man of the heart" cannot stage a play to be seen of men. For many years ships that plowed the Pacific were taken into dry dock where, by a long, laborious process the hundreds of pounds of barnacles attaching themselves to the bottom of the ship during her voyage were cut loose. It was finally discovered that when the ships sailed into the fresh waters of Lake Washington the barnacles loosed their grip, and it was easy to rid the vessels of them. To turn the church into a dry dock and use hammers and chisels of legalism to separate men from things of the world that have attached to them and to which they are attached, is fruitless labor. Steer them into the fresh waters of saving and sanctifying grace, and the things that are evil will drop off naturally.

"Cleansed from all inward *sin*." Again, note the emphasized word *sin.* Entire sanctification cleanses from all inward *sin,* and nothing but sin.

HUMANITY

When sin is cleansed away, the man remains with all the characteristics of a human being. He still has his human infirmities and limitations, and this is not at all inconsistent with purity of heart. God made man and He destroys nothing He has made, but He does destroy the thing that would destroy man. One may have a body that is imperfect in many respects, yet enjoy perfect health. A man may be lame or he may have lost an arm, and still have perfect health. He might be disfigured by an accident or have a deformity, without his health being affected. He may be short of stature, or have weak mental powers, but possess perfect health. He may be so limited in natural abilities that he cannot do a thousand things others can do, and still enjoy as perfect health as does anyone. He could have an ill-proportioned body but a healthy one.

So one may be burdened with a variety of infirmities and shortcomings, and at the same time have perfect spiritual health. If some good men had not put infirmities in the category of sin, they would not have opposed the doctrine of Christian perfection so earnestly. These good men have often said that Paul's "thorn in the flesh" was remaining sin. Paul called it "mine infirmities," and he did not confound it with sin. It could not have been inbred sin for it was "given unto" him long after he was born, immediately following his third heaven experience. Paul prayed three times for its removal, and the answer was, "My grace is sufficient for thee." If the thorn had been inbred sin, the prayer would have been answered in its removal. Upon the denial of his request, he said, "I will glory in my infirmities." Would he have gloried in the presence of sin? "The Spirit helpeth our infirmities," but He does not help indwelling sin. The body of sin is to be destroyed.

INFIRMITIES

Fletcher has pointed out that Paul, in writing to Timothy, said, "Them that sin rebuke before all, that others also may fear" (1 Tim. 5:20), but he writes to the Romans, "We then that are strong ought to bear the infirmities of the weak" (Rom. 15:1). We are to stop the sinner in his course, as far as that can be done, by rebuke, but we are to strengthen the infirmities of the weak, to inspire him in his course. The willful sin of the wicked and the mistakes of the Christian cannot be put in the same class. When the walks and streets are covered with ice, sober people go through unsteady movements that greatly resemble the actions of intoxicated persons. The strange movements of the sober man are caused by external conditions to which it is difficult for him to adjust, whereas the staggering of the intoxicated man is caused by internal conditions created by alcohol. That is the difference between mistakes and sins.

"We have this treasure" of perfect love in an "earthen vessel," and the vessel may be marred and misshapen. A faulty head may cause us to carry out the purposes of a pure heart in a very blundering manner. Perfection of love does not imply perfection of understanding. Wesley made it clear that errors in judgment are not only consistent with perfect love; but may even be occasioned by perfect love, for love would lead one to consider some persons better than they are. Purity of heart is not demonstrated by errorless judgment but in the humble confession of error. Paul was infallibly inspired in the hours of special revelation by the Spirit. Outside such hours he could make mistakes. He called the high priest a

EARTHEN VESSELS

"whited wall" in holy indignation against his unwarranted attack. When he was told it was the high priest, he humbly apologized because of the Bible injunction against speaking evil of the rulers of the people. He admitted his ignorance and exhibited his holiness.

Dr. Daniel Steele, in his *Milestone Papers,* the second part of which might well be called a "Sanctified Pilgrim's Progress," after describing the blessedness of citizenship in the goodly land of Perfect Love, said, "There are old residents of this country who are by no means favorites of mine, and I cut their acquaintence as much as possible, such as Ignorance, Forgetfulness, Misjudgment, Error, Inadvertence, Failure, and a large family by the name of Infirmity. In fact I have repeatedly cast my vote for their exclusion, but they insist that they have a right to remain, since no statute lies against them.

"They say that they are grossly wronged when confounded with an odious foreigner called Sin, who slightly resembles them, but is wholly different in moral character. I must confess that a close observation, extended through several years, demonstrates the justice of their plea. Hence I live in peace with these old citizens, but do not delight in their society" (208).

Infirmities are the weak offspring of the weak father, Humanity. Sins are the wicked offspring of a wicked father, Depravity. We regret the infirmities and repent of the sins. Depravity and his offspring "the old man with his deeds" may be "put off" now. Infirmities will be put off when "this mortal shall have put on immortality," and our humanity is glorified.

We may be ashamed of the unattractive and blundering citizens of the goodly land of Perfect Love that are our most intimate relatives, but they help to keep us humble, whereas sins, that claim kinship with us from long association, stimulate pride in the heart, for they have a genealogy reaching back to Lucifer, the first proud pretender to Godhood.

Then there are the constitutional passions and desires. These . . . are not extinguished by any degree of grace. They are a fire created in our being for benevolent purposes. This fire could not be extinguished without killing the man. The fire was put there to warm the house of life, but when it leaps out of the fireplace it destroys the house. A patient in a hospital is running a high temperature and becomes delirious. In this state he grows violent and strikes the nurse, the doctor, or a friend. What is to be done? Hurry him to the operating room and amputate the hand that struck the blows? No. Hold him in subjection until the temperature is reduced to normal and the delirium dissipated, and the medicine can be administered to cure the disease back of the fever and violence. Then the normal heat and energy of health may be directed to constructive ends. Holiness brings health, which means normalcy, and the normal temperature of natural desires contributes to life instead of consuming it.

Then there are passions that are purely spiritual. They could not be destroyed without annihilating the spiritual nature of man. Wesley held, concerning those whom he called "the truly meek," in his second discourse "Upon Our Lord's Sermon on the Mount," "They do not desire to extinguish any of the passions which God has for wise ends implanted in their nature; but they have the mastery of all: they hold them all in subjection, and employ them only in subservience to those ends. And thus even the harsher and more unpleasing passions are applicable to the noblest purposes; even hatred, and anger, and fear, when engaged against sin, and regulated by faith and love, are as walls and bulwarks to the soul, so that wicked one cannot approach to hurt it."

SPIRITUAL PASSIONS

With this, all responsible Wesleyan teachers agree. Dr. Nathan Bangs was one of the most powerful exponents of the doctrine of entire sanctification. He echoes Wesley in these words, concerning the sanctified man. "He has a strict and suitable government over all the passions and appetites of his soul and body; so much so that none of these are permitted to usurp dominion over him. His sanctified heart and enlightened understanding having mounted the throne; under their dictation he exercises a controlling influence over all his passions and appetites, keeping them in subjection to the dominion of grace—the grace of sanctification.

"Instead of being a slave to them, he makes them his servants, and while they obey his commands, they administer to his pleasure and advance his temporal and spiritual interests. His passions of love, hate, desire, aversion, all his affinities and antipathies, of whatever sort or degree, his fears and hopes, are all sanctified, fixed on their right objects and directed to their right ends. . . . All the passions of his nature are sanctified and made subservient to the highest, most holy, and most enduring interests—not excepting his ambition, which is now directed to the loftiest aims, impelling him forward in the conscientious use of all the means within his grasp for the attainment of God's glory, in his own and the salvation of his fellow-men."

Supreme love does not kill any of the driving forces of life, but bridles them, so they move with controlled energy in the right direction. Gilbert K. Chesterton is a strange witness, speaking better than he knew, perhaps, concerning a great saint in a strange setting. He says of St. Francis of Assisi, who was a man of passionate nature, "He had wheeled his charger clean around, but there was no halt or check in the thundering impetuosity of his charge. There was nothing negative about it; it was not a regimen or a stoical simplicity of life. It was not self-denial merely in the sense of self-control. It was as positive as a passion; it had all the air of being as positive as a pleasure."

Jesus sent His disciples to loose a colt that He might ride it to Jerusalem. The only explanation to be given was, "The Lord hath need of him." The colt was one on which never man sat, yet the mastery of Jesus was so complete that the unbroken animal was perfectly tame and tractable, even in the midst of a shouting throng, waving palm branches. "The Lord hath need of" all our constitutional powers. Under the misrule of sin they are wild and fractious, but Christ can tame them and harness them to His highest purposes. "The carnal mind is enmity against God: for it is not subject to the law of God, neither indeed can be" (Rom. 8:7). It is intractable and cannot be harnessed and driven in the right direction. It is the work of the devil, which Christ came to destroy. But the human element is His own work, and He recovers and cleanses it for His own uses.

Heavenly fire quenches only the hellfire in the breast, and controls the human fire. Referring to this heavenly fire of "the love of God shed abroad in our hearts," Adam Clarke wrote, "Every *flame* that rises from this pure and vigorous fire must be pleasing in God's sight: it *consumes* what is *unholy, refines* every *passion* and *appetite: sublimes* the whole, and *assimilates* all to itself." So entire sanctification does not mutilate or amputate any of our essential human qualities. It does not dehumanize us but does purify us for effective action in a new realm.

Herein lies the possibility of temptation to a holy man. Adam was created holy, but he was tempted and sinned. Jesus, the second Adam, was holy and was tempted in all points like as we are, yet without sin. The garden temptation and the wilderness temptation are examples of Satan's approach to the pure in heart. The only approach possible is through that which is good and desirable. He tempts to a misuse of good things, an excessive attention to them, a misplacing or misdirecting them.

TEMPTATION

Paul experienced what Archbishop Trench had in mind when he

said, "By a mighty wonderstroke of grace the polarity in the man is shifted; the flesh, that was the positive pole, has become the negative, and the spirit, which was before the negative, is henceforth the positive." But Paul knew he could be tempted to reshift the polarity, so he said he kept his body under lest after having preached to others he should become a castaway. The natural powers must be kept in their place. If Satan can make a breach in the outworks, he can take the citadel, so there he makes his attack, since he has no point of contact in the purified heart. Paul was a holy man, but it was necessary that he have a thorn in the flesh, not to save him from pride, but to guard him against being exalted through the abundance of the revelations. Spiritual pride may come in through the skylight when Satan appears as an angel of light. Because we trust God, the devil may suggest that we give an unwarranted and spectacular demonstration of it by presuming on the divine intervention in a plunge from the pinnacle of the temple.

PERSONAL PECULIARITIES

God has made man with as many types of individuality as there are individuals, and when He sanctifies men He does not pour them into the same mold or run them through an assembly line, reconstructing all by the same pattern. Our individual characteristics and peculiarities remain, purified for normal self-expression. Washing one's face does not change its distinctive features, but rather makes them more distinct. Many individual peculiarities are expressions of human infirmities.

Wesley, in his sermon "On Temptation," raises the question, "Can we expect to find any temptation in those who are perfected in love?" He answers, "Even those . . . who are now really perfect in love, may still be an occasion of temptation to you, for they are still encompassed with infirmity. They may be dull of apprehension; they may have a natural heedlessness; they may have too lively an imagination, or a treacherous memory: And any of these may cause little improprieties, either in speech or behavior, which, though not sinful in themselves, may try all the grace you have. . . . So, proper was the answer which a saint of God (now in Abraham's bosom) gave me some years ago. I said, 'Jenny, surely now your mistress and you can neither of you be a trial to the other, as God has saved you both from sin!' 'O, sir,' said she, 'if we were saved from sin, we still have infirmities enough to try all the grace that God has given us'" (Sermon 82).

These infirmities associated with personal peculiarities may furnish the great adversary with an occasion to create division. "O cunning enemy that to catch a saint, with saints dost bait the hook," exclaimed one of Shakespeare's characters. "Forbearing one another in love" is the rule of the sanctified.

A Final Summary[2]

What J. Paul Taylor calls a preview and uses as a foreword, is here used, in part, as an epilogue. The warnings and exhortations found here constitute a fitting and in a sense a climactic close for this anthology.

A Preview of the Finished Foundation

DOCTRINE AND EXPERIENCE

Every serious Christian is concerned about foundations. "If the foundations be destroyed, what can the righteous do?" asked an ancient Psalmist, and since some of the greatest dangers that threaten the Church, originate in the Church, the question might be varied by asking, "If the foundations be not properly laid, what can the Church do?" If the foundations are of sand, the superstructure will match its weakness with wood, hay, and stubble. If the foundations of the Church, the earthly Zion, are like the foundations of the holy city, made of precious stones, the only fitting superstructure will be of "gold, silver, and precious stones." Unless we have a solid doctrinal foundation, we cannot have a solid experimental foundation, for doctrine is the blueprint, the pattern for experience.

THE WESLEYAN FOUNDATION

It is often assumed that justification is the foundation, while holiness of heart is the superstructure at which one works as long as he lives. On the contrary, entire holiness is a part of the foundation. It is the top layer of stones finishing the foundation. It was said of John Dempster, as a preacher, that "he laid his foundation in the heavens and built upward." Jude urges his "beloved" brethren, "build up yourselves on your most holy faith." Wesley comments on these words, "Than which none can be more holy in itself, or more conducive to the most refined and exalted holiness." When sanctification is "entire," the foundation is completed. It is laid in "the heavenly places" of a high and "most holy faith," and on that lofty foundation one may build upward forever.

We may take it for granted that we stand, theoretically, on a

2. *Holiness, the Finished Foundation,* 9-11.

platform of Wesleyan entire sanctification, but unless this platform becomes a launching pad from which we ascend into the heights of holy experience, the doctrine will ultimately go by default and become a dead letter, and history would teach that by one more step it will become a queer relic in the church museum. *We will continue thoroughly to believe the doctrine and to teach it with confidence and effectiveness as we have the experience.*[3] Interest in abstractions cannot be sustained for any great length of time, unless the abstractions crystallize into concrete experience.

On the other hand, the doctrinal waymarks must be clear and correct, or men will not find their way to the "highway of holiness."

DOCTRINE MUST BE CLEAR

Not many stumble into the way. We joyfully admit, with John Fletcher, that "some gracious persons—pious and inconsistent antinomians—speak against Christian perfection with their lips but cannot help following hard after it with their hearts; and while they do so, they sometimes attain the thing, although they continue to quarrel with the name. These perfect imperfectionists undoubtedly adorn the doctrine of Christ far more than the imperfect, hypocritical perfectionists—and God, who looks at the simplicity of the heart more than at the consistency of the judgment, pities their mistakes and accepts their works." But we are aware, as was Fletcher, that while the exceptional individual may find his way in spite of faulty directions, the masses will miss the road, unless the directions are specific and perpetually repeated.

When the doctrine is not preached clearly and with power, people do not hunger for the experience. If they do not hunger for it

POSSESSION PROMPTS PREACHING

intensely, they will not seek it. If they do not seek it, they will not find it. If they do not find it, they will not witness to it. Out of the church where this fatal lack occurs, one or more persons may enter the ministry. Not being in possession of the joyful experience, they will fail to preach it with assurance, and the vicious circle begins once more to do its devastating work on the spiritual life of the church. If the preacher has a pure heart, he will preach heart purity as naturally as he breathes, and people will hunger for a like experience. If they hunger, they will seek and find, and finding, they will witness to it. Then out of such a group, some men may be called to preach the everlasting gospel, and they will declare its offer of full salvation to believers. Thus a gracious, instead of a vicious

---

3. Italics added. *Editor.*

circle is repeated, and an increasing number find their way into the inheritance of those who are sanctified.

We should be reminded often that not all that glitters in the name of holiness is the pure gold of genuine holiness. Paul speaks of "true holiness" in Eph. 4:24. The inference may be drawn that there is an imitation holiness. Every valuable thing is matched by rival substitutes bearing acceptable labels. Numerous counterfeits of holiness, claiming the divine image and superscription, are in circulation and pass current with those lacking in spiritual discernment. By every legitimate test they are without the qualities for which the coin of the kingdom is distinguished. They do not ring true. In the balances of the sanctuary they are found wanting in solid substance. Exposure to an evil atmosphere tarnishes their false brightness, and an acid baptism of trial makes havoc of their pretense.

More than theoretical interest attaches to a question involving the eternal defeat or triumph of the soul. God, being what He is, has built the whole system of redemption along the lines of unchangeable truth, and, of moral necessity, can save men only in conformity with this arrangement. "Thus saith the Lord God, Behold, I lay in Zion for a foundation a stone, a tried stone, a precious corner stone, a sure foundation: . . . Judgment also will I lay to the line, and righteousness to the plummet: and the hail shall sweep away the refuge of lies, and the waters shall overflow the hiding place" (Isa. 28:16-17). The cornerstone is in perfect alignment with the divine nature of eternal righteousness in the One who laid it. That stone gives law to every angle of the wall. Each living stone in the edifice, from foundation to pinnacle, takes its position according to a horizontal line of prescribed conduct stretching away into eternity, and to a plummet of required character, reaching heaven high, both dimensions being determined by Christ, the living Truth.

HOLINESS THE FOUNDATION STONE

Wherever the winds of false doctrine, raised by prejudice or pride, have swung the man-made plummet like a pendulum, from one extreme to the other, refuges of lies have been reared, out of plumb, and daubed with the untempered mortar of carnal self-confidence. Being precariously balanced, these false sanctuaries usually collapse of their own weight without the visitation of a shattering earthquake or a sweeping storm, leaving the once deluded but now disillusioned soul without a sheltering habitation. Sound thinking on the subject of holiness is as necessary to solid, symmetrical experience as a correct plumb line and level are to the building of a good house. Deviation from the straight line, toward a superfluity of natural claims, or in the opposite direction toward a shortage of supernatural qualities, spell equal disaster.

A SCRIPTURAL STANDARD

John Fletcher, the seraphic defender of the Wesleyan doctrine, said, "If you will hit a mark, you must know where it is. Some people aim at Christian perfection, but mistaking it for *angelical perfection,* they shoot above the mark, miss it, and then peevishly give up their hopes. Others place the mark as much too low; hence it is that you hear them profess to have attained Christian perfection, when they have not so much as attained the mental serenity of a philosopher, or the candor of a good-natured, conscientious heathen." Hence the peril of raising false standards. The morbidly introspective will collapse in the presence of a standard higher than the one presented in the Scriptures. Others are inclined to presumption, and to set the standard too low is to encourage them to fall short of the divine requirements and take everything for granted. Whatever peace either class feels, will be the peace of carnal security, and the fruits of holiness will not be in evidence. They will become a liability to the Church, if not a reproach.

EXEMPLARS ARE NEEDED

Exponents of the standard should exemplify the standard. While opposing erroneous and inadequate views of the subject, they should demonstrate the beauty of holiness. It is unfortunate when men engage in unholy debates about holiness of heart. It damages the Church when Christlikeness of character is discussed in an unchristlike manner. When the sweetest thing in the world is defended with bitterness, and "the faith once delivered unto the saints" is contended for contentiously, the world discredits the thing represented rather than its unworthy representative. Unattractive examples of the professed experience provide no valid argument against its possibility but are painful demonstrations of its need. However, unregenerate men, who are always on the defensive, do not follow this line of reasoning, and the low-living professor of high attainments is an occasion of stumbling to them. When the talk and the walk agree, a breach is made in the defenses of the loudest critic.

Holy men may be branded by unholy men as Puritans or Pharisees because the purity of the holy condemns their impurity, but while the passions of the heart shout condemnation, the convictions of the heart whisper commendation. Black has more respect for white than for neutral gray. Voltaire could viciously attack the Church, but when an opponent asked him, "Where, in all history, will you find a life as beautiful as the life of Jesus of Nazareth?" the famous sceptic replied, "You will find a life just as beautiful in the vicarage of Madeley in Shropshire." Fletcher would have said, "I am crucified with Christ: nevertheless I live; yet not I, but Christ liveth in me," but the estimate is significant, coming from such a source. Gibbon, on various occasions, said that the beautiful character of William Law had done more to make Christianity credible to him than had all the volumes of polemics and apologetics he had read.

THE BIBLE IS THE SOURCE

But where shall we find the pattern and the power for such elevated character? The Church would be in grave danger if every man had an interpretation of his own and boasted with one of Mrs. Browning's characters,

> "I have a pattern on my nail,
> I will carve the world new after it."

We find the pattern in the mount of God or receive it from others who have found it there. In the 18th century there appeared a conjunction of stars of the first magnitude in the spiritual realm. Most prominent among them were John Wesley, John Fletcher, and Adam Clarke. We joyfully take these stars as our guiding lights, for they moved in an orbit of undeviating loyalty to the Holy Scriptures. We shall not be in danger of what has been lightly called "Wesleyolatry" if we follow the teachings of the great founder of Methodism, for he was, as he declared, "a man of one Book," and to follow him is to follow the Book.

Bibliography

Anderson, T. M., comp. and ed. *Our Holy Faith.* Kansas City: Beacon Hill Press of Kansas City, 1965.

Arthur, William. *The Tongue of Fire.* London: Epworth Press, n.d.

Baker, Eric S. *The Faith of a Methodist.* London: Epworth Press, 1958.

Bassett, Paul, and Greathouse, William M. *Exploring Christian Holiness.* Vol. 2, *The Historical Foundations.* Kansas City: Beacon Hill Press of Kansas City, 1984.

Binney, Amos. *The Theological Compend.* Cincinnati: Swormatedt and Poe, 1858.

Bunting, Jabez. *Bunting's Sermons.* 2 vols. New York: Carlton & Porter, 1863.

Byrum, Russell R. *Christian Theology.* Ed. by Arlo F. Newell. Anderson, Ind.: Warner Press, 1982. Gospel Trumpet Company, 1925.

Carter, Charles W., ed. *A Contemporary Wesleyan Theology.* 2 vols. Grand Rapids: Francis Asbury Press (Zondervan), 1983.

———. *The Person and Ministry of the Holy Spirit.* Grand Rapids: Baker Book House, 1974.

Cell, John Croft. *The Rediscovery of John Wesley.* New York: Henry Holt and Co., 1935.

Chiles, Robert E. *Theological Transition in American Methodism.* New York: Abingdon Press, 1965.

Curtis, Olin Alfred. *The Christian Faith.* Grand Rapids: Kregel Publications, 1956. First ed., 1905.

Field, Benjamin. *The Student's Handbook of Christian Theology.* New York: Methodist Book Concern, 1887.

Finney, Charles G. *Lectures on Systematic Theology.* Grand Rapids: Wm. B. Eerdmans Publishing Co., 1951. First pub., 1846; rev. by J. H. Fairchild, 1878.

———. *The Promise of the Spirit: Charles G. Finney on Christian Holiness.* Comp. and ed. by Timothy L. Smith. Minneapolis: Bethany Fellowship, 1980.

Flew, R. Newton. *The Idea of Perfection in Christian Theology.* London: Oxford University Press, 1934.

Foster, Randolph S. *Nature and Blessedness of Christian Purity.* New York: Carlton & Porter, 1851.

Gamertsfelder, S. J. *Systematic Theology.* Harrisburg, Pa.: Evangelical Publishing House, 1921.

Geiger, Kenneth E., comp. *The Word and the Doctrine.* Kansas City: Beacon Hill Press of Kansas City, 1965.

Gray, Frederick Albert. *Christian Theology.* 2 vols. Anderson, Ind.: Warner Press, 1946.

Greathouse, William M., and Bassett, Paul. *Exploring Christian Holiness.* Vol. 2, *The Historical Foundations.* Kansas City: Beacon Hill Press of Kansas City, 1984.

Grider, J. Kenneth. *Entire Sanctification: The Distinctive Doctrine of Wesleyanism.* Kansas City: Beacon Hill Press of Kansas City, 1980.

Hills, Aaron M. *Fundamental Christian Theology.* 2 vols. Pasadena, Calif.: C. J. Kinne, 1931.

———. *Holiness and Power.* Jamestown, N.C.: Newby Book Room, n.d. Orig. pub. by M. W. Knapp, Cincinnati, 1897.

Hogue, Wilson T. *The Holy Spirit.* Chicago: William B. Rose, Agent, 1916.

Jessup, Harry E. *Foundations of Doctrine.* Chicago: Chicago Evangelistic Institute, 1938.

Knight, John A. *In His Likeness.* Kansas City: Beacon Hill Press of Kansas City, 1976.

———. *The Holiness Pilgrimage.* Kansas City: Beacon Hill Press of Kansas City, 1973.

Lee, Luther. *Elements of Theology.* Syracuse, N.Y.: Samuel Lee, 1861.

Lindstrom, Harald. *Wesley and Sanctification.* London: Epworth Press, n.d. First Swedish ed., 1946.

McCumber, W. E. *Holiness in the Prayers of St. Paul.* Kansas City: Beacon Hill Press, 1955.

———. *Holy God, Holy People.* Kansas City: Beacon Hill Press of Kansas City, 1982.

Metz, Donald S. *Studies in Biblical Holiness.* Kansas City: Beacon Hill Press of Kansas City, 1971.

Miley, John. *Systematic Theology.* 2 vols. New York: Methodist Book Concern, 1892.

Mitchell, T. Crichton. *Great Holiness Classics.* Vol. 2, *The Wesley Century.* Kansas City: Beacon Hill Press of Kansas City, 1984.

Neely, Thomas B. *Doctrinal Standards of Methodism.* New York: Fleming H. Revell Company, 1918.

Outler, Albert C. *Theology in the Wesleyan Spirit.* Nashville: Tidings, 1975.

Peters, John L. *Christian Perfection and American Methodism.* Nashville: Abingdon, 1956.

Pope, William Burt. *A Compendium of Christian Theology,* 3 vols. London: Wesleyan Conference Office, 1880.

———. *A Higher Catechism of Theology.* London: T. Woolmer, 1883.

Purkiser, W. T. *Exploring Christian Holiness.* Vol. 1, *The Biblical Foundations.* Kansas City: Beacon Hill Press of Kansas City, 1983.

———, ed. *Exploring Our Christian Faith.* Kansas City: Beacon Hill Press, 1960.

———, with Richard S. Taylor and Willard H. Taylor. *God, Man, and Salvation.* Kansas City: Beacon Hill Press of Kansas City, 1977.

Ralston, Thomas N. *Elements of Divinity.* Ed. by T. O. Summers. Nashville: Publishing House of M.E. Church, South, 1921. Original work, 1847.

Raymond, Miner. *Systematic Theology.* 3 vols. Cincinnati: Hitchcock & Walden, 1877.

Sangster, W. E. *The Path to Perfection.* New York: Abingdon-Cokesbury Press, 1945.

Sheldon, Henry C. *A System of Christian Doctrine.* Rev. ed. New York: Eaton and Mains, 1912.

Steele, Daniel. *Love Enthroned: Essays in Evangelical Perfection.* New York: Nelson & Phillips, 1875.

———. *The Gospel of the Comforter.* Boston: Christian Witness Co., 1897.

———. *The Holy Spirit, the Conservator of Orthodoxy.* Boston: McDonald and Gill, n.d.

Summers, Thomas O. *Systematic Theology.* 2 vols. Ed. by John Tigert. Nashville: Publishing House of the M.E. Church, South, 1888.

Taylor, J. Paul. *Holiness, the Finished Foundation.* Winona Lake, Ind.: Light and Life Press, 1963.

Taylor, Richard S. *Exploring Christian Holiness.* Vol. 3, *The Theological Formulation.* Kansas City: Beacon Hill Press of Kansas City, 1985.

———. *A Right Conception of Sin.* Kansas City: Nazarene Publishing House, 1939. Rev., 1945.

———, ed. *Beacon Dictionary of Theology.* Kansas City: Beacon Hill Press of Kansas City, 1983.

Turner, George Allen. *The Vision Which Transforms: Is Christian Perfection Scriptural?* Kansas City: Beacon Hill Press, 1964.

Wakefield, Samuel A. *A Complete System of Christian Theology.* Cincinnati: Cranston and Stowe, 1869.

Watson, Richard. *Theological Institutes.* 2 vols. Ed. by J. M'Clintock. New York: Carlton & Lanahan, 1850.

Wilcox, Leslie D. *Be Ye Holy.* Cincinnati: Revivalist Press, 1956.

———, ed. *Profiles in Wesleyan Theology.* Vol. 1. Salem, Ohio: Schmul Publishing Company, Inc., 1983.

Wiley, H. Orton. *Christian Theology.* 3 vols. Kansas City: Nazarene Publishing House, 1942.

Williams, Colin W. *John Wesley's Theology Today.* London: Epworth Press, 1960.

Wynkoop, Mildred Bangs. *Foundations of Wesleyan-Arminian Theology.* Kansas City: Beacon Hill Press of Kansas City, 1967.

———. *A Theology of Love.* Kansas City: Beacon Hill Press of Kansas City, 1972.

Author Index

Subject Index

Index of Scripture References